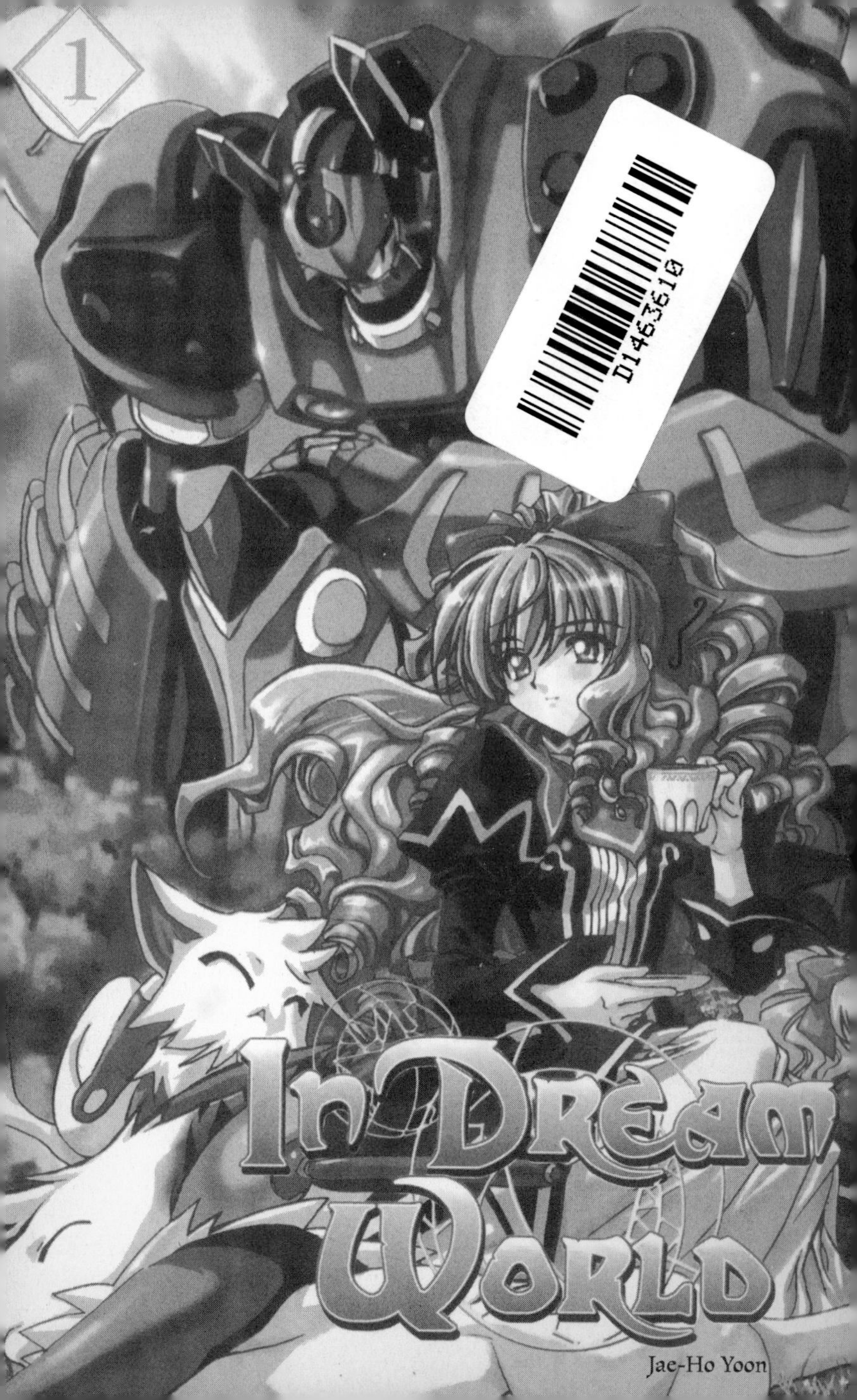
1
In Dream World
Jae-Ho Yoon

In Dream World Vol. 1
Created by Jae-Ho Yoon

Translation - Jihae Hong
English Adaptation - Michael French
Copy Editor - Adam Arnold
Associate Editor - Troy Lewter
Retouch and Lettering - Abelardo Bigting
Production Artist - Jason Milligan
Cover Design - Jorge Negrete

Editor - Luis Reyes
Digital Imaging Manager - Chris Buford
Pre-Press Manager - Antonio DePietro
Production Managers - Jennifer Miller and Mutsumi Miyazaki
Art Director - Matt Alford
Managing Editor - Jill Freshney
VP of Production - Ron Klamert
President and C.O.O. - John Parker
Publisher and C.E.O. - Stuart Levy

A  Manga

TOKYOPOP Inc.
5900 Wilshire Blvd. Suite 2000
Los Angeles, CA 90036

E-mail: info@TOKYOPOP.com
Come visit us online at www.TOKYOPOP.com

ISBN: 1-59532-516-6

First TOKYOPOP printing: April 2005
10 9 8 7 6 5 4 3 2 1
Printed in the USA

In Dream World

Volume 1

By
Jae-Ho Yoon

TOKYOPOP®

HAMBURG // LONDON // LOS ANGELES // TOKYO

CONTENTS

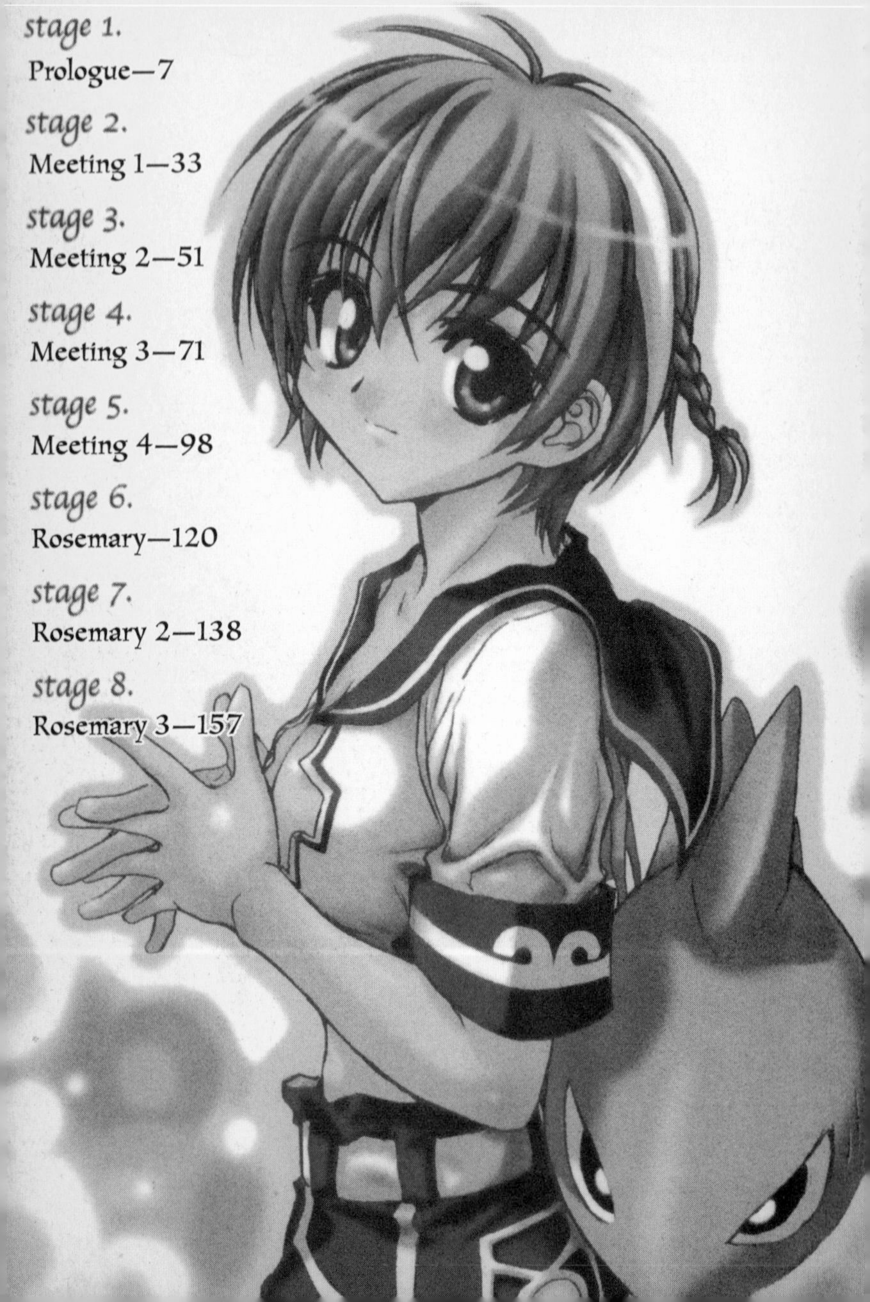

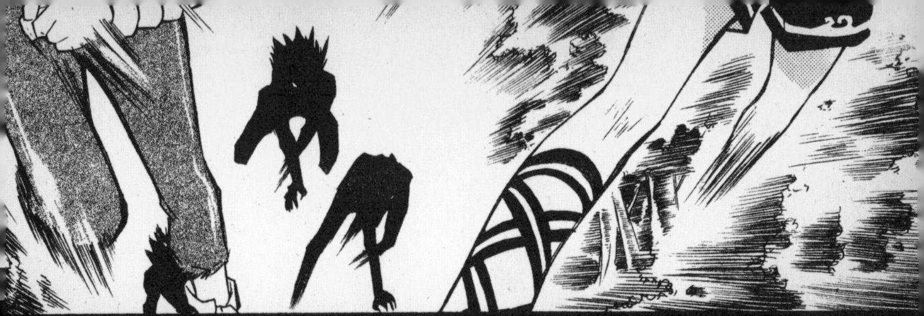

The In Dream World Project

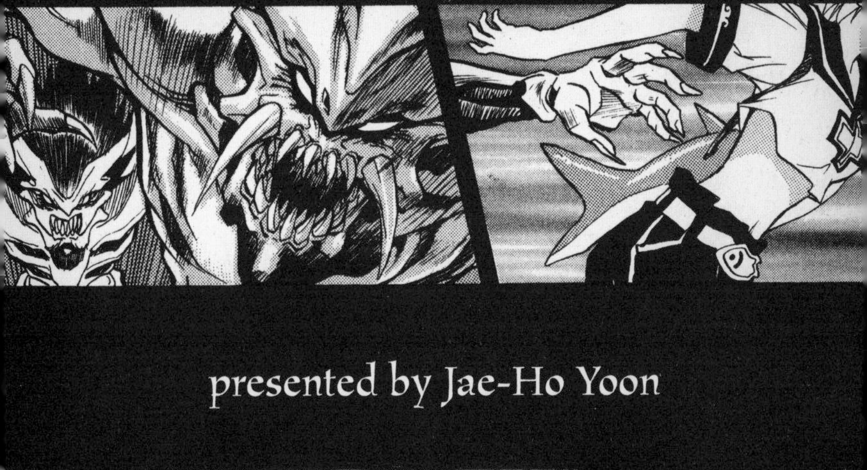

presented by Jae-Ho Yoon

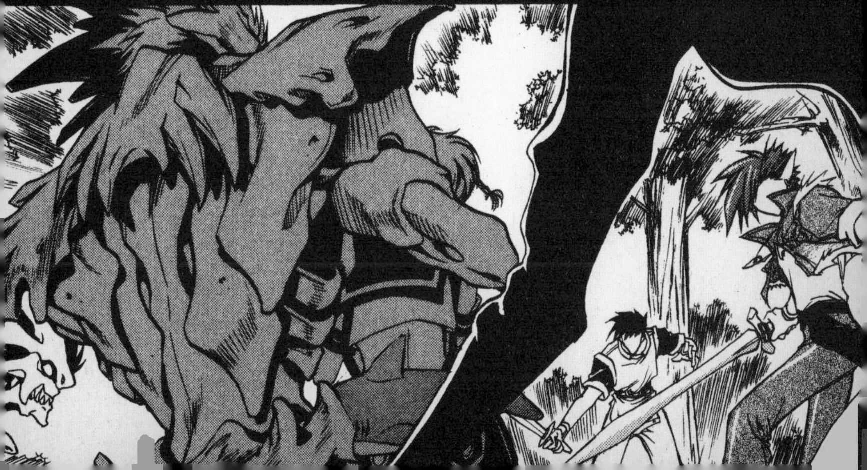

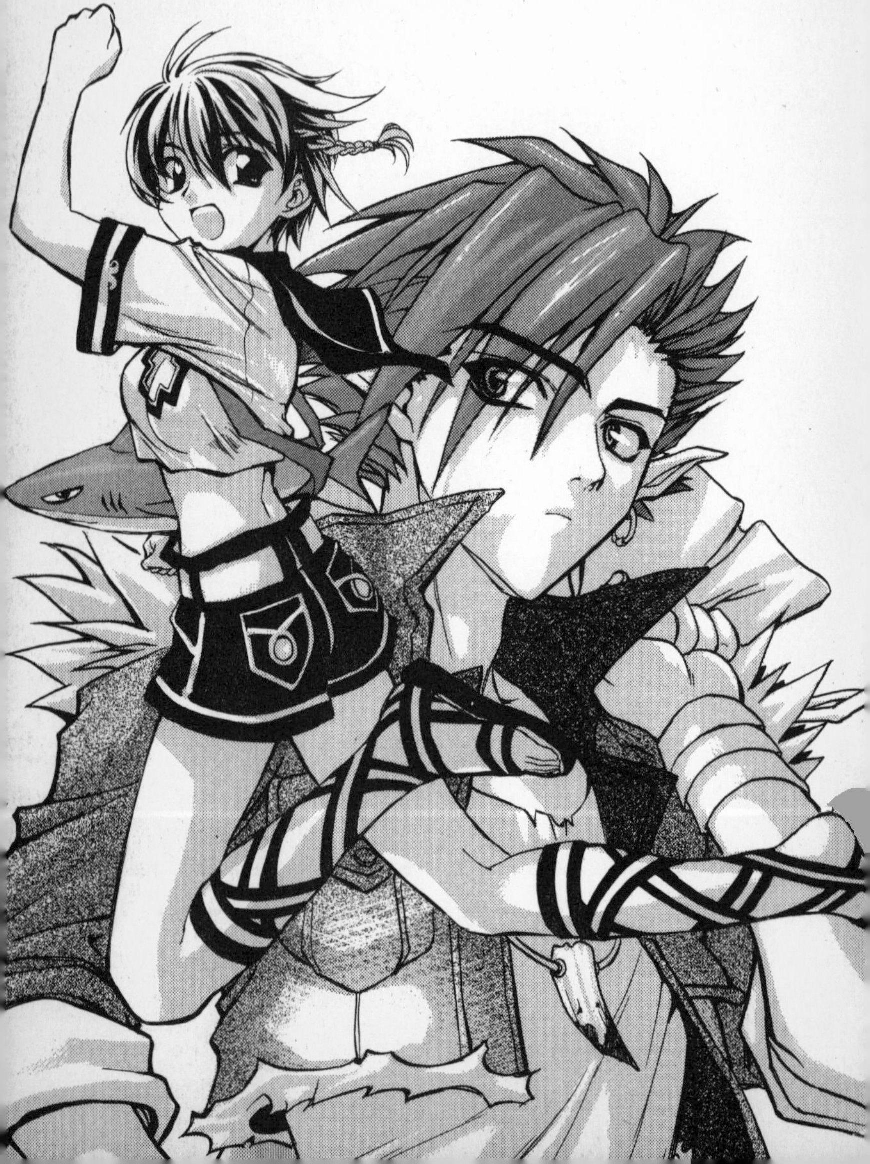

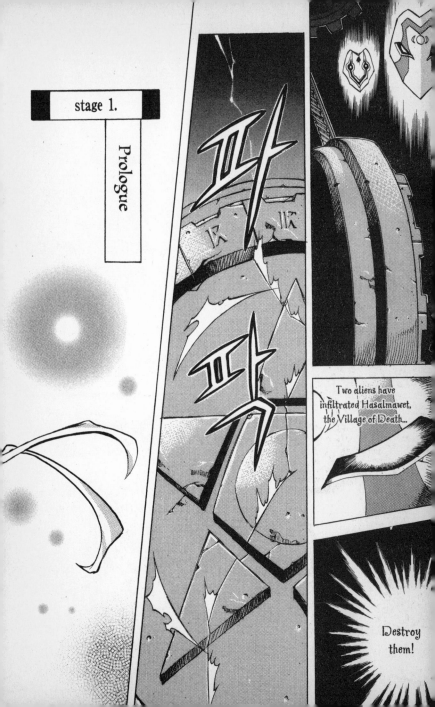

stage 1.

Prologue

Two aliens have infiltrated Hasalmawet, the Village of Death...

Destroy them!

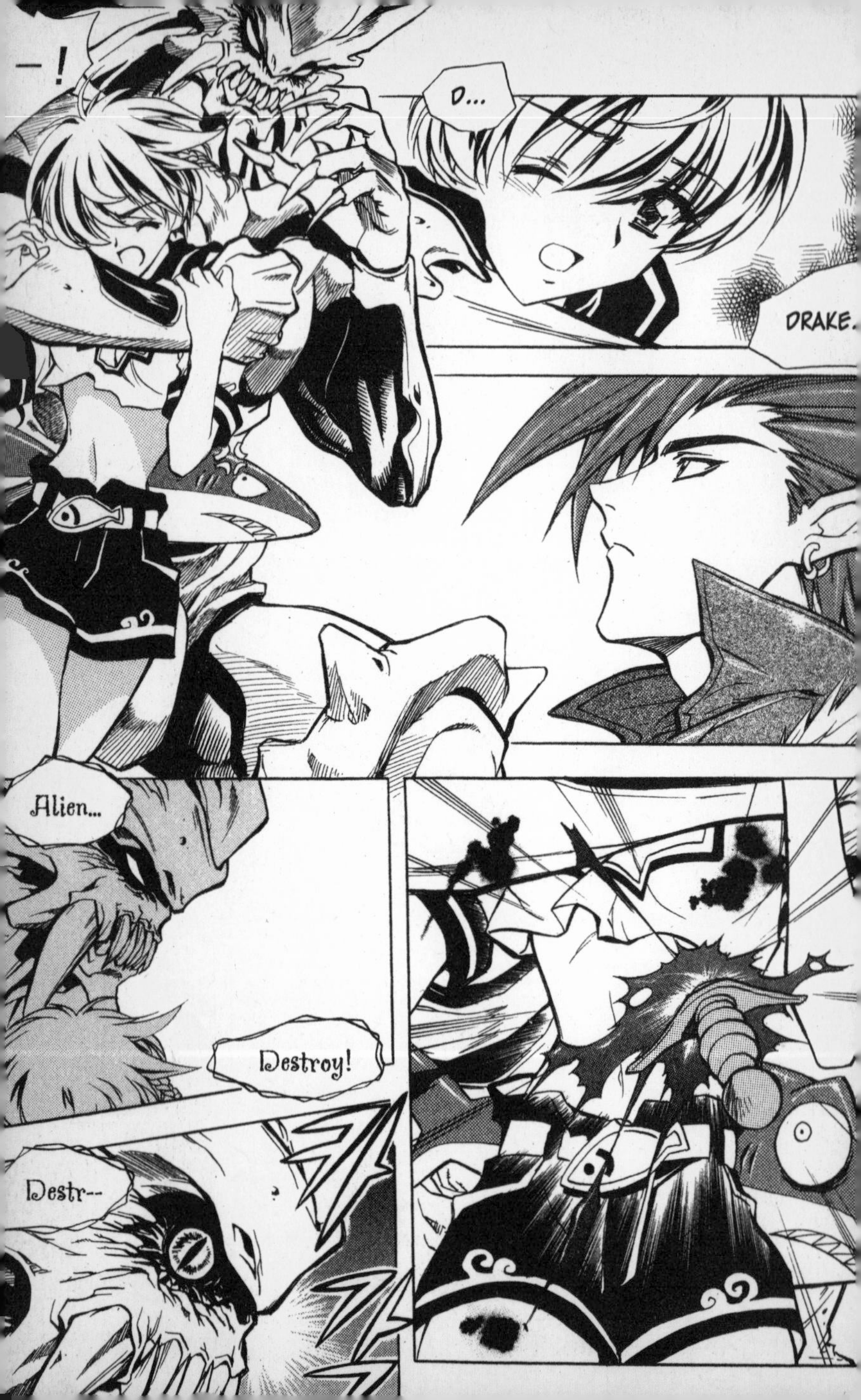
—!
D...
DRAKE.
Alien...
Destroy!
Destr--

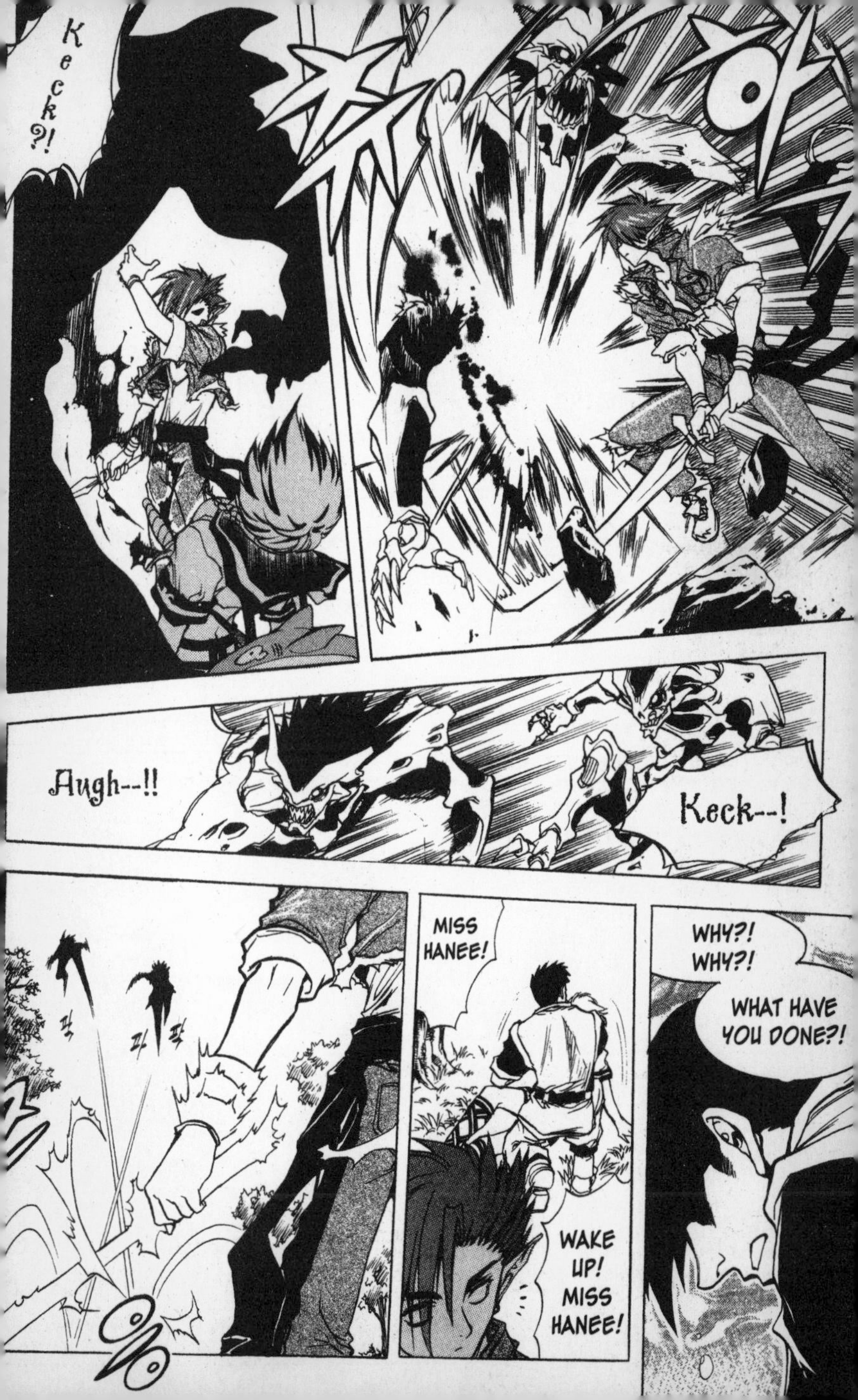
Keck?!
Augh--!!
Keck--!
MISS HANEE!
WAKE UP! MISS HANEE!
WHY?! WHY?!
WHAT HAVE YOU DONE?!

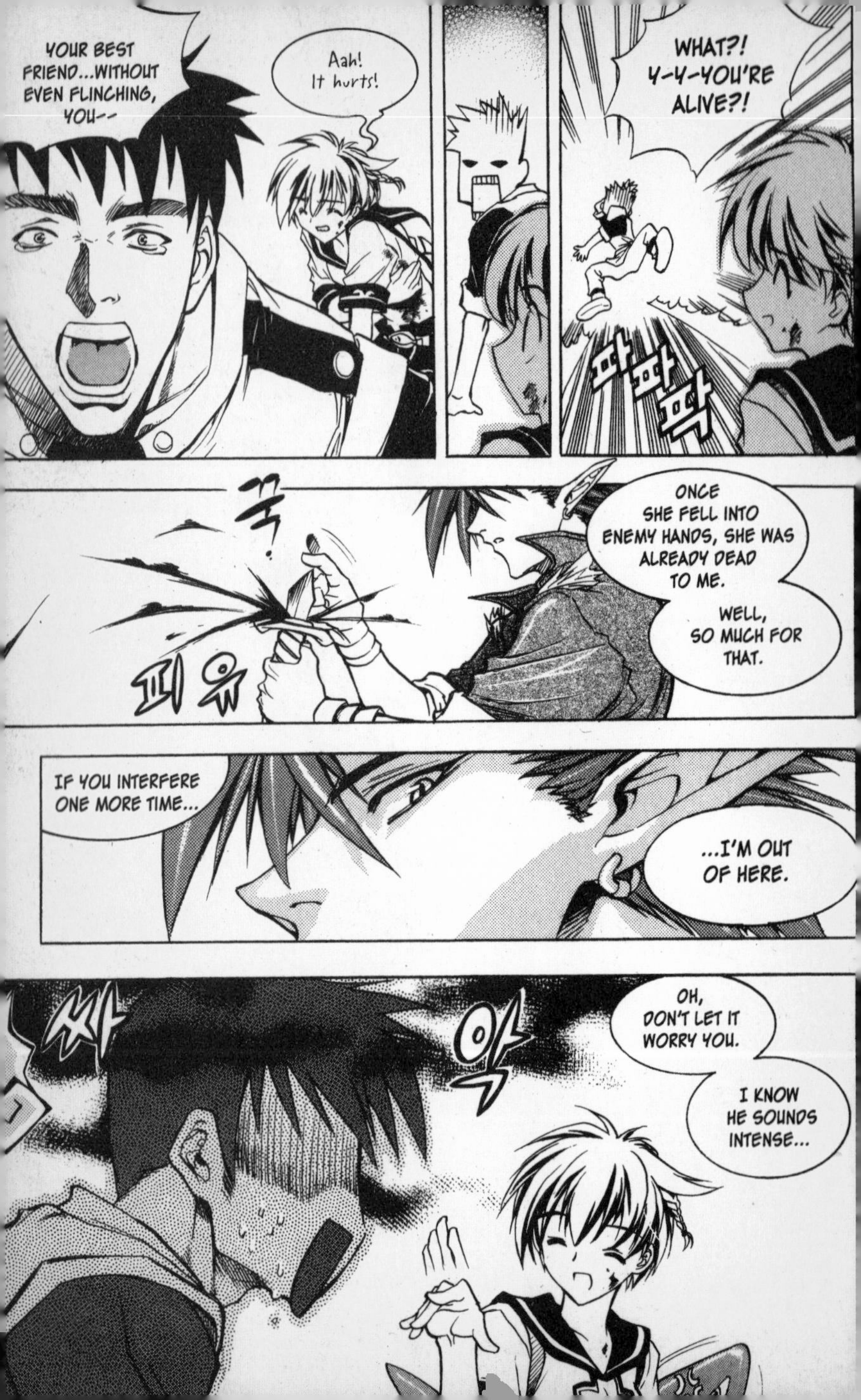
YOUR BEST FRIEND...WITHOUT EVEN FLINCHING, YOU--
Aah! It hurts!
WHAT?! Y-Y-YOU'RE ALIVE?!
파파팍
ONCE SHE FELL INTO ENEMY HANDS, SHE WAS ALREADY DEAD TO ME.
WELL, SO MUCH FOR THAT.
피유
IF YOU INTERFERE ONE MORE TIME...
...I'M OUT OF HERE.
OH, DON'T LET IT WORRY YOU.
I KNOW HE SOUNDS INTENSE...

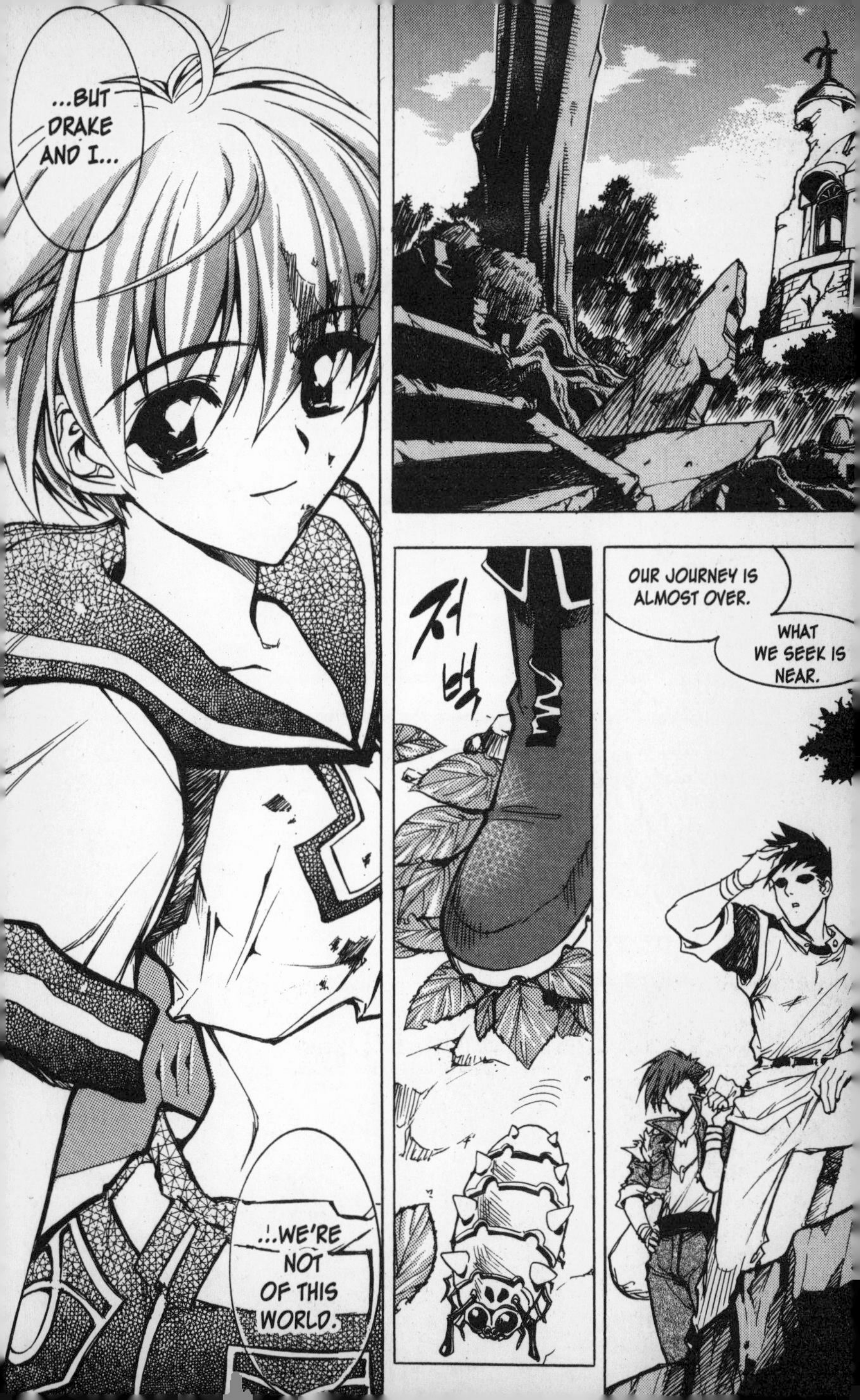
...BUT DRAKE AND I...
...WE'RE NOT OF THIS WORLD.
저벅
OUR JOURNEY IS ALMOST OVER.
WHAT WE SEEK IS NEAR.

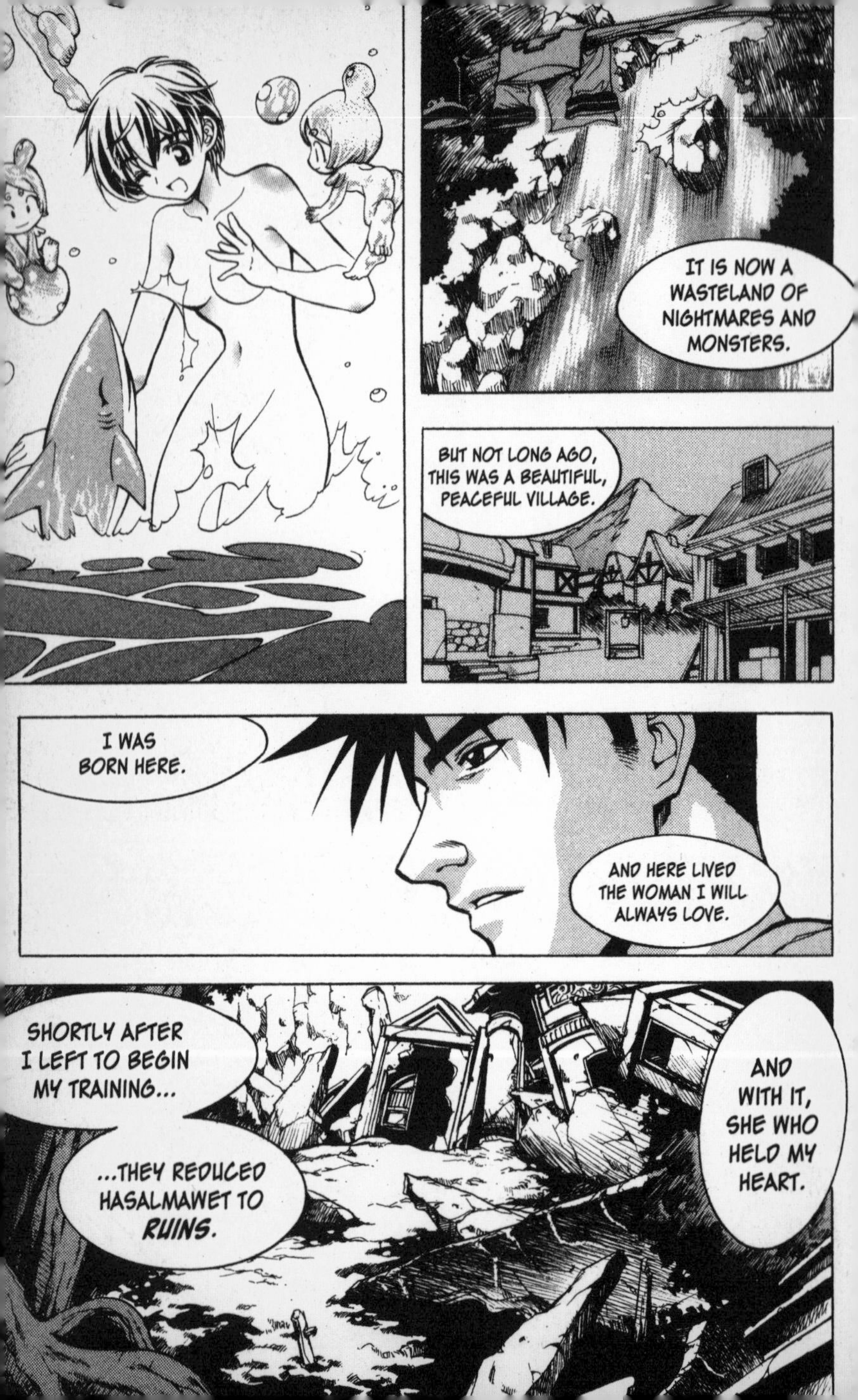
IT IS NOW A WASTELAND OF NIGHTMARES AND MONSTERS.
BUT NOT LONG AGO, THIS WAS A BEAUTIFUL, PEACEFUL VILLAGE.
I WAS BORN HERE.
AND HERE LIVED THE WOMAN I WILL ALWAYS LOVE.
SHORTLY AFTER I LEFT TO BEGIN MY TRAINING...
...THEY REDUCED HASALMAWET TO RUINS.
AND WITH IT, SHE WHO HELD MY HEART.

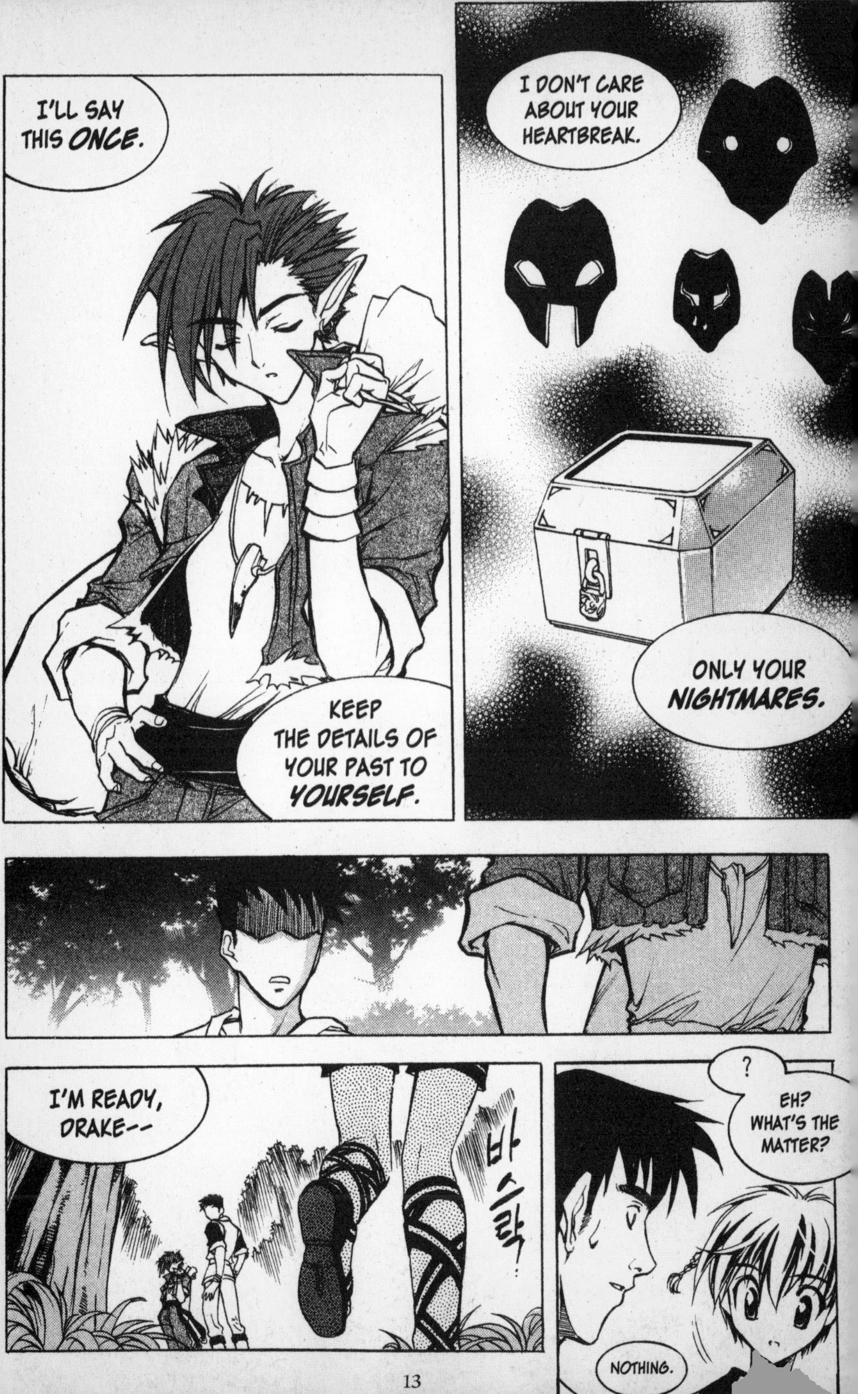
I'LL SAY THIS ONCE.
KEEP THE DETAILS OF YOUR PAST TO YOURSELF.
I DON'T CARE ABOUT YOUR HEARTBREAK.
ONLY YOUR NIGHTMARES.
I'M READY, DRAKE--
바스락!
?
EH? WHAT'S THE MATTER?
NOTHING.

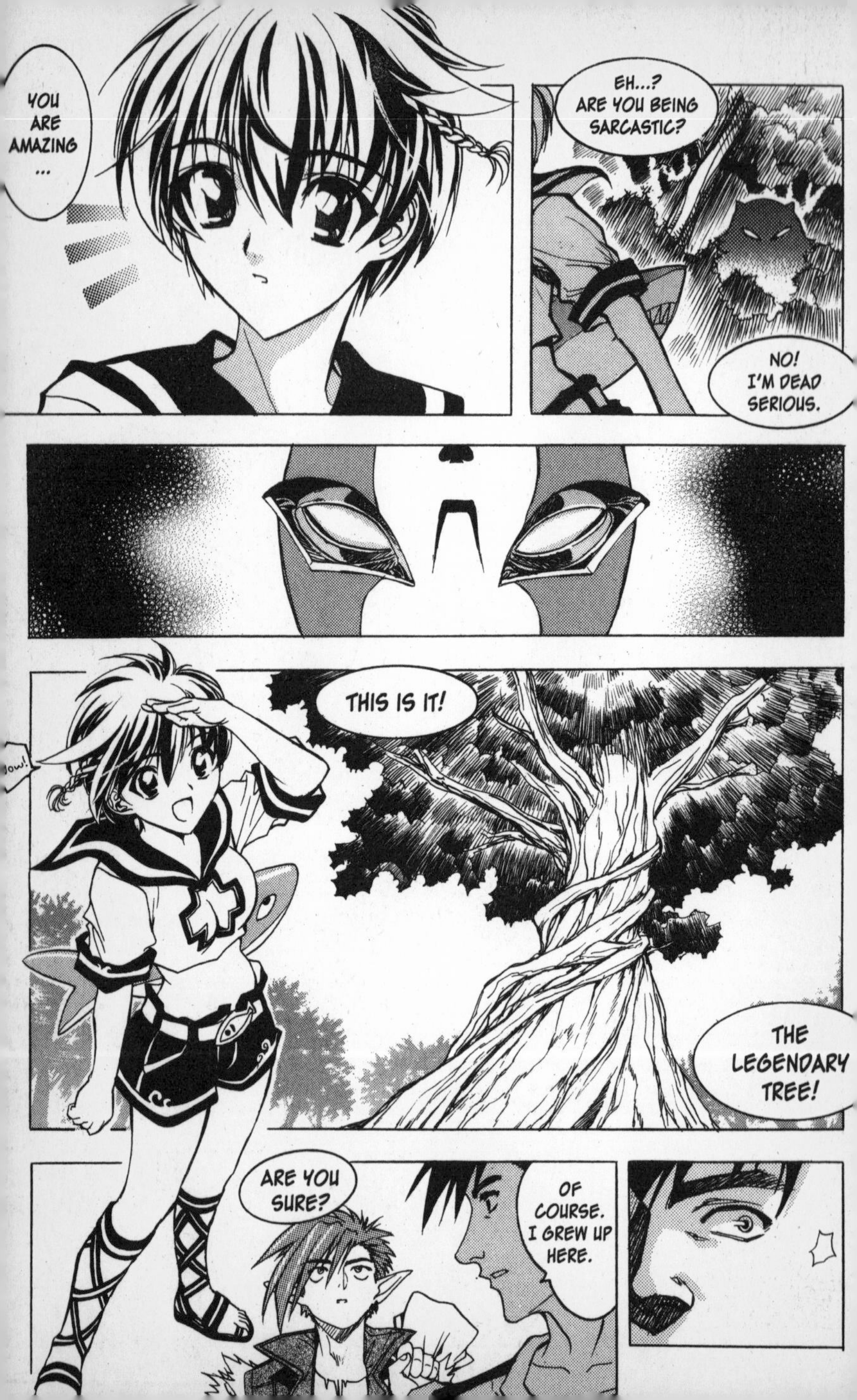
YOU ARE AMAZING ...
EH...? ARE YOU BEING SARCASTIC?
NO! I'M DEAD SERIOUS.
THIS IS IT!
THE LEGENDARY TREE!
ARE YOU SURE?
OF COURSE. I GREW UP HERE.

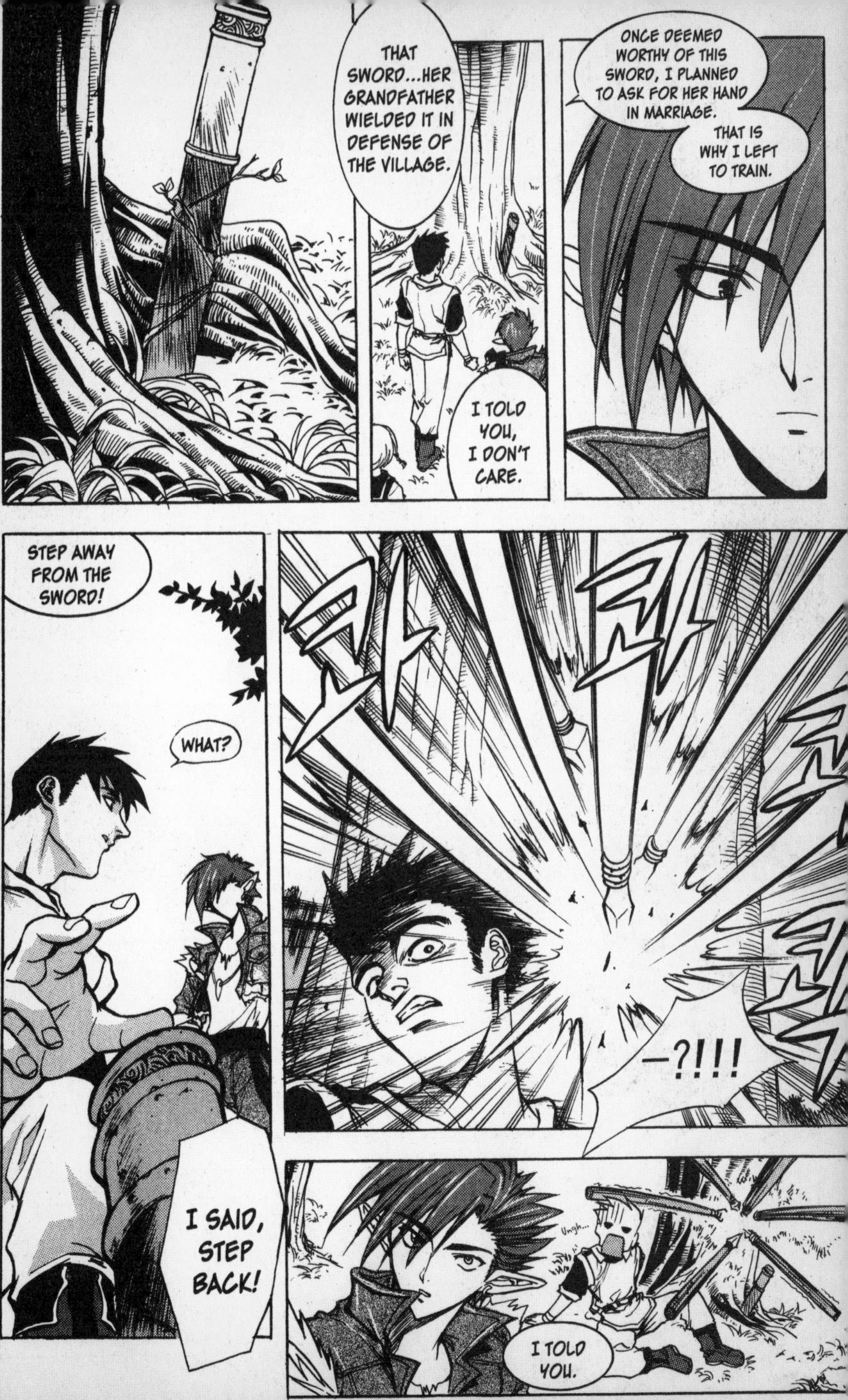
THAT SWORD...HER GRANDFATHER WIELDED IT IN DEFENSE OF THE VILLAGE.
I TOLD YOU, I DON'T CARE.
ONCE DEEMED WORTHY OF THIS SWORD, I PLANNED TO ASK FOR HER HAND IN MARRIAGE.
THAT IS WHY I LEFT TO TRAIN.
STEP AWAY FROM THE SWORD!
WHAT?
I SAID, STEP BACK!
—?!!!
Ungh...
I TOLD YOU.

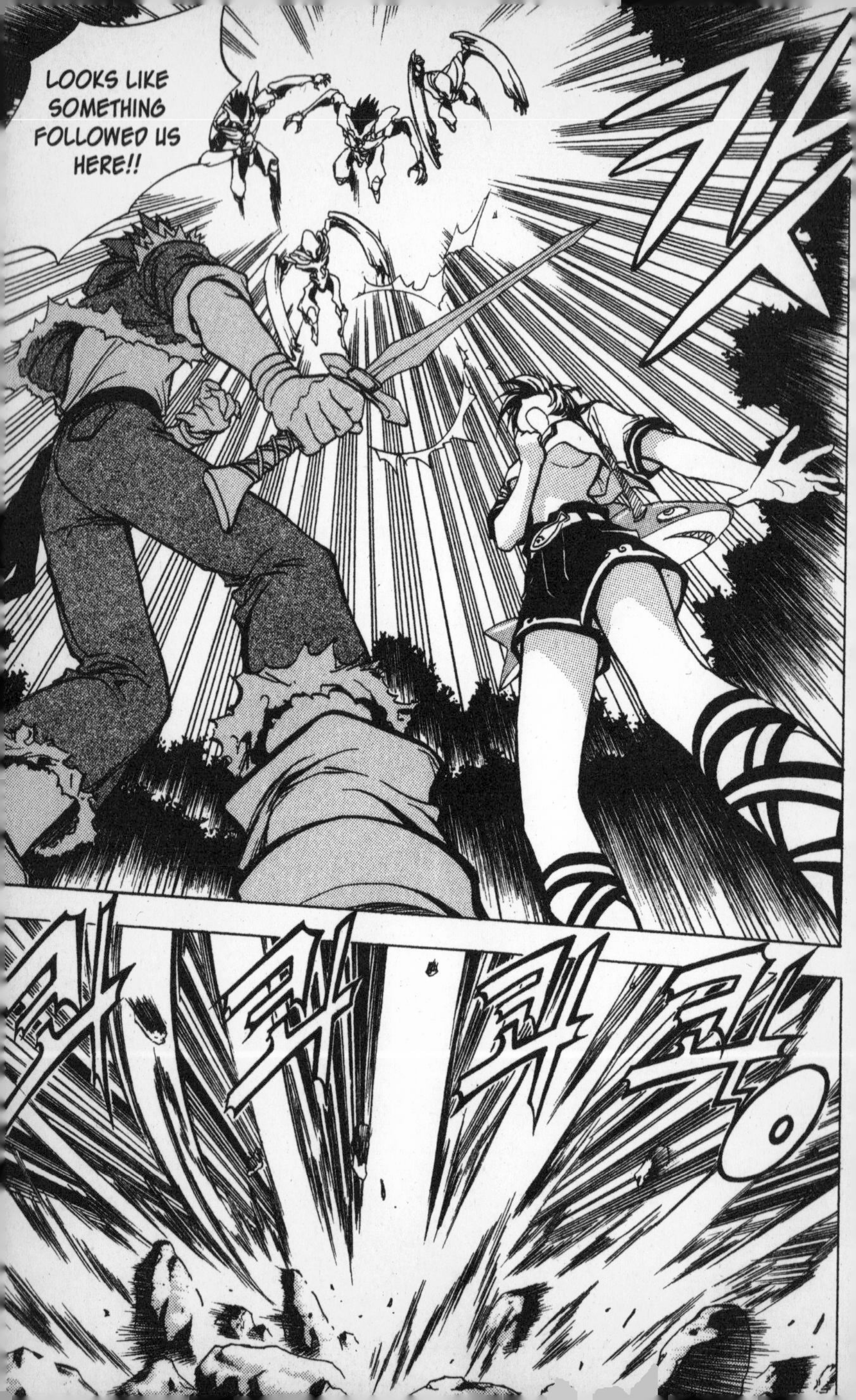
LOOKS LIKE SOMETHING FOLLOWED US HERE!!

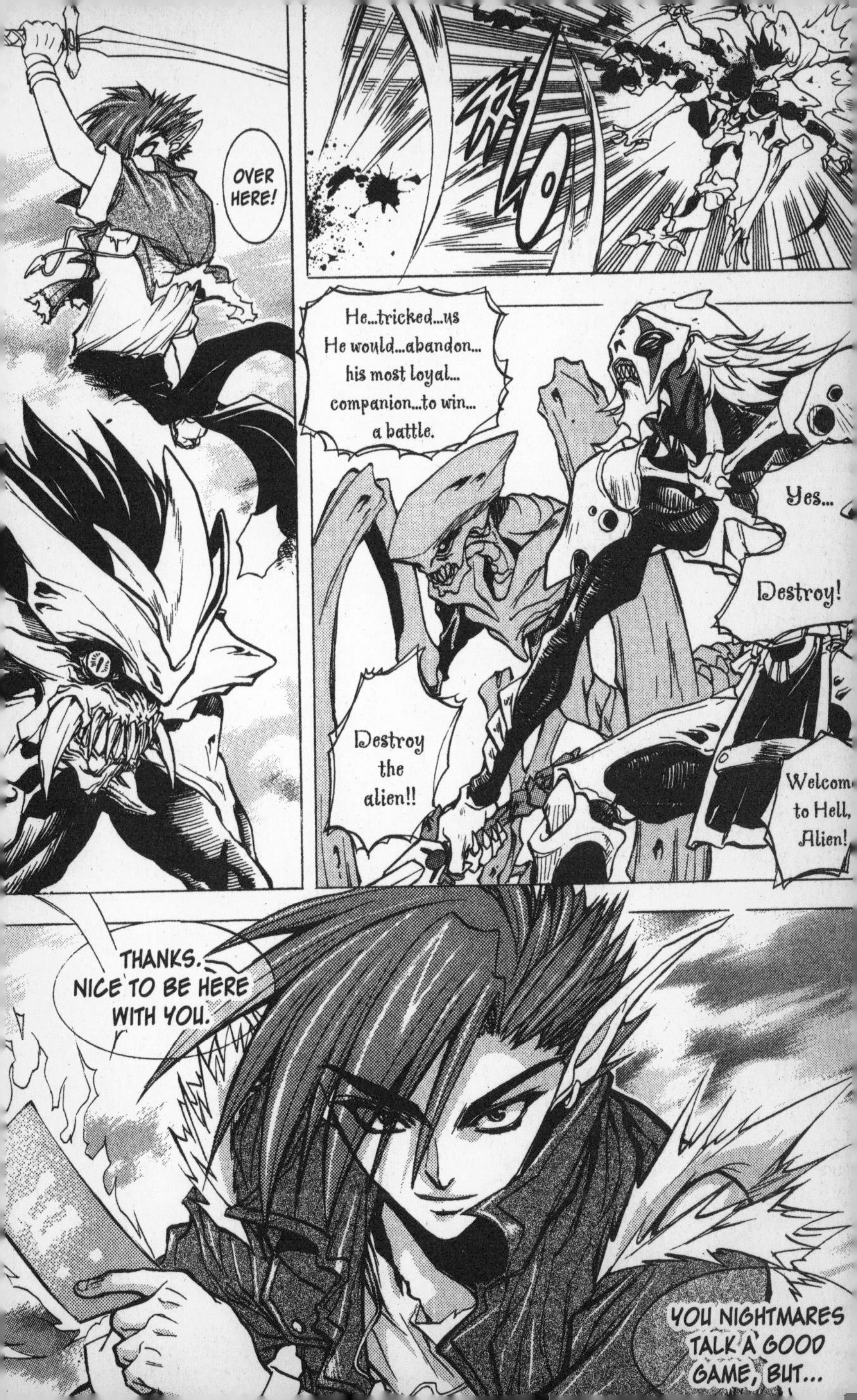
OVER HERE!
He...tricked...us He would...abandon... his most loyal... companion...to win... a battle.
Yes...
Destroy!
Destroy the alien!!
Welcome to Hell, Alien!
THANKS. NICE TO BE HERE WITH YOU.
YOU NIGHTMARES TALK A GOOD GAME, BUT...

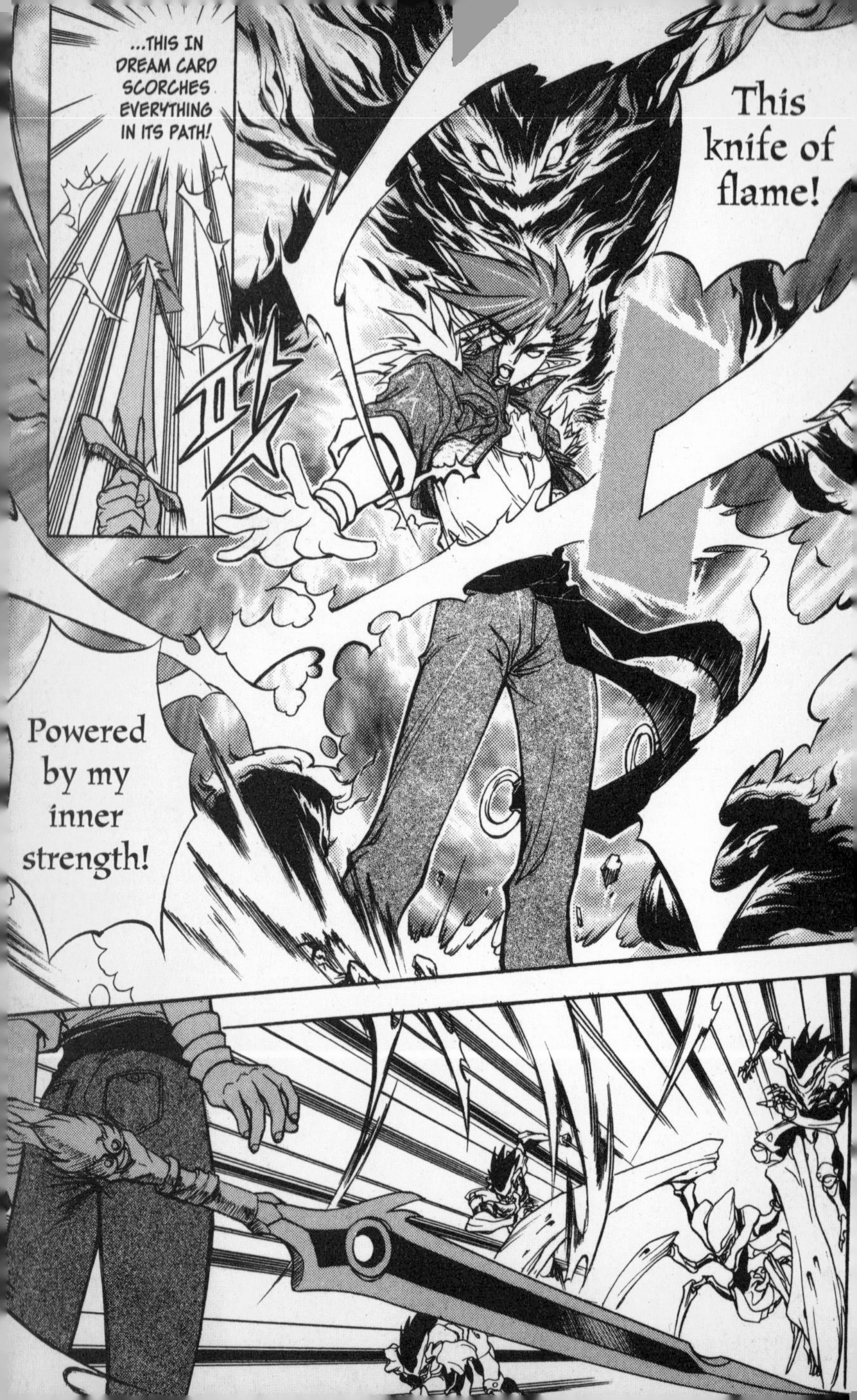
...THIS IN DREAM CARD SCORCHES EVERYTHING IN ITS PATH!
This knife of flame!
Powered by my inner strength!

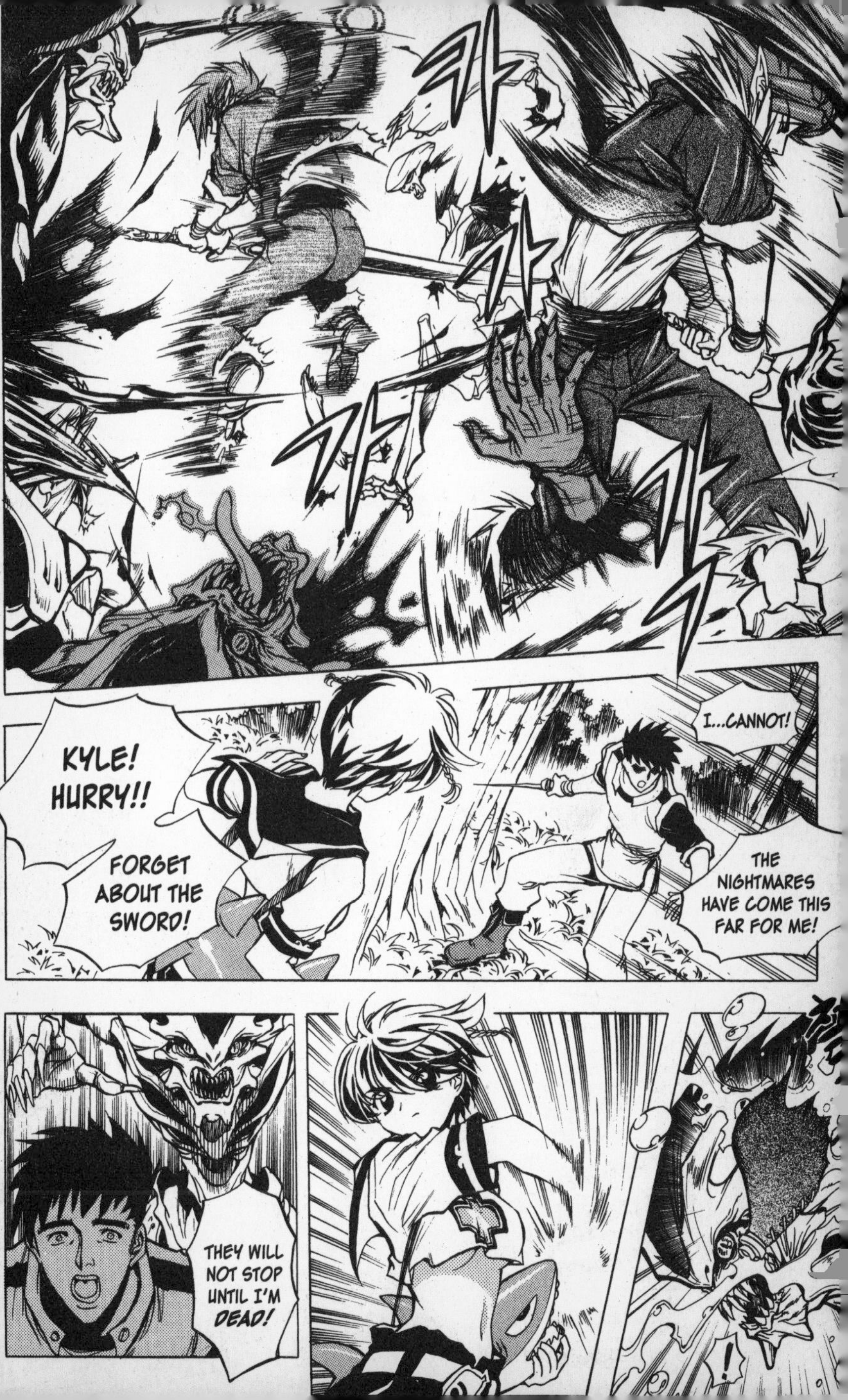
KYLE! HURRY!!
FORGET ABOUT THE SWORD!
I...CANNOT!
THE NIGHTMARES HAVE COME THIS FAR FOR ME!
THEY WILL NOT STOP UNTIL I'M DEAD!
!

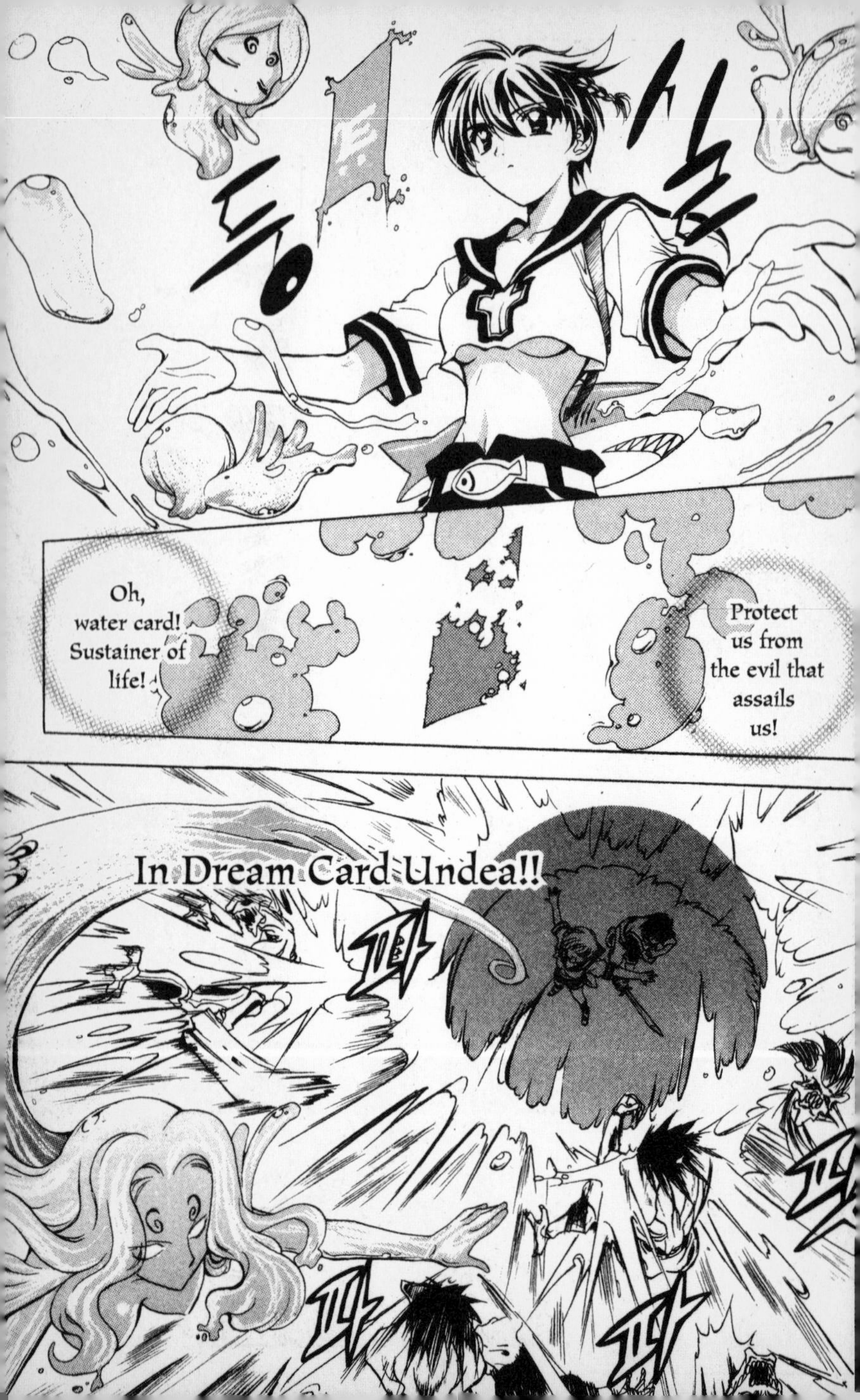
Oh, water card! Sustainer of life!
Protect us from the evil that assails us!
In Dream Card Undea!!

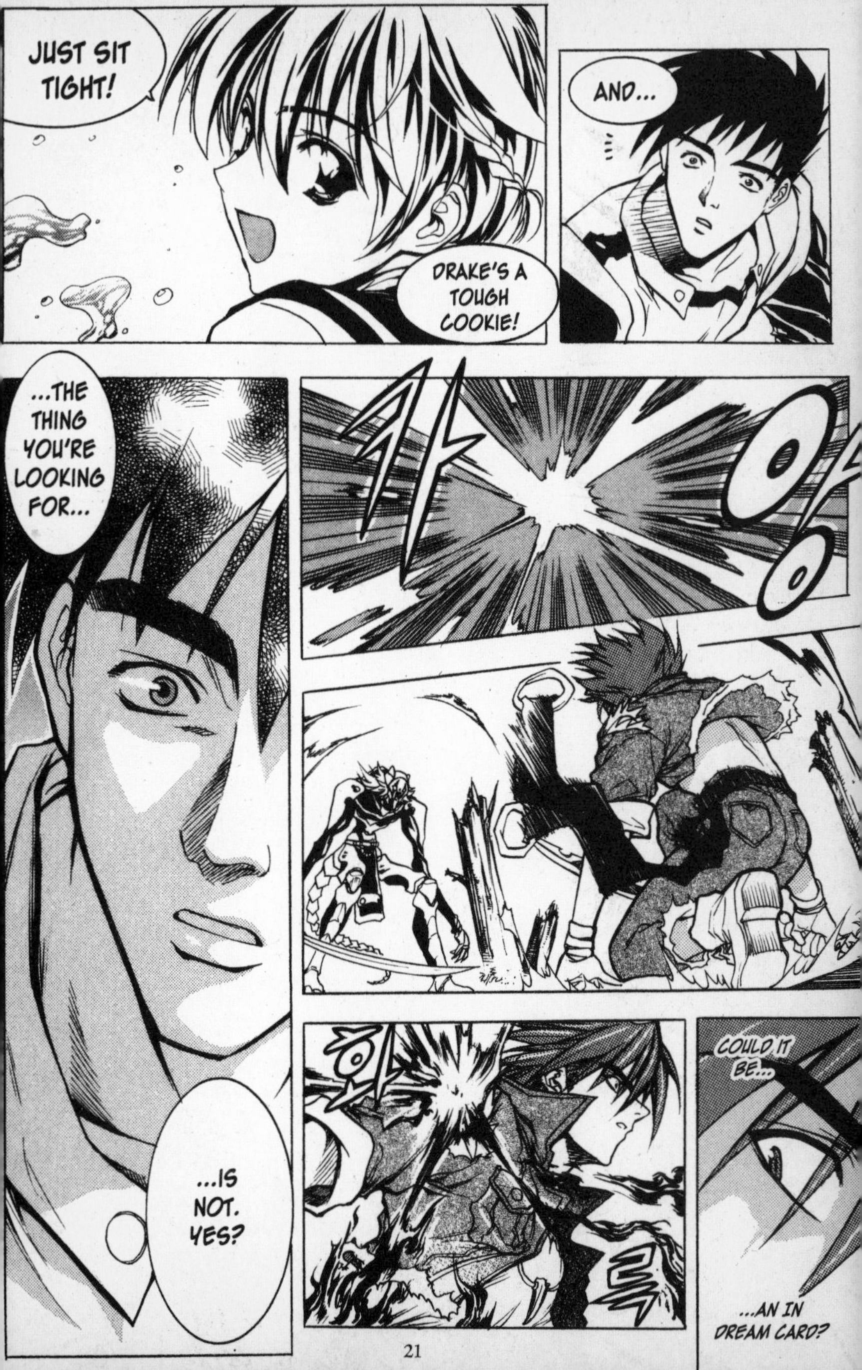
JUST SIT TIGHT!
DRAKE'S A TOUGH COOKIE!
AND...
...THE THING YOU'RE LOOKING FOR...
...IS NOT. YES?
COULD IT BE...
...AN IN DREAM CARD?

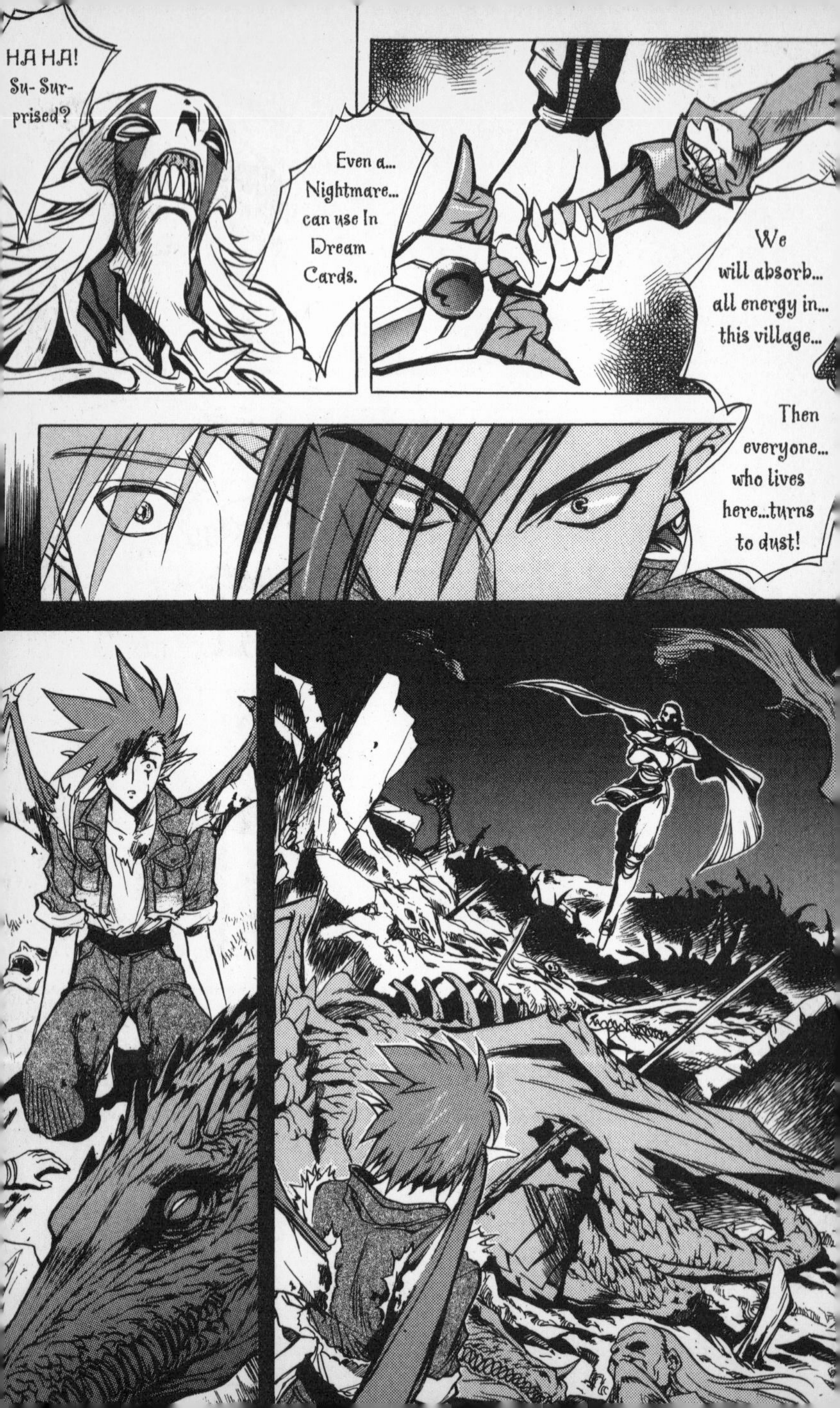
HA HA! Su- Surprised?
Even a... Nightmare... can use In Dream Cards.
We will absorb... all energy in... this village...
Then everyone... who lives here...turns to dust!

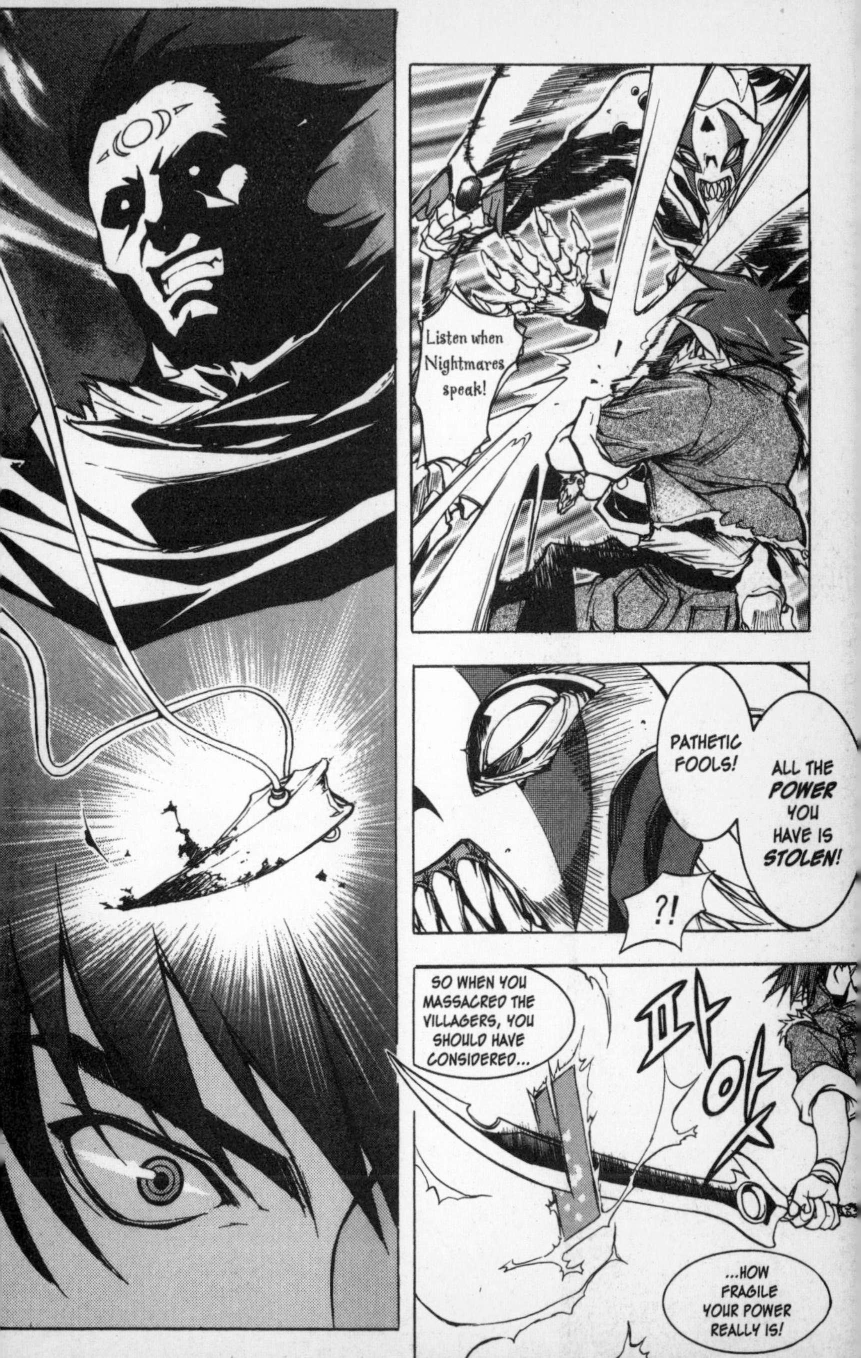
Listen when Nightmares speak!
PATHETIC FOOLS!
ALL THE POWER YOU HAVE IS STOLEN!
?!
SO WHEN YOU MASSACRED THE VILLAGERS, YOU SHOULD HAVE CONSIDERED...
파앗
...HOW FRAGILE YOUR POWER REALLY IS!

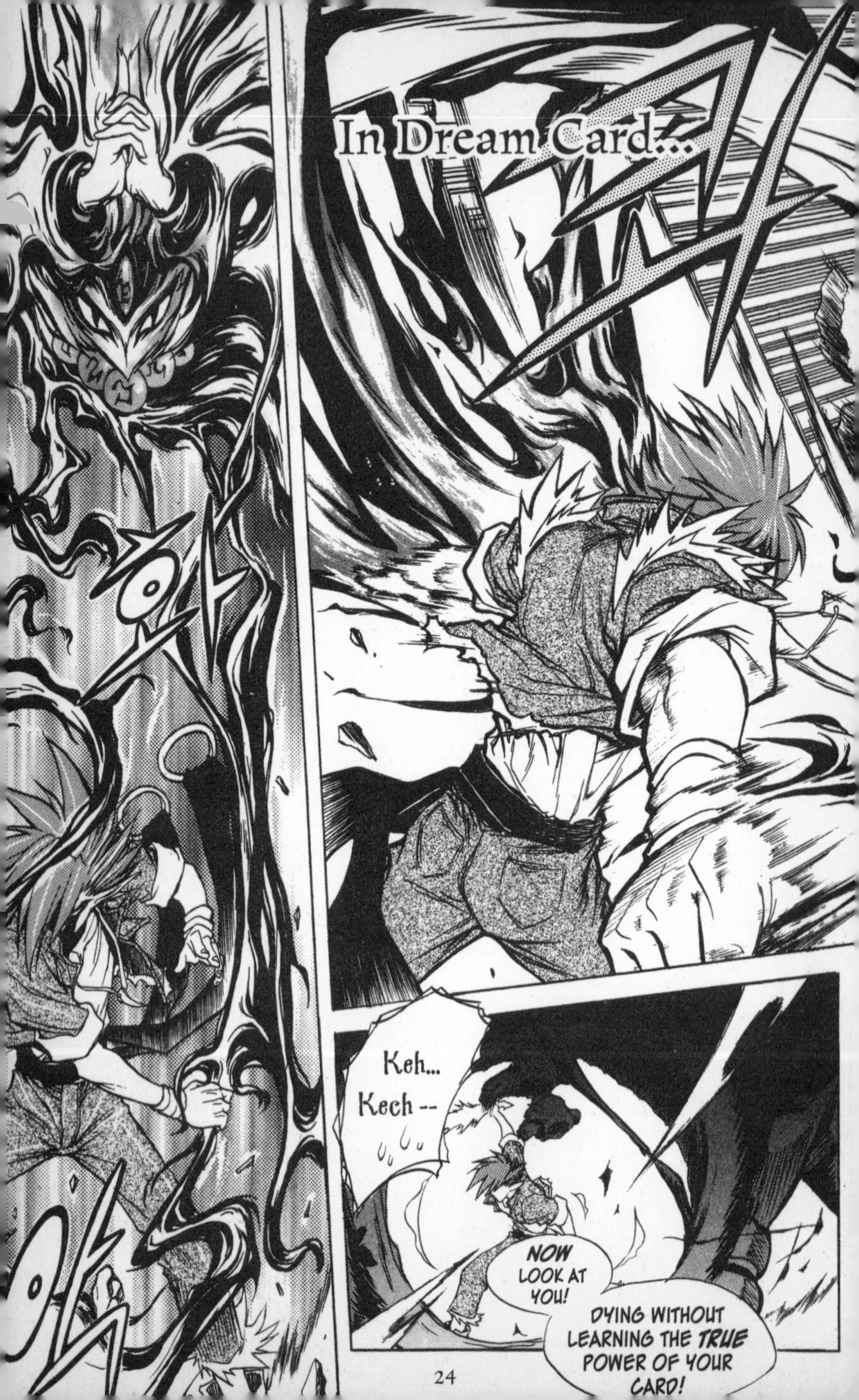
In Dream Card...
Keh... Kech --
NOW LOOK AT YOU!
DYING WITHOUT LEARNING THE TRUE POWER OF YOUR CARD!

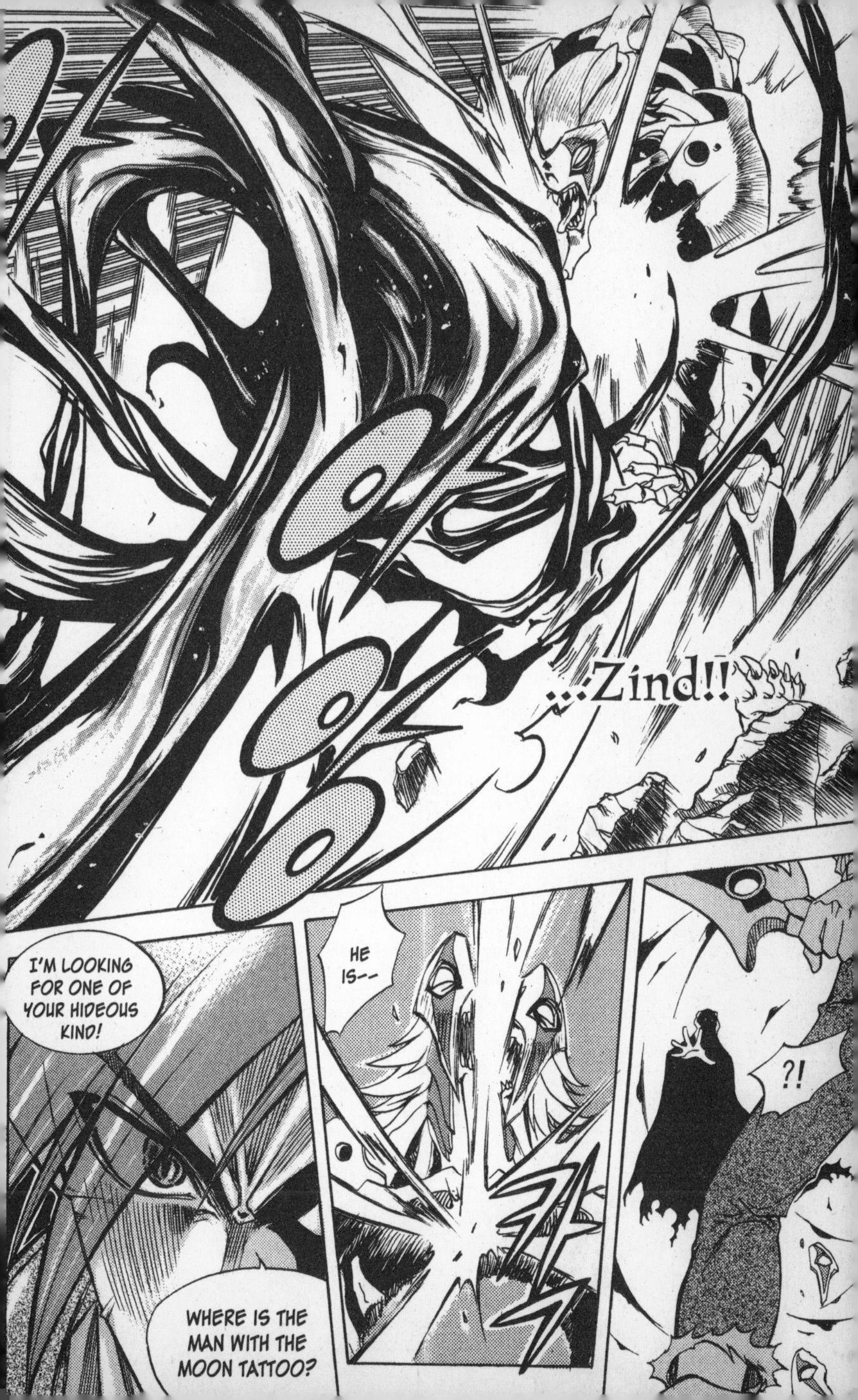
...Zind!!
I'M LOOKING FOR ONE OF YOUR HIDEOUS KIND!
WHERE IS THE MAN WITH THE MOON TATTOO?
HE IS--
?!

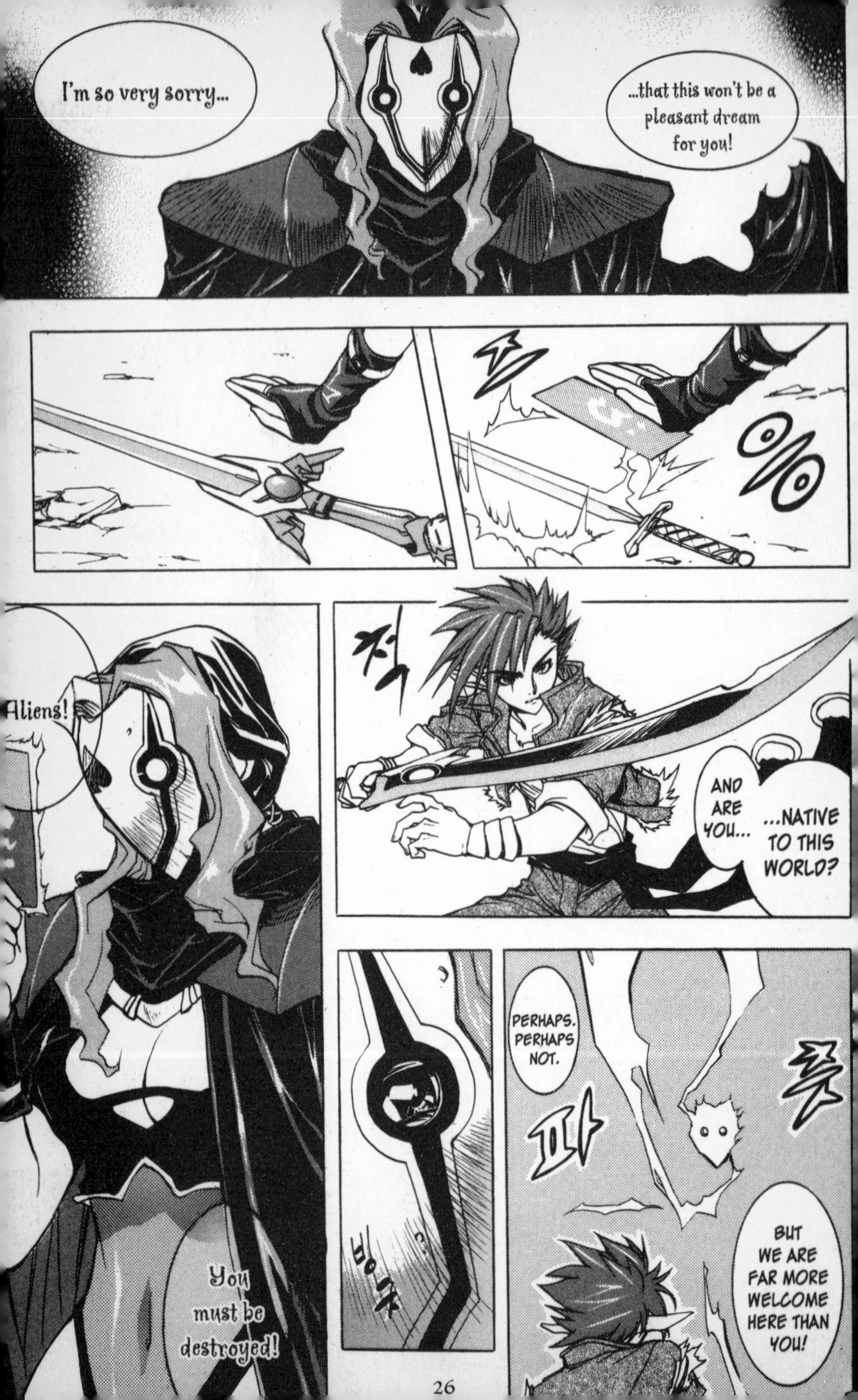
I'm so very sorry...
...that this won't be a pleasant dream for you!
Aliens!
You must be destroyed!
AND ARE YOU...
...NATIVE TO THIS WORLD?
PERHAPS. PERHAPS NOT.
BUT WE ARE FAR MORE WELCOME HERE THAN YOU!

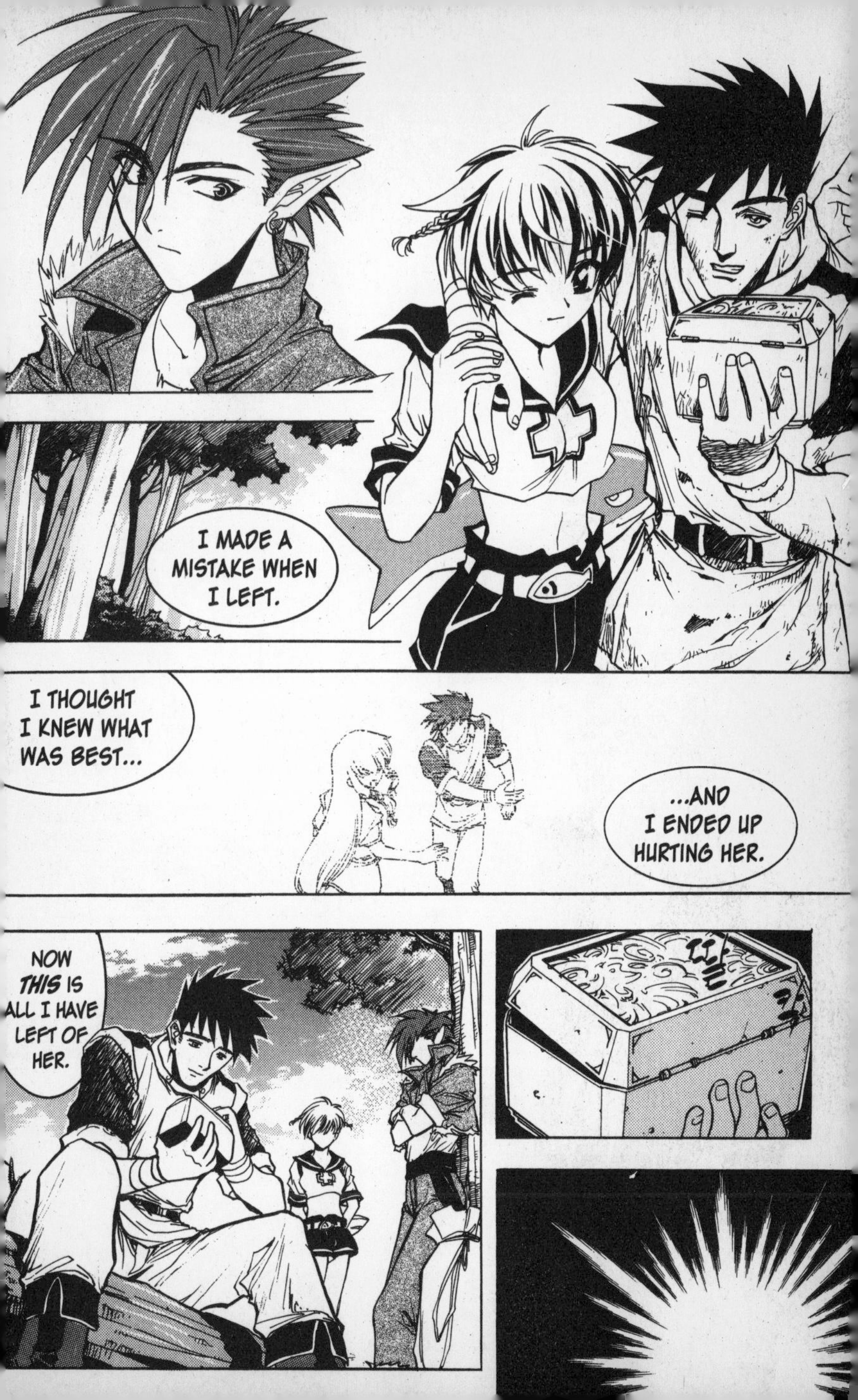
I MADE A MISTAKE WHEN I LEFT.
I THOUGHT I KNEW WHAT WAS BEST...
...AND I ENDED UP HURTING HER.
NOW *THIS* IS ALL I HAVE LEFT OF HER.

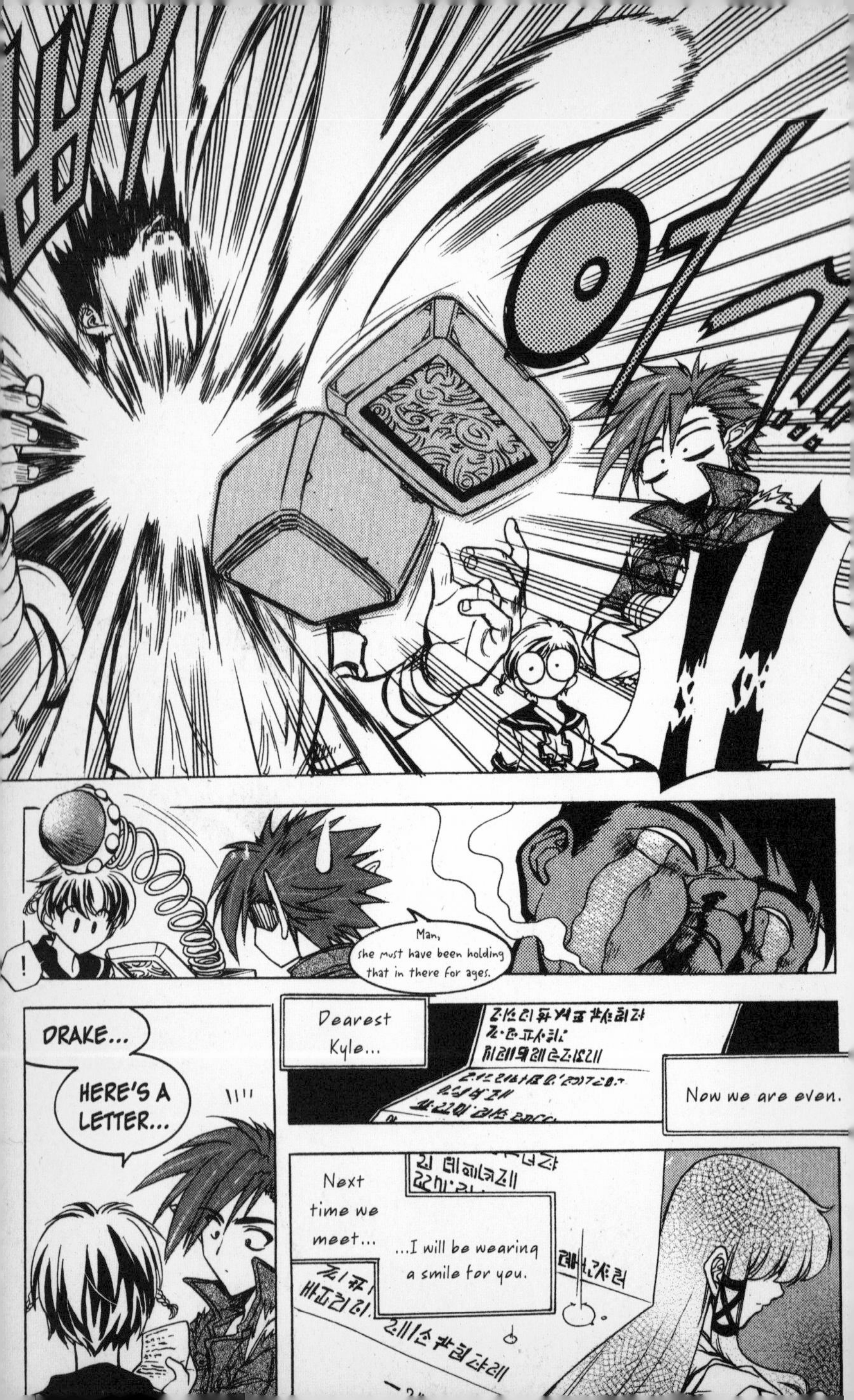
!
Man, she must have been holding that in there for ages.
DRAKE...
HERE'S A LETTER...
Dearest Kyle...
Now we are even.
Next time we meet...
...I will be wearing a smile for you.

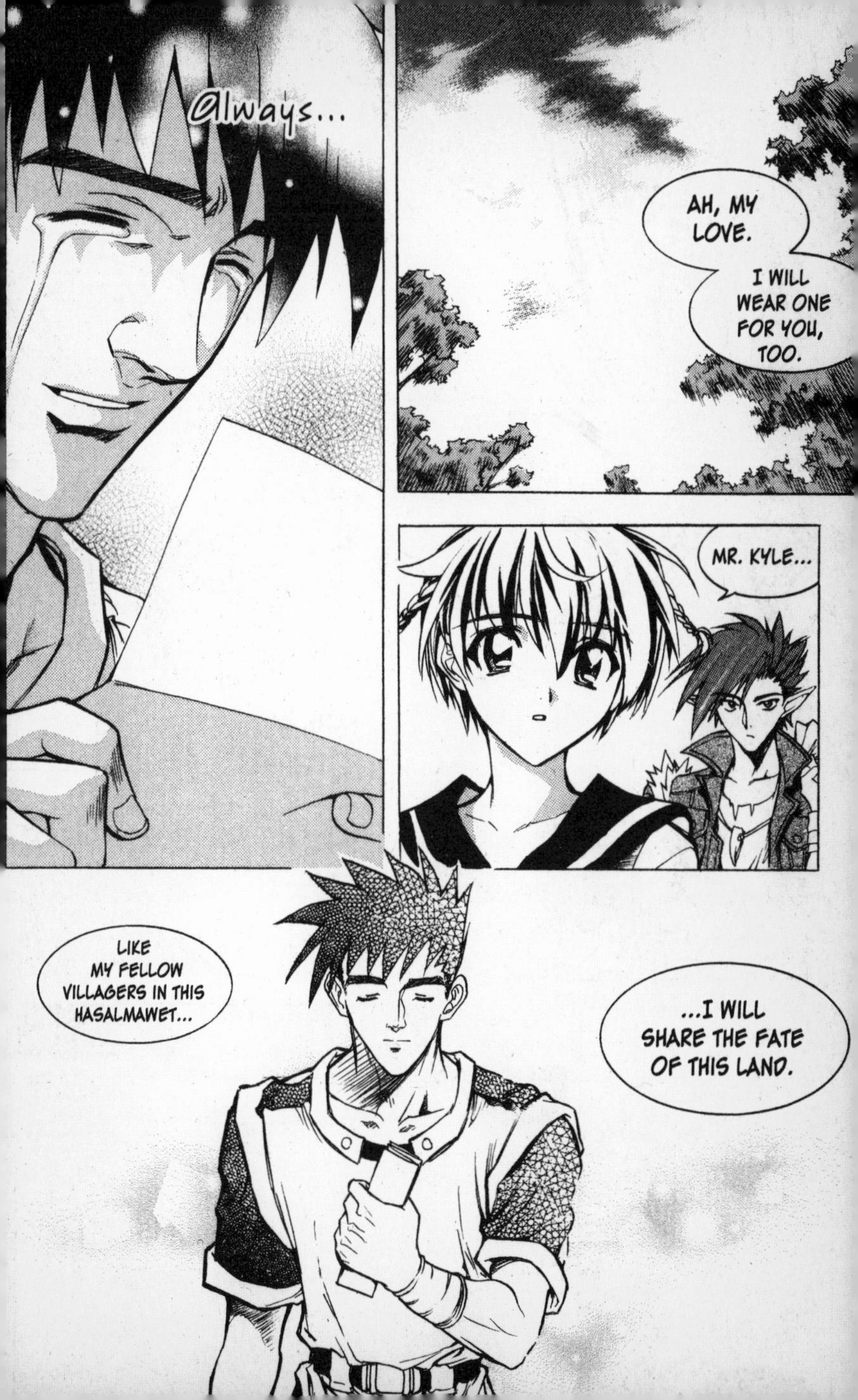
Always...
AH, MY LOVE.
I WILL WEAR ONE FOR YOU, TOO.
MR. KYLE...
LIKE MY FELLOW VILLAGERS IN THIS HASALMAWET...
...I WILL SHARE THE FATE OF THIS LAND.

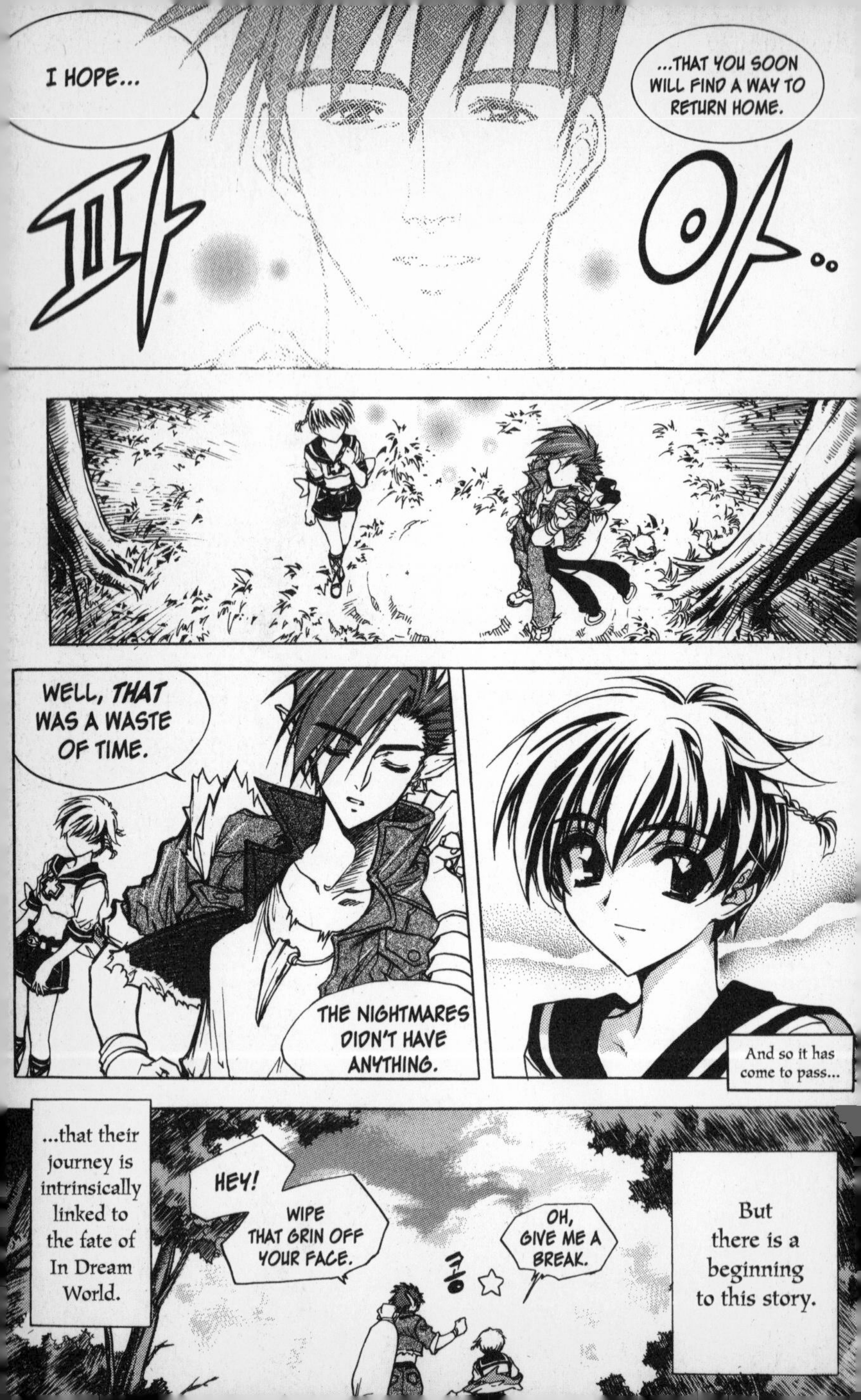
I HOPE...
파
...THAT YOU SOON WILL FIND A WAY TO RETURN HOME.
아..
WELL, *THAT* WAS A WASTE OF TIME.
THE NIGHTMARES DIDN'T HAVE ANYTHING.
And so it has come to pass...
...that their journey is intrinsically linked to the fate of In Dream World.
HEY!
WIPE THAT GRIN OFF YOUR FACE.
OH, GIVE ME A BREAK.
But there is a beginning to this story.

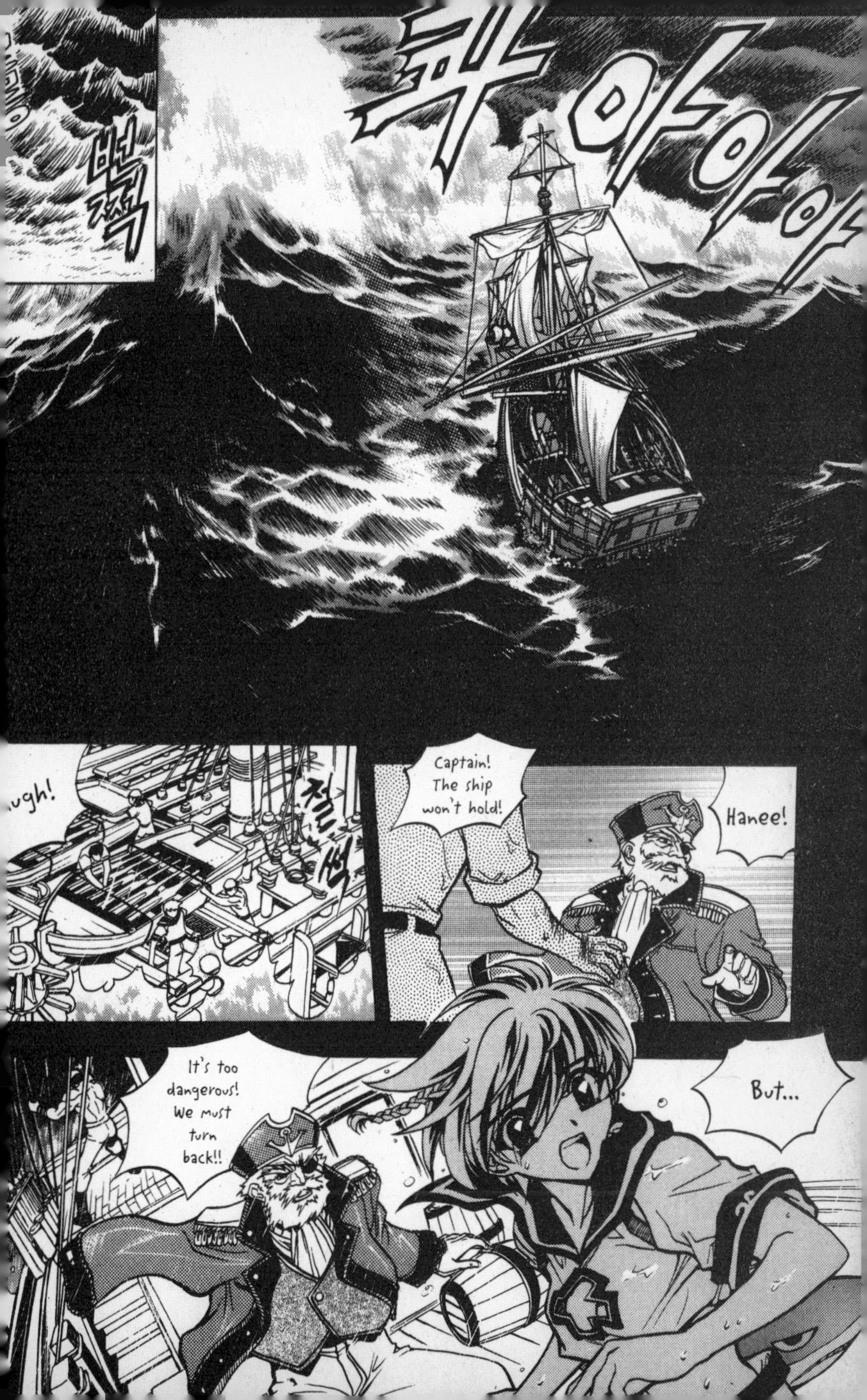

번쩍
화아아아
철썩
Captain! The ship won't hold!
Hanee!
It's too dangerous! We must turn back!!
But...

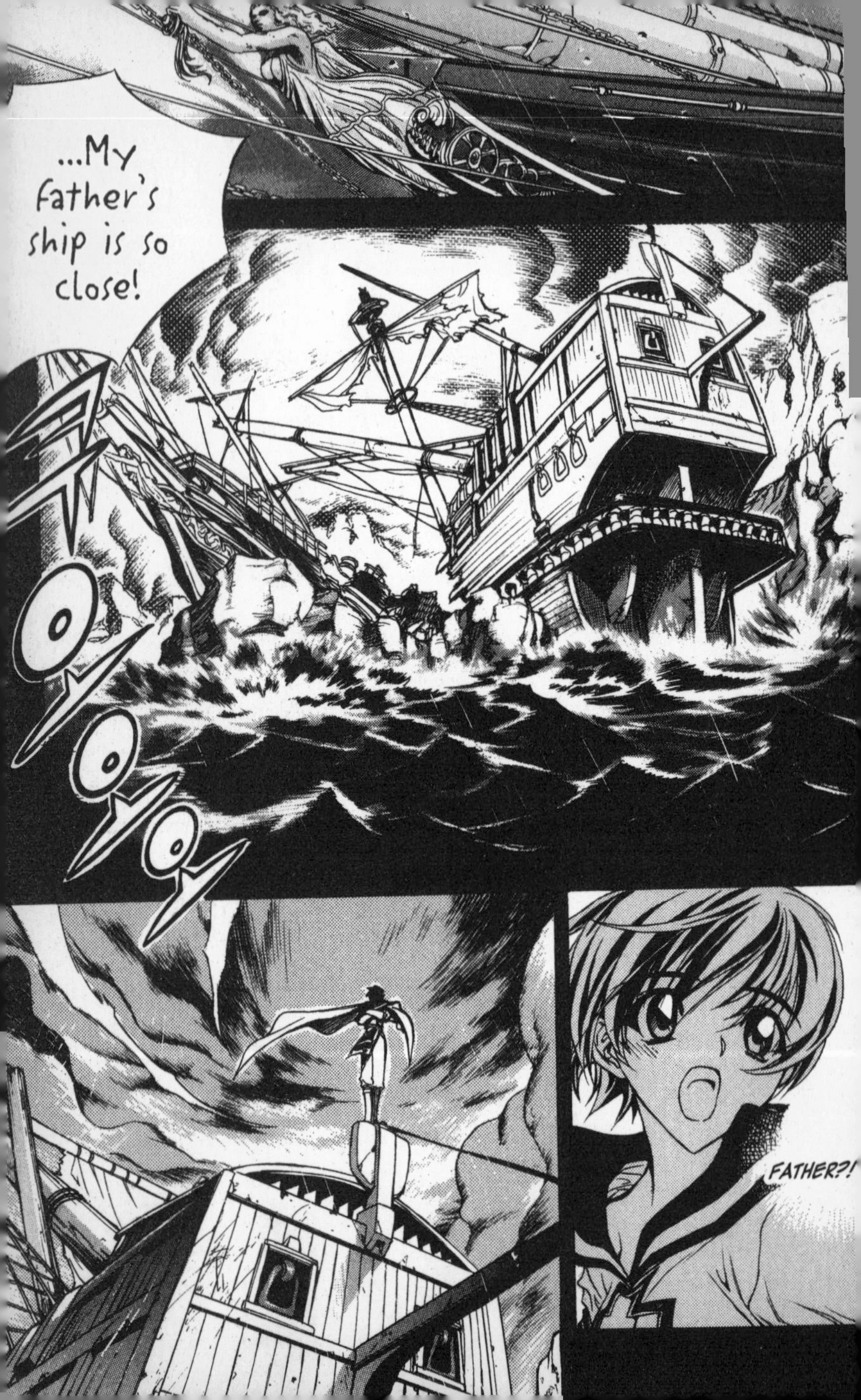
...My father's ship is so close!
FATHER?!

stage 2.

Meeting 1

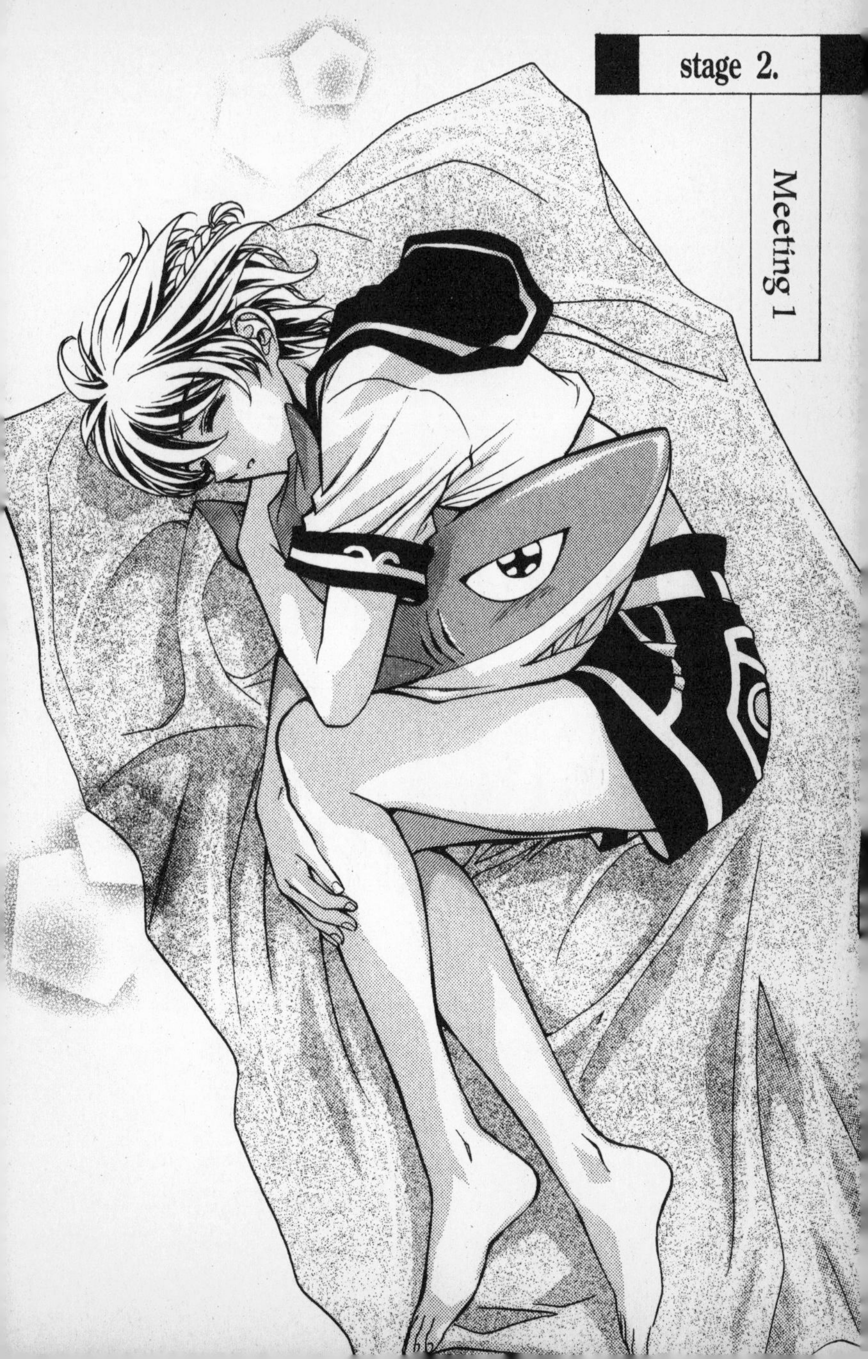

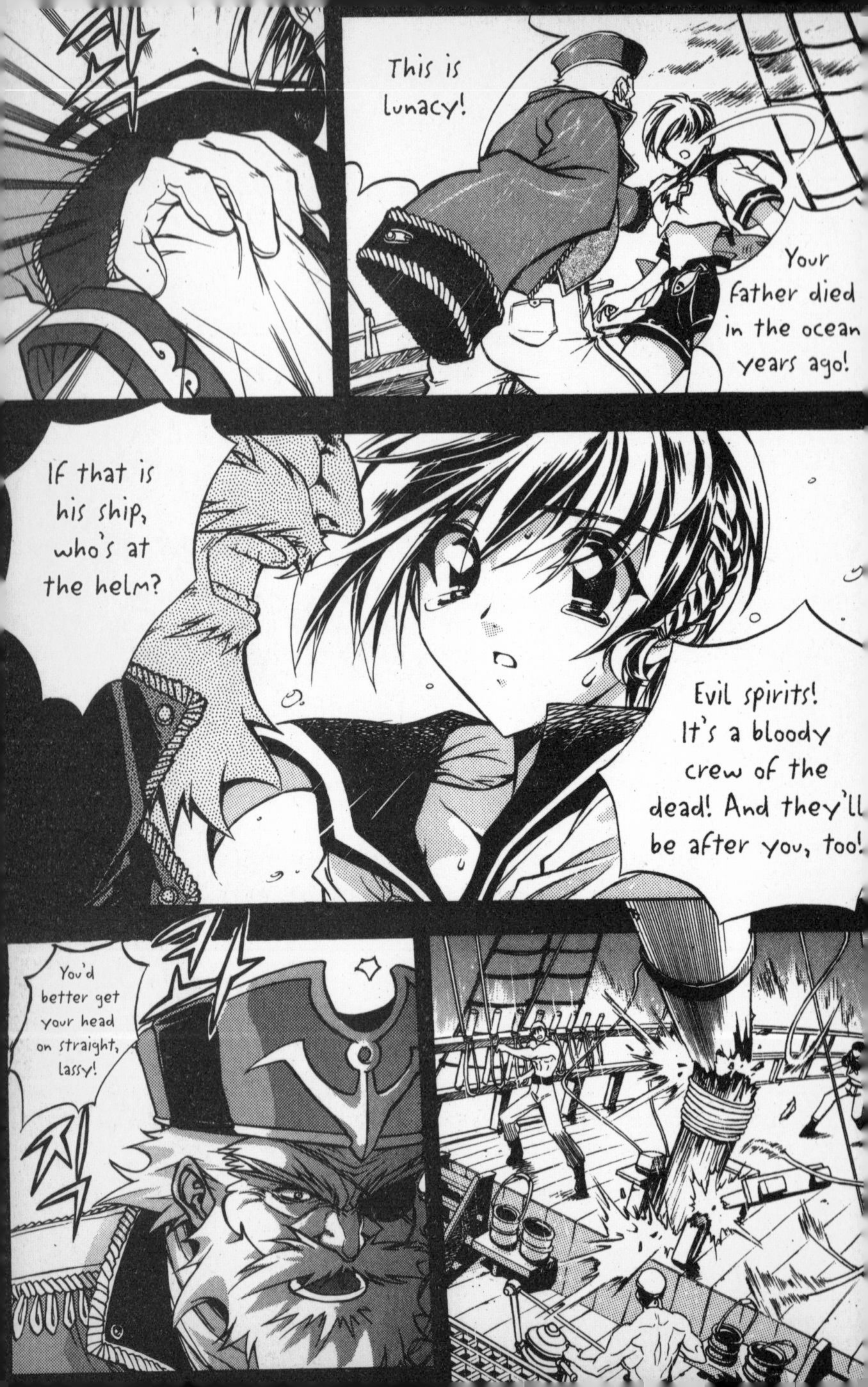

This is lunacy!
Your father died in the ocean years ago!
If that is his ship, who's at the helm?
Evil spirits! It's a bloody crew of the dead! And they'll be after you, too!
You'd better get your head on straight, lassy!

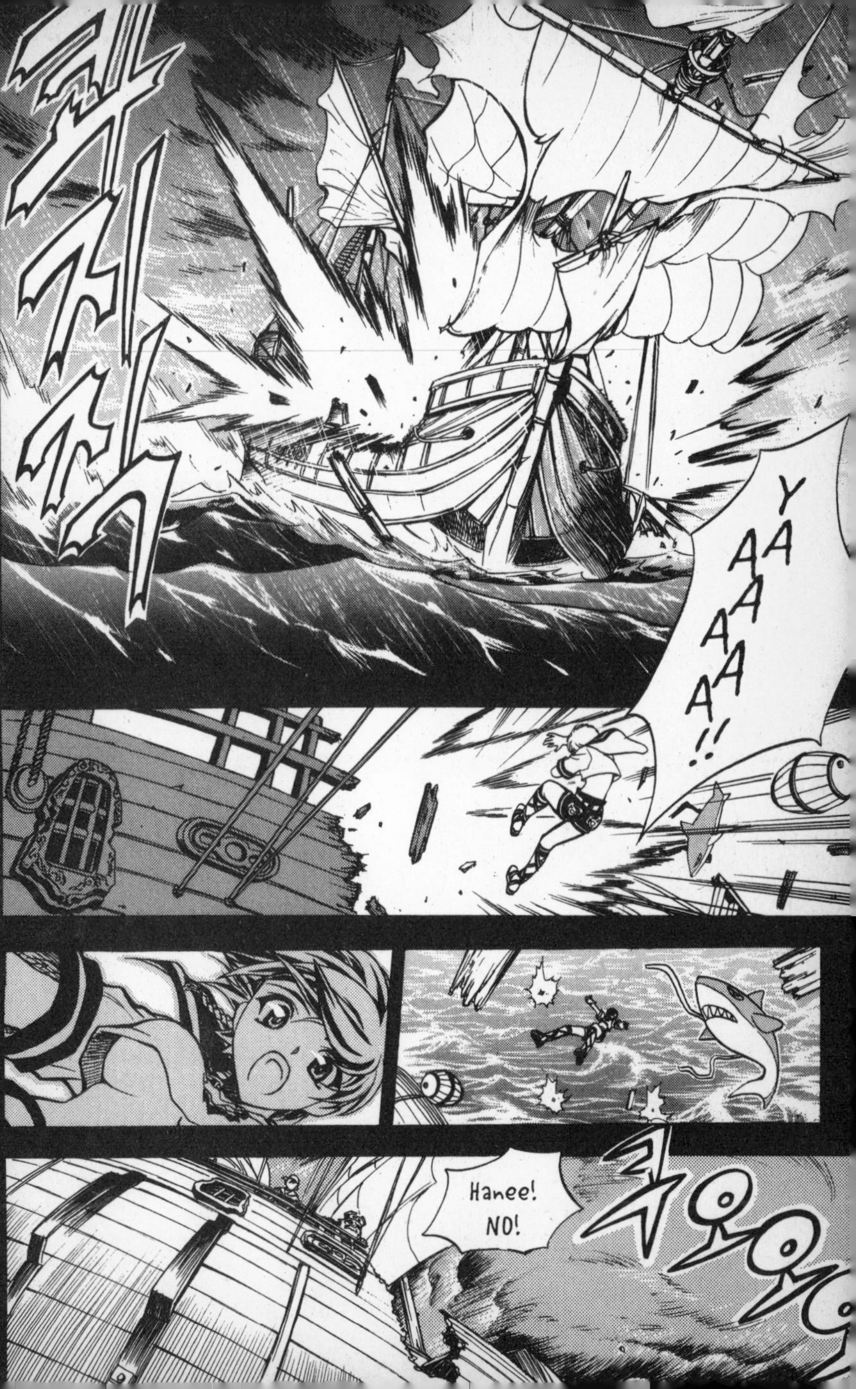
YAAAAAA!!
Hanee! NO!

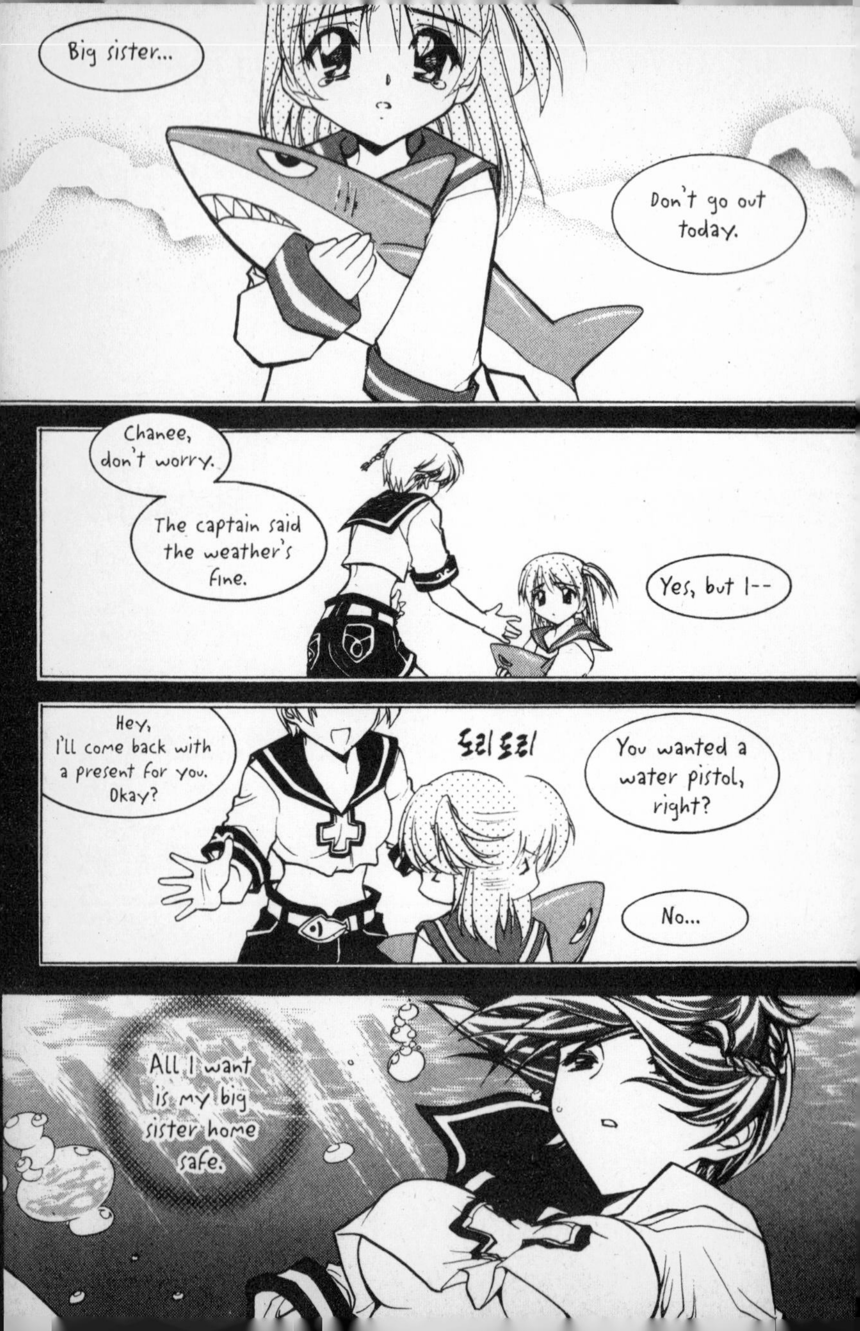
Big sister...
Don't go out today.
Chanee, don't worry.
The captain said the weather's fine.
Yes, but I--
Hey, I'll come back with a present for you. Okay?
도리도리
You wanted a water pistol, right?
No...
All I want is my big sister home safe.

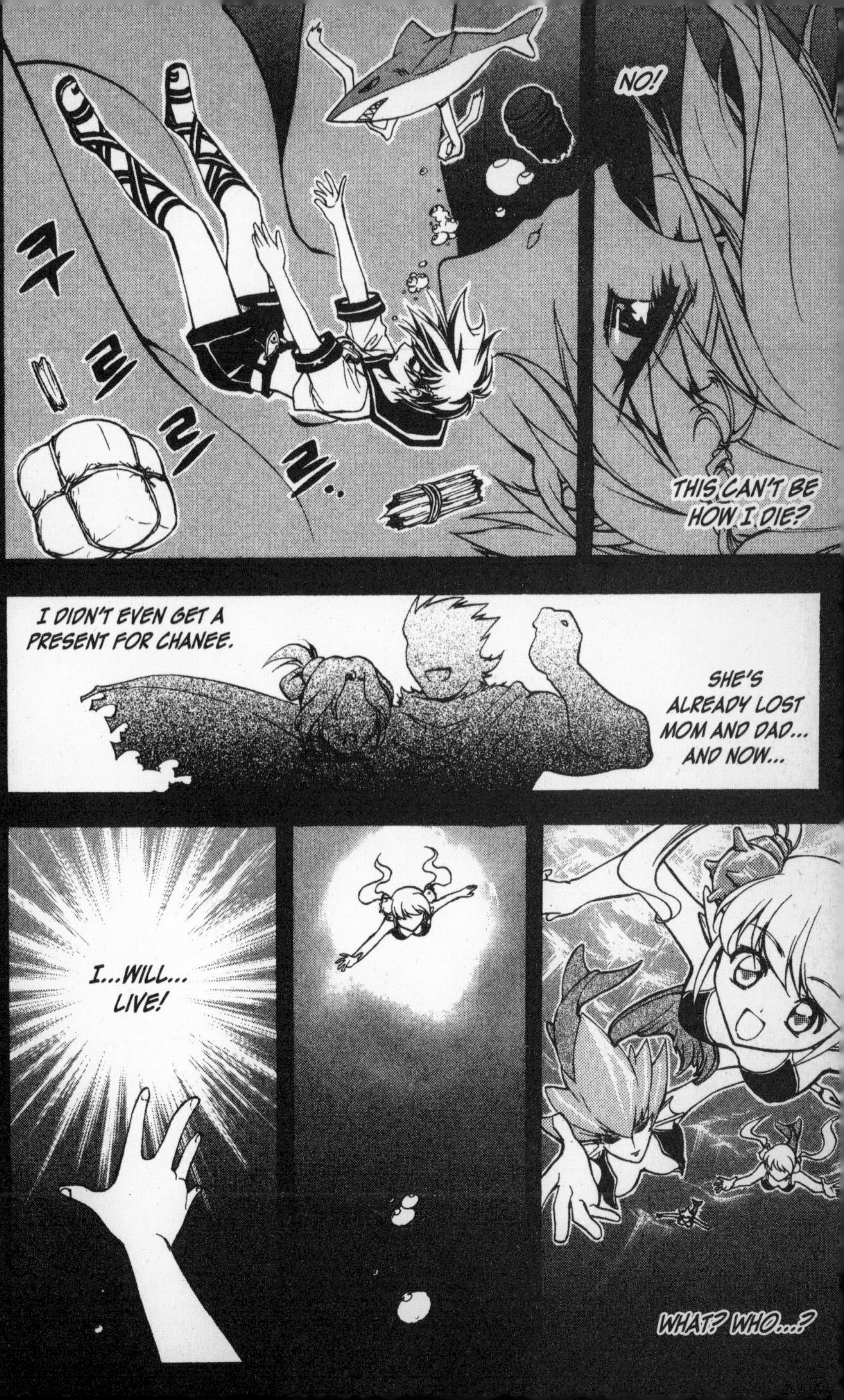
NO!
THIS CAN'T BE HOW I DIE?
I DIDN'T EVEN GET A PRESENT FOR CHANEE.
SHE'S ALREADY LOST MOM AND DAD... AND NOW...
I...WILL... LIVE!
WHAT? WHO...?

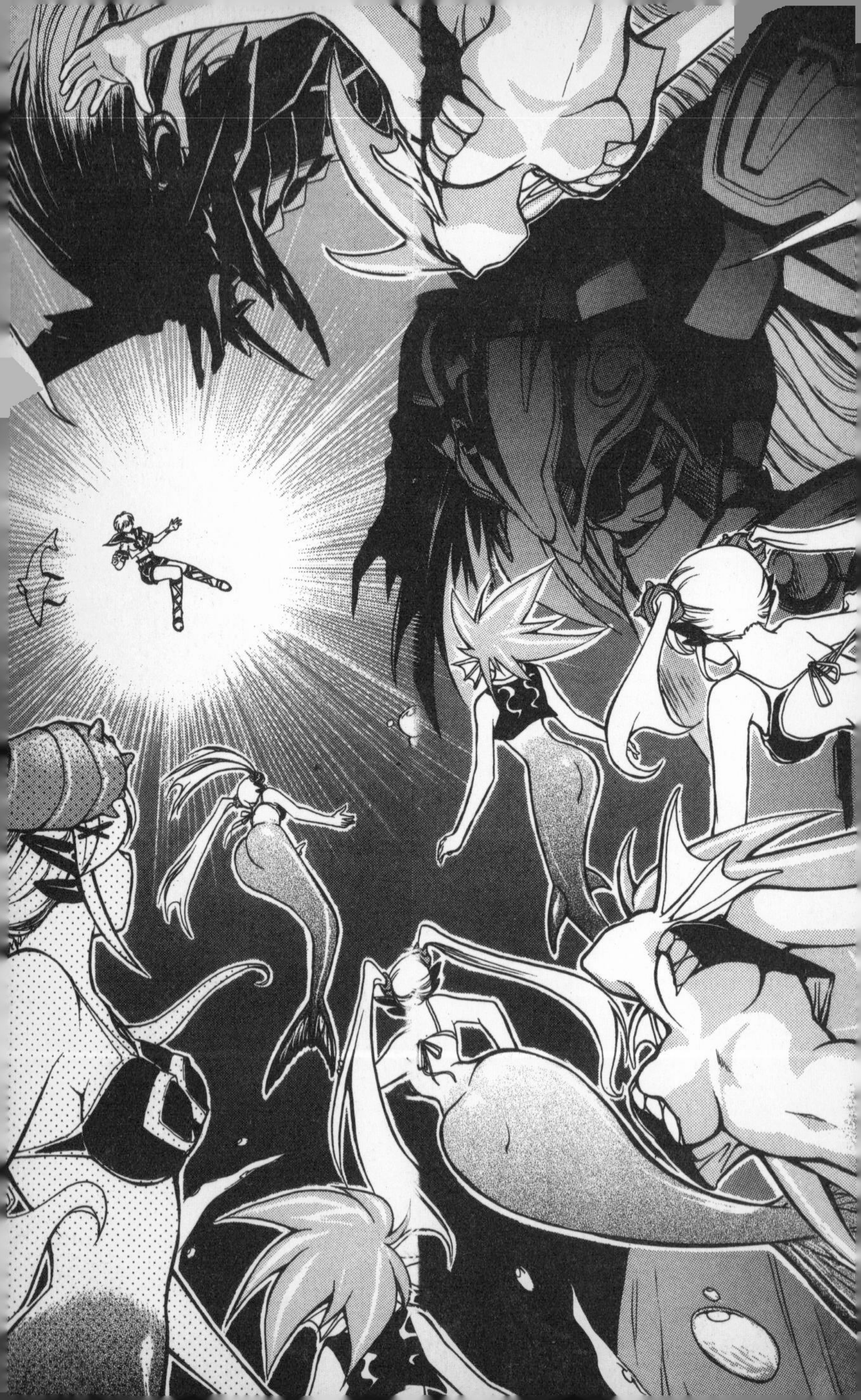

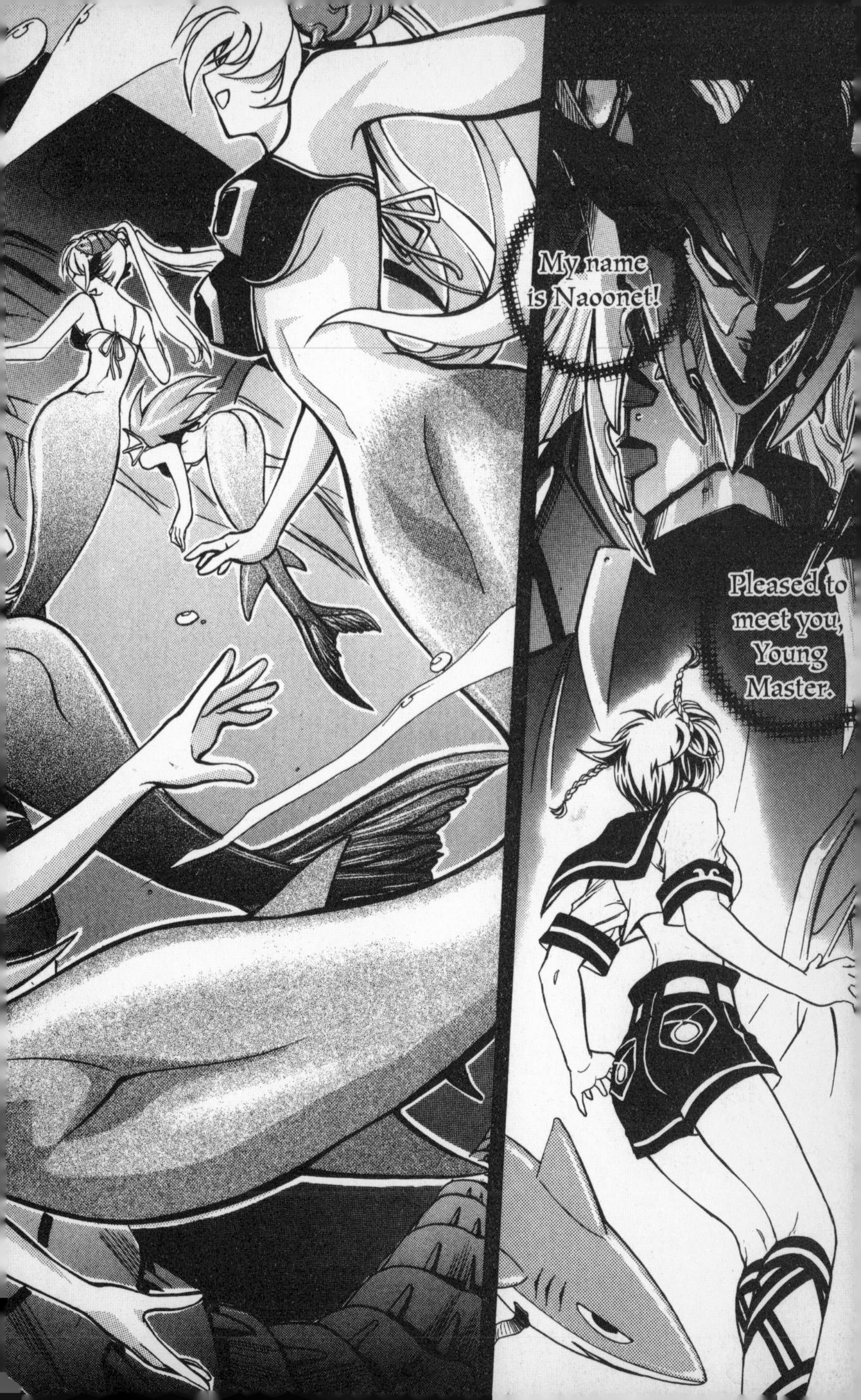
My name is Naoonet!
Pleased to meet you, Young Master.

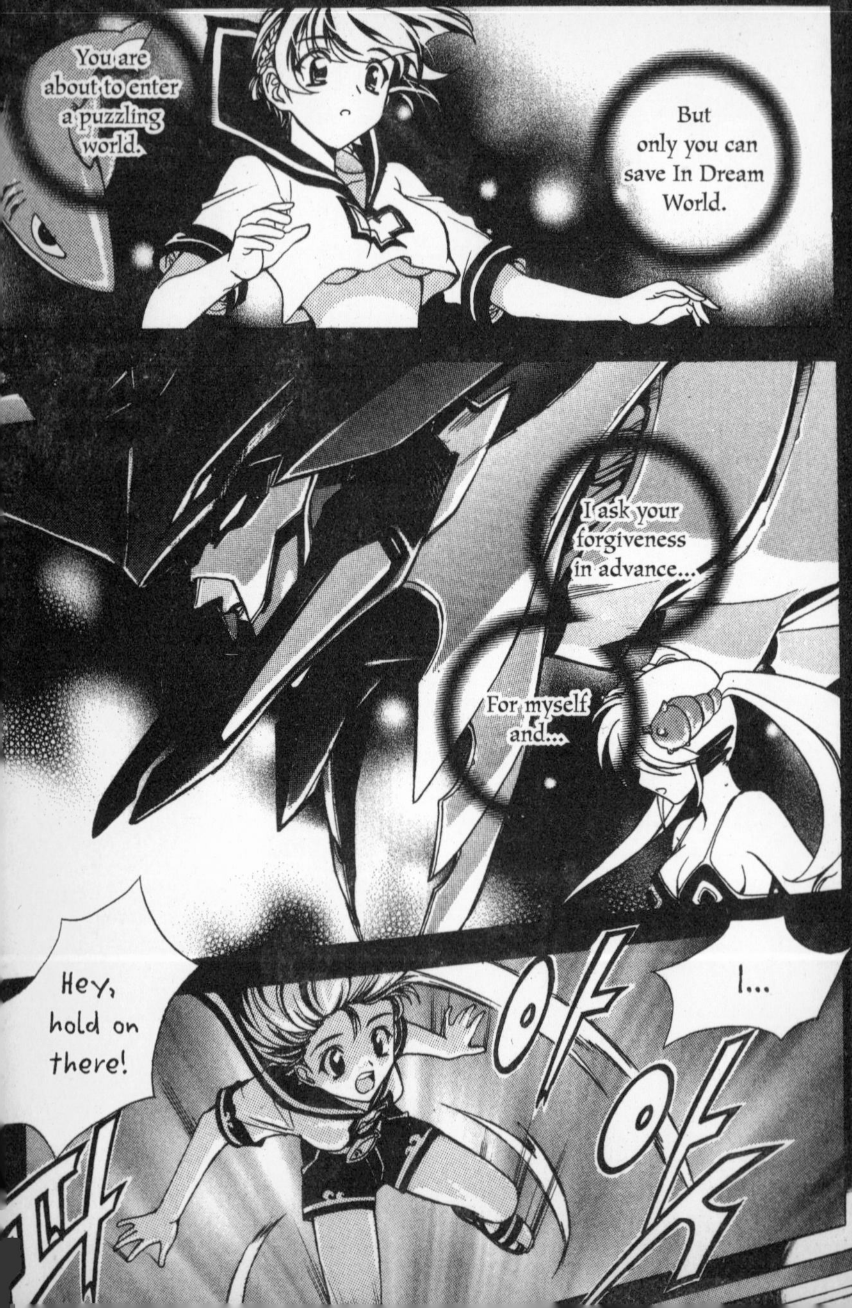
You are about to enter a puzzling world.
But only you can save In Dream World.
I ask your forgiveness in advance...
For myself and...
Hey, hold on there!
I...

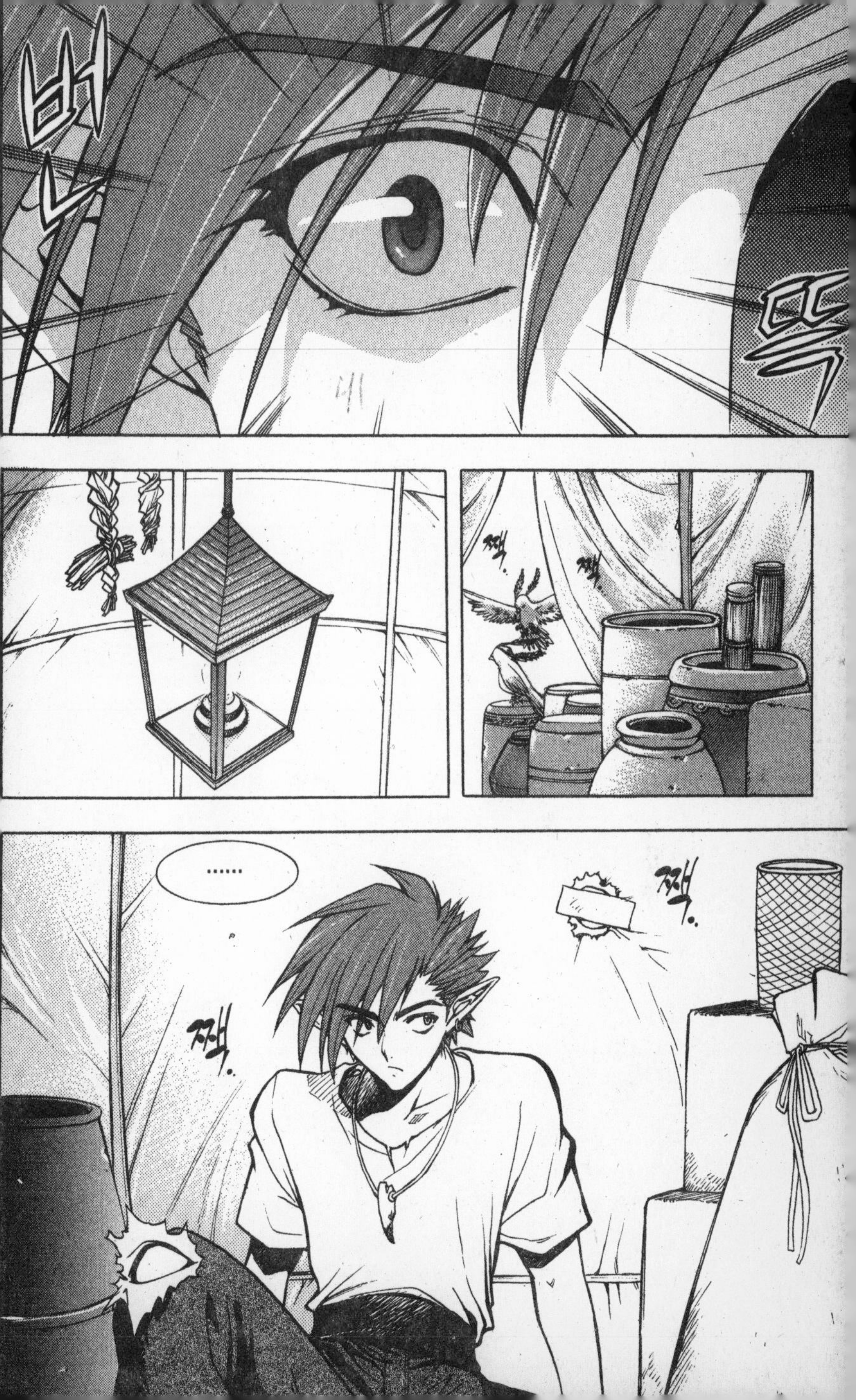

번
뜩
네
짹.
짹
......
짹..
짹..

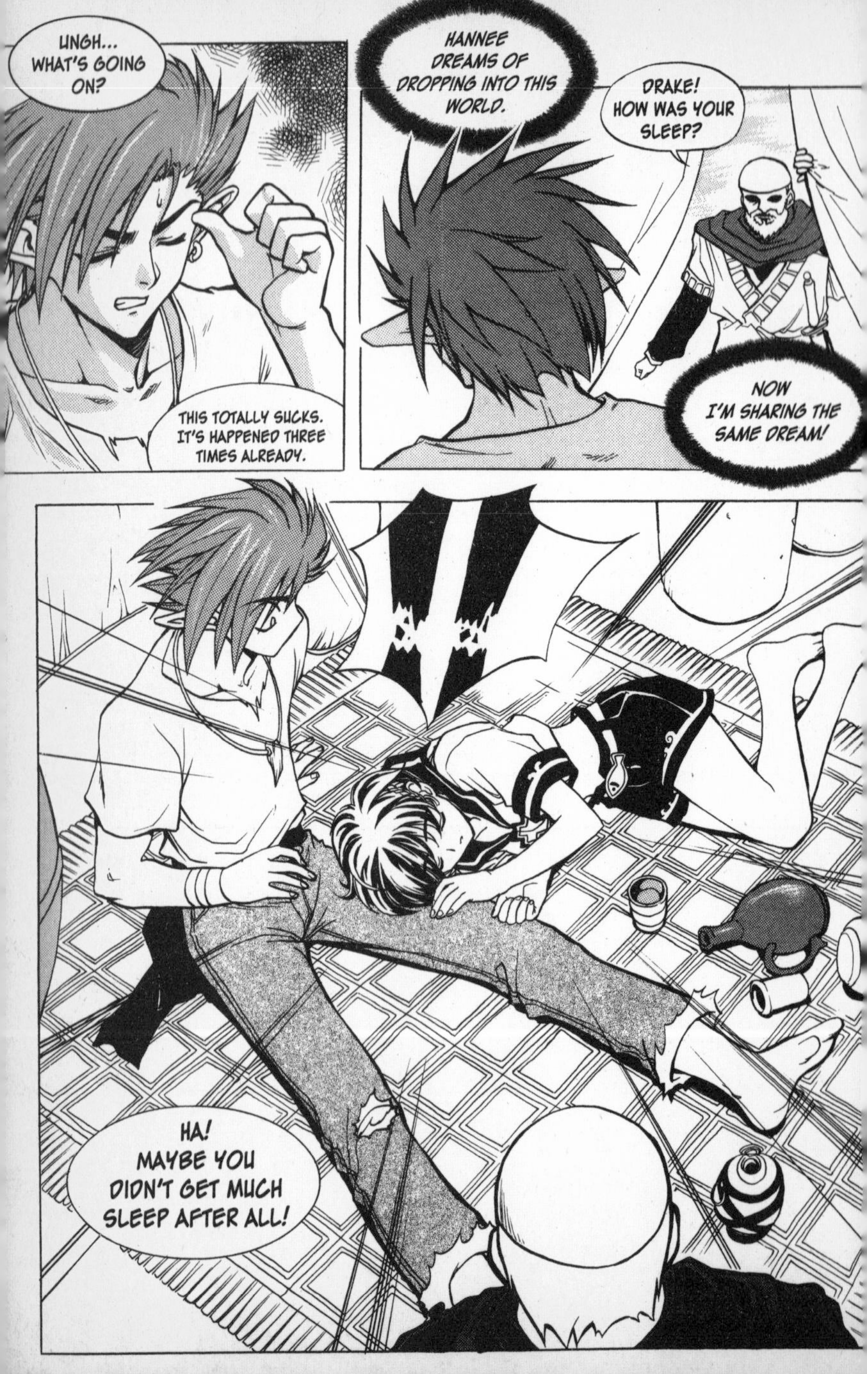
UNGH... WHAT'S GOING ON?
THIS TOTALLY SUCKS. IT'S HAPPENED THREE TIMES ALREADY.
HANNEE DREAMS OF DROPPING INTO THIS WORLD.
DRAKE! HOW WAS YOUR SLEEP?
NOW I'M SHARING THE SAME DREAM!
HA! MAYBE YOU DIDN'T GET MUCH SLEEP AFTER ALL!

Hm...Sharkie, you lost weight...

YOU --!

I DON'T CARE IF YOU *ARE* DREAMING! WATCH WHERE YOU PUT YOUR HANDS!

OUCH!

※ You look so svelte.

I KNOW, I KNOW.

WOMEN! CAN'T LIVE WITH 'EM, CAN'T --

SHUT UP, OLD MAN!

HMPH! WELL, YOU GUYS WORKED A LOT YESTERDAY.

NO WONDER YOU'RE TIRED AND CRANKY.

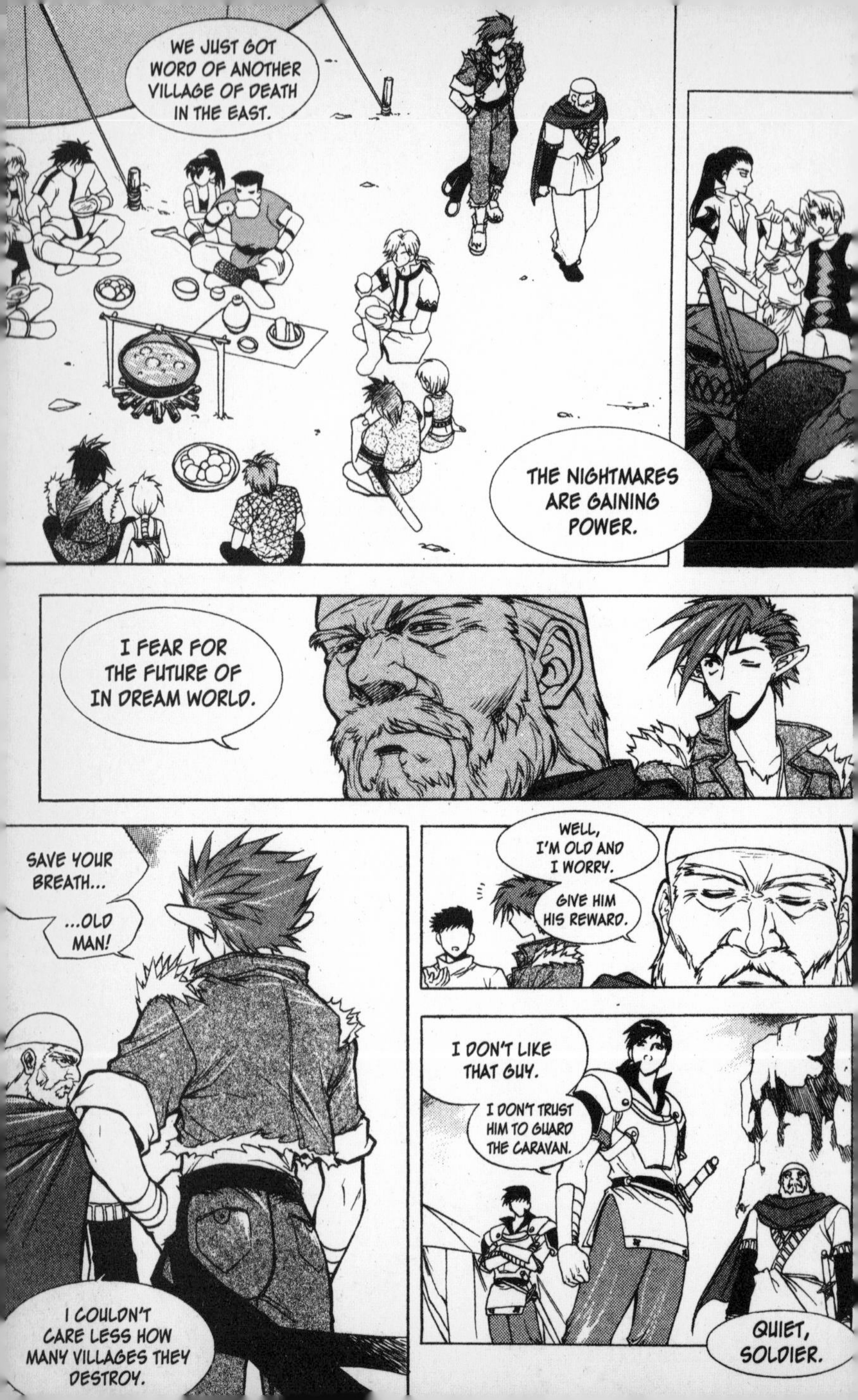
WE JUST GOT WORD OF ANOTHER VILLAGE OF DEATH IN THE EAST.
THE NIGHTMARES ARE GAINING POWER.
I FEAR FOR THE FUTURE OF IN DREAM WORLD.
SAVE YOUR BREATH...
...OLD MAN!
I COULDN'T CARE LESS HOW MANY VILLAGES THEY DESTROY.
WELL, I'M OLD AND I WORRY.
GIVE HIM HIS REWARD.
I DON'T LIKE THAT GUY.
I DON'T TRUST HIM TO GUARD THE CARAVAN.
QUIET, SOLDIER.

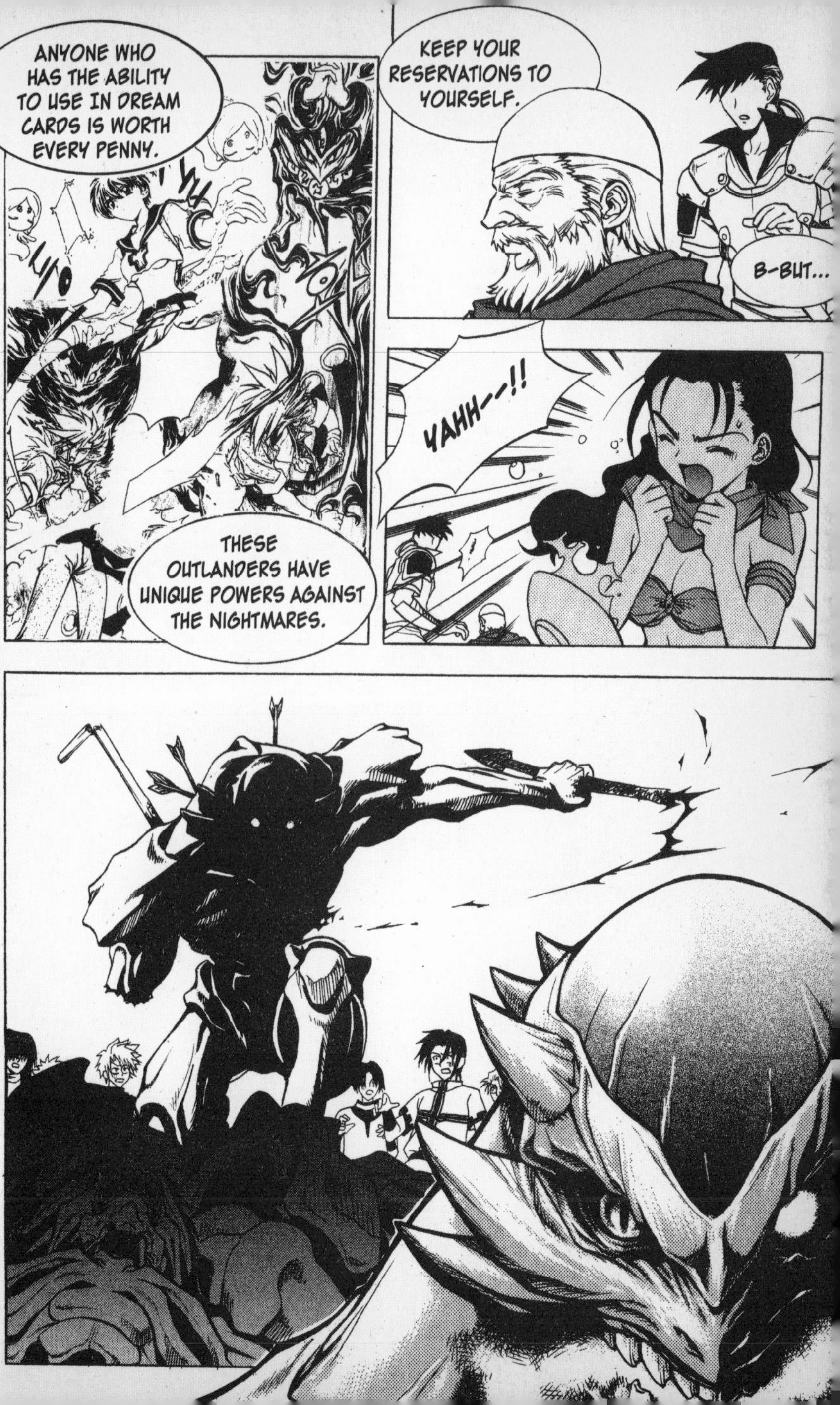
ANYONE WHO HAS THE ABILITY TO USE IN DREAM CARDS IS WORTH EVERY PENNY.
THESE OUTLANDERS HAVE UNIQUE POWERS AGAINST THE NIGHTMARES.
KEEP YOUR RESERVATIONS TO YOURSELF.
B-BUT...
YAHH--!!

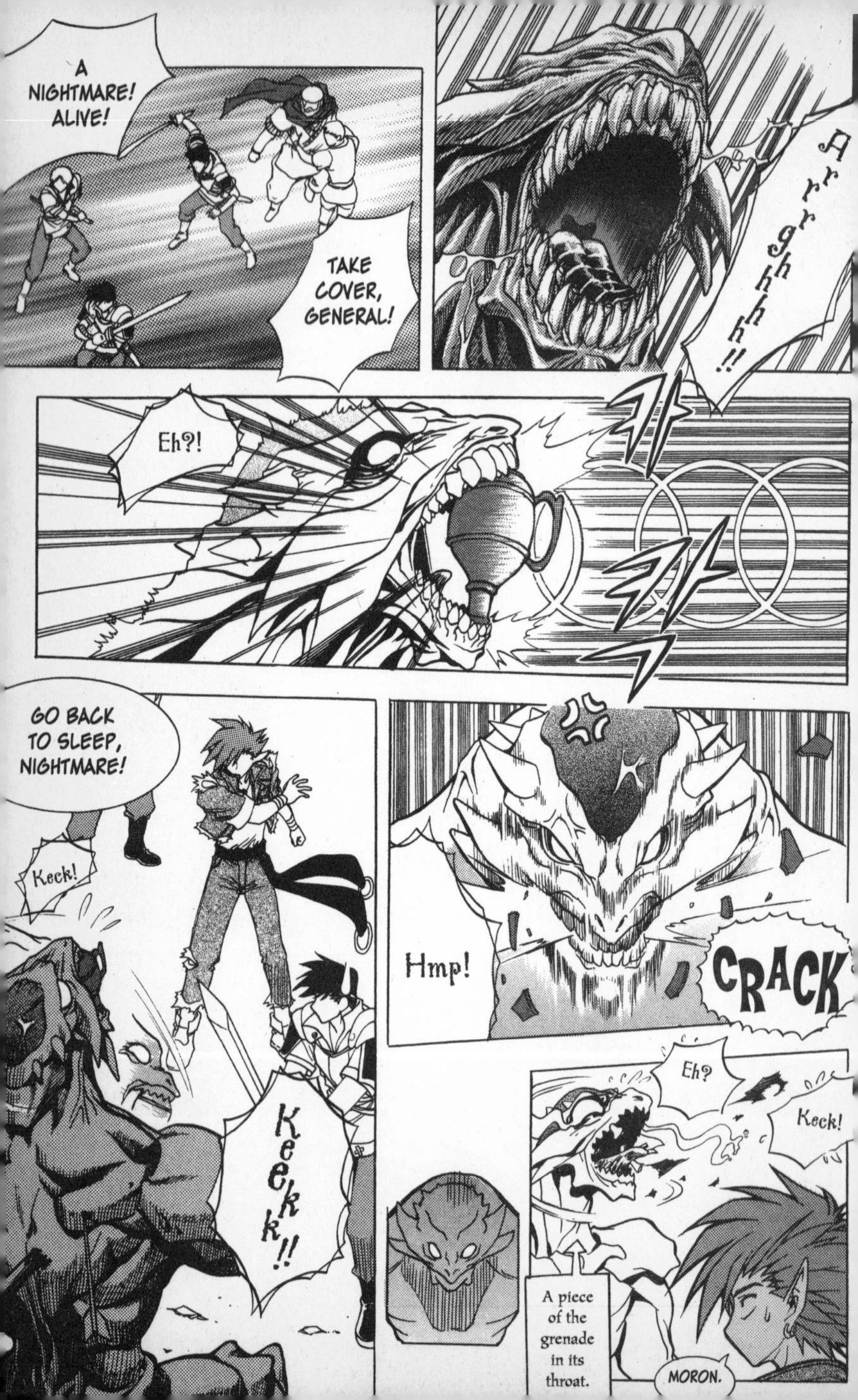
A NIGHTMARE! ALIVE!
TAKE COVER, GENERAL!
Arrrghhhh!!
Eh?!
GO BACK TO SLEEP, NIGHTMARE!
Keek!
Keekk!!
Hmp!
CRACK
A piece of the grenade in its throat.
Eh?
Keek!
MORON.

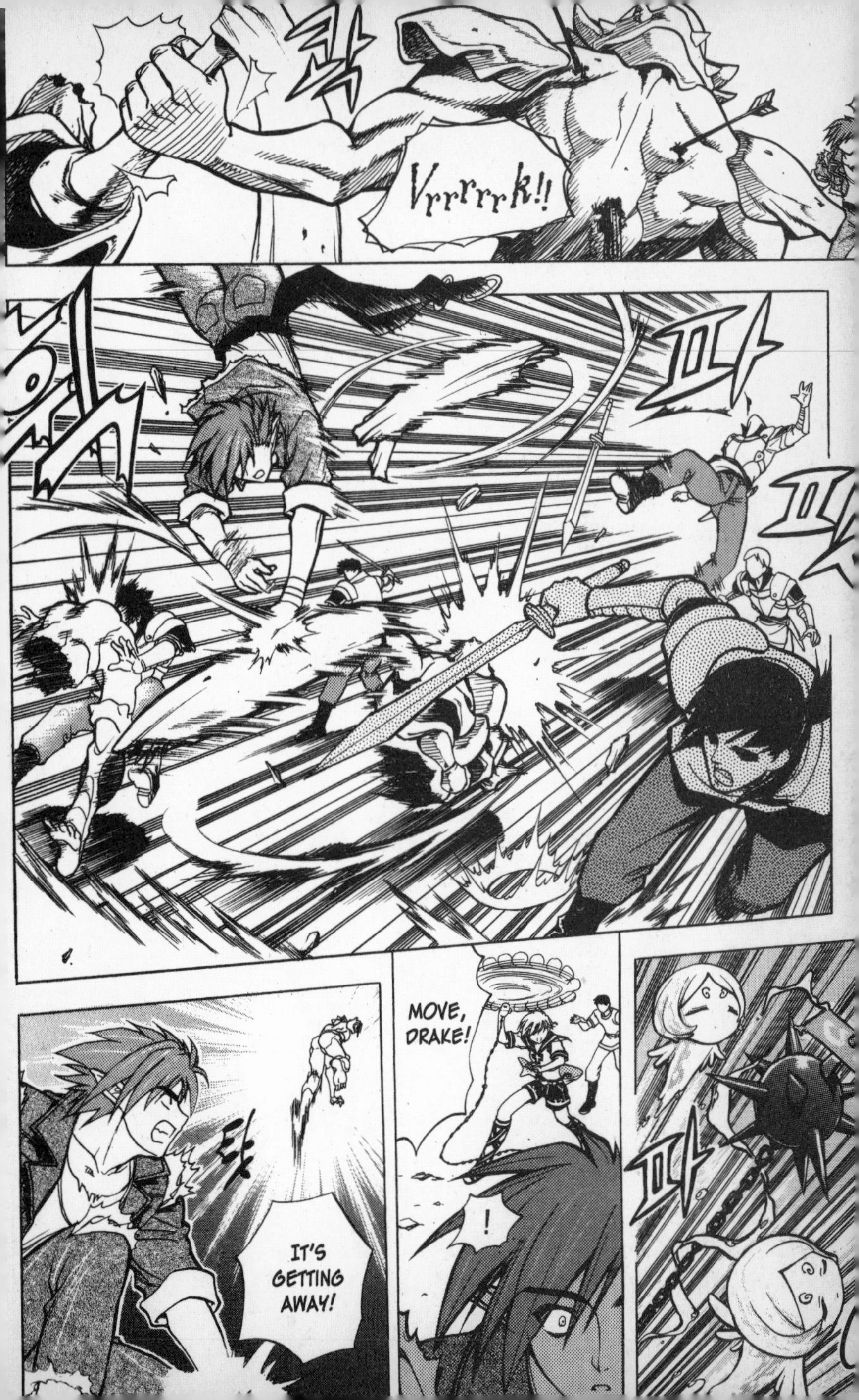
Vrrrrrk!!
IT'S GETTING AWAY!
MOVE, DRAKE!
!

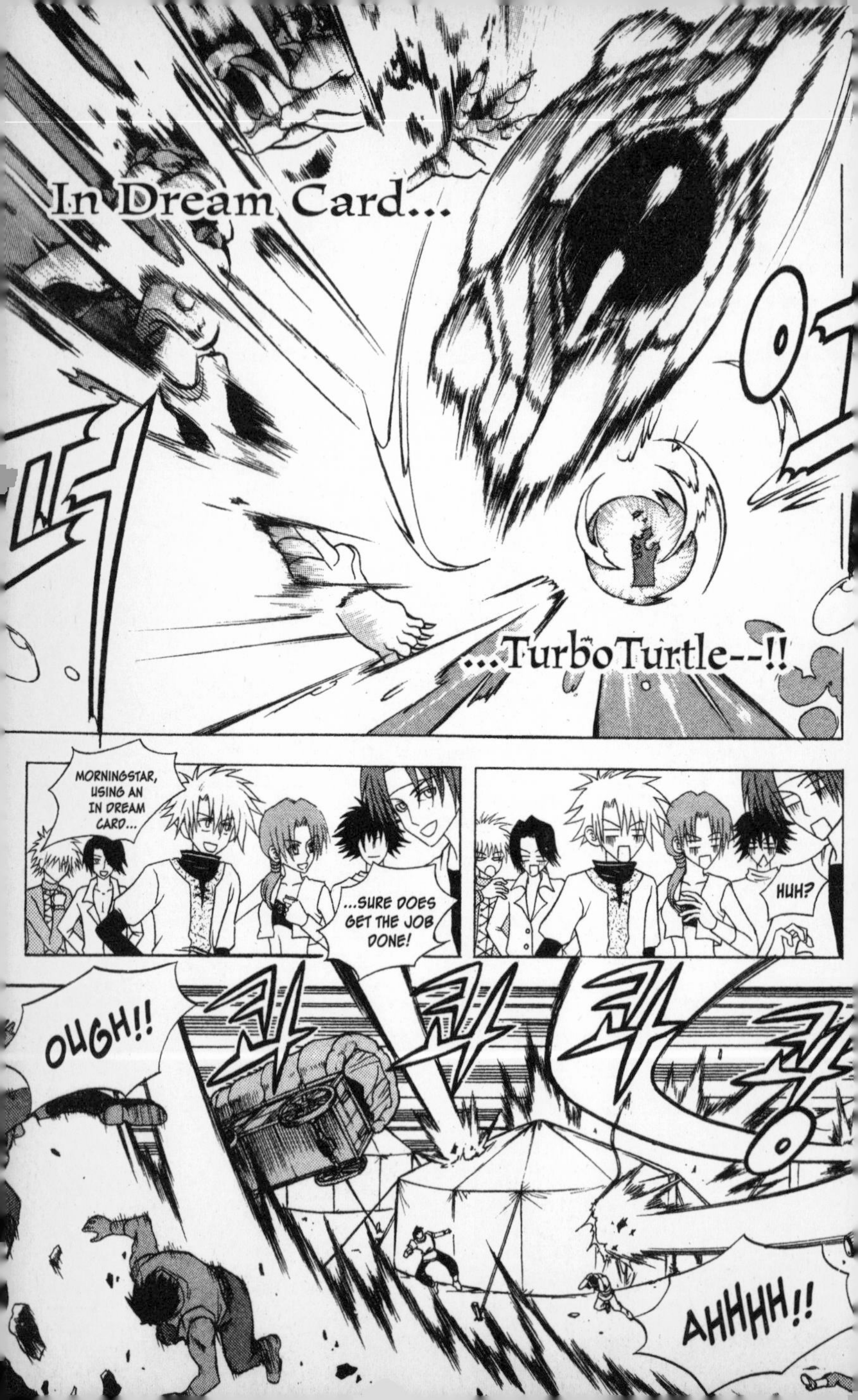
In Dream Card...
...TurboTurtle--!!
MORNINGSTAR, USING AN IN DREAM CARD...
...SURE DOES GET THE JOB DONE!
HUH?
OUGH!!
AHHHH!!

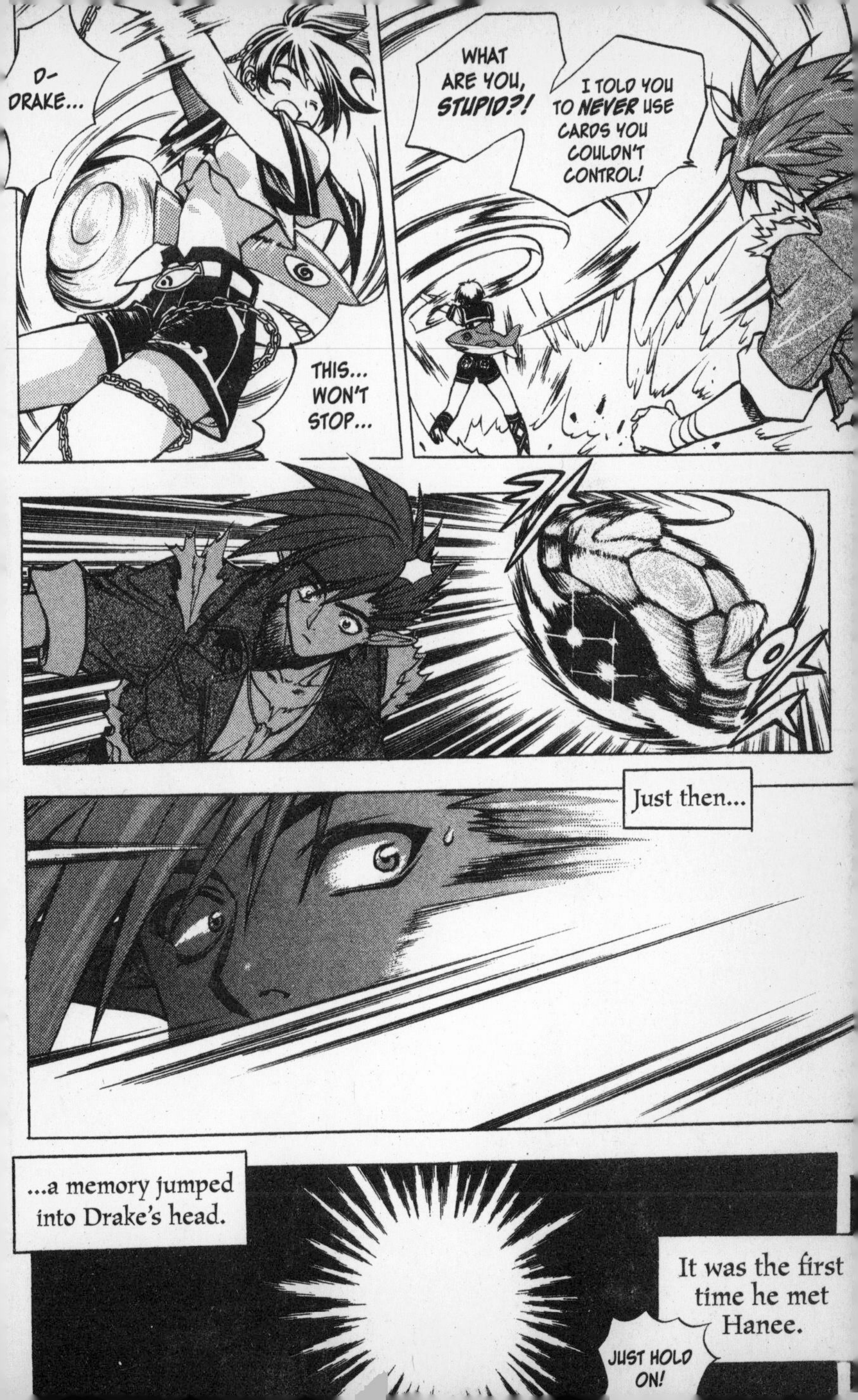

D-
DRAKE...
THIS...
WON'T
STOP...
WHAT
ARE YOU,
STUPID?!
I TOLD YOU
TO NEVER USE
CARDS YOU
COULDN'T
CONTROL!
Just then...
...a memory jumped
into Drake's head.
It was the first
time he met
Hanee.
JUST HOLD
ON!

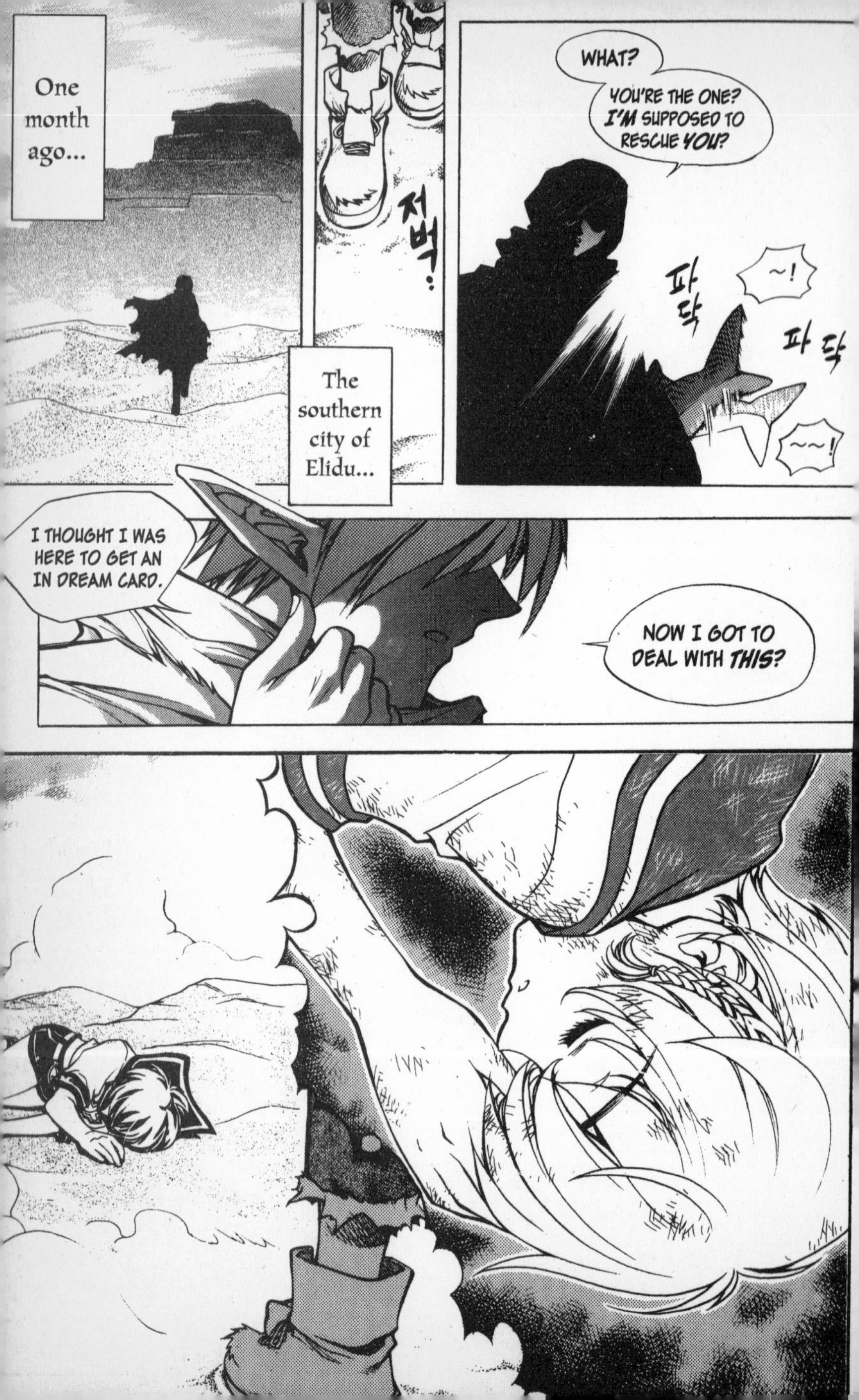

One month ago...
저벅!
The southern city of Elidu...
WHAT?
YOU'RE THE ONE? I'M SUPPOSED TO RESCUE YOU?
파닥
~!
파닥
~~!
I THOUGHT I WAS HERE TO GET AN IN DREAM CARD.
NOW I GOT TO DEAL WITH THIS?

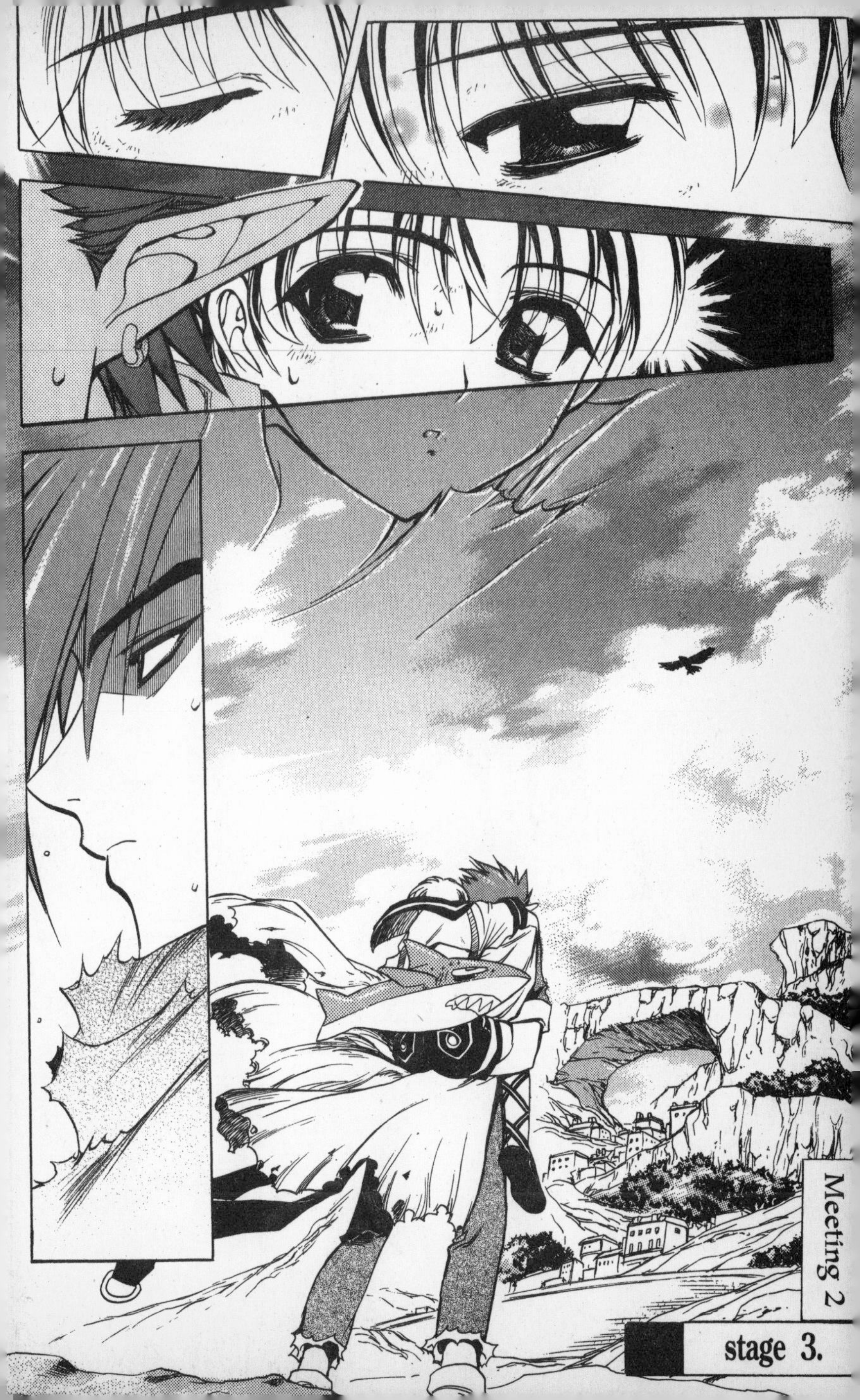
Meeting 2
stage 3.

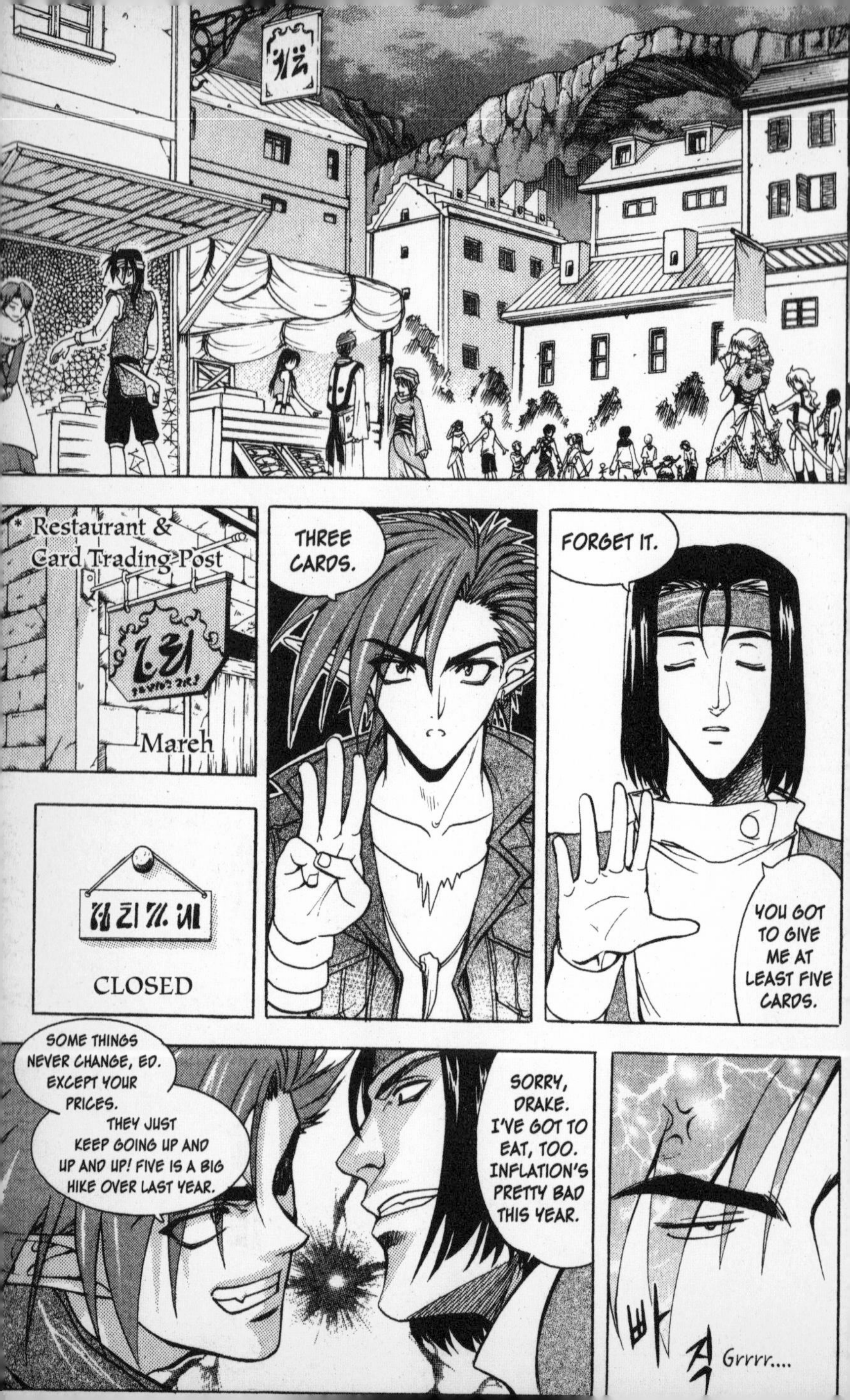
* Restaurant & Card Trading Post
Mareh
CLOSED
THREE CARDS.
FORGET IT.
YOU GOT TO GIVE ME AT LEAST FIVE CARDS.
SOME THINGS NEVER CHANGE, ED. EXCEPT YOUR PRICES.
THEY JUST KEEP GOING UP AND UP AND UP! FIVE IS A BIG HIKE OVER LAST YEAR.
SORRY, DRAKE. I'VE GOT TO EAT, TOO. INFLATION'S PRETTY BAD THIS YEAR.
Grrrr....

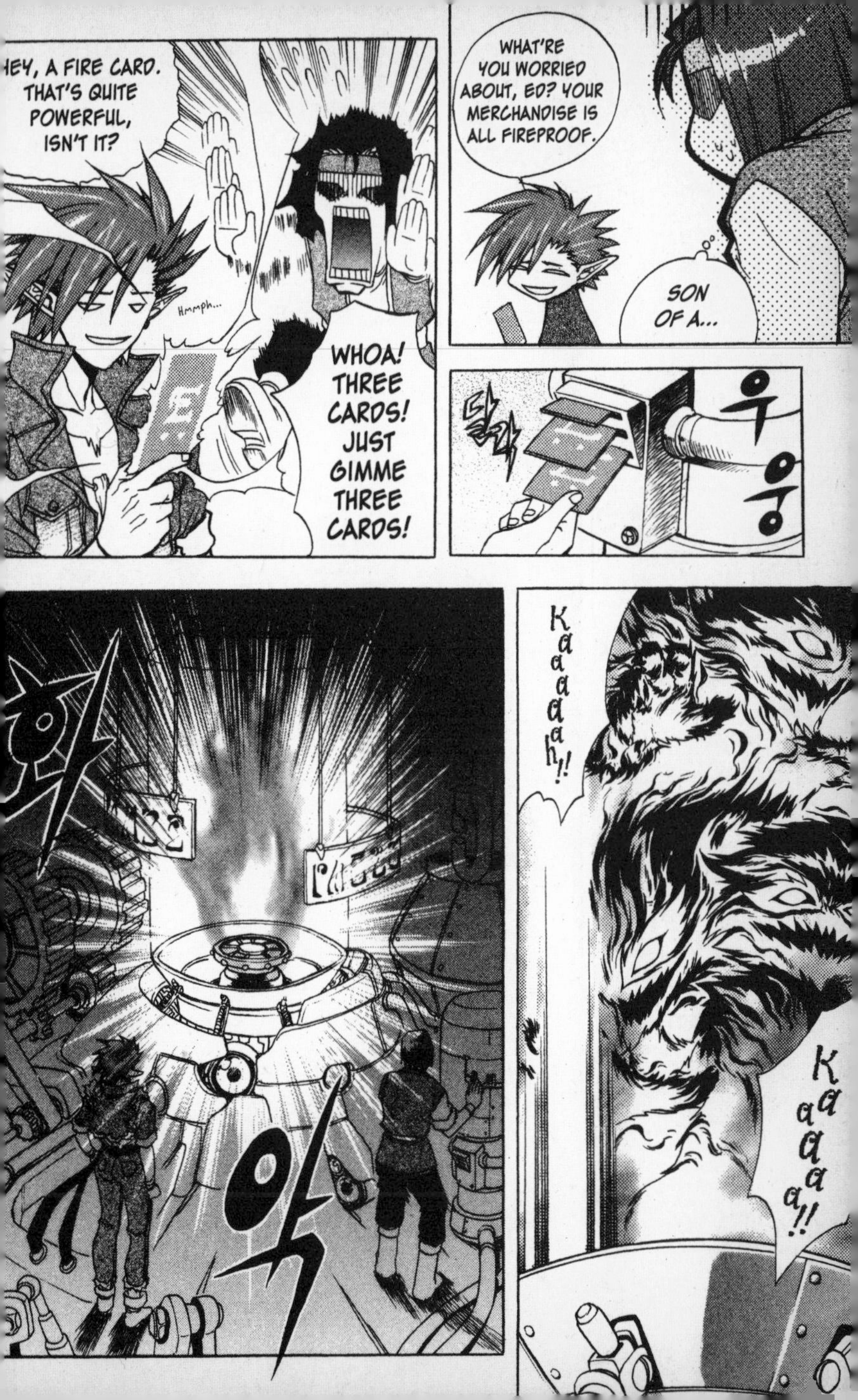
HEY, A FIRE CARD. THAT'S QUITE POWERFUL, ISN'T IT?
Hmmph...
WHOA! THREE CARDS! JUST GIMME THREE CARDS!
WHAT'RE YOU WORRIED ABOUT, ED? YOUR MERCHANDISE IS ALL FIREPROOF.
SON OF A...
우웅
Kaaaaah!!
Kaaaaaa!!

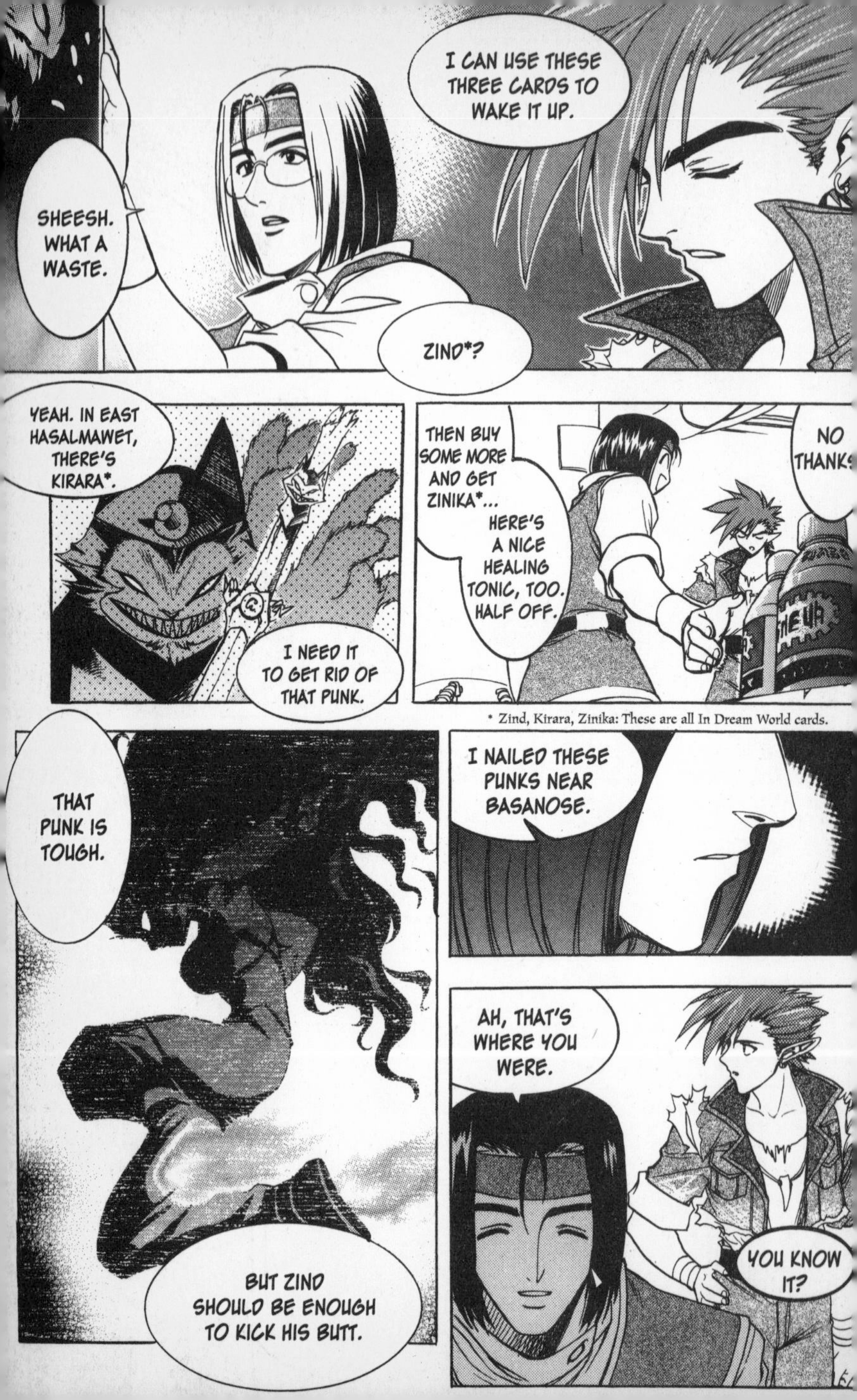
I CAN USE THESE THREE CARDS TO WAKE IT UP.
SHEESH. WHAT A WASTE.
ZIND*?
YEAH. IN EAST HASALMAWET, THERE'S KIRARA*.
I NEED IT TO GET RID OF THAT PUNK.
THEN BUY SOME MORE AND GET ZINIKA*...
HERE'S A NICE HEALING TONIC, TOO. HALF OFF.
NO THANKS
THAT PUNK IS TOUGH.
BUT ZIND SHOULD BE ENOUGH TO KICK HIS BUTT.
I NAILED THESE PUNKS NEAR BASANOSE.
AH, THAT'S WHERE YOU WERE.
YOU KNOW IT?

* Zind, Kirara, Zinika: These are all In Dream World cards.

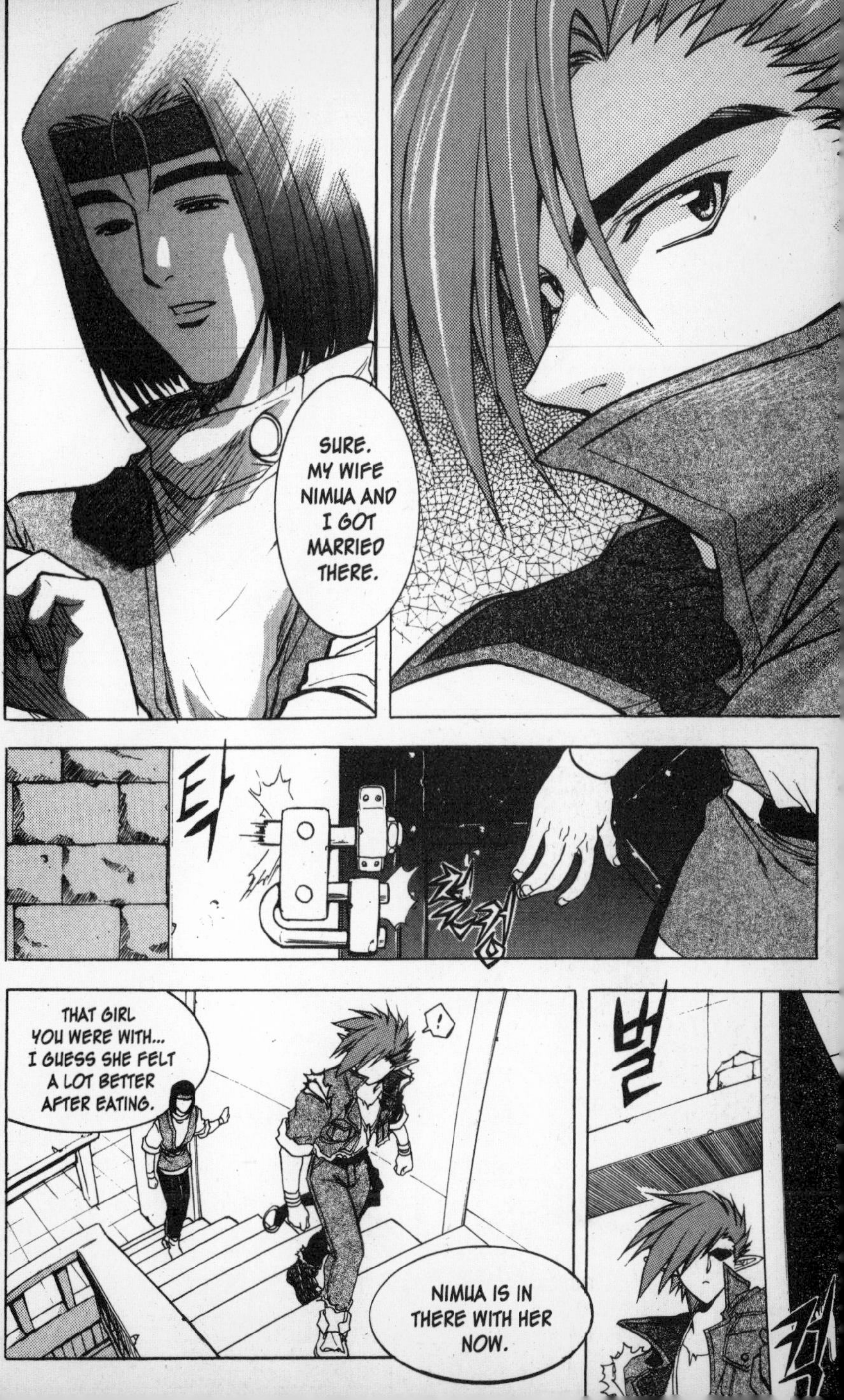
SURE. MY WIFE NIMUA AND I GOT MARRIED THERE.
탁
THAT GIRL YOU WERE WITH... I GUESS SHE FELT A LOT BETTER AFTER EATING.
!
NIMUA IS IN THERE WITH HER NOW.
벌

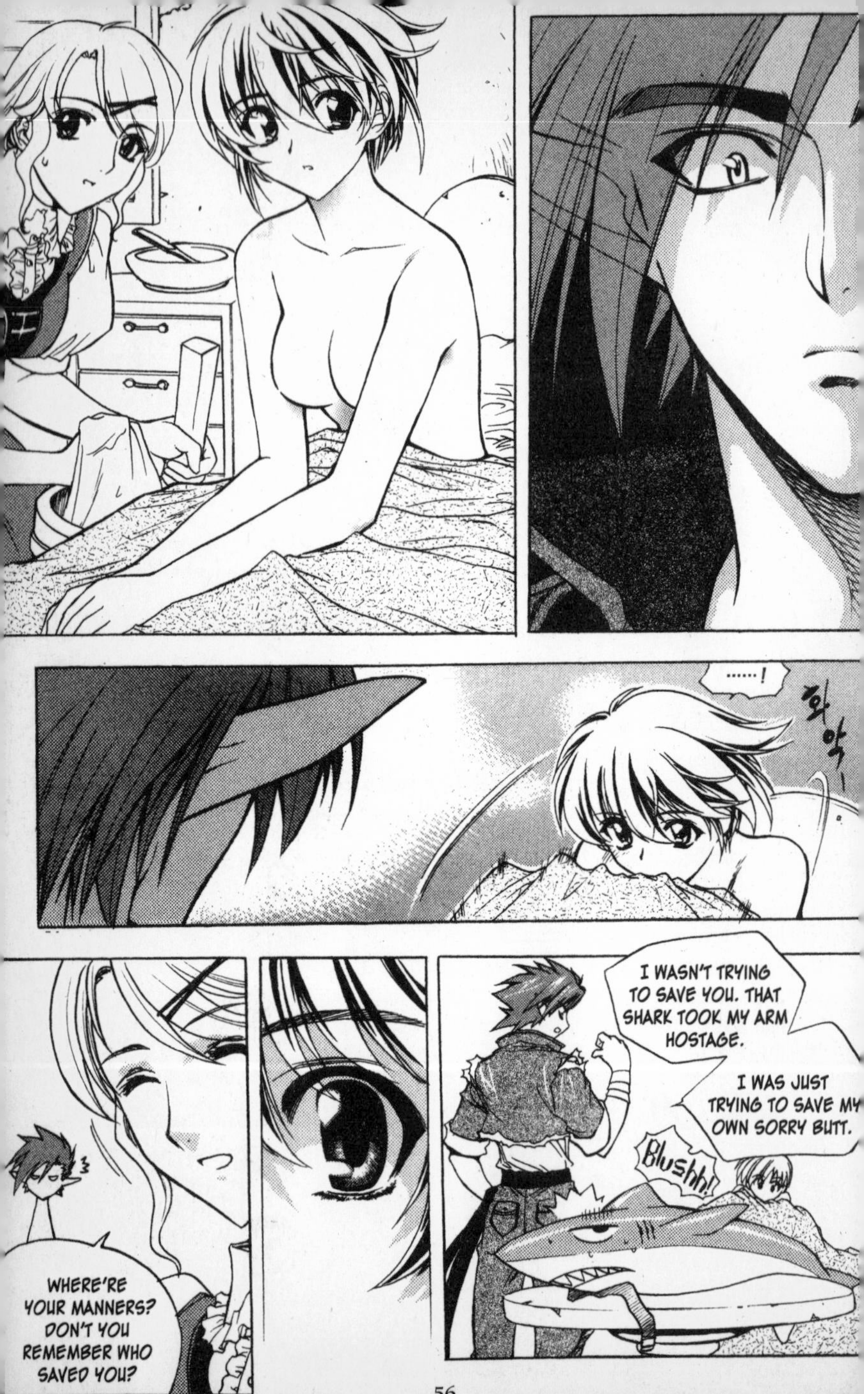
......!
화악
WHERE'RE YOUR MANNERS? DON'T YOU REMEMBER WHO SAVED YOU?
I WASN'T TRYING TO SAVE YOU. THAT SHARK TOOK MY ARM HOSTAGE.
I WAS JUST TRYING TO SAVE MY OWN SORRY BUTT.
Blushh!

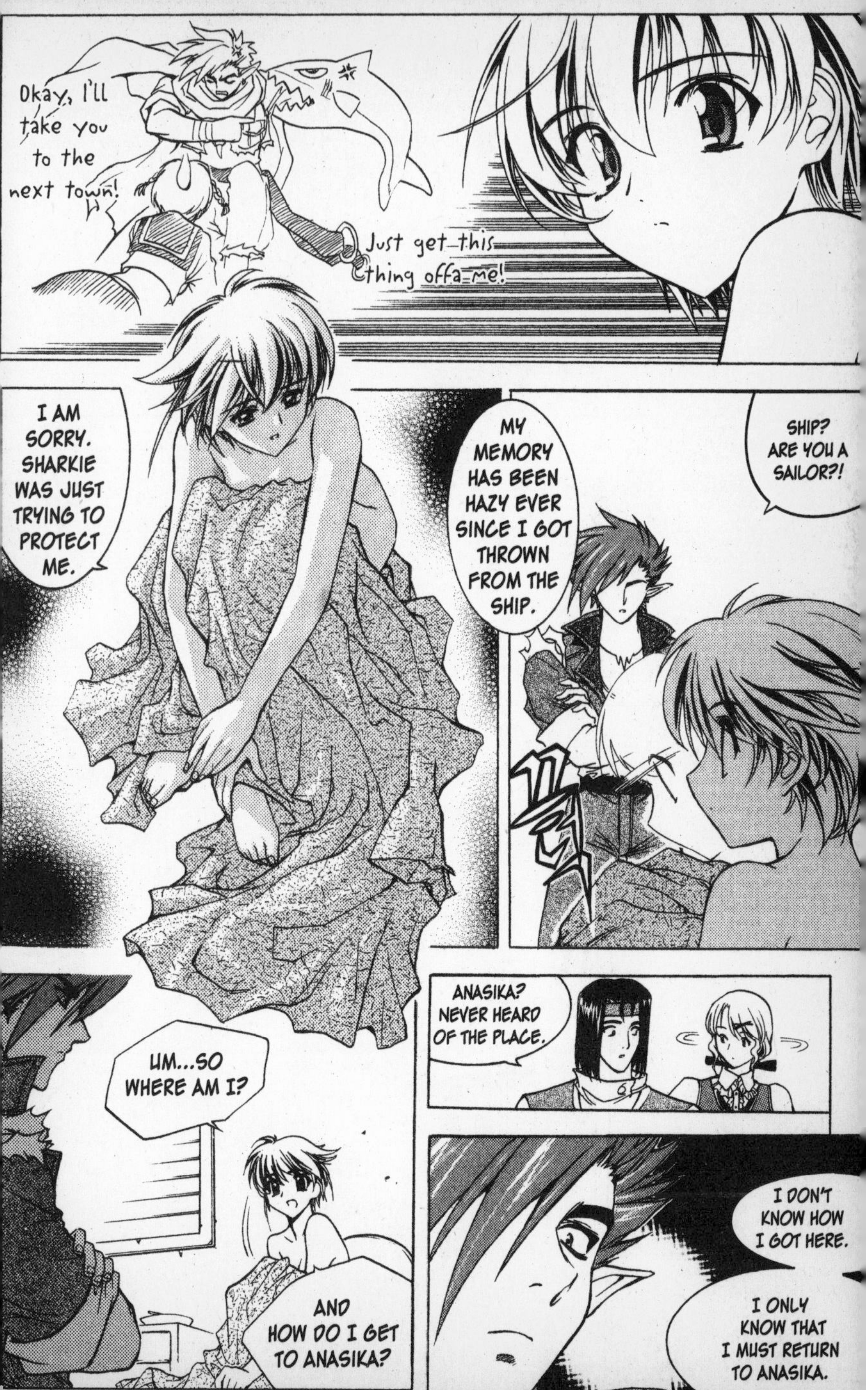
Okay, I'll take you to the next town!
Just get this thing offa me!
I AM SORRY. SHARKIE WAS JUST TRYING TO PROTECT ME.
MY MEMORY HAS BEEN HAZY EVER SINCE I GOT THROWN FROM THE SHIP.
SHIP? ARE YOU A SAILOR?!
UM...SO WHERE AM I?
AND HOW DO I GET TO ANASIKA?
ANASIKA? NEVER HEARD OF THE PLACE.
I DON'T KNOW HOW I GOT HERE.
I ONLY KNOW THAT I MUST RETURN TO ANASIKA.

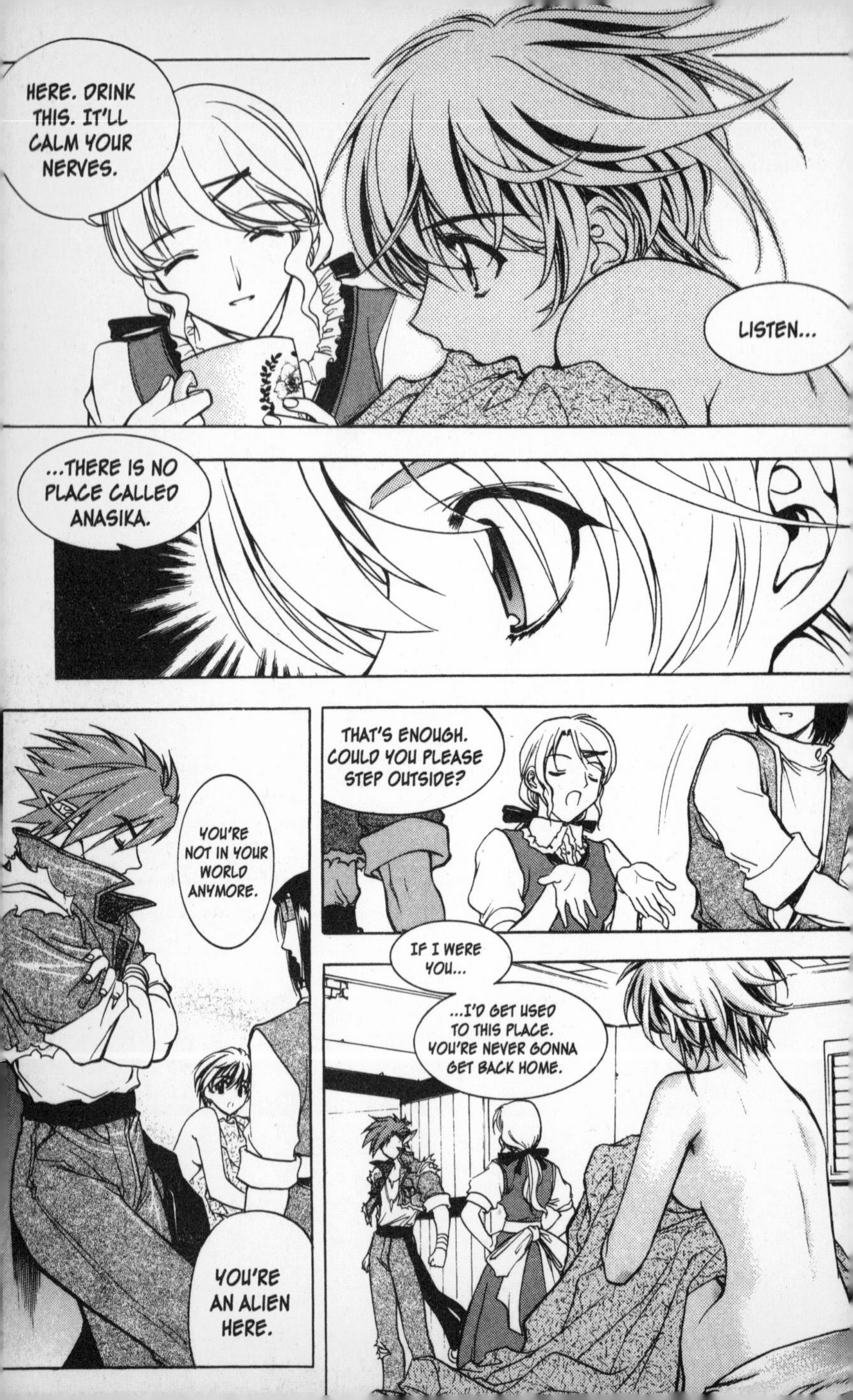
HERE. DRINK THIS. IT'LL CALM YOUR NERVES.
LISTEN...
...THERE IS NO PLACE CALLED ANASIKA.
YOU'RE NOT IN YOUR WORLD ANYMORE.
YOU'RE AN ALIEN HERE.
THAT'S ENOUGH. COULD YOU PLEASE STEP OUTSIDE?
IF I WERE YOU...
...I'D GET USED TO THIS PLACE. YOU'RE NEVER GONNA GET BACK HOME.

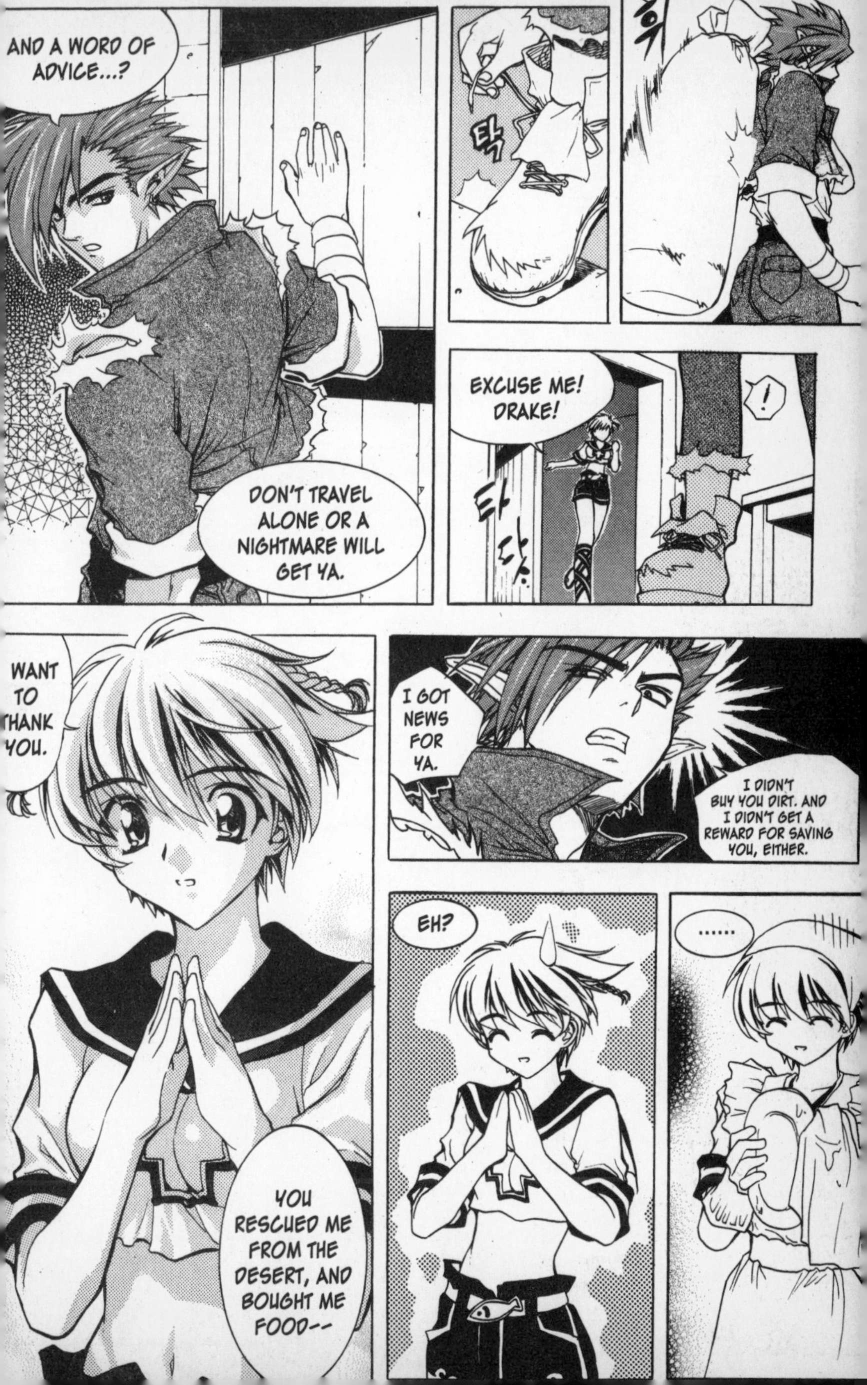
AND A WORD OF ADVICE...?
DON'T TRAVEL ALONE OR A NIGHTMARE WILL GET YA.
탁
휙
EXCUSE ME! DRAKE!
!
타 닥
WANT TO THANK YOU.
YOU RESCUED ME FROM THE DESERT, AND BOUGHT ME FOOD--
I GOT NEWS FOR YA.
I DIDN'T BUY YOU DIRT. AND I DIDN'T GET A REWARD FOR SAVING YOU, EITHER.
EH?
......

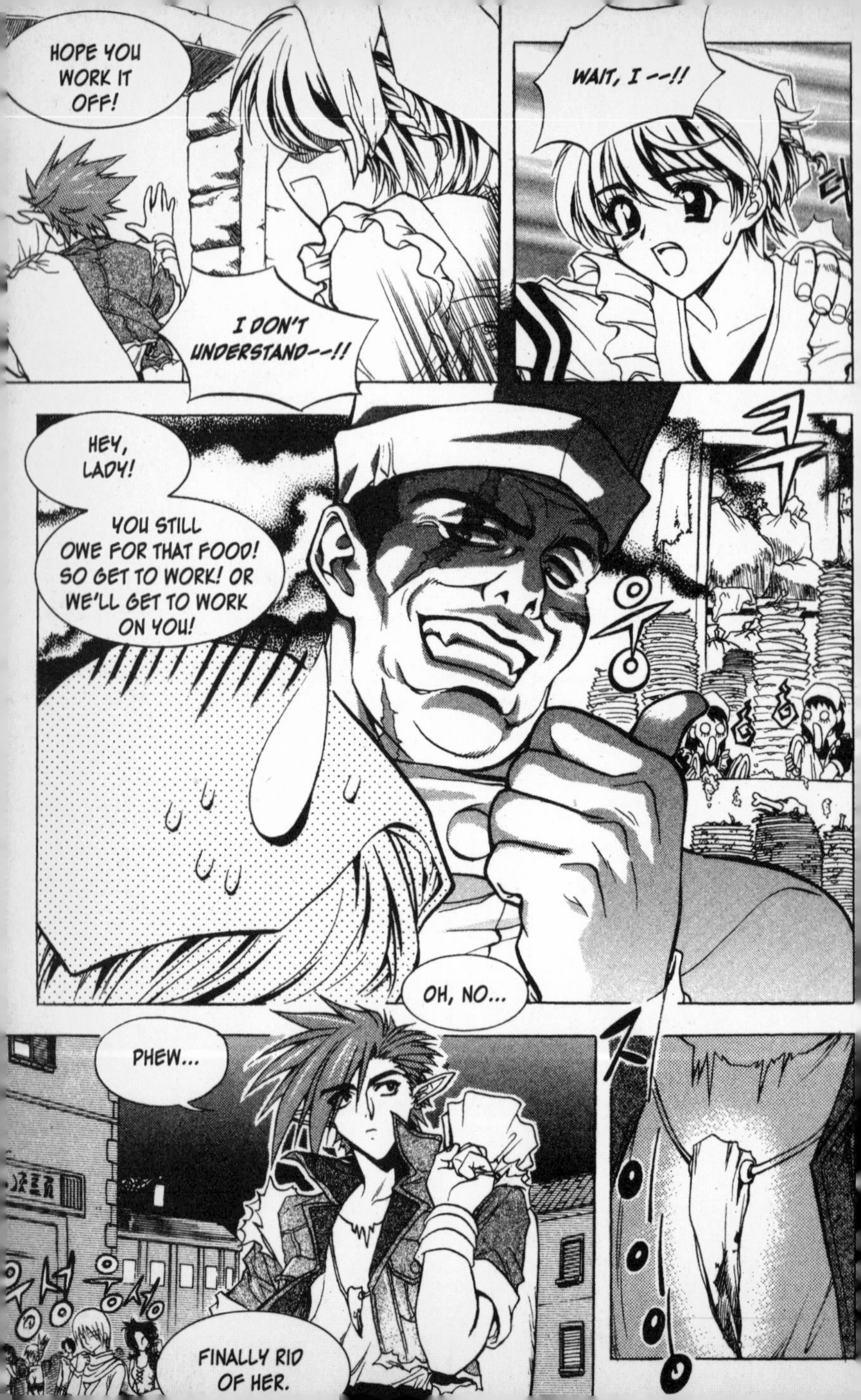
HOPE YOU WORK IT OFF!
I DON'T UNDERSTAND--!!
WAIT, I --!!
HEY, LADY!
YOU STILL OWE FOR THAT FOOD! SO GET TO WORK! OR WE'LL GET TO WORK ON YOU!
OH, NO...
PHEW...
FINALLY RID OF HER.

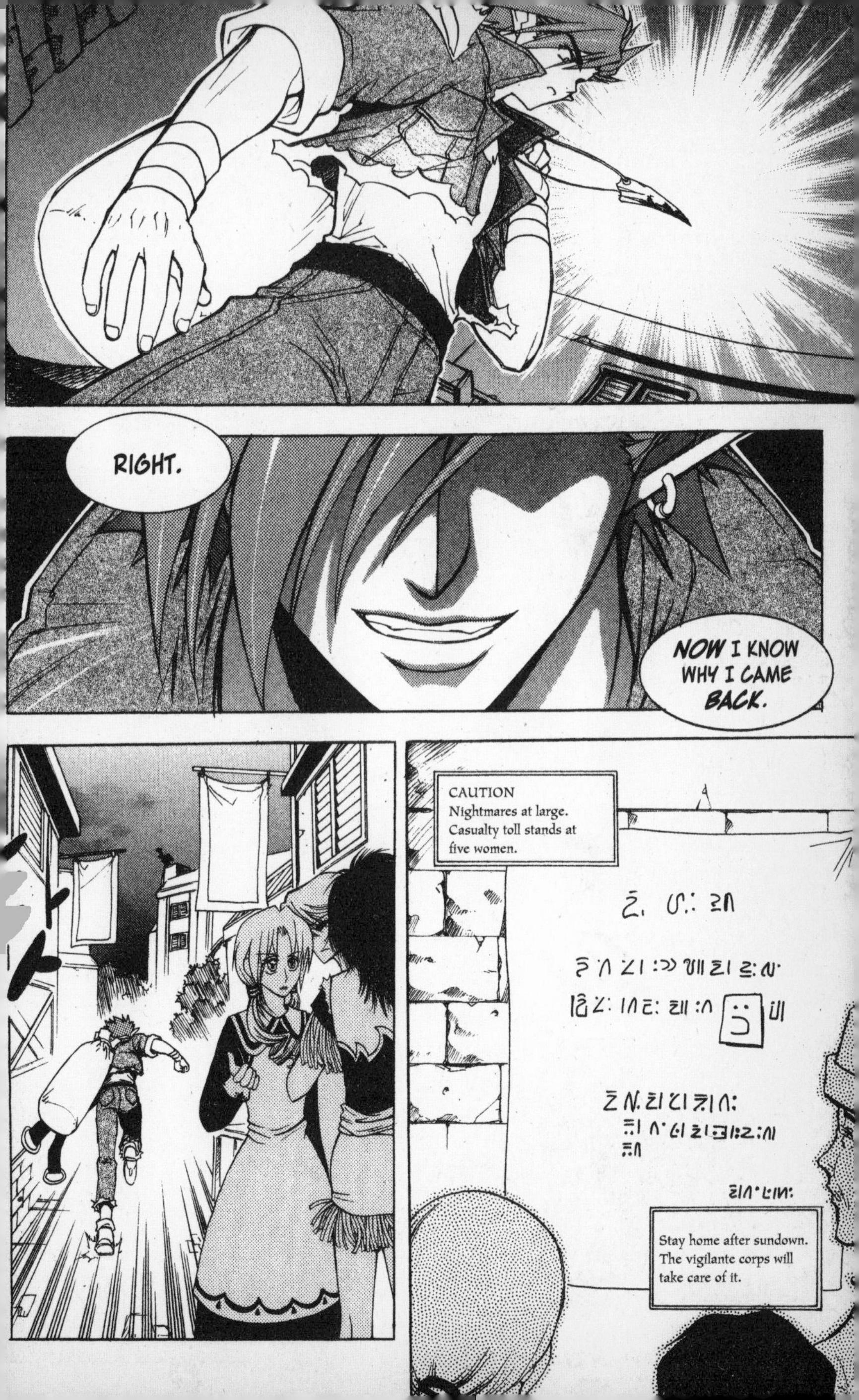
RIGHT.
NOW I KNOW WHY I CAME BACK.
CAUTION
Nightmares at large.
Casualty toll stands at five women.
Stay home after sundown.
The vigilante corps will take care of it.

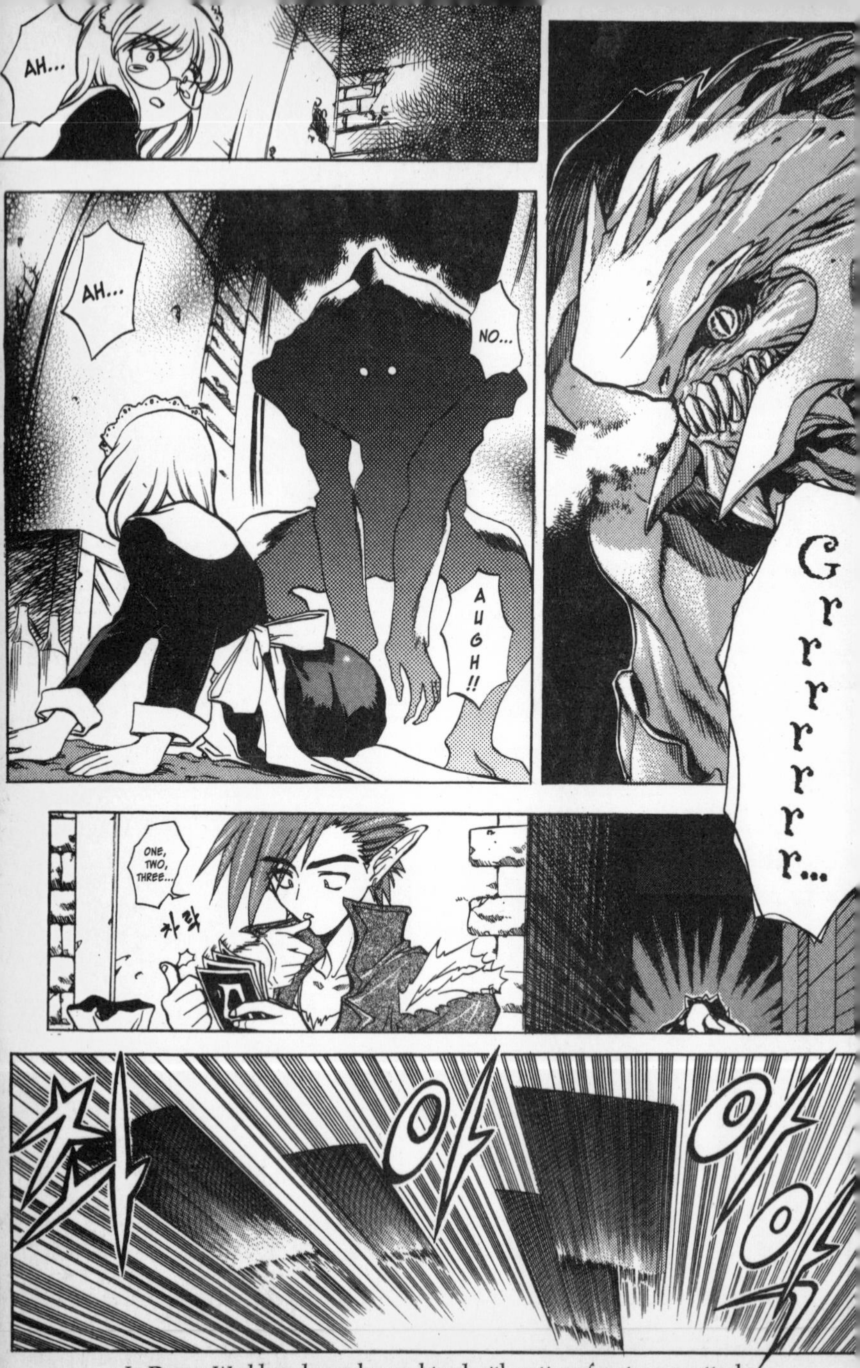
AH...
AH...
NO...
AUGH!!
Grrrrrrrr...
ONE, TWO, THREE...

In Dream World cards can be combined with potions for stronger attacks.

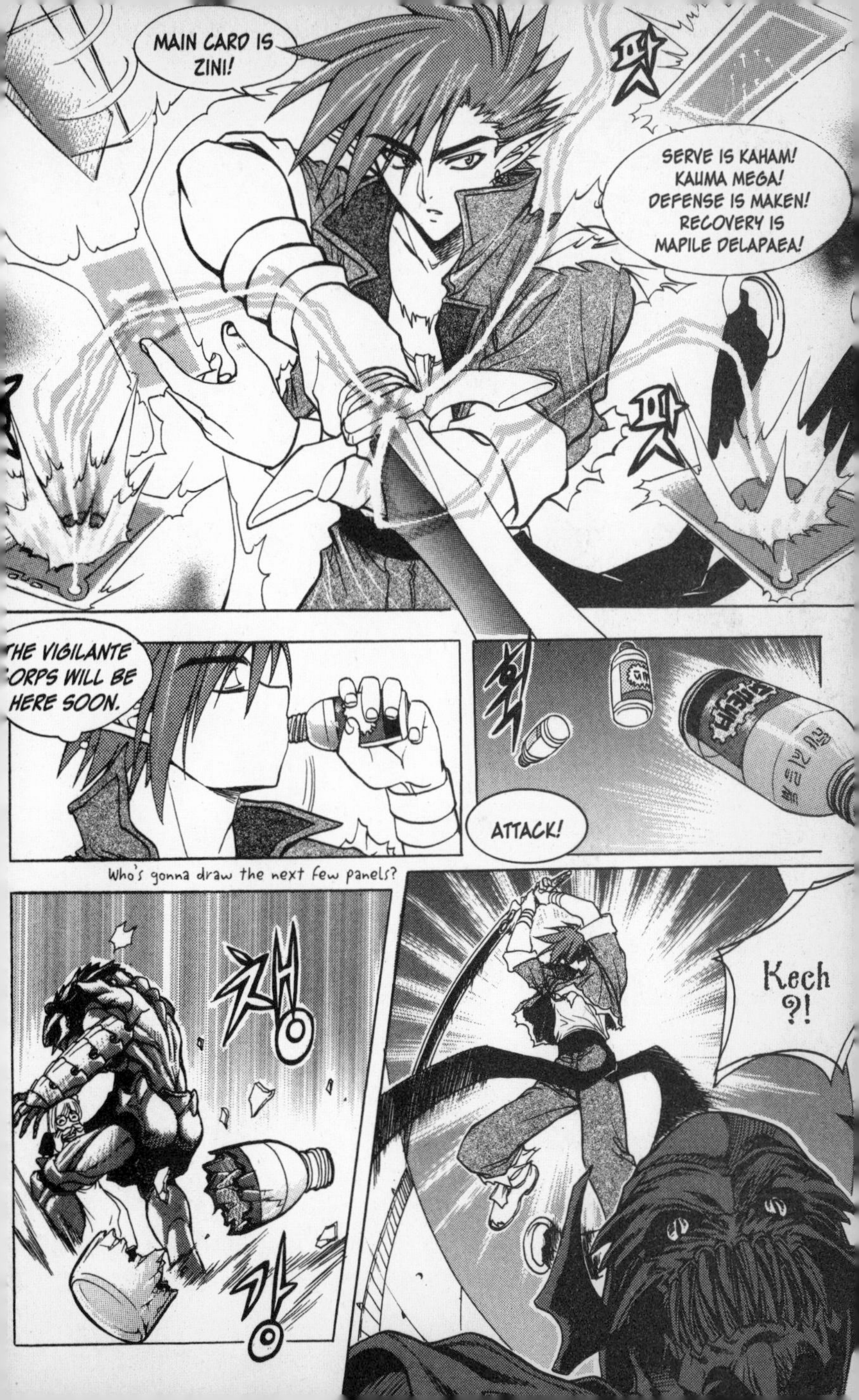
MAIN CARD IS ZINI!
SERVE IS KAHAM! KAUMA MEGA! DEFENSE IS MAKEN! RECOVERY IS MAPILE DELAPAEA!
THE VIGILANTE CORPS WILL BE HERE SOON.
ATTACK!
Who's gonna draw the next few panels?
Kech ?!

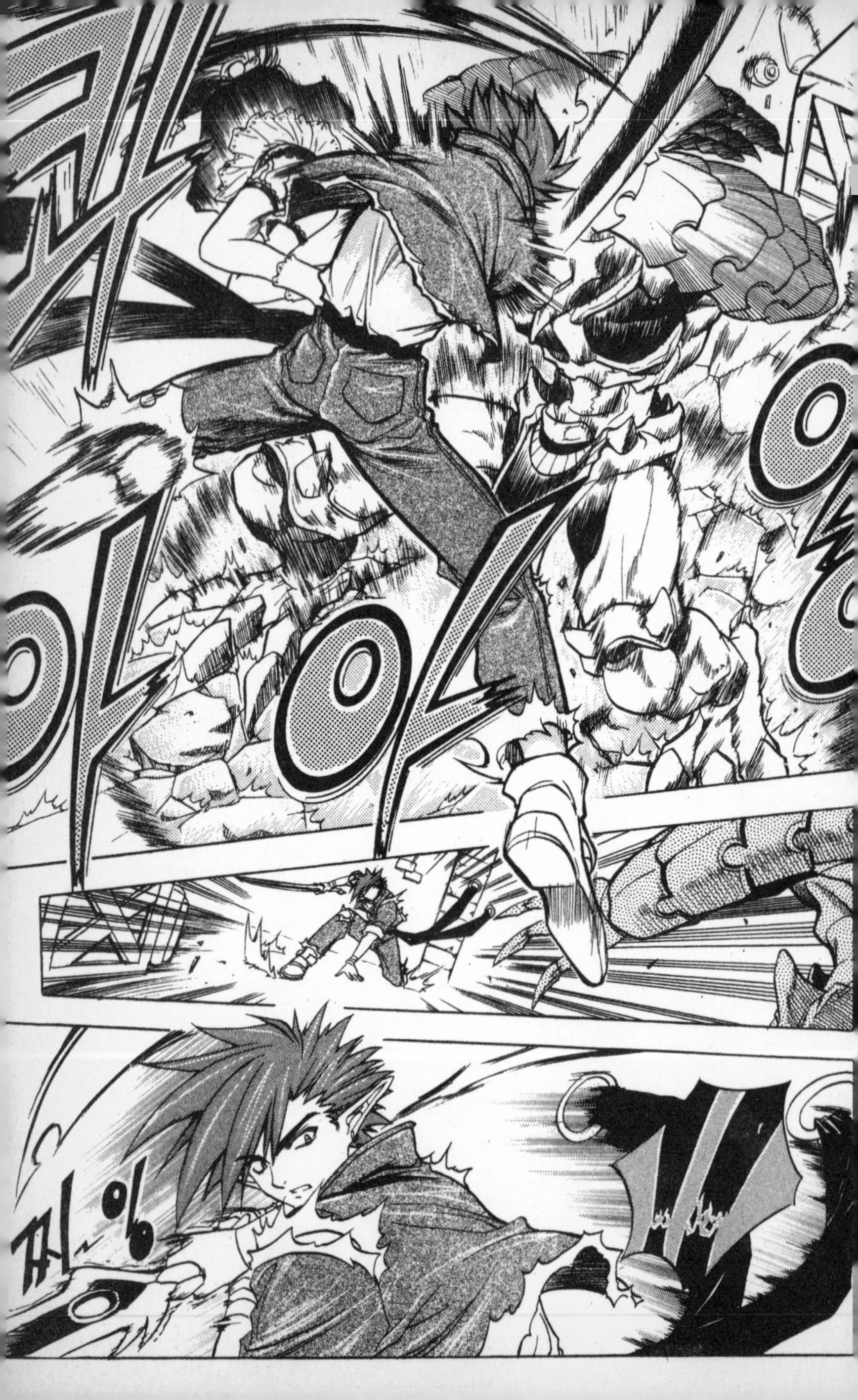

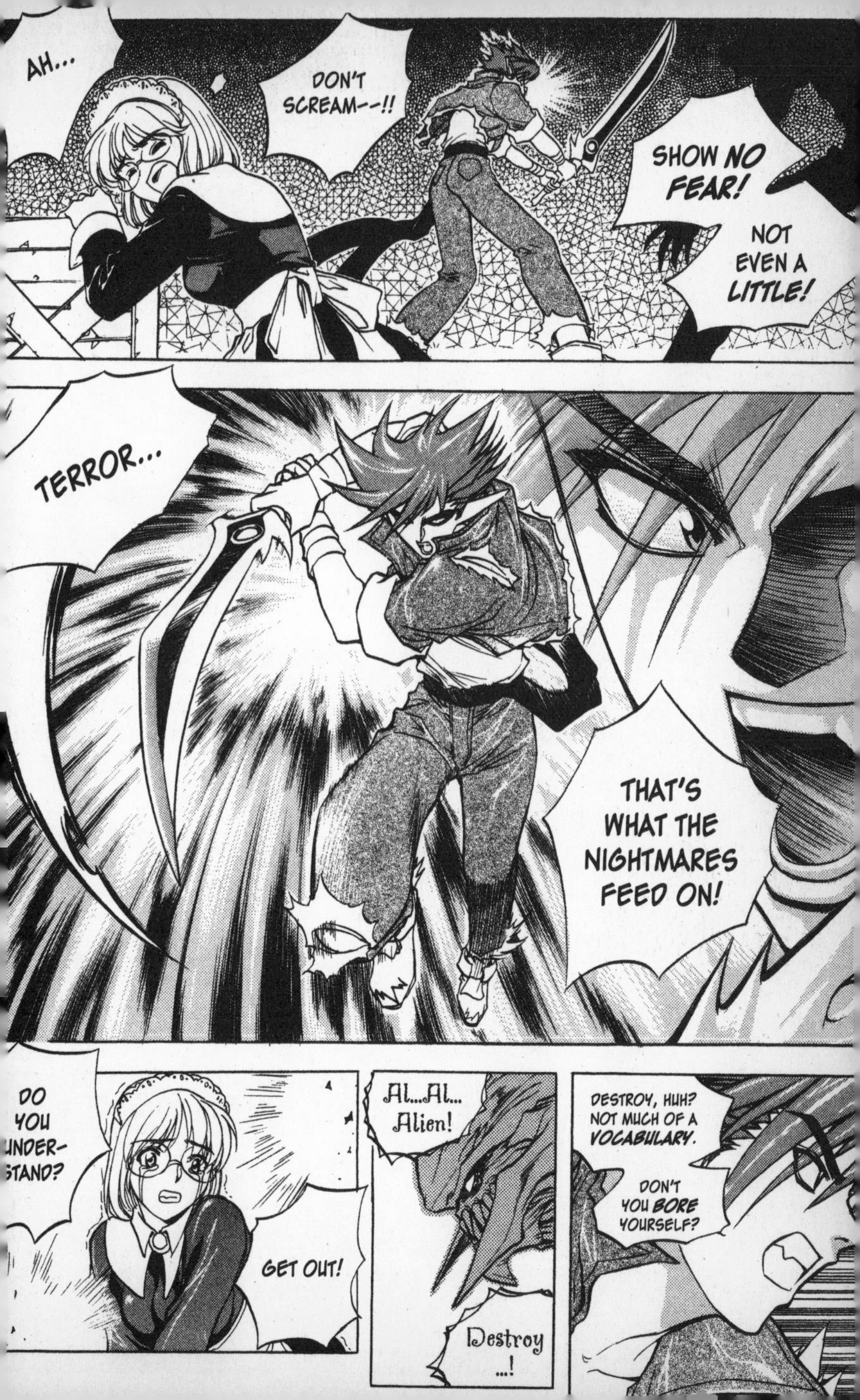
AH...
DON'T SCREAM--!!
SHOW NO FEAR!
NOT EVEN A LITTLE!
TERROR...
THAT'S WHAT THE NIGHTMARES FEED ON!
DO YOU UNDER-STAND?
GET OUT!
Al...Al... Alien!
Destroy ...!
DESTROY, HUH? NOT MUCH OF A VOCABULARY.
DON'T YOU BORE YOURSELF?

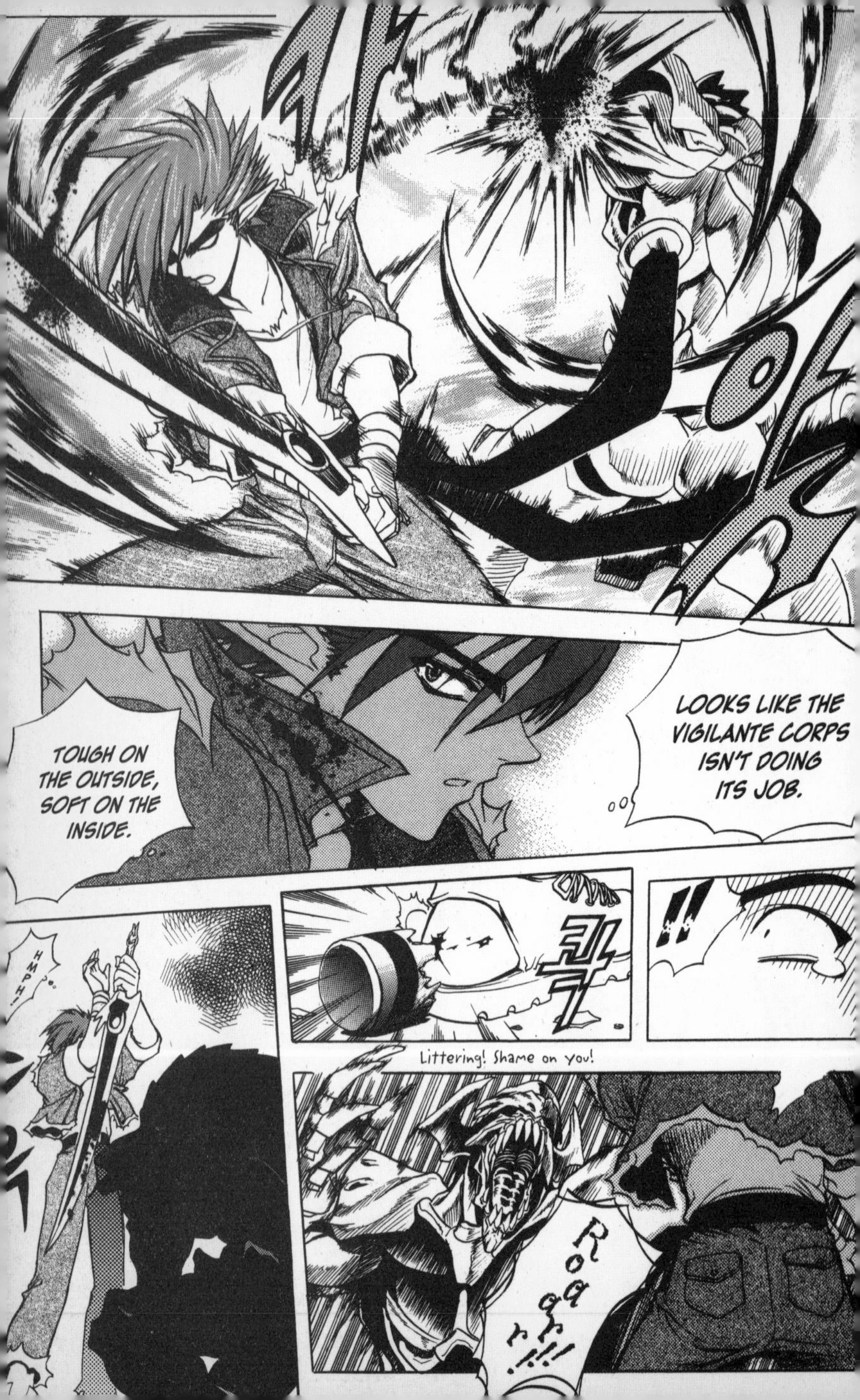
TOUGH ON THE OUTSIDE, SOFT ON THE INSIDE.
LOOKS LIKE THE VIGILANTE CORPS ISN'T DOING ITS JOB.
HMPH!
!!
Littering! Shame on you!
Roaarr!!!

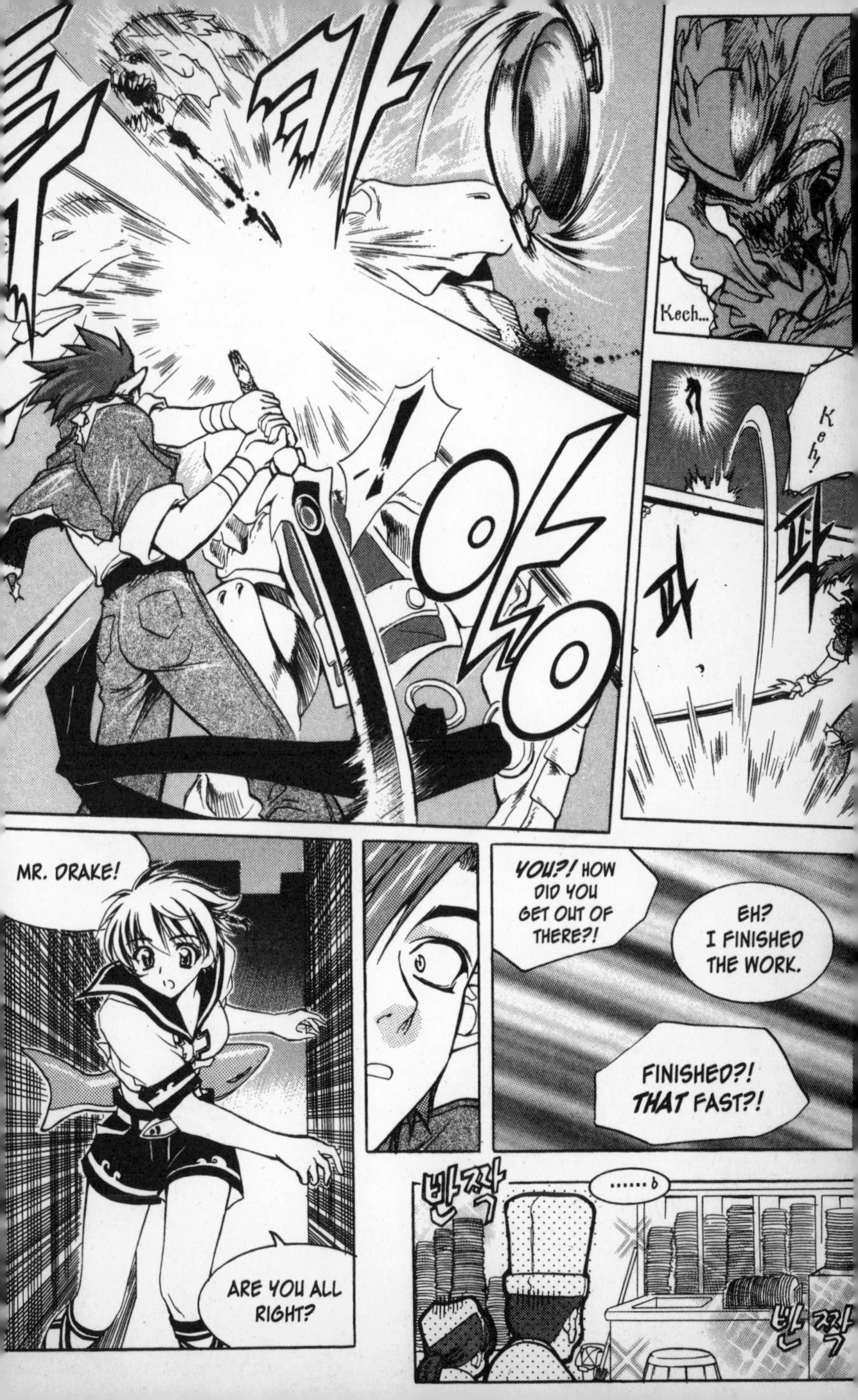
Kech...
Keh!
파
파
MR. DRAKE!
ARE YOU ALL RIGHT?
YOU?! HOW DID YOU GET OUT OF THERE?!
EH? I FINISHED THE WORK.
FINISHED?! THAT FAST?!
반짝
......♭
반짝

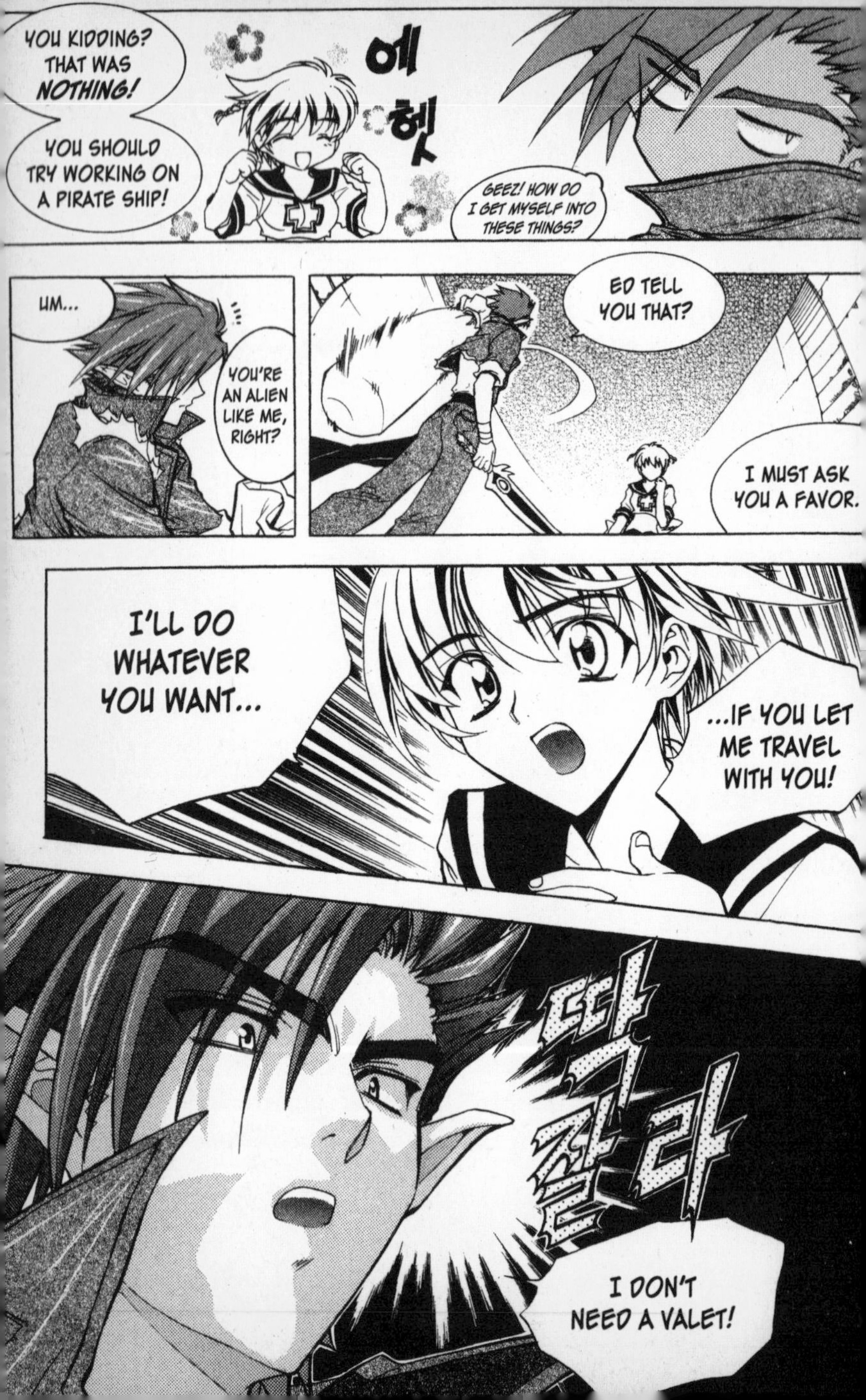
YOU KIDDING? THAT WAS *NOTHING!*
YOU SHOULD TRY WORKING ON A PIRATE SHIP!
예헷
GEEZ! HOW DO I GET MYSELF INTO THESE THINGS?
UM...
YOU'RE AN ALIEN LIKE ME, RIGHT?
ED TELL YOU THAT?
I MUST ASK YOU A FAVOR.
I'LL DO WHATEVER YOU WANT...
...IF YOU LET ME TRAVEL WITH YOU!
딱 잘라
I DON'T NEED A VALET!

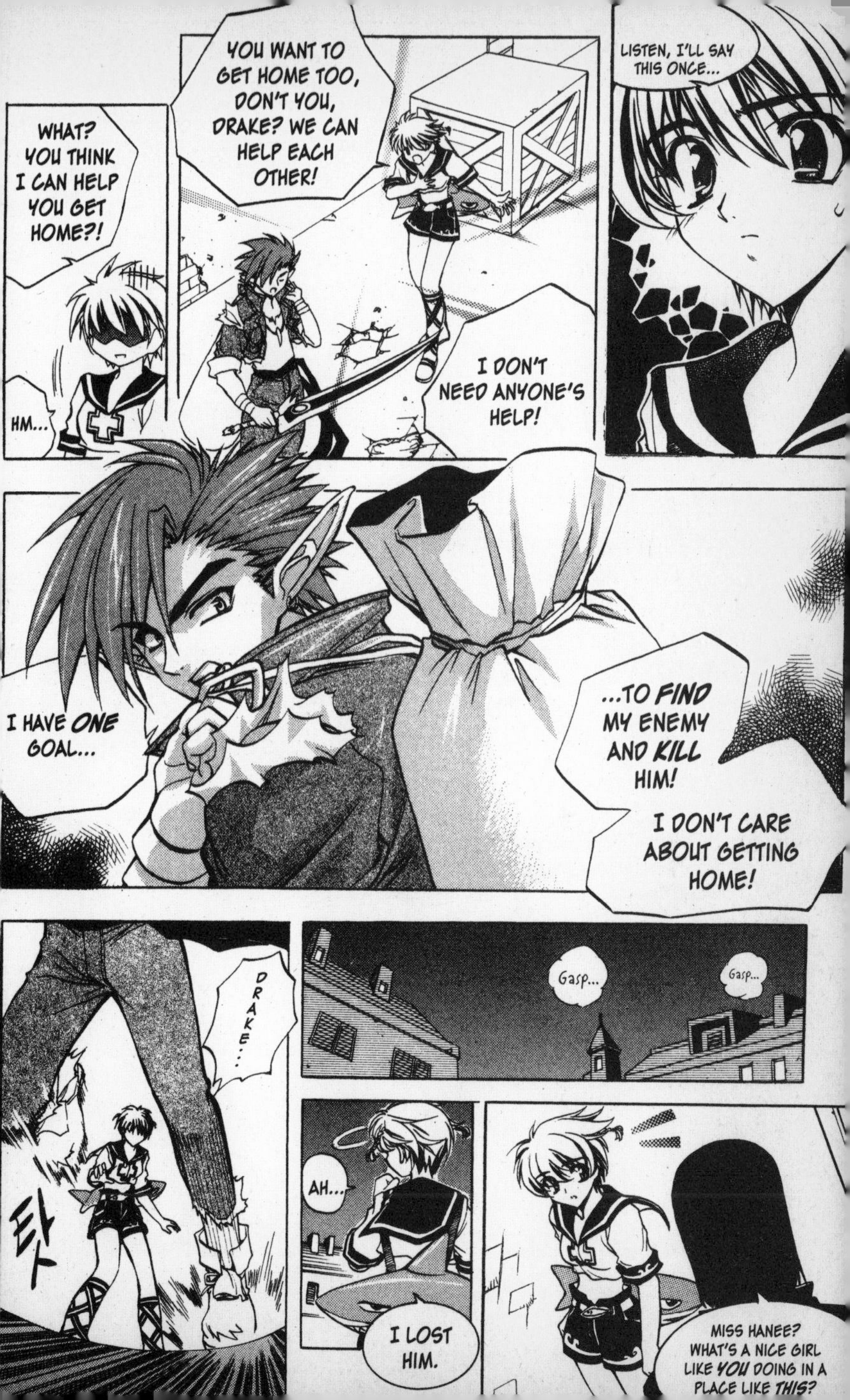
WHAT? YOU THINK I CAN HELP YOU GET HOME?!
HM...
YOU WANT TO GET HOME TOO, DON'T YOU, DRAKE? WE CAN HELP EACH OTHER!
I DON'T NEED ANYONE'S HELP!
LISTEN, I'LL SAY THIS ONCE...
I HAVE ONE GOAL...
...TO FIND MY ENEMY AND KILL HIM!
I DON'T CARE ABOUT GETTING HOME!
DRAKE...
탁
Gasp...
Gasp...
AH...
I LOST HIM.
MISS HANEE? WHAT'S A NICE GIRL LIKE YOU DOING IN A PLACE LIKE THIS?

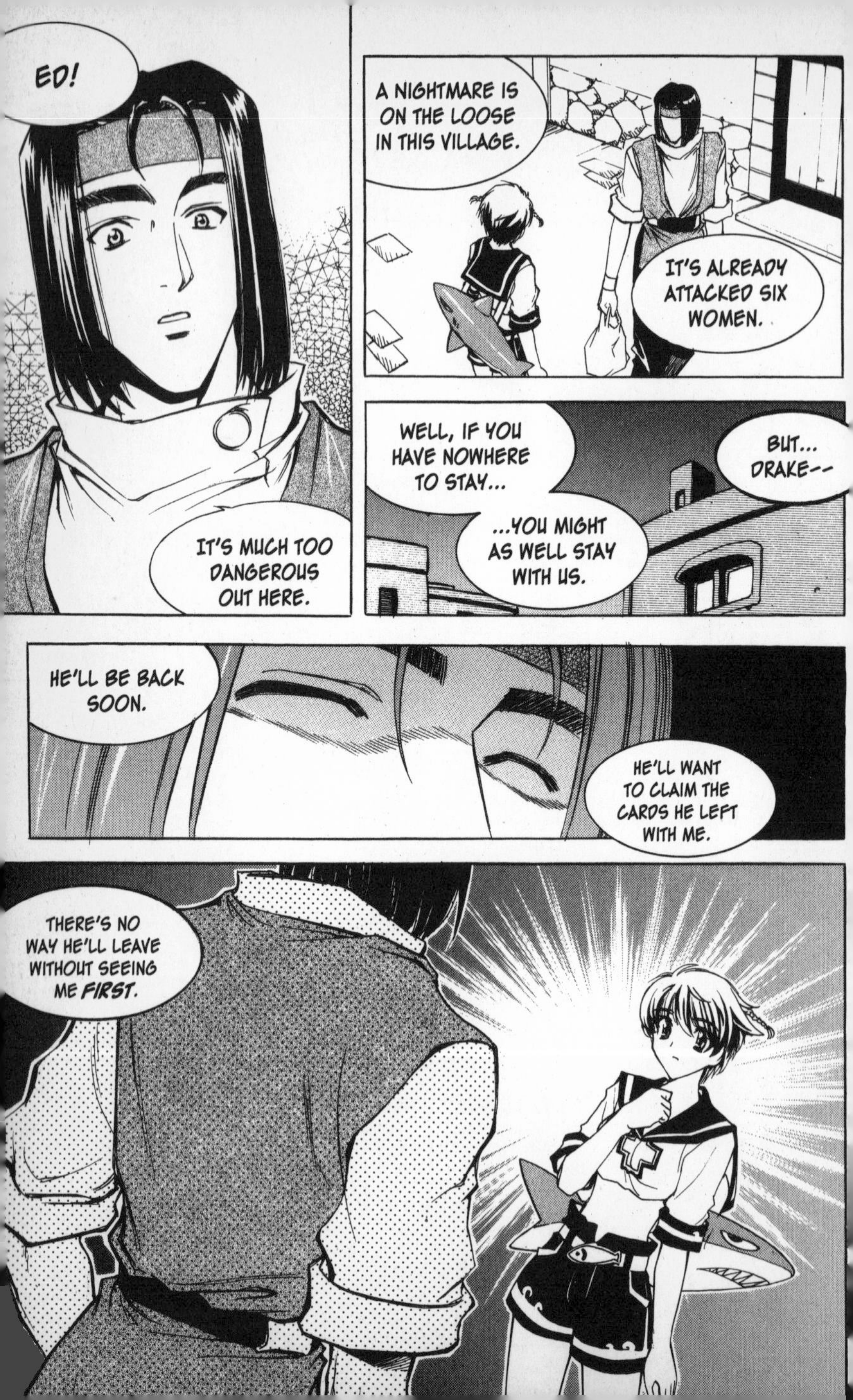
ED!
IT'S MUCH TOO DANGEROUS OUT HERE.
A NIGHTMARE IS ON THE LOOSE IN THIS VILLAGE.
IT'S ALREADY ATTACKED SIX WOMEN.
WELL, IF YOU HAVE NOWHERE TO STAY...
...YOU MIGHT AS WELL STAY WITH US.
BUT... DRAKE--
HE'LL BE BACK SOON.
HE'LL WANT TO CLAIM THE CARDS HE LEFT WITH ME.
THERE'S NO WAY HE'LL LEAVE WITHOUT SEEING ME *FIRST*.

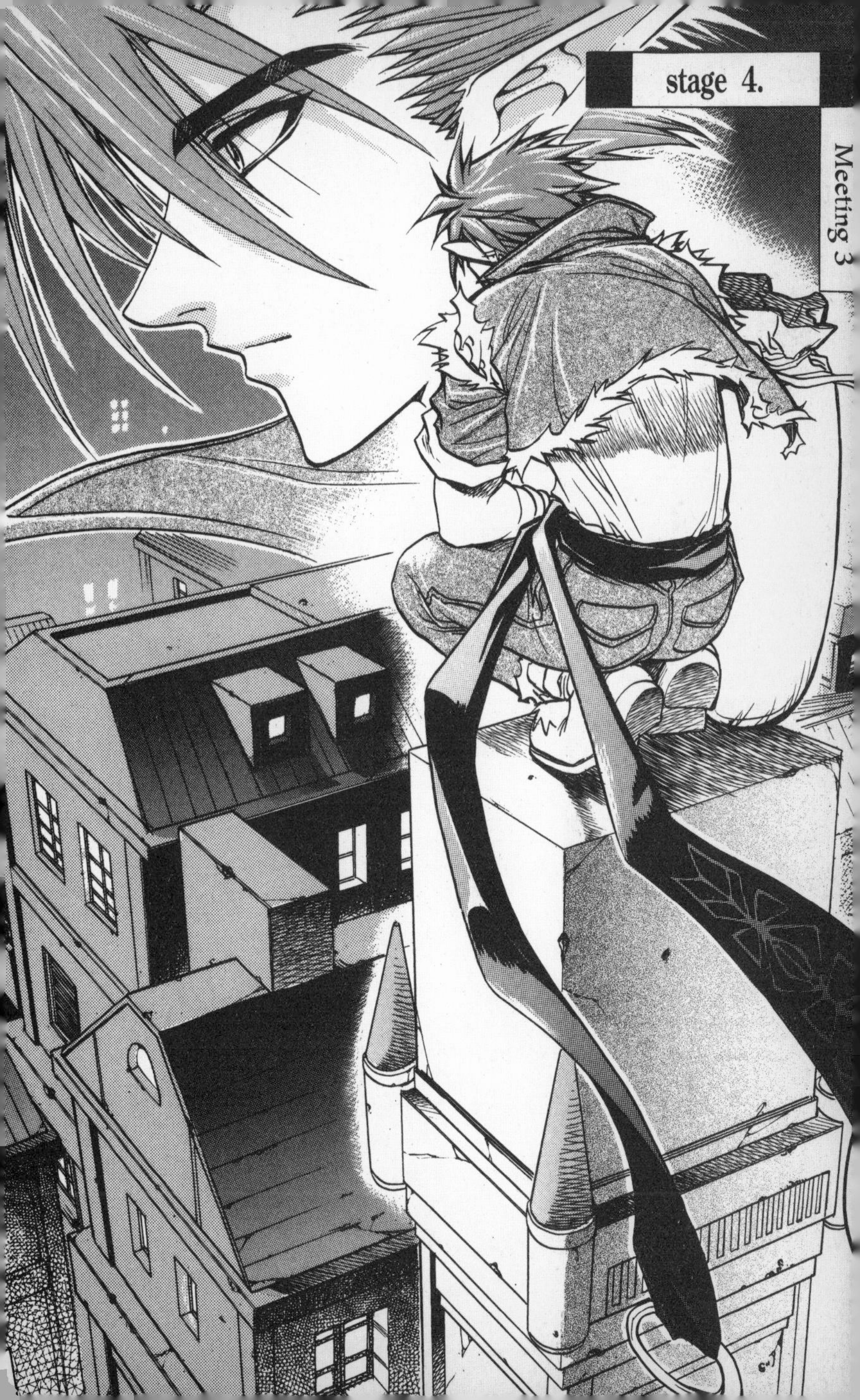
stage 4.
Meeting 3

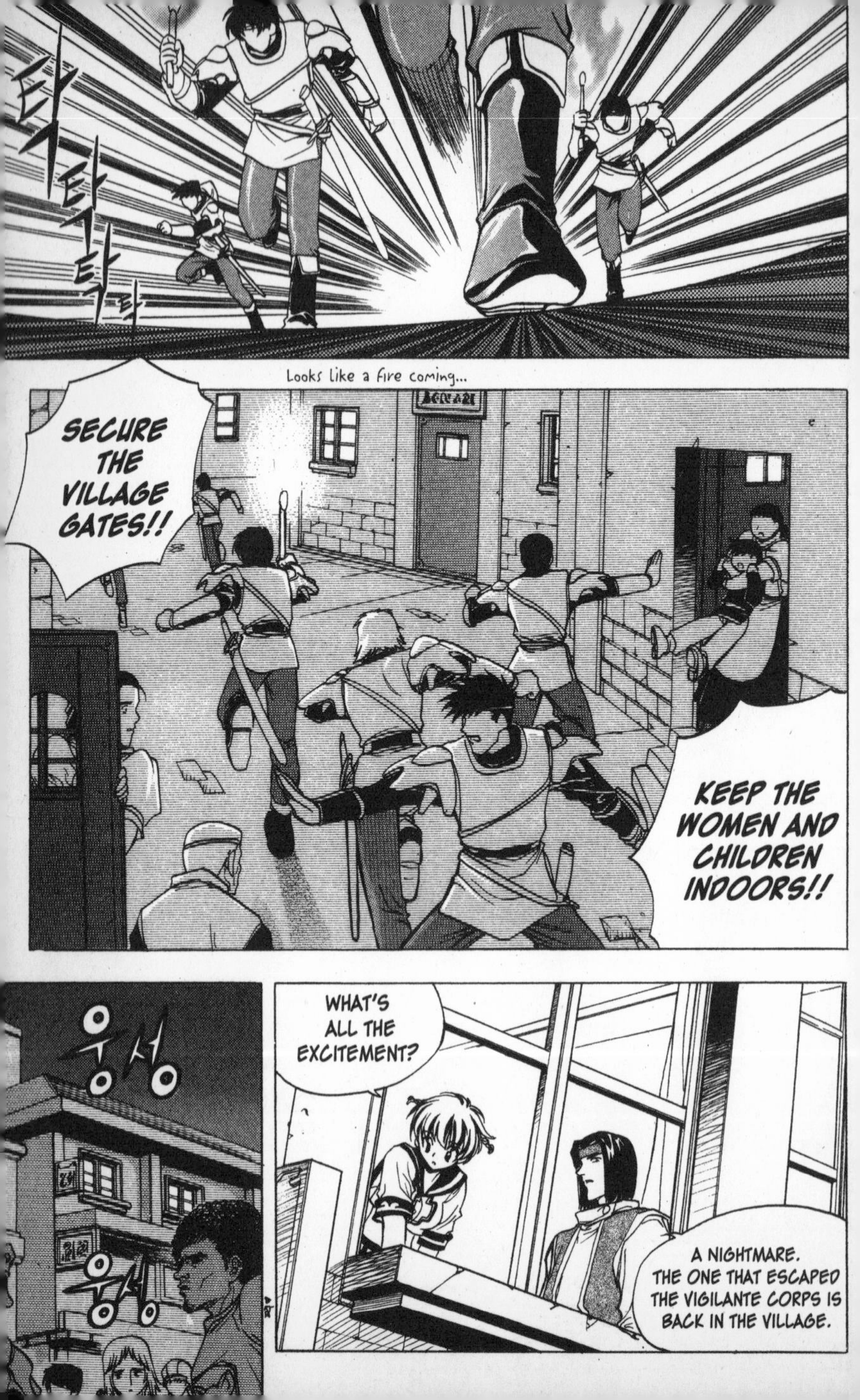
Looks like a fire coming...
SECURE THE VILLAGE GATES!!
KEEP THE WOMEN AND CHILDREN INDOORS!!
웅성
웅성
WHAT'S ALL THE EXCITEMENT?
A NIGHTMARE. THE ONE THAT ESCAPED THE VIGILANTE CORPS IS BACK IN THE VILLAGE.

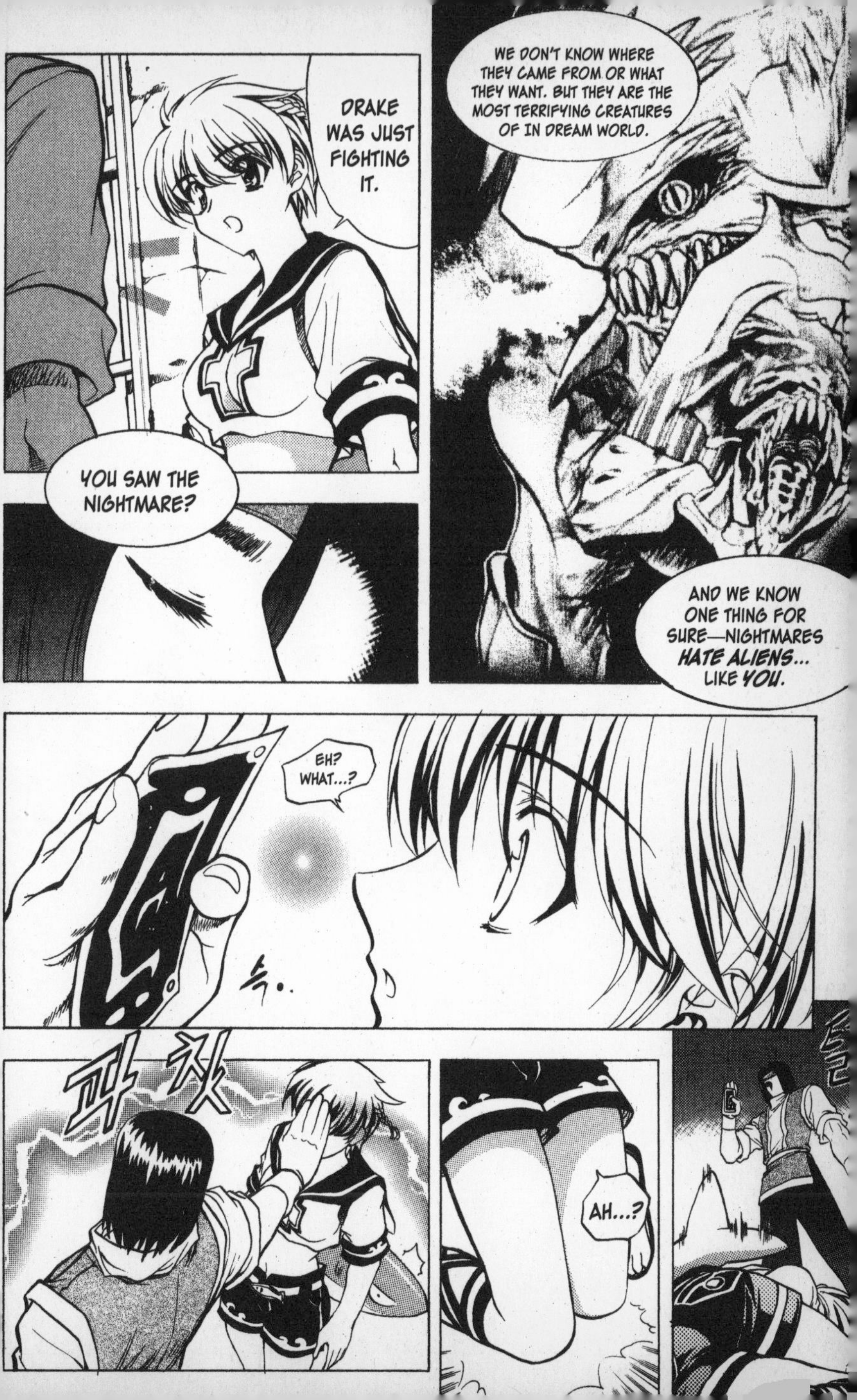
DRAKE WAS JUST FIGHTING IT.
YOU SAW THE NIGHTMARE?
WE DON'T KNOW WHERE THEY CAME FROM OR WHAT THEY WANT. BUT THEY ARE THE MOST TERRIFYING CREATURES OF IN DREAM WORLD.
AND WE KNOW ONE THING FOR SURE—NIGHTMARES ***HATE ALIENS...*** LIKE ***YOU.***
EH? WHAT...?
파 칫
AH...?

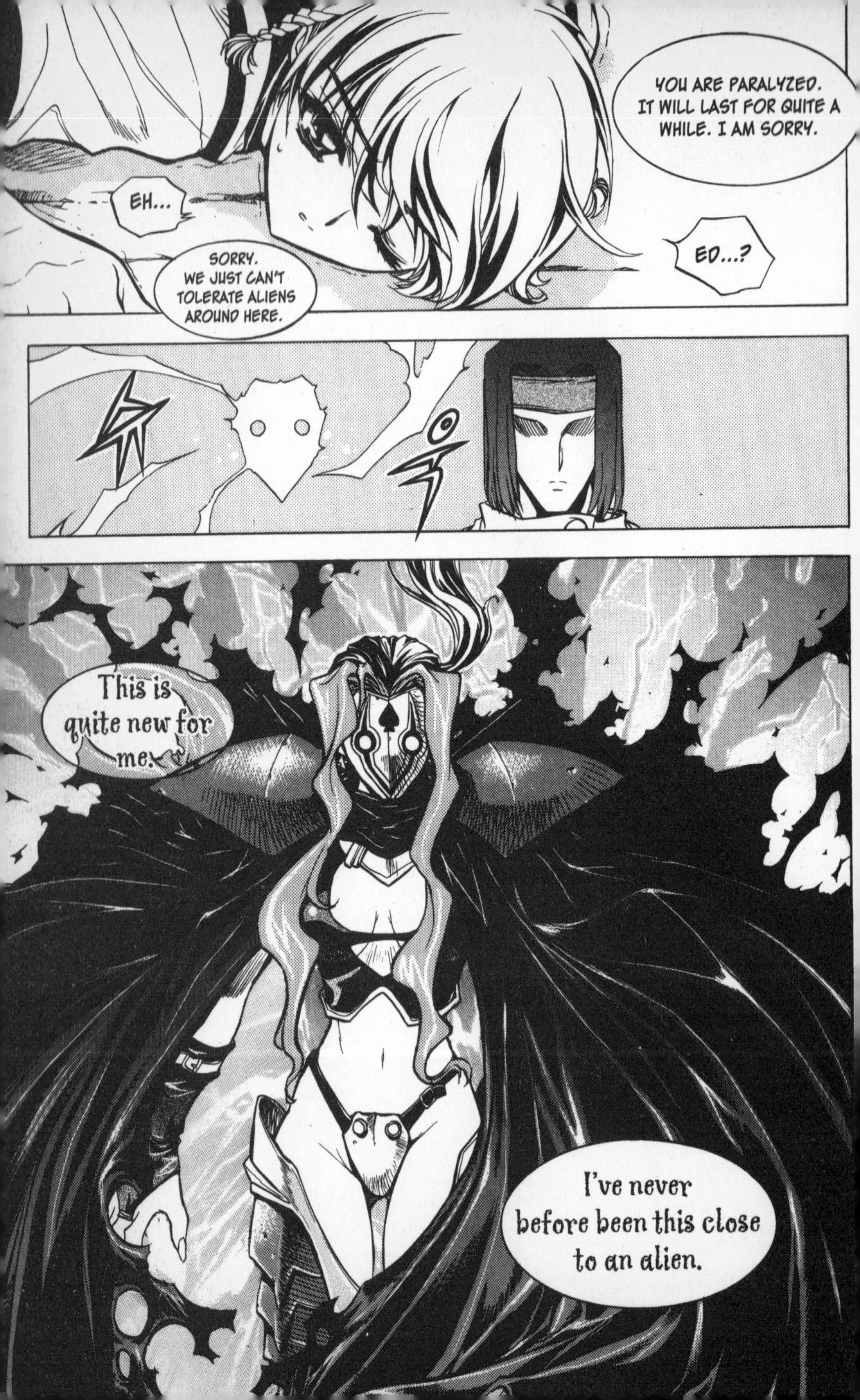
EH...
SORRY. WE JUST CAN'T TOLERATE ALIENS AROUND HERE.
YOU ARE PARALYZED. IT WILL LAST FOR QUITE A WHILE. I AM SORRY.
ED...?
This is quite new for me.
I've never before been this close to an alien.

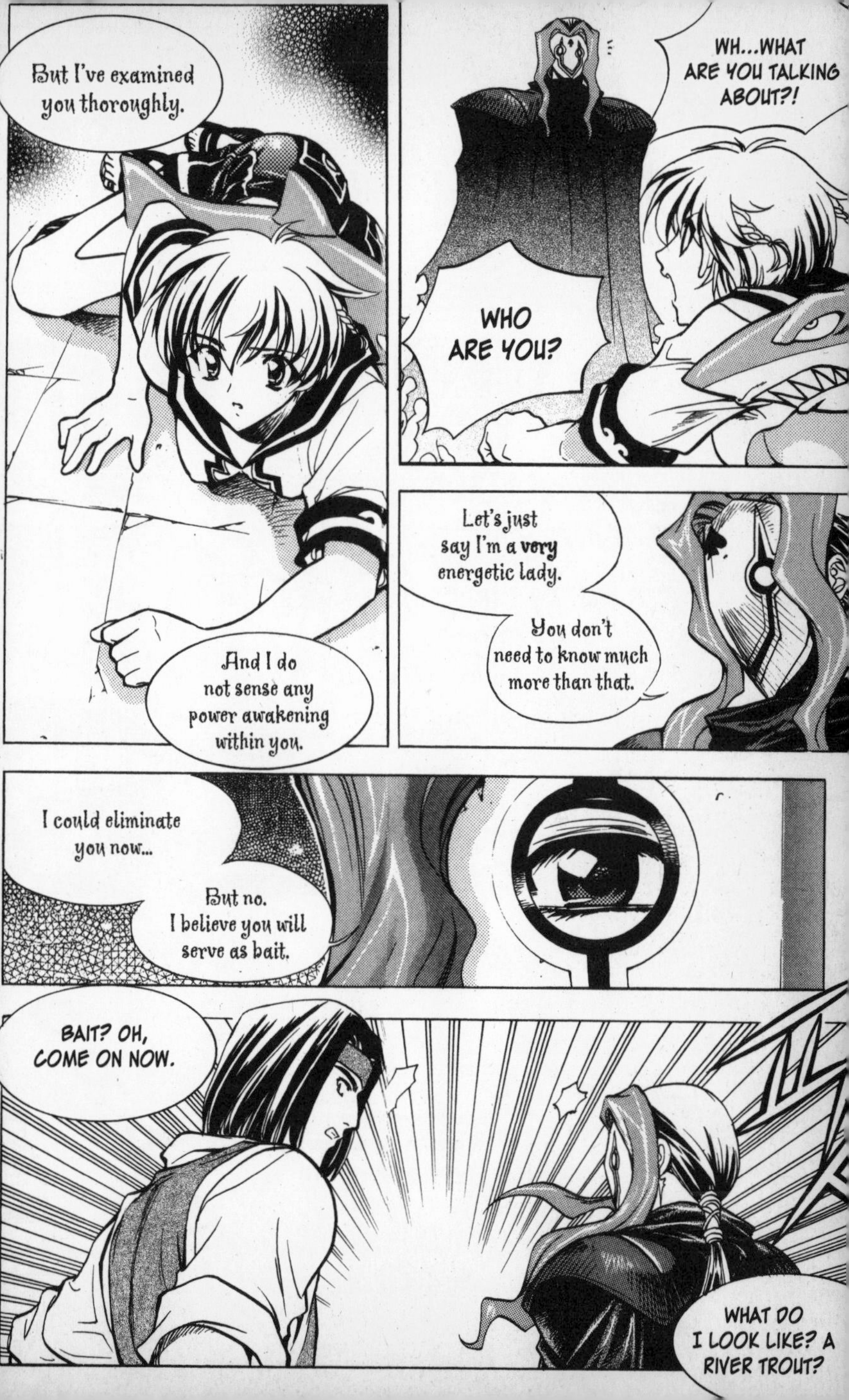
But I've examined you thoroughly.
And I do not sense any power awakening within you.
WH...WHAT ARE YOU TALKING ABOUT?!
WHO ARE YOU?
Let's just say I'm a **very** energetic lady.
You don't need to know much more than that.
I could eliminate you now...
But no. I believe you will serve as bait.
BAIT? OH, COME ON NOW.
WHAT DO I LOOK LIKE? A RIVER TROUT?

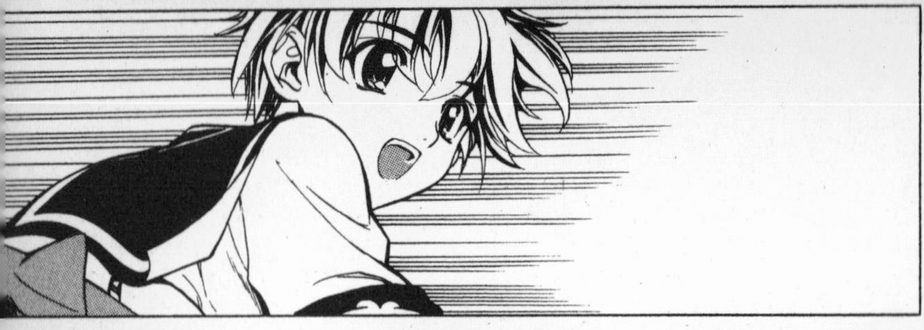

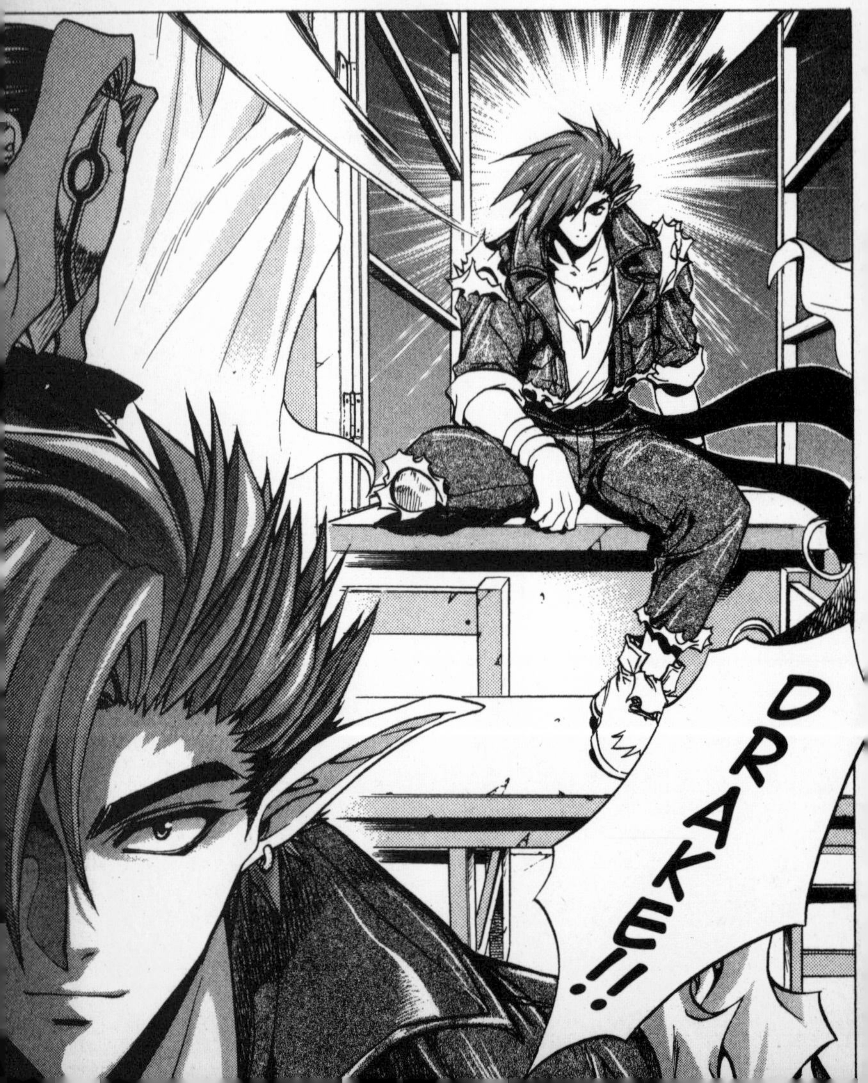
DRAKE!!

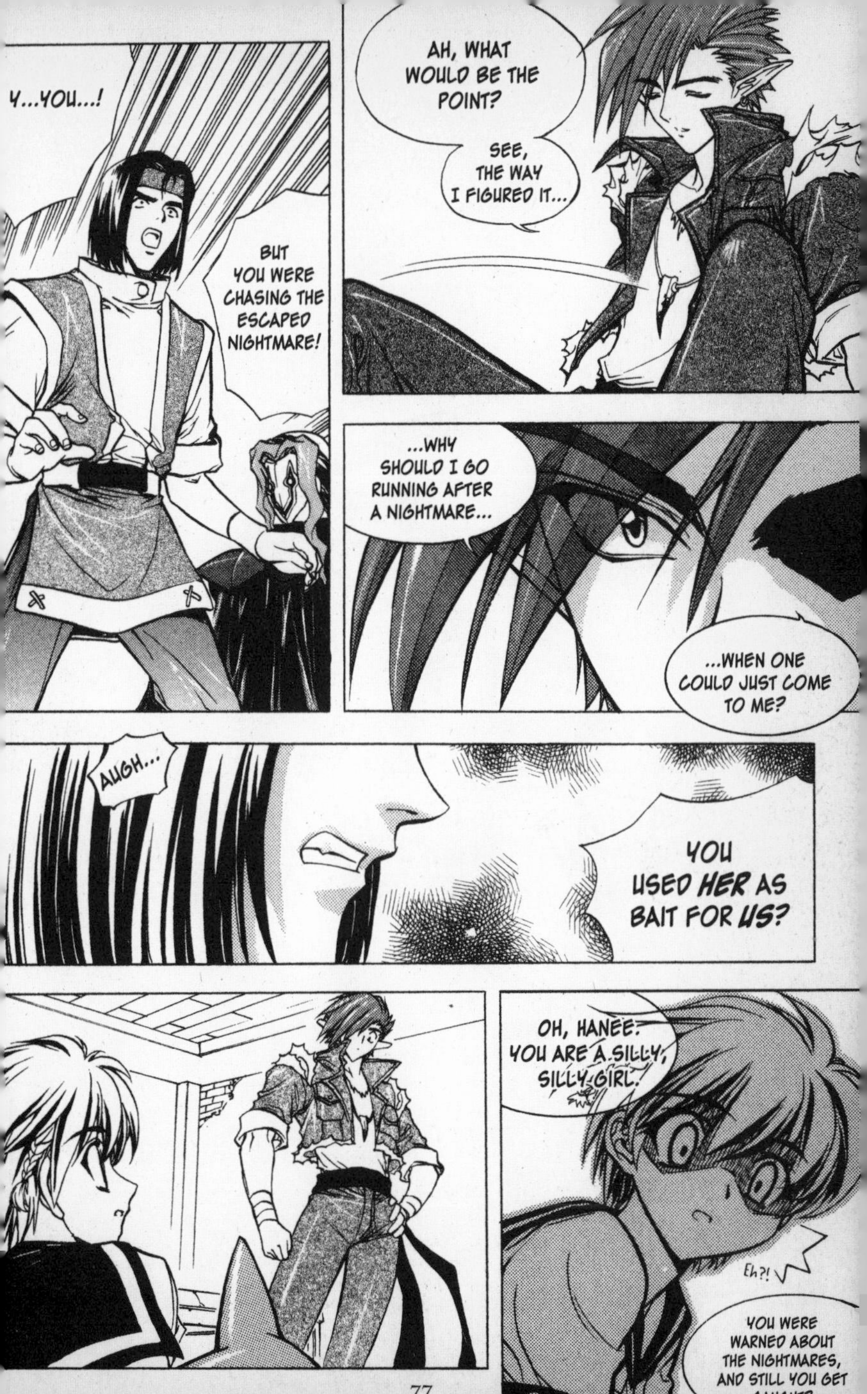
Y...YOU...!
BUT YOU WERE CHASING THE ESCAPED NIGHTMARE!
AH, WHAT WOULD BE THE POINT?
SEE, THE WAY I FIGURED IT...
...WHY SHOULD I GO RUNNING AFTER A NIGHTMARE...
...WHEN ONE COULD JUST COME TO ME?
AUGH...
YOU USED HER AS BAIT FOR US?
OH, HANEE. YOU ARE A SILLY, SILLY GIRL.
Eh?!
YOU WERE WARNED ABOUT THE NIGHTMARES, AND STILL YOU GET CAUGHT?

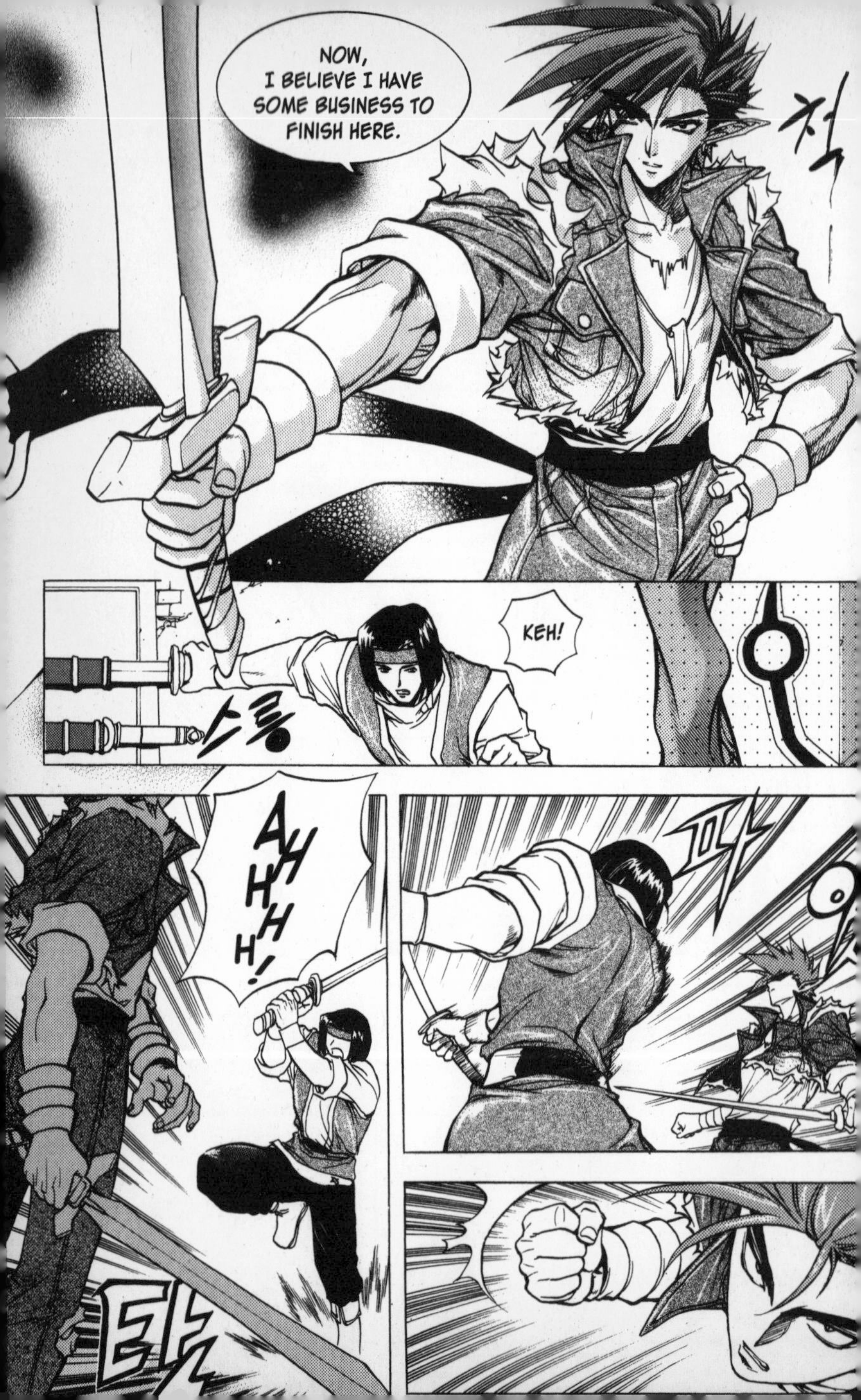
NOW, I BELIEVE I HAVE SOME BUSINESS TO FINISH HERE.
KEH!
스릉
AHHHHH!

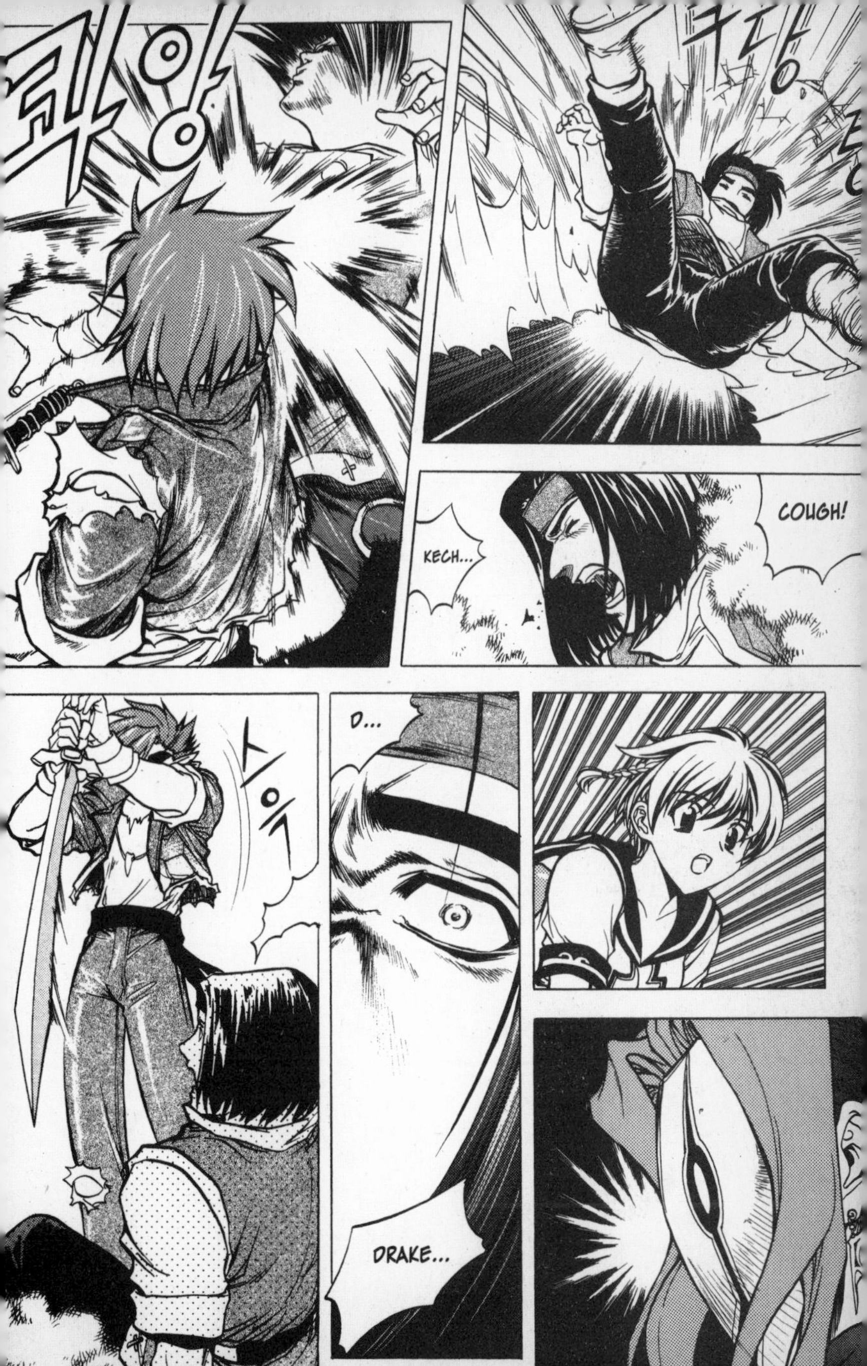
KECH...
COUGH!
D...
DRAKE...

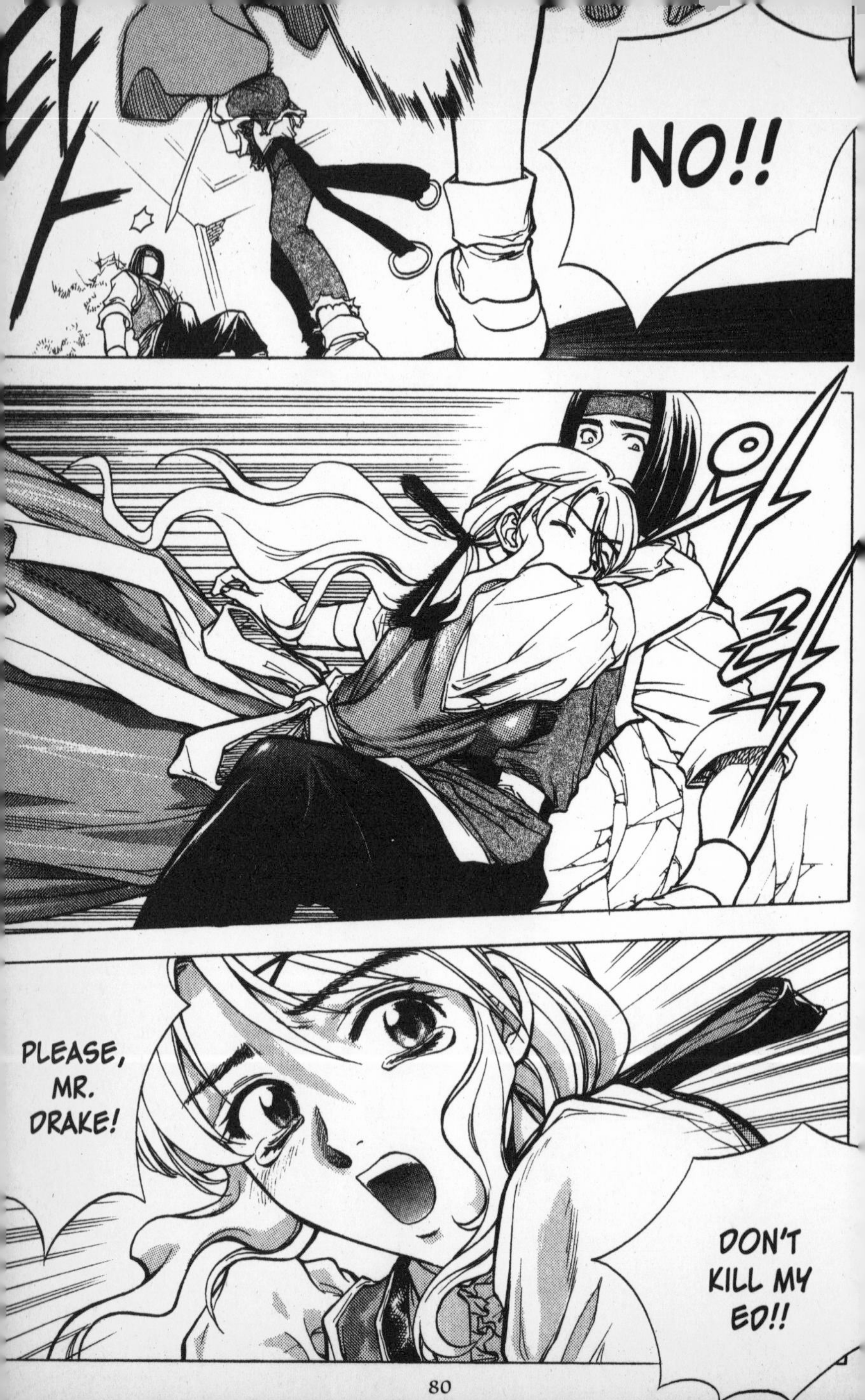
NO!!
PLEASE, MR. DRAKE!
DON'T KILL MY ED!!

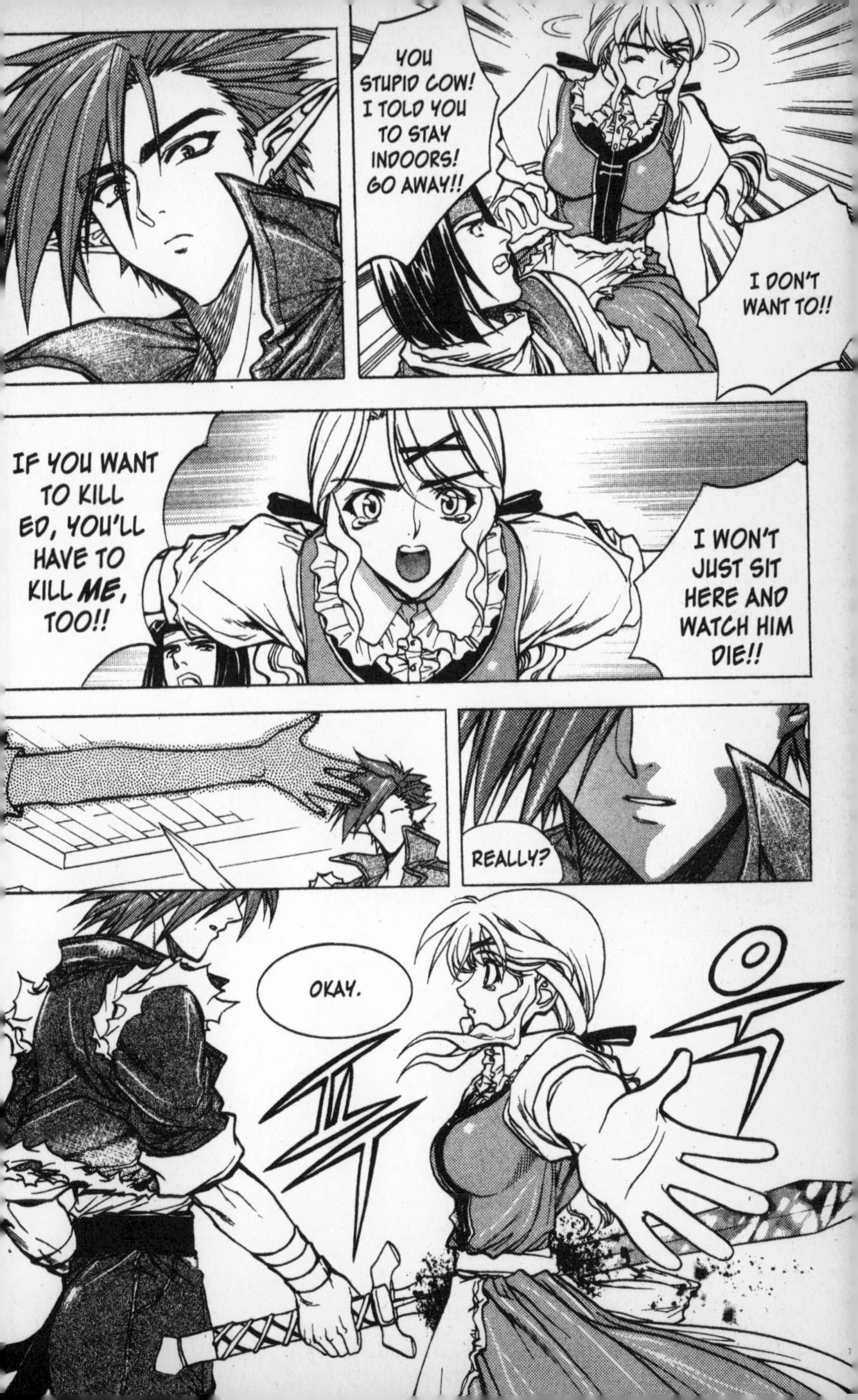
YOU STUPID COW! I TOLD YOU TO STAY INDOORS! GO AWAY!!
I DON'T WANT TO!!
IF YOU WANT TO KILL ED, YOU'LL HAVE TO KILL *ME*, TOO!!
I WON'T JUST SIT HERE AND WATCH HIM DIE!!
REALLY?
OKAY.

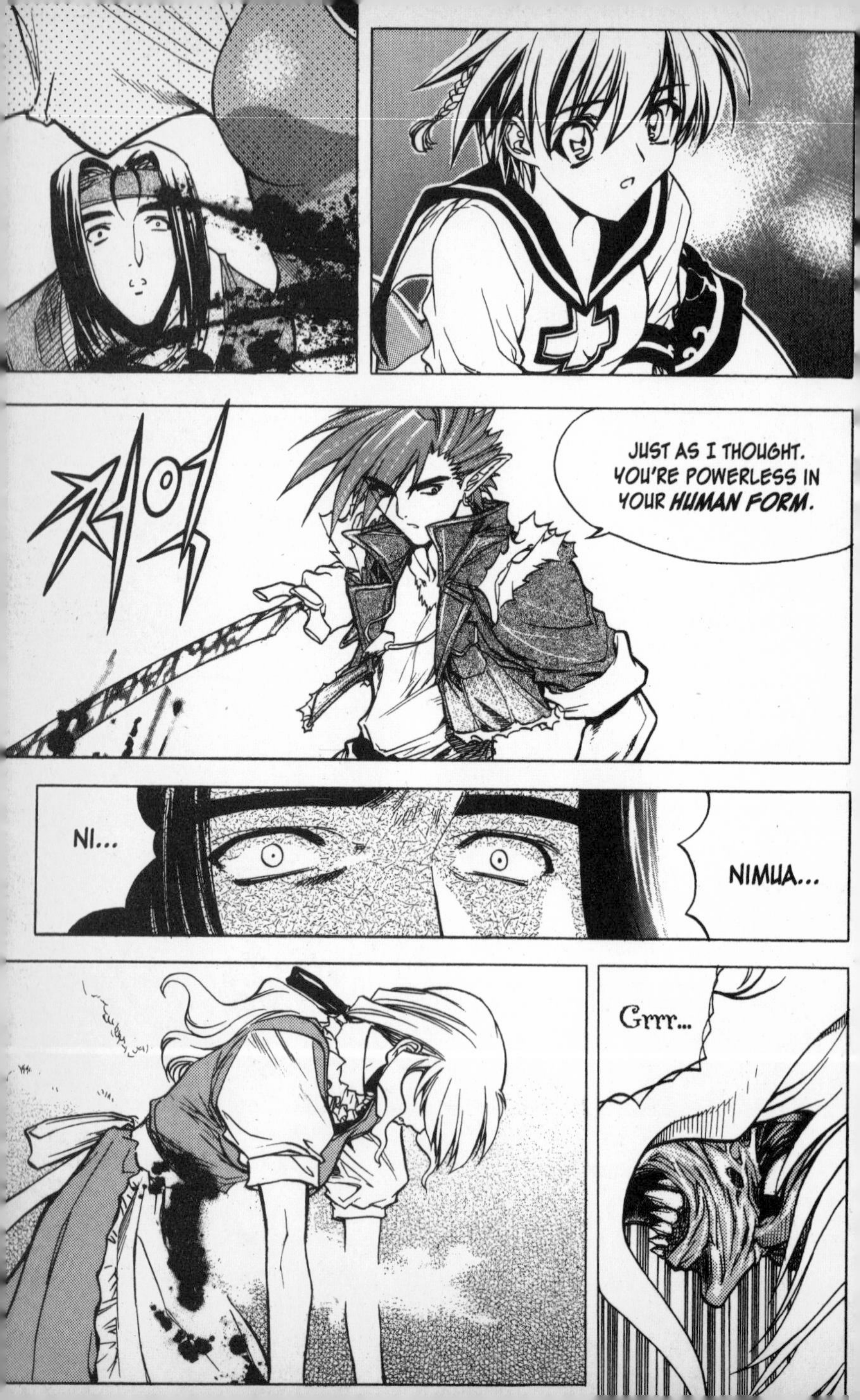
JUST AS I THOUGHT. YOU'RE POWERLESS IN YOUR **HUMAN FORM**.
NI...
NIMUA...
Grrr...

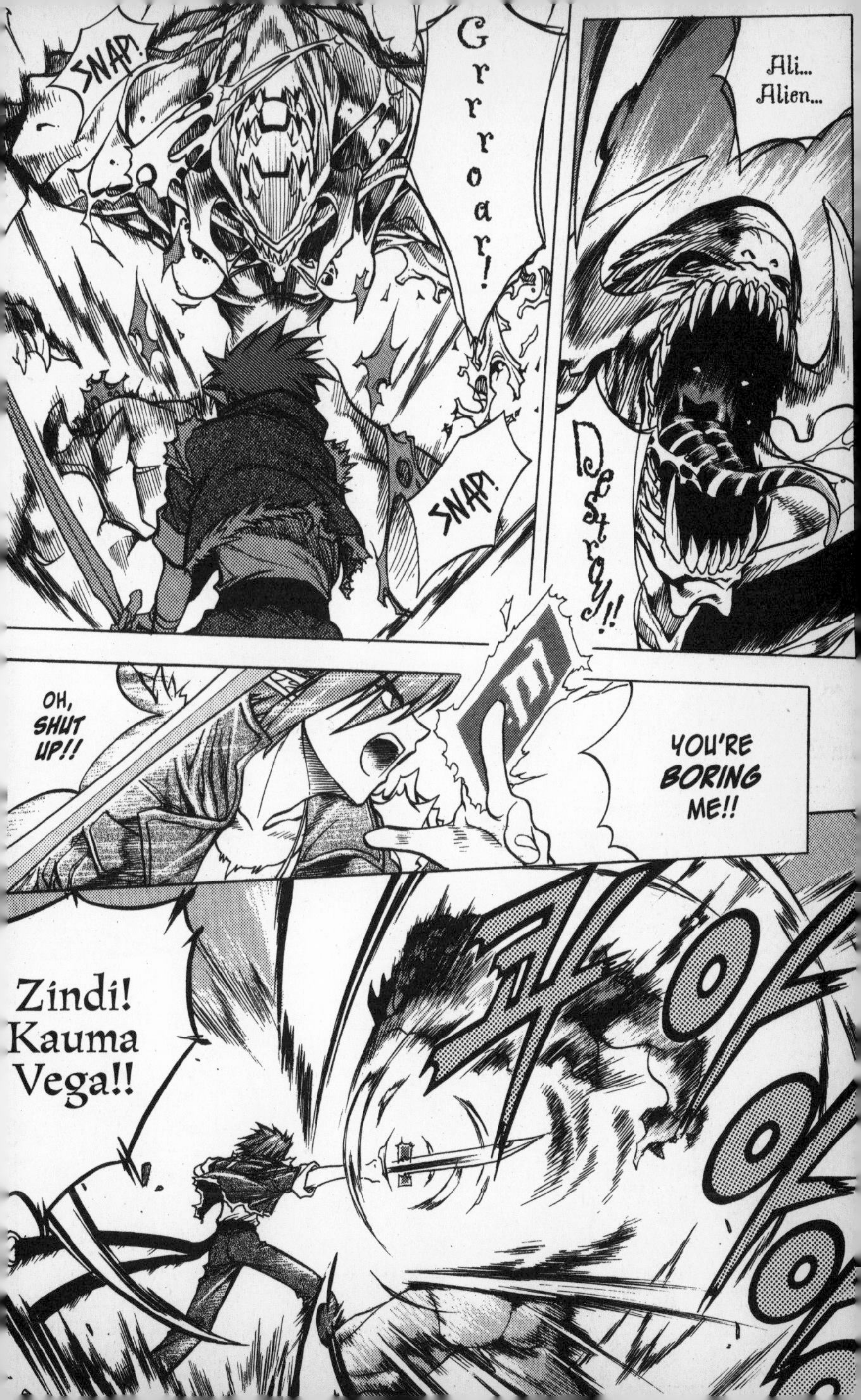
SNAP!
Grrroar!
SNAP!
Ali... Alien...
Destroy!!
OH, SHUT UP!!
YOU'RE BORING ME!!
Zindi! Kauma Vega!!

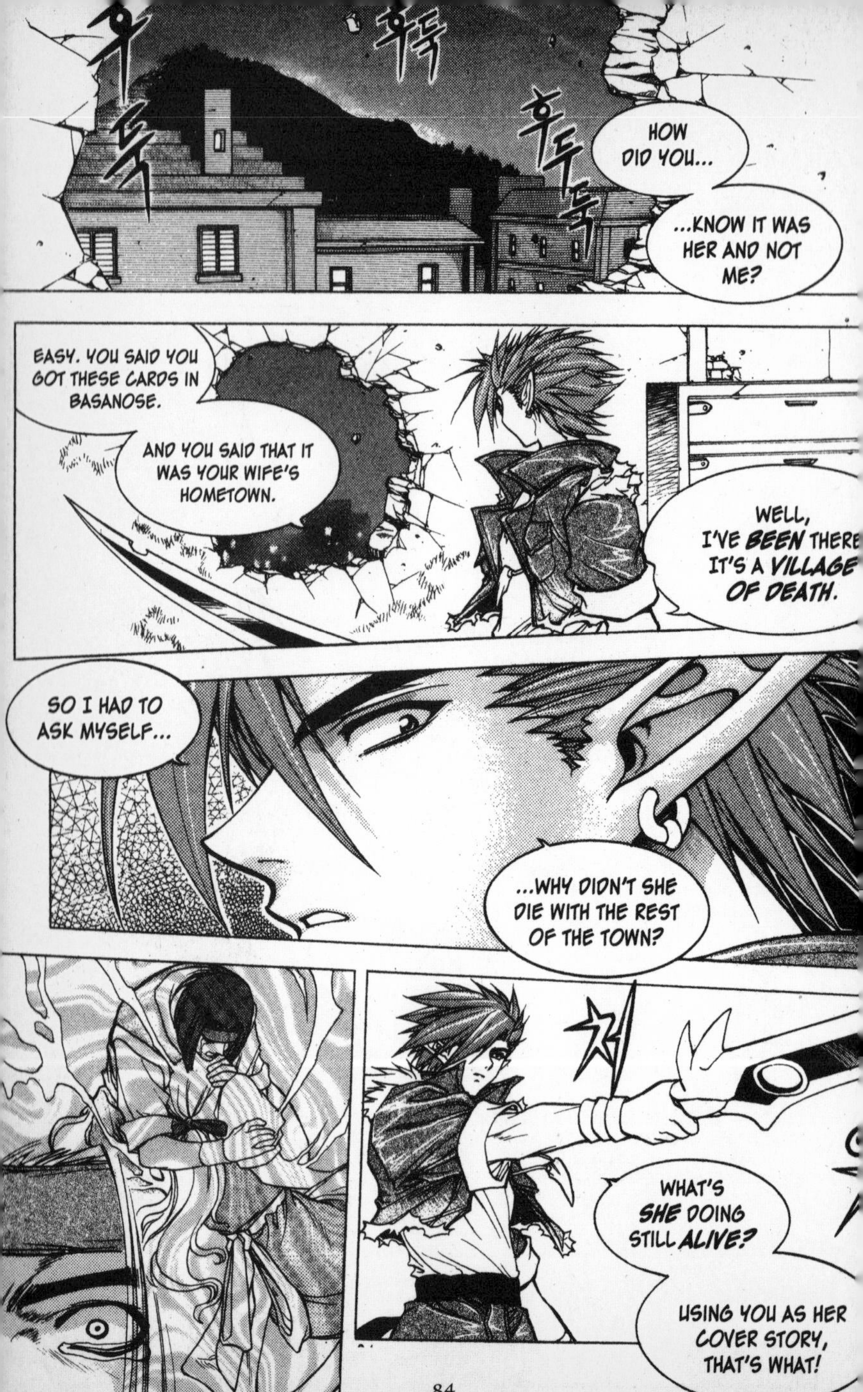
HOW DID YOU...
...KNOW IT WAS HER AND NOT ME?
EASY. YOU SAID YOU GOT THESE CARDS IN BASANOSE.
AND YOU SAID THAT IT WAS YOUR WIFE'S HOMETOWN.
WELL, I'VE BEEN THERE. IT'S A VILLAGE OF DEATH.
SO I HAD TO ASK MYSELF...
...WHY DIDN'T SHE DIE WITH THE REST OF THE TOWN?
WHAT'S SHE DOING STILL ALIVE?
USING YOU AS HER COVER STORY, THAT'S WHAT!

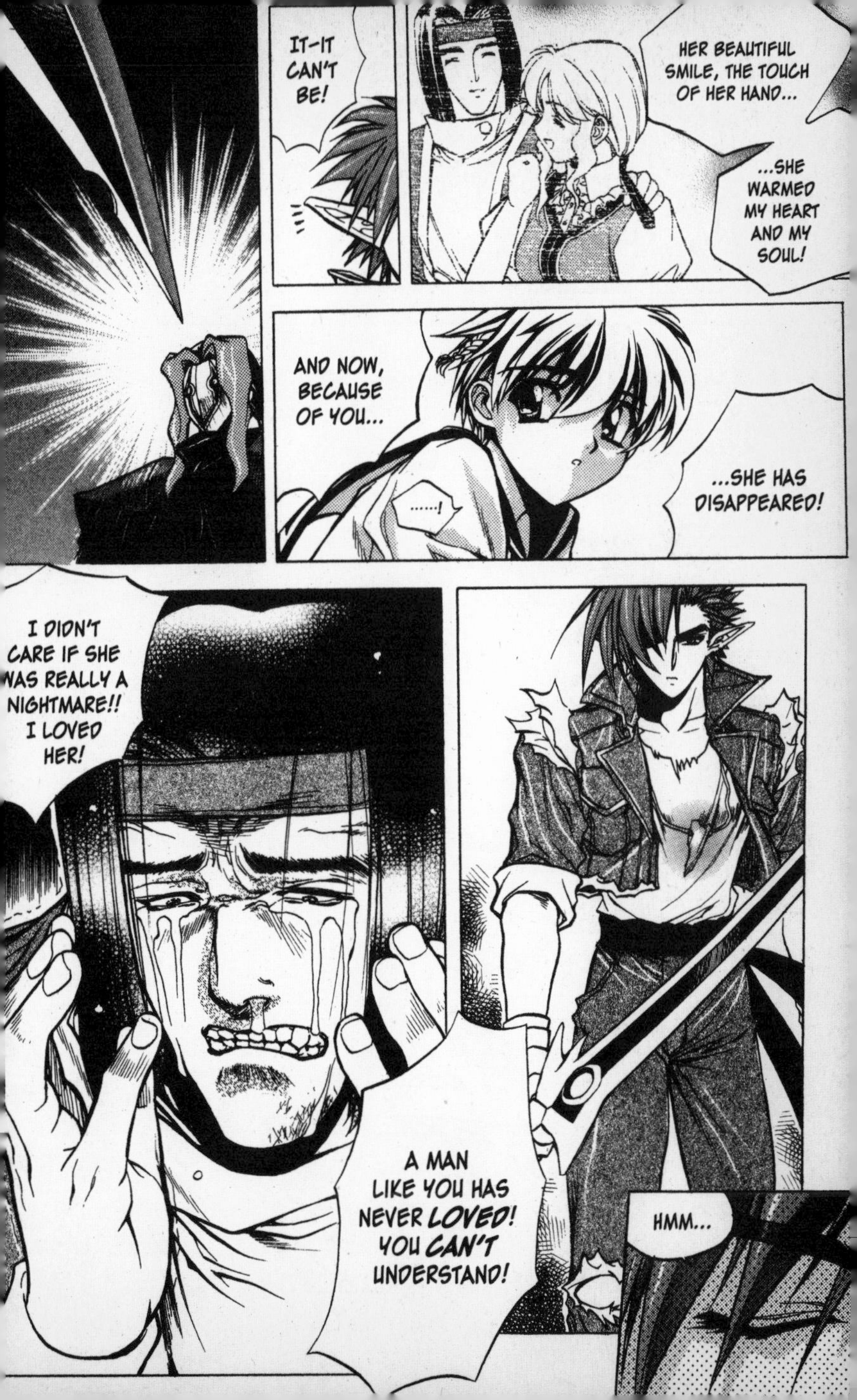
IT-IT CAN'T BE!
HER BEAUTIFUL SMILE, THE TOUCH OF HER HAND...
...SHE WARMED MY HEART AND MY SOUL!
AND NOW, BECAUSE OF YOU...
......!
...SHE HAS DISAPPEARED!
I DIDN'T CARE IF SHE WAS REALLY A NIGHTMARE!! I LOVED HER!
A MAN LIKE YOU HAS NEVER LOVED! YOU CAN'T UNDERSTAND!
HMM...

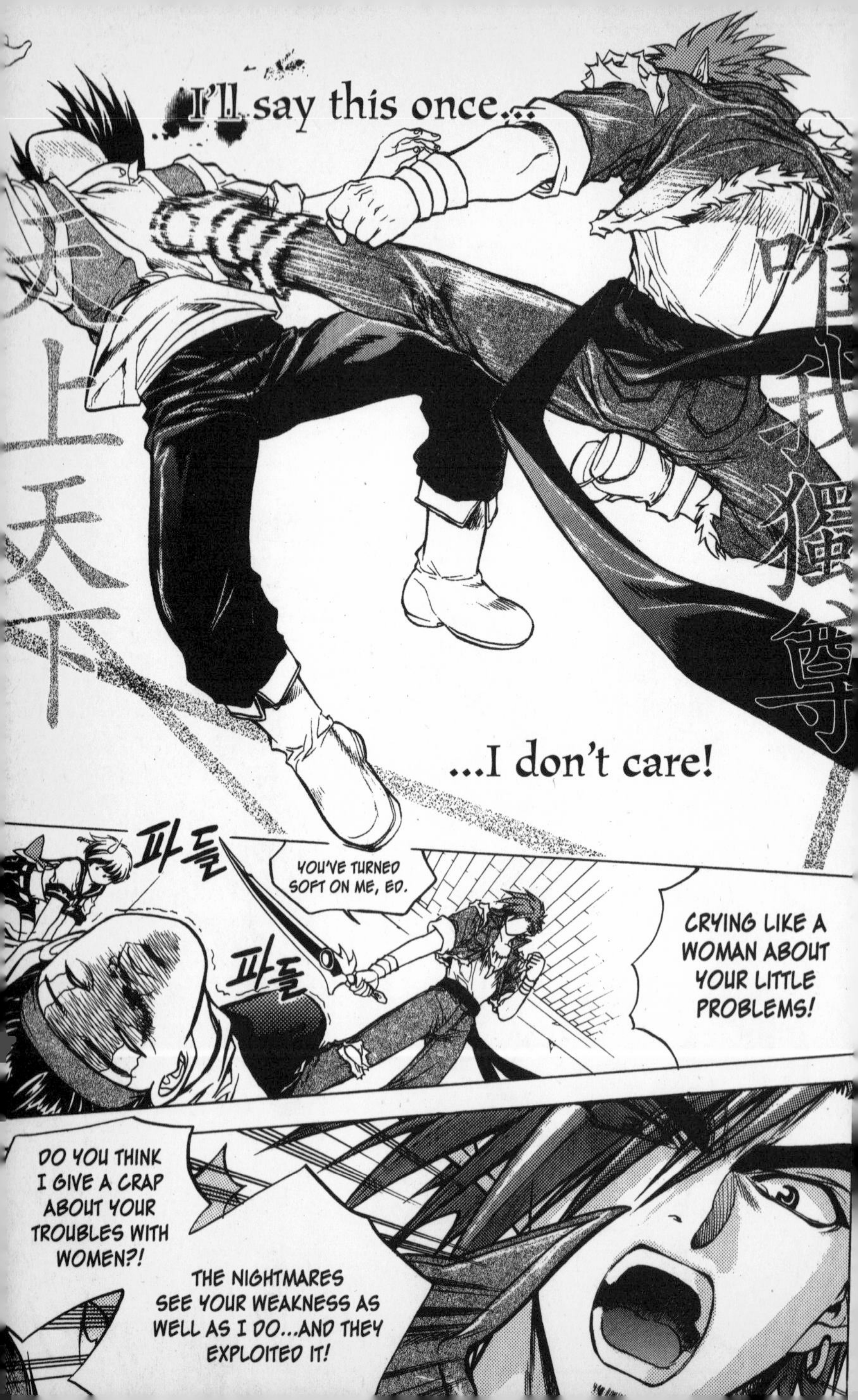
I'll say this once...
天上天下
唯我獨尊
...I don't care!
파들
YOU'VE TURNED SOFT ON ME, ED.
파들
CRYING LIKE A WOMAN ABOUT YOUR LITTLE PROBLEMS!
DO YOU THINK I GIVE A CRAP ABOUT YOUR TROUBLES WITH WOMEN?!
THE NIGHTMARES SEE YOUR WEAKNESS AS WELL AS I DO...AND THEY EXPLOITED IT!

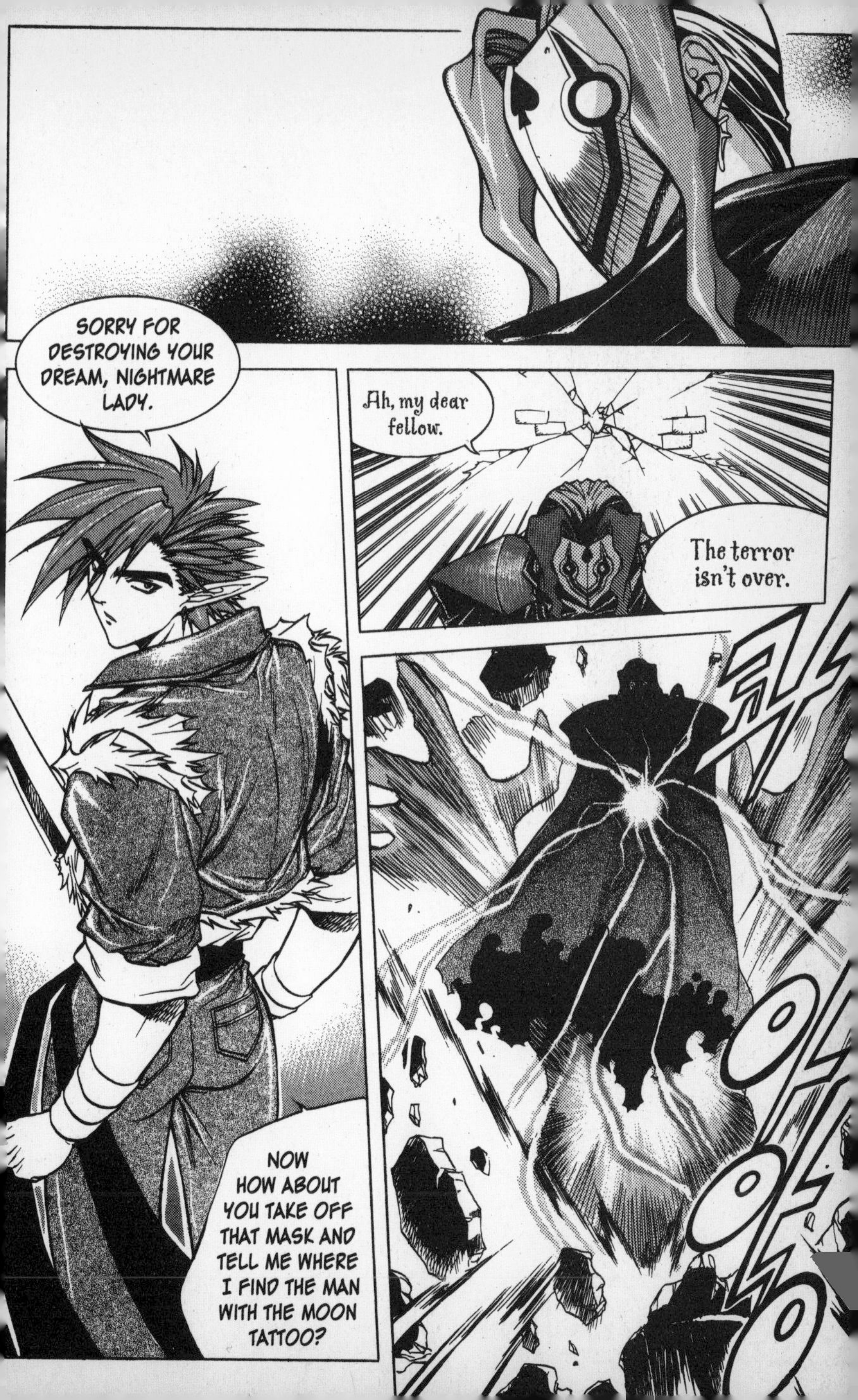
SORRY FOR DESTROYING YOUR DREAM, NIGHTMARE LADY.
NOW HOW ABOUT YOU TAKE OFF THAT MASK AND TELL ME WHERE I FIND THE MAN WITH THE MOON TATTOO?
Ah, my dear fellow.
The terror isn't over.

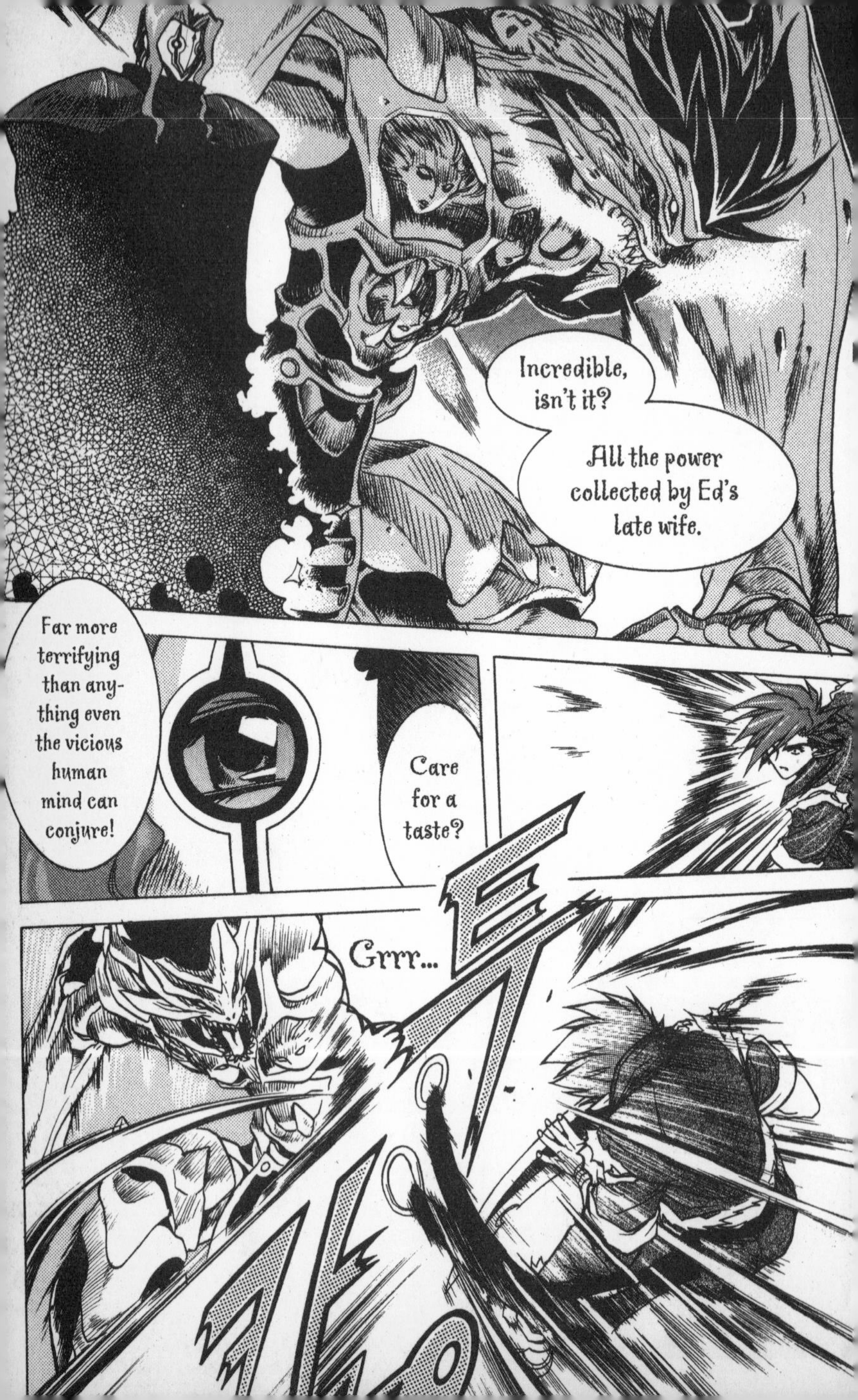
Incredible, isn't it?
All the power collected by Ed's late wife.
Far more terrifying than anything even the vicious human mind can conjure!
Care for a taste?
Grrr...

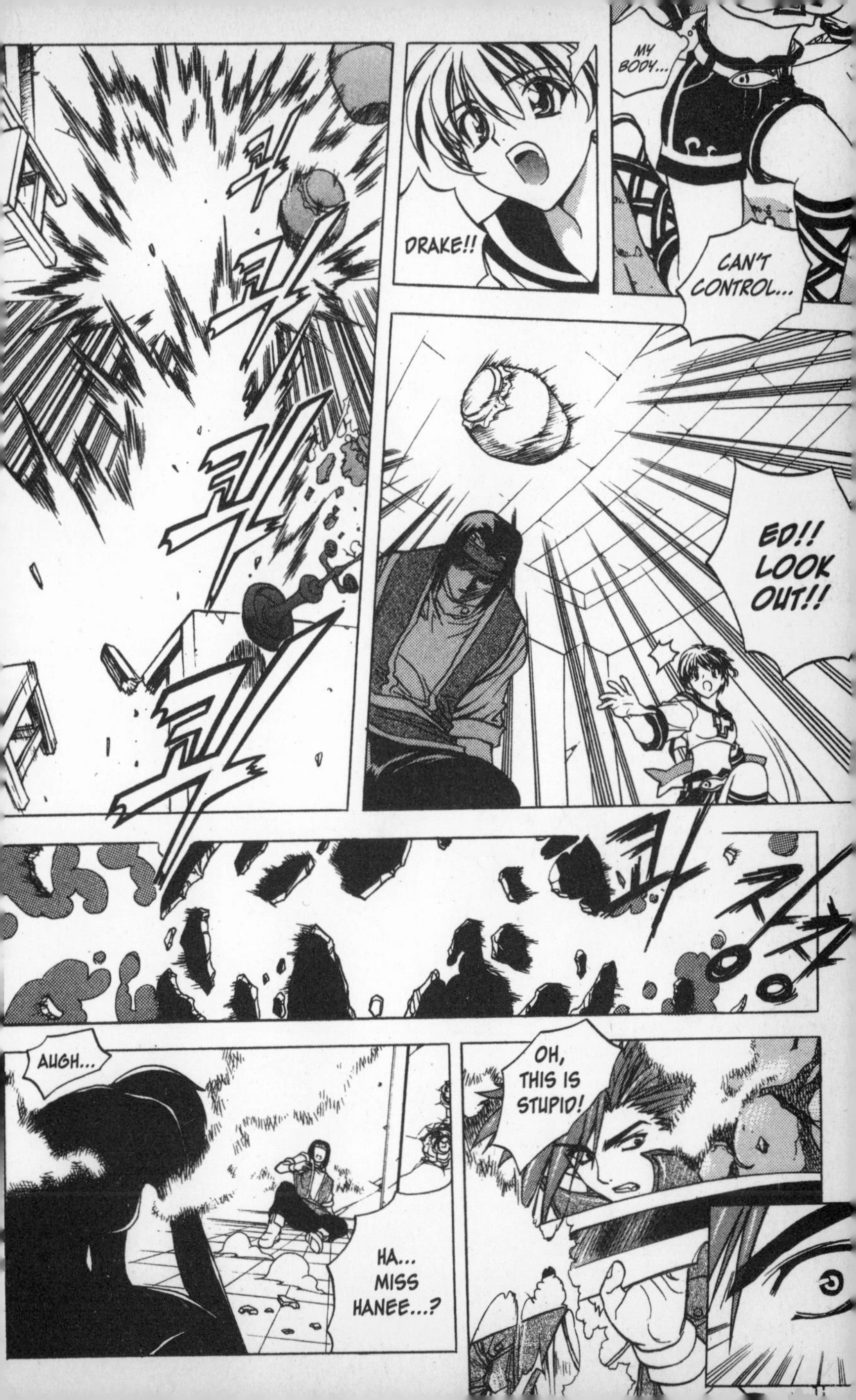
DRAKE!!
MY BODY...
CAN'T CONTROL...
ED!! LOOK OUT!!
AUGH...
HA... MISS HANEE...?
OH, THIS IS STUPID!

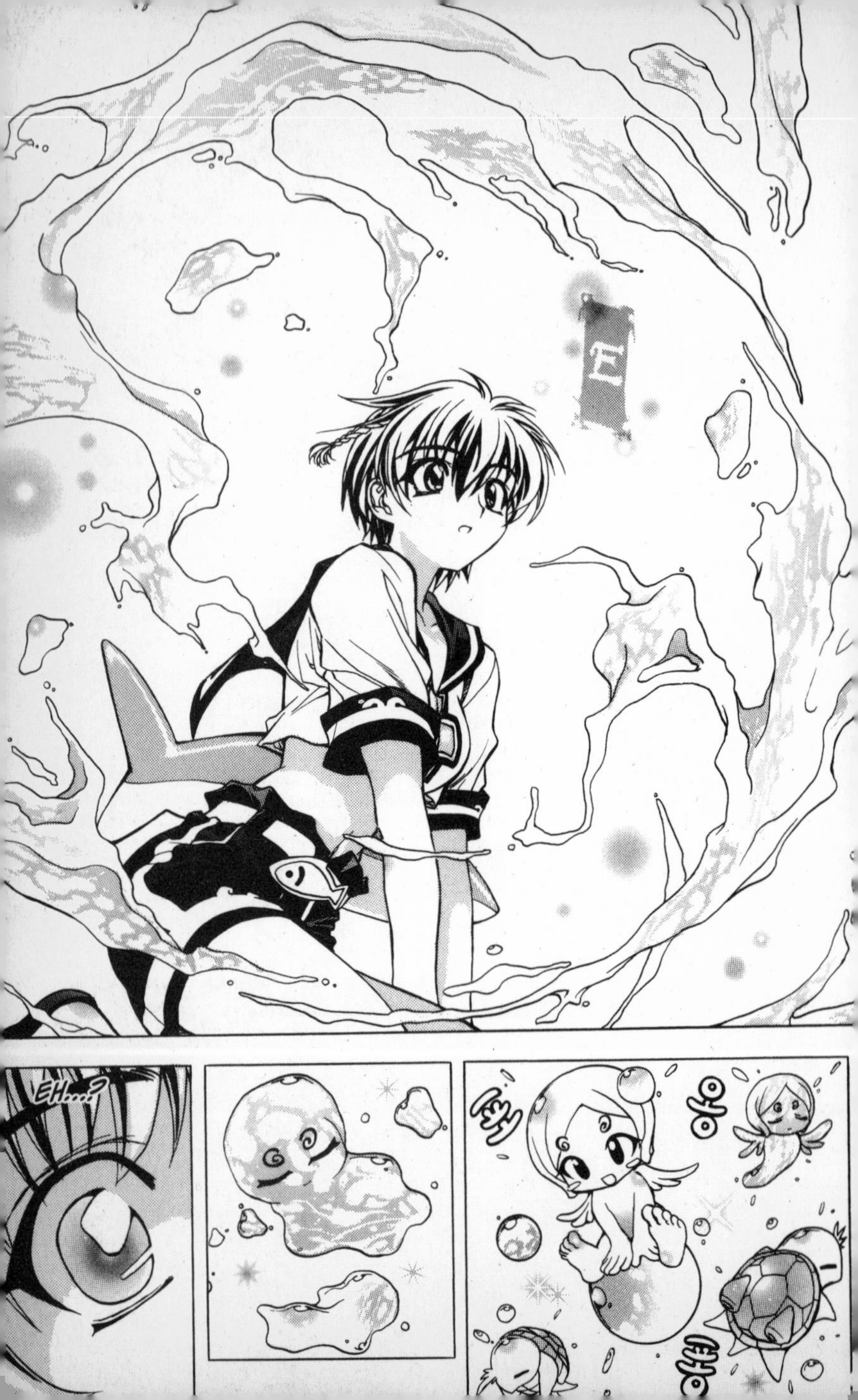
EH...?

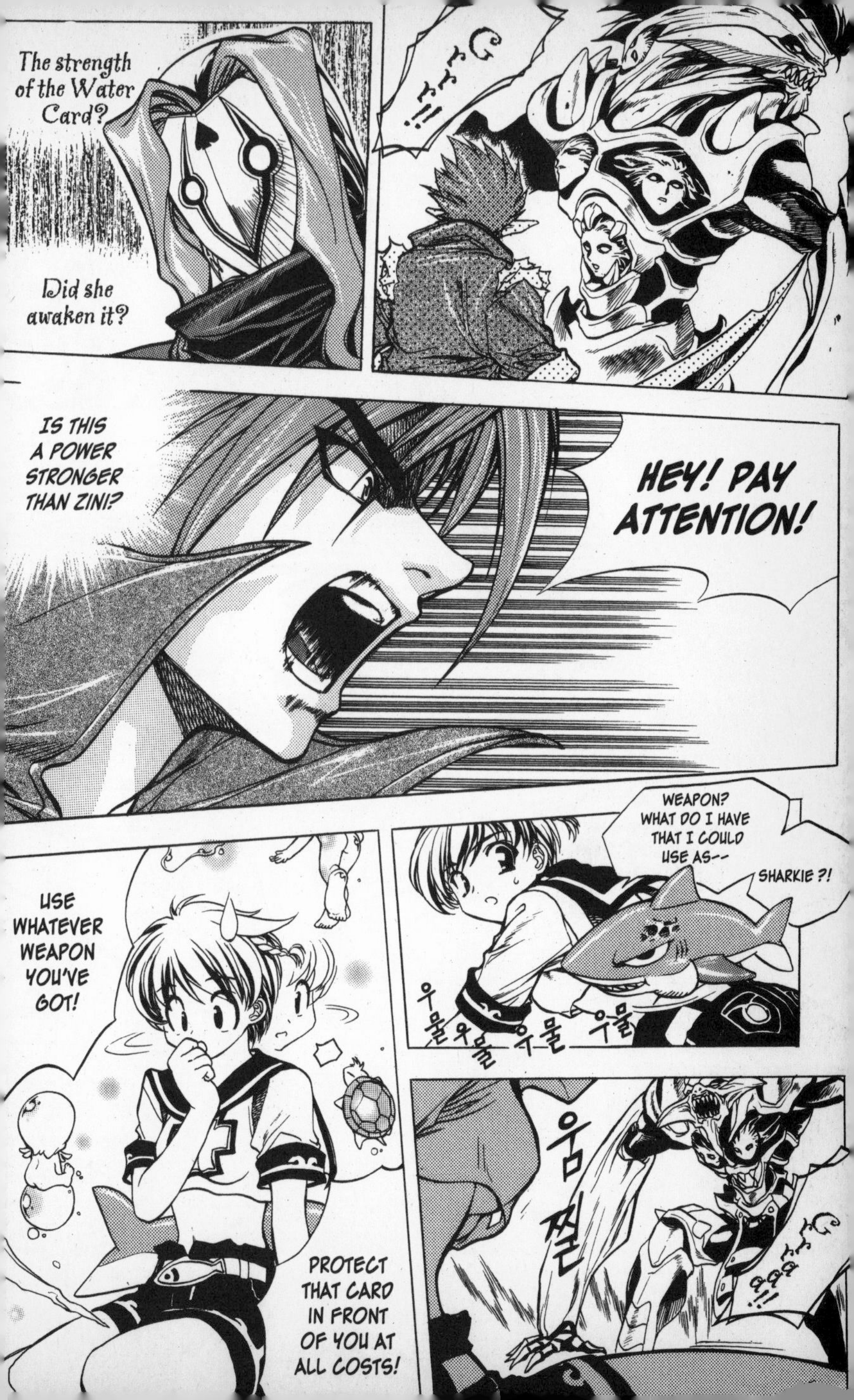
The strength of the Water Card?
Did she awaken it?
Grrr!!!
IS THIS A POWER STRONGER THAN ZINI?
HEY! PAY ATTENTION!
USE WHATEVER WEAPON YOU'VE GOT!
PROTECT THAT CARD IN FRONT OF YOU AT ALL COSTS!
WEAPON? WHAT DO I HAVE THAT I COULD USE AS--
SHARKIE ?!
우물우물 우물 우물
움찔
Grraa!!!

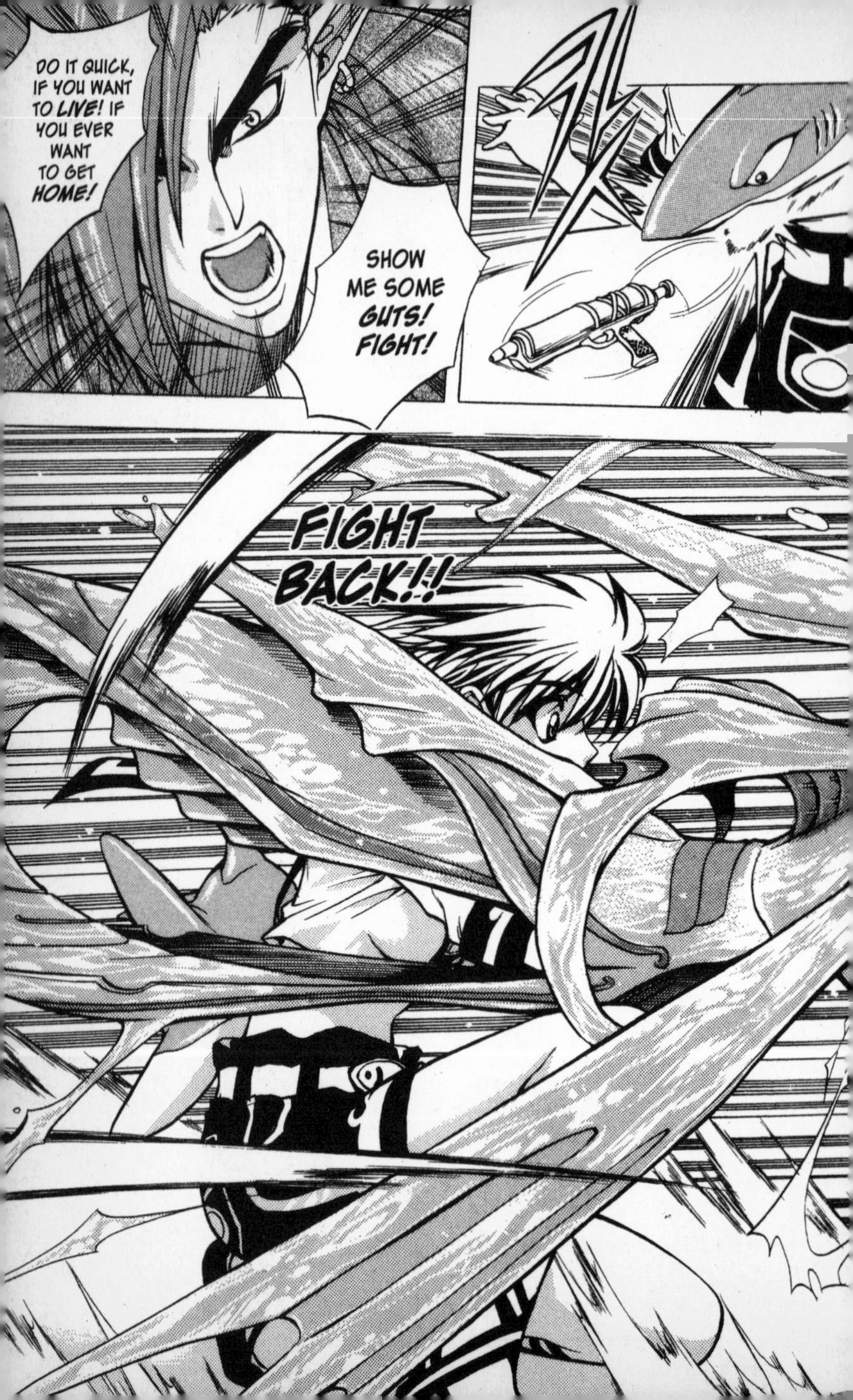
DO IT QUICK, IF YOU WANT TO LIVE! IF YOU EVER WANT TO GET HOME!
SHOW ME SOME GUTS! FIGHT!
FIGHT BACK!!

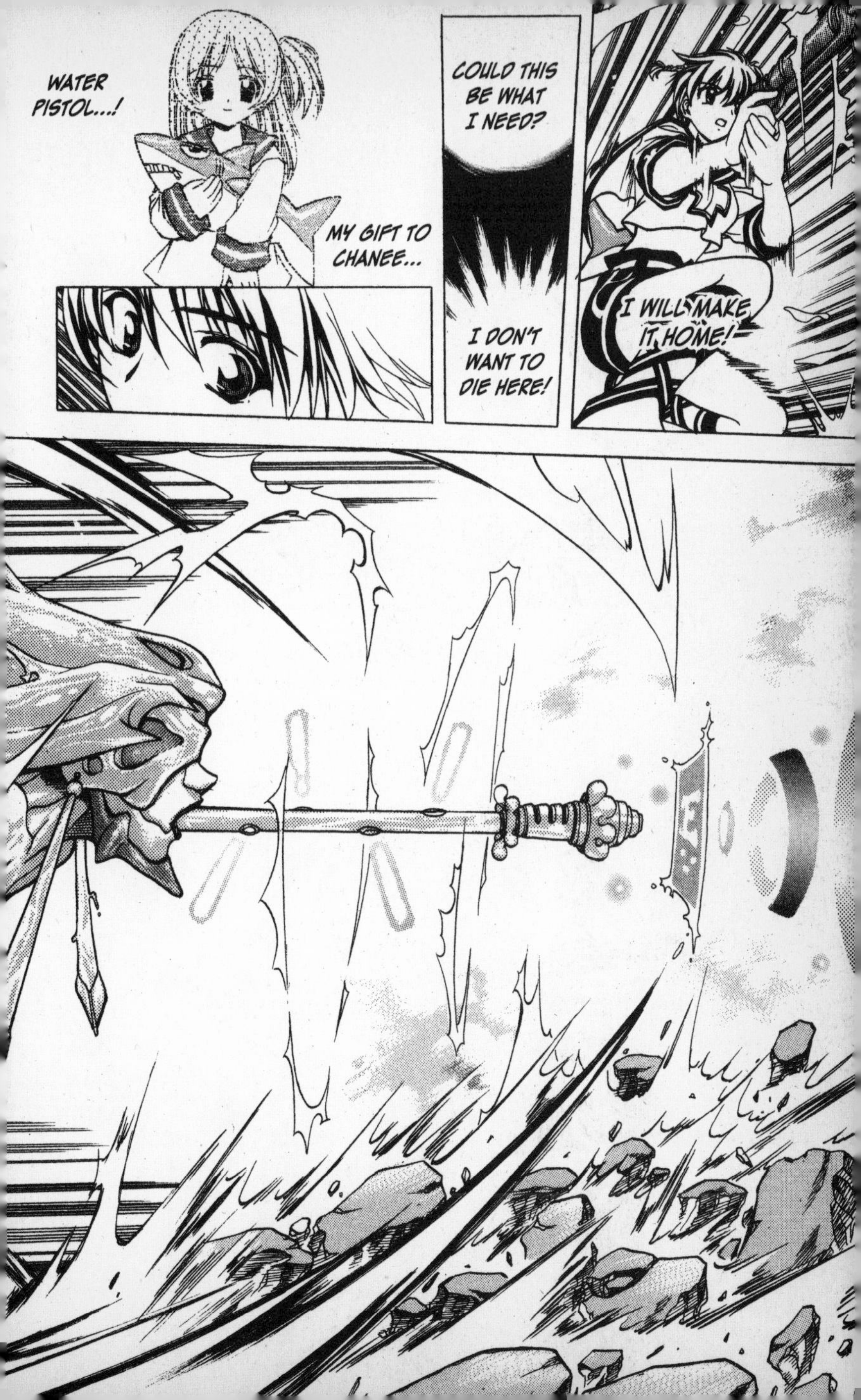
WATER PISTOL...!
MY GIFT TO CHANEE...
COULD THIS BE WHAT I NEED?
I DON'T WANT TO DIE HERE!
I WILL MAKE IT HOME!

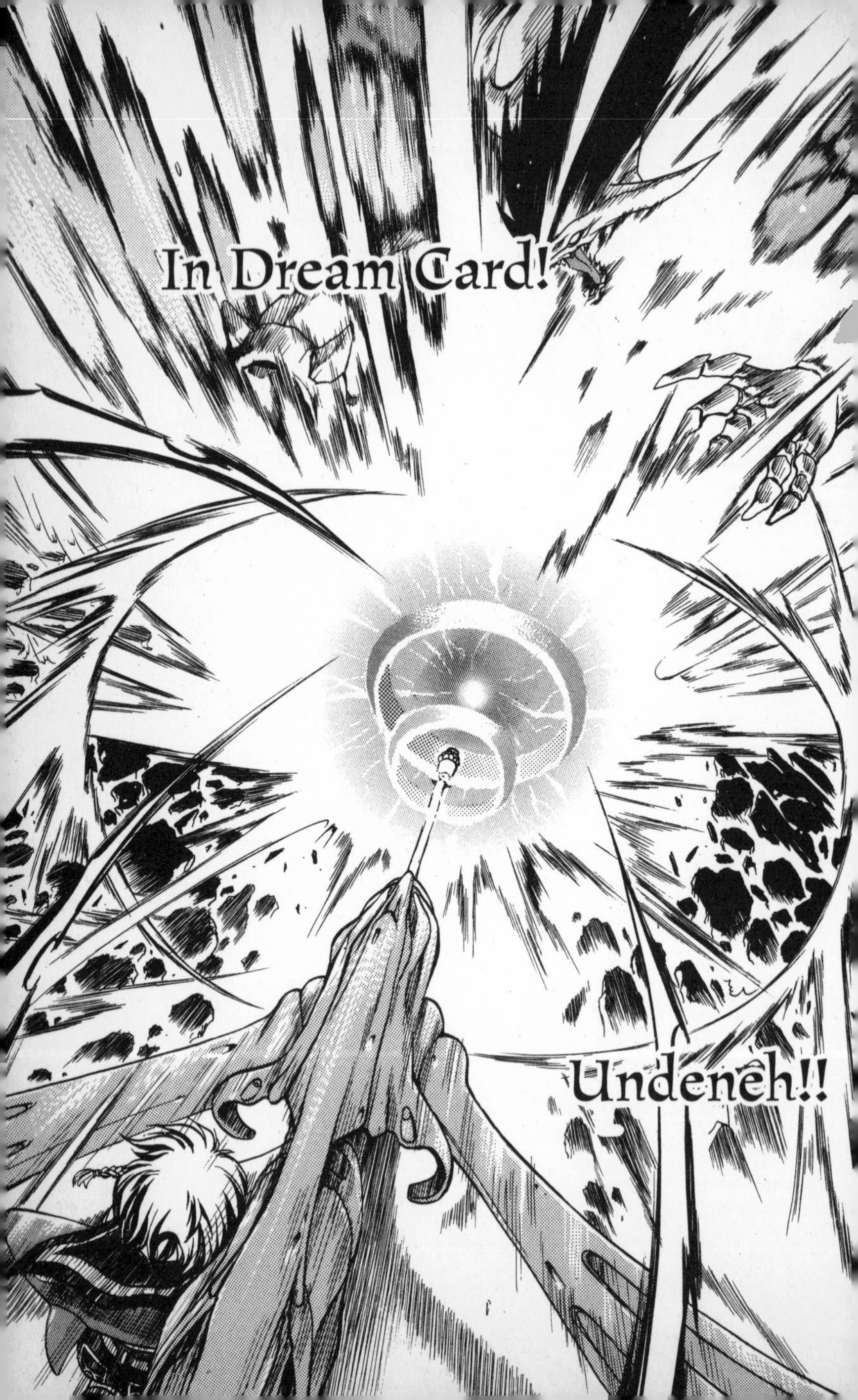
In Dream Card!
Undeneh!!

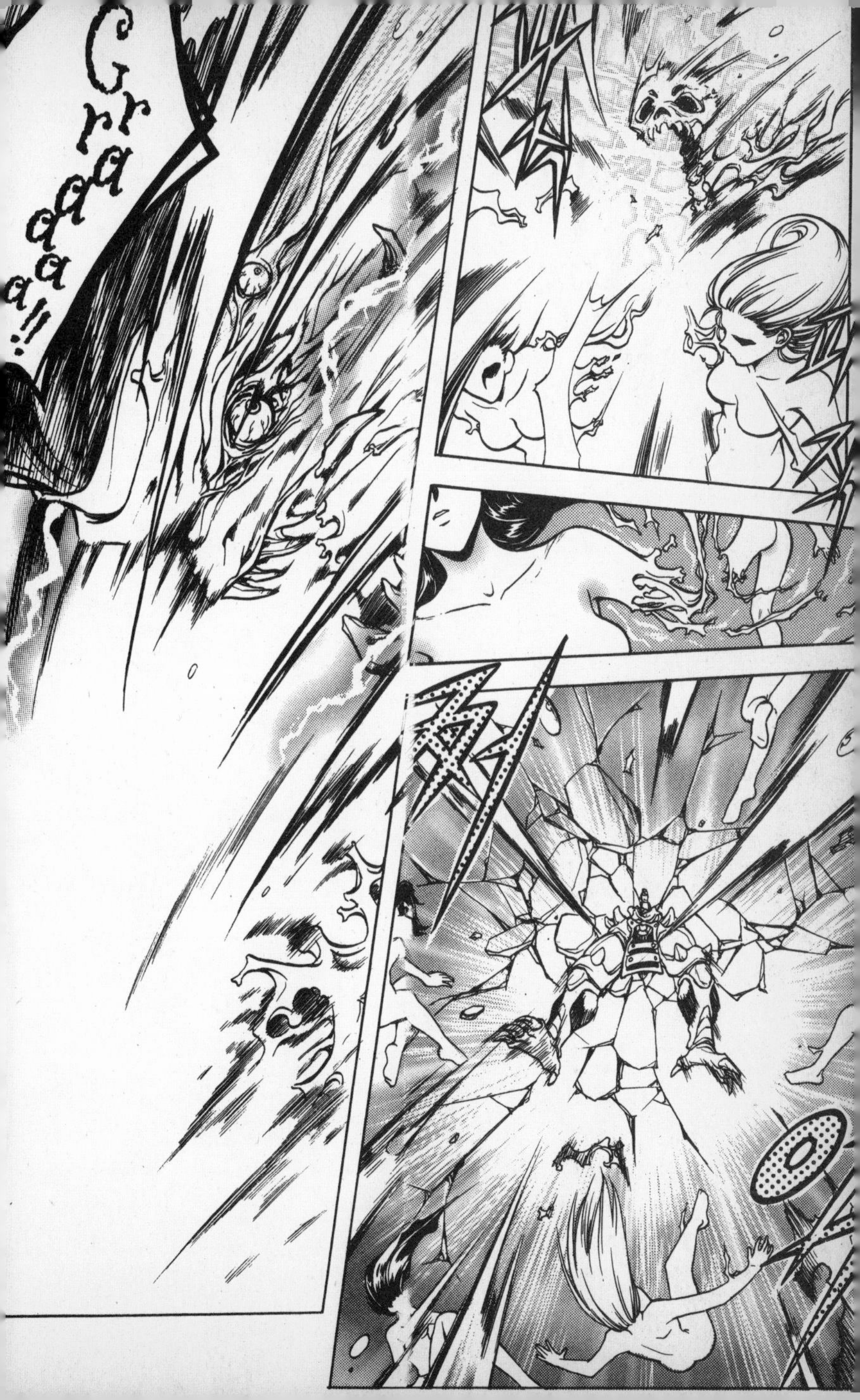
Graaaaa!!

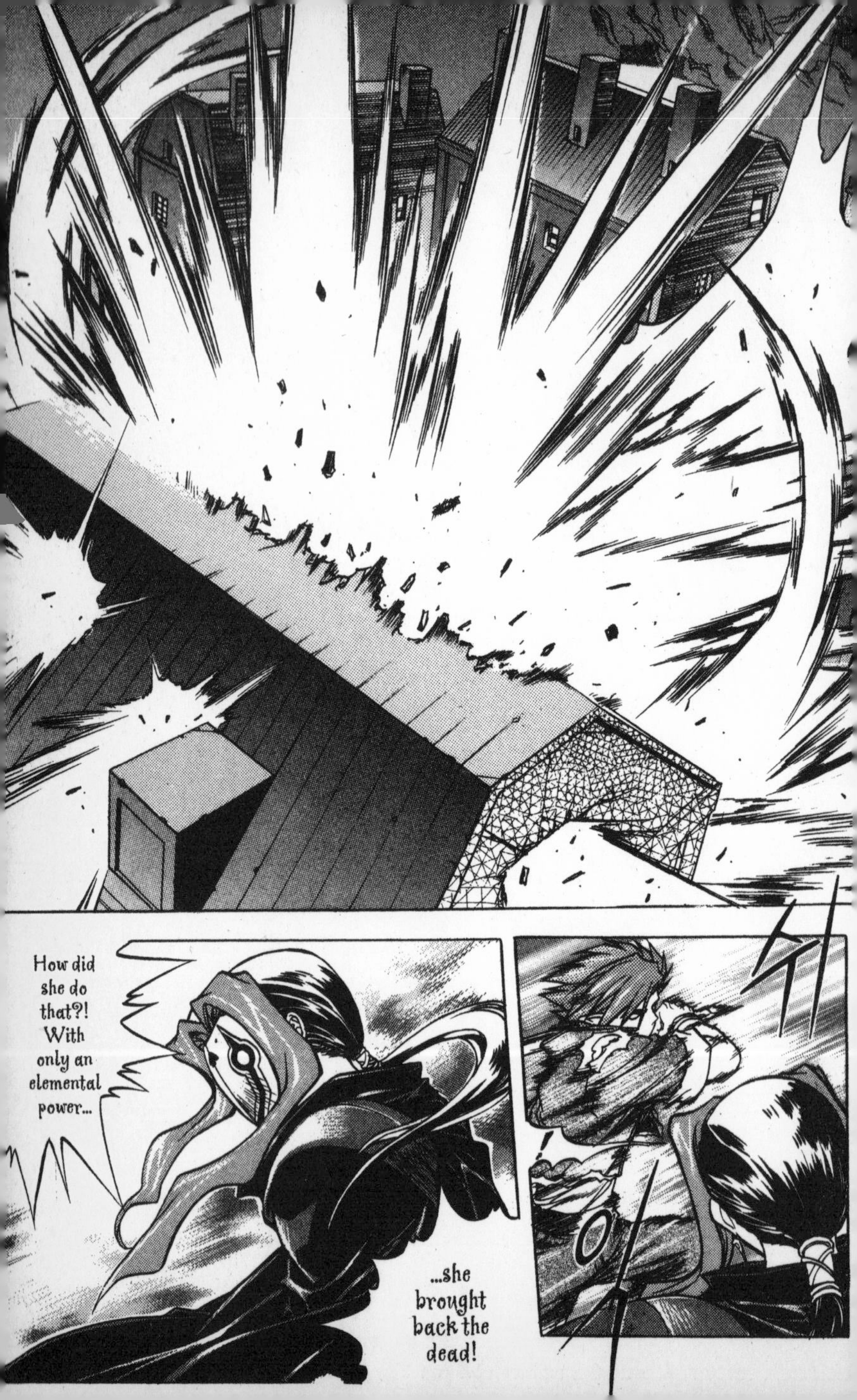
How did she do that?! With only an elemental power...
...she brought back the dead!

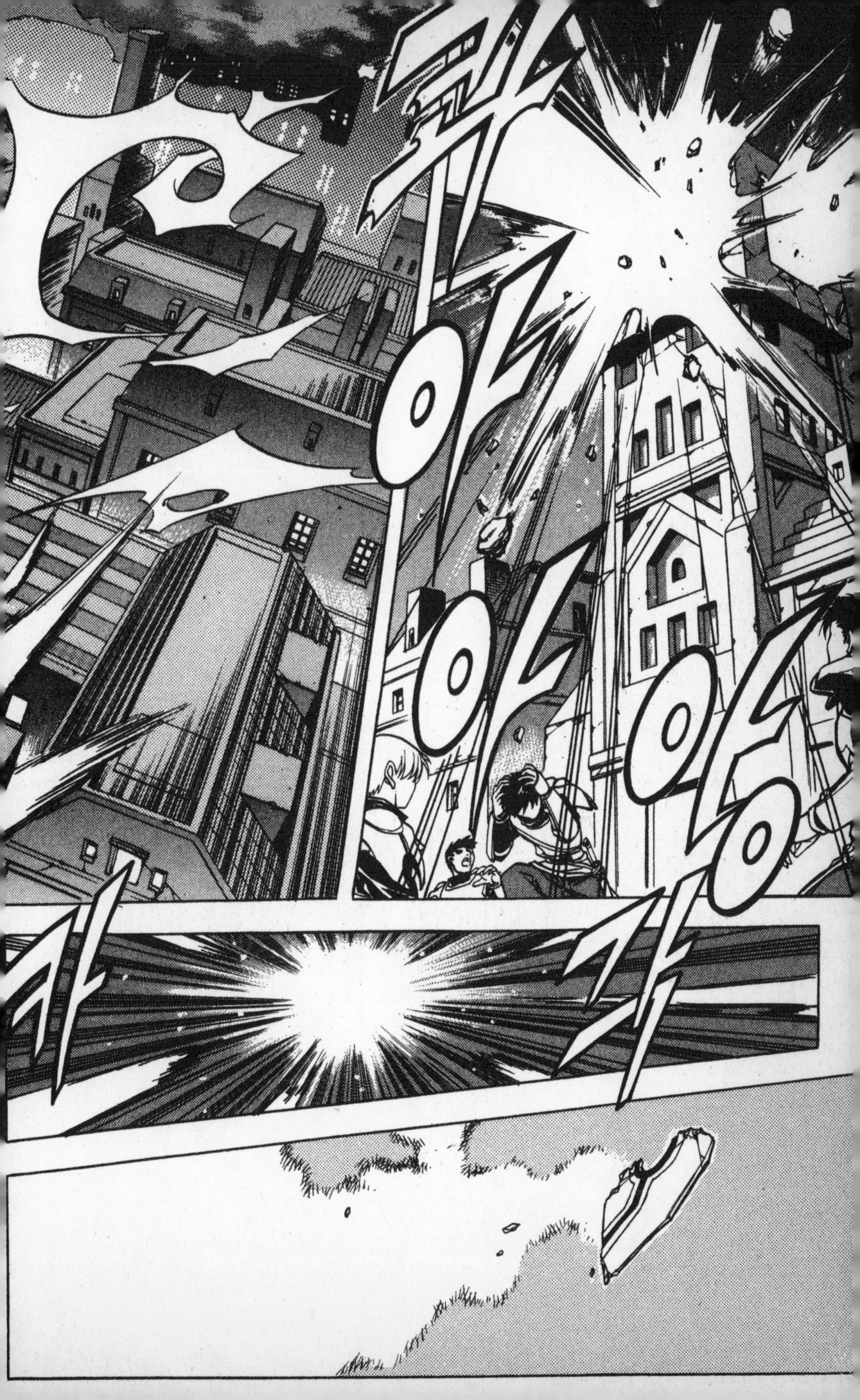

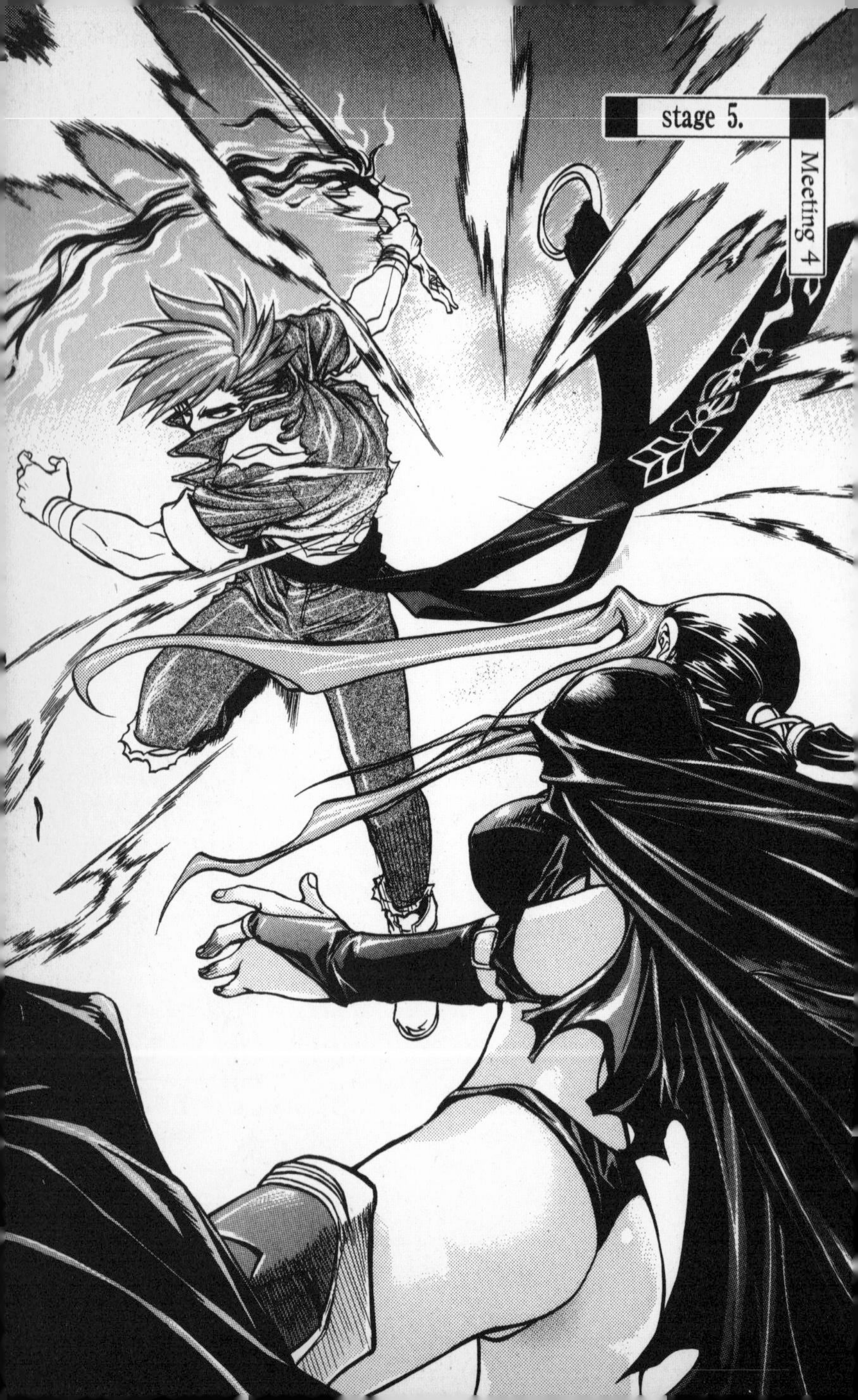
stage 5.
Meeting 4

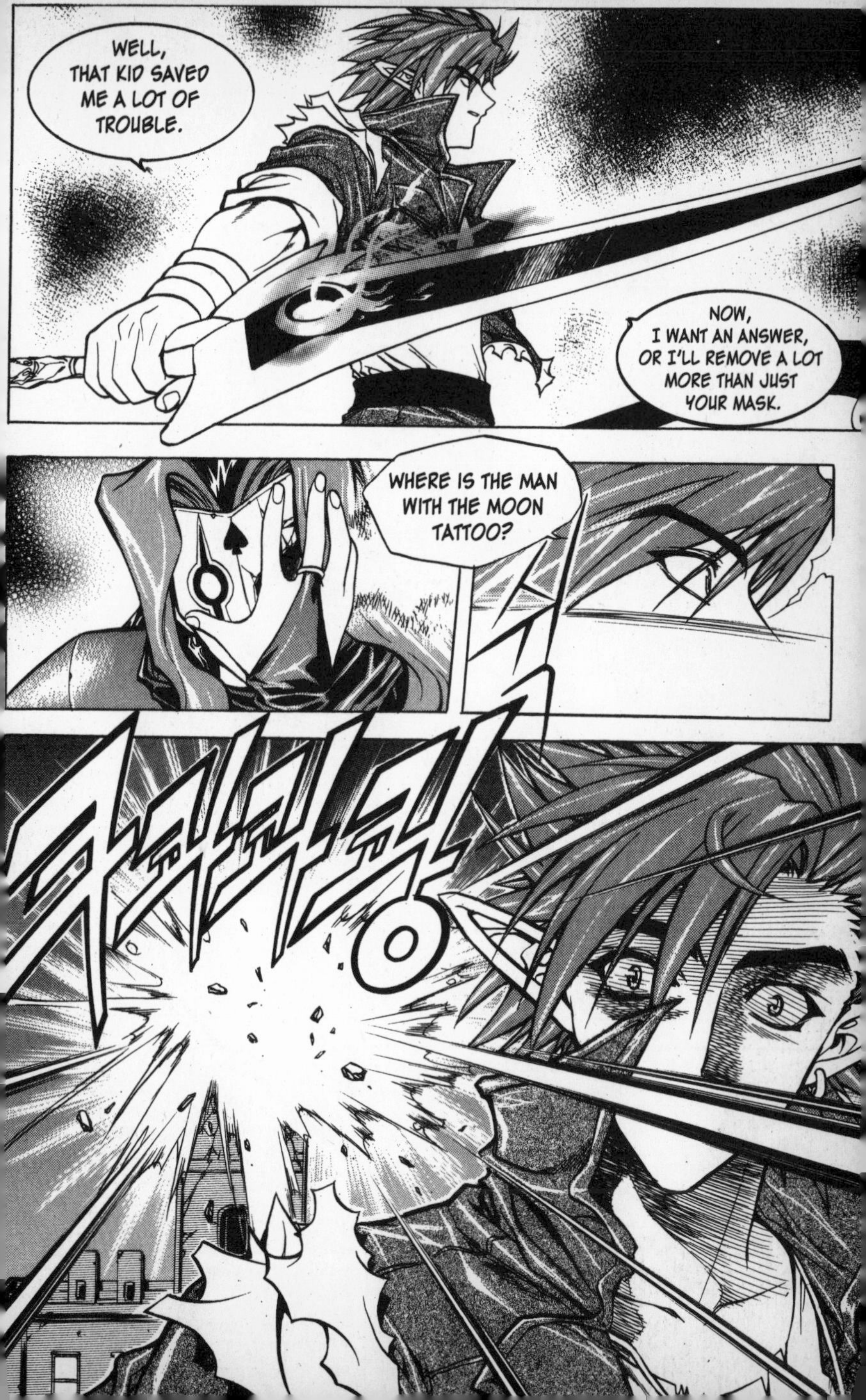
WELL, THAT KID SAVED ME A LOT OF TROUBLE.
NOW, I WANT AN ANSWER, OR I'LL REMOVE A LOT MORE THAN JUST YOUR MASK.
WHERE IS THE MAN WITH THE MOON TATTOO?

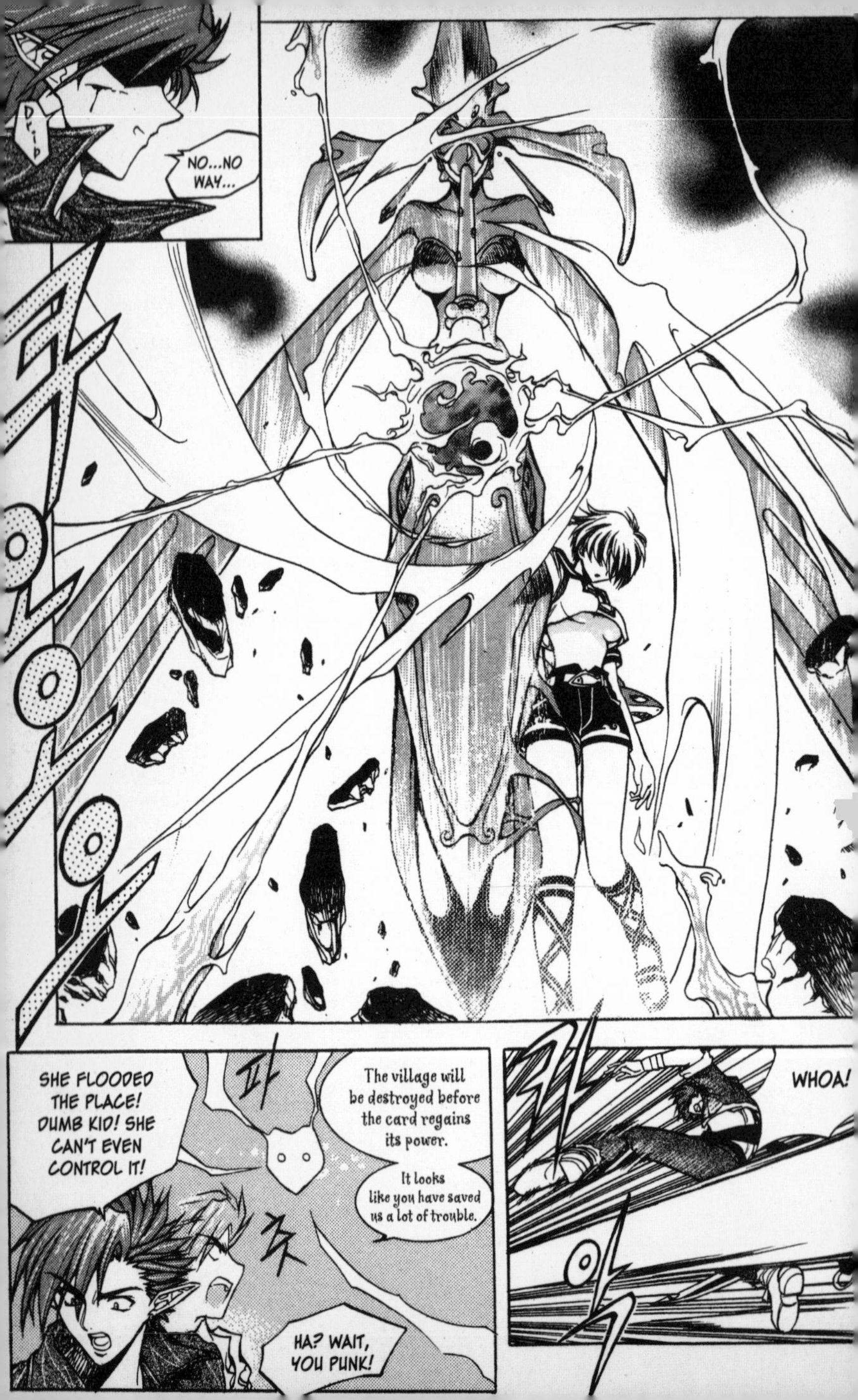
Drip
NO...NO WAY...
SHE FLOODED THE PLACE! DUMB KID! SHE CAN'T EVEN CONTROL IT!
The village will be destroyed before the card regains its power.
It looks like you have saved us a lot of trouble.
HA? WAIT, YOU PUNK!
WHOA!

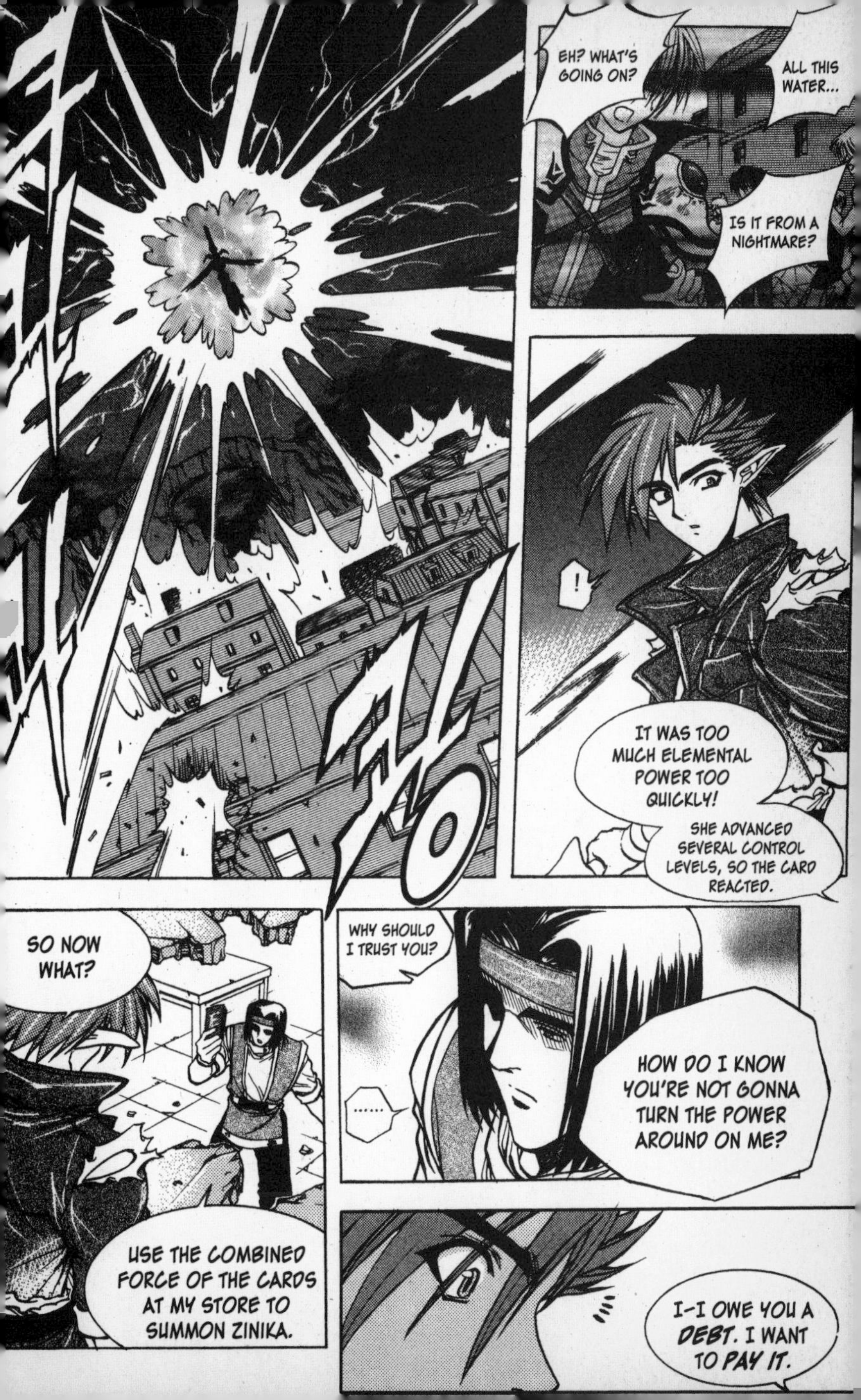
EH? WHAT'S GOING ON?
ALL THIS WATER...
IS IT FROM A NIGHTMARE?
!
IT WAS TOO MUCH ELEMENTAL POWER TOO QUICKLY!
SHE ADVANCED SEVERAL CONTROL LEVELS, SO THE CARD REACTED.
SO NOW WHAT?
USE THE COMBINED FORCE OF THE CARDS AT MY STORE TO SUMMON ZINIKA.
WHY SHOULD I TRUST YOU?
......
HOW DO I KNOW YOU'RE NOT GONNA TURN THE POWER AROUND ON ME?
I-I OWE YOU A *DEBT*. I WANT TO *PAY IT*.

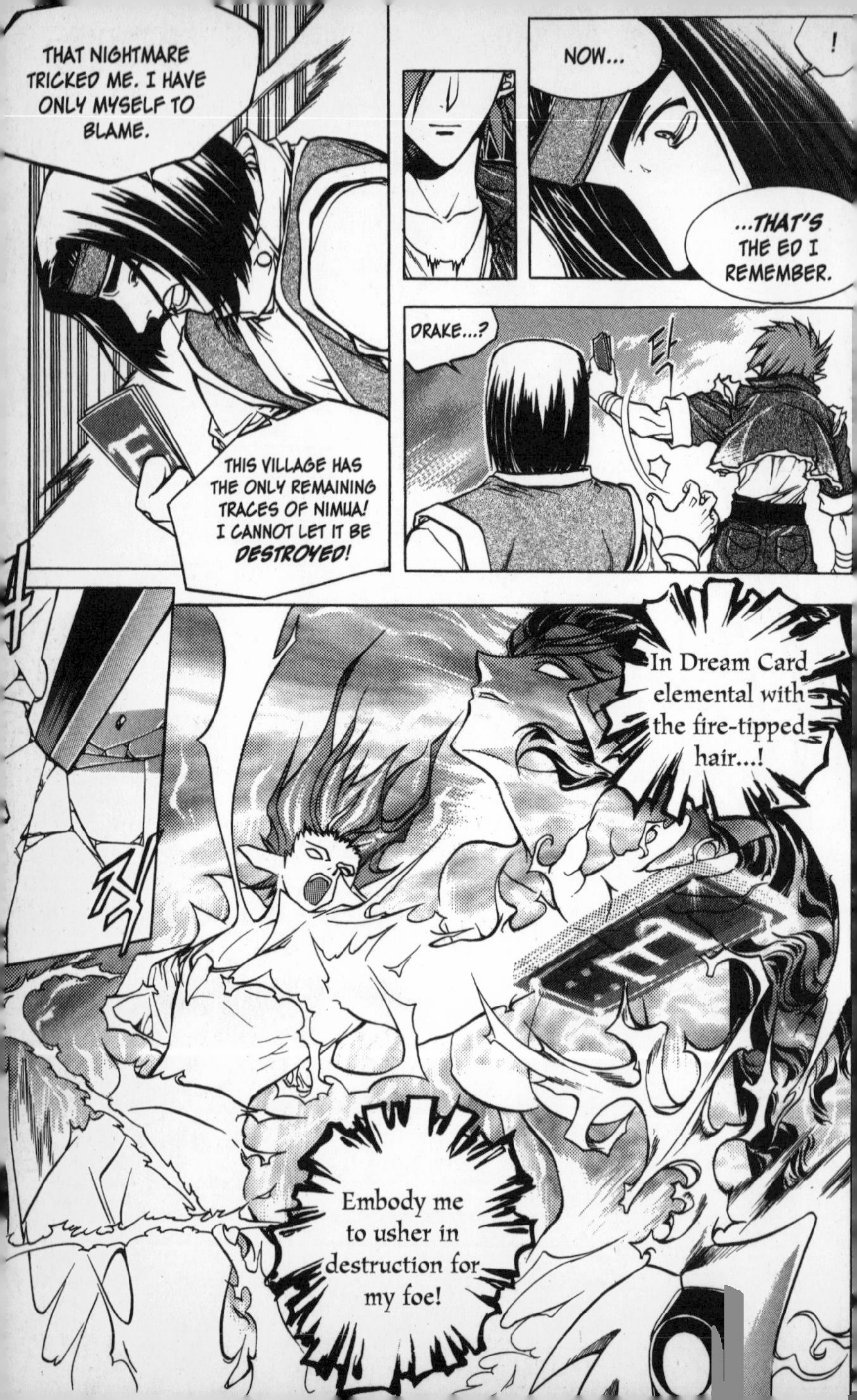
THAT NIGHTMARE TRICKED ME. I HAVE ONLY MYSELF TO BLAME.
THIS VILLAGE HAS THE ONLY REMAINING TRACES OF NIMUA! I CANNOT LET IT BE DESTROYED!
NOW...
...THAT'S THE ED I REMEMBER.
!
DRAKE...?
In Dream Card elemental with the fire-tipped hair...!
Embody me to usher in destruction for my foe!

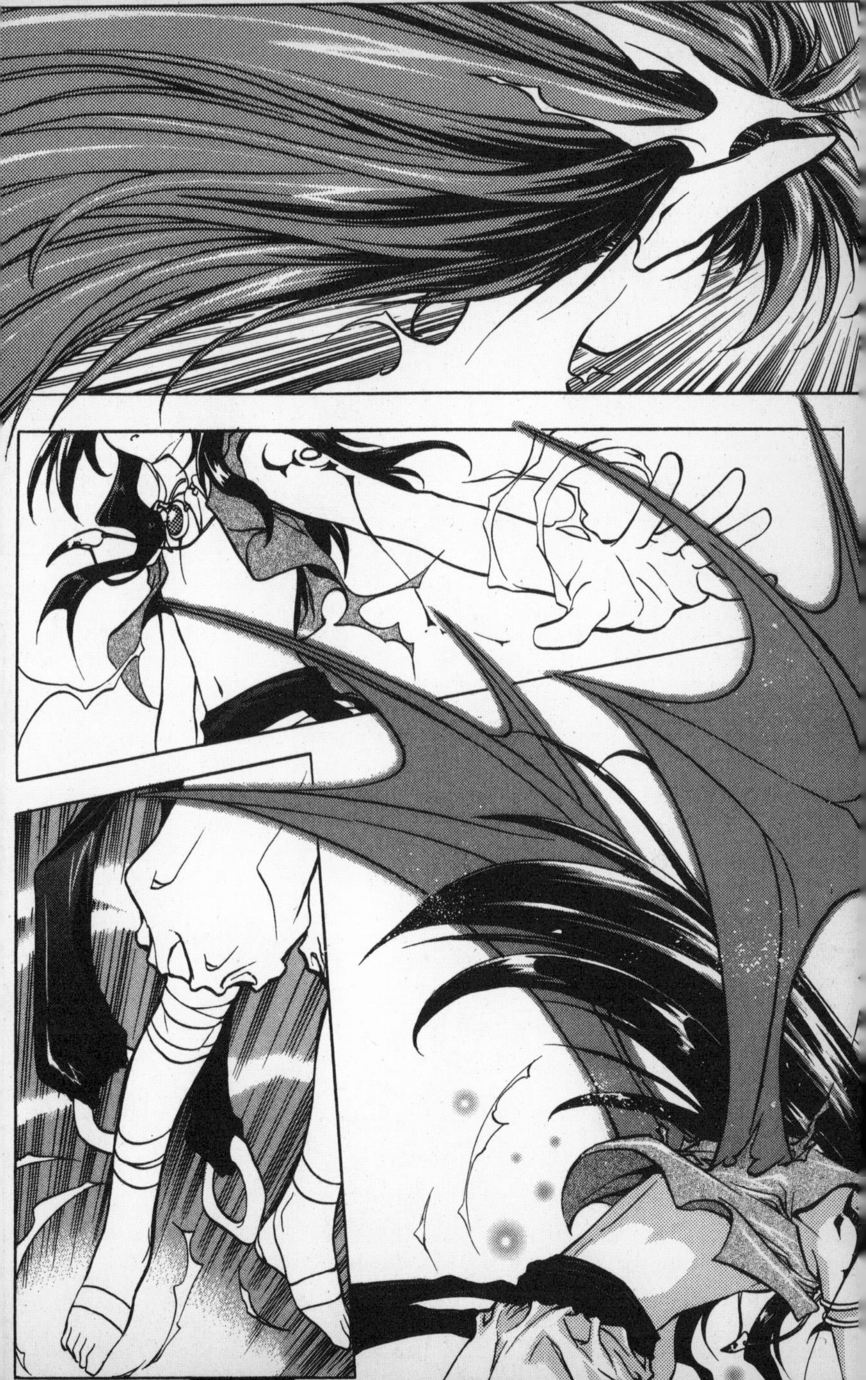

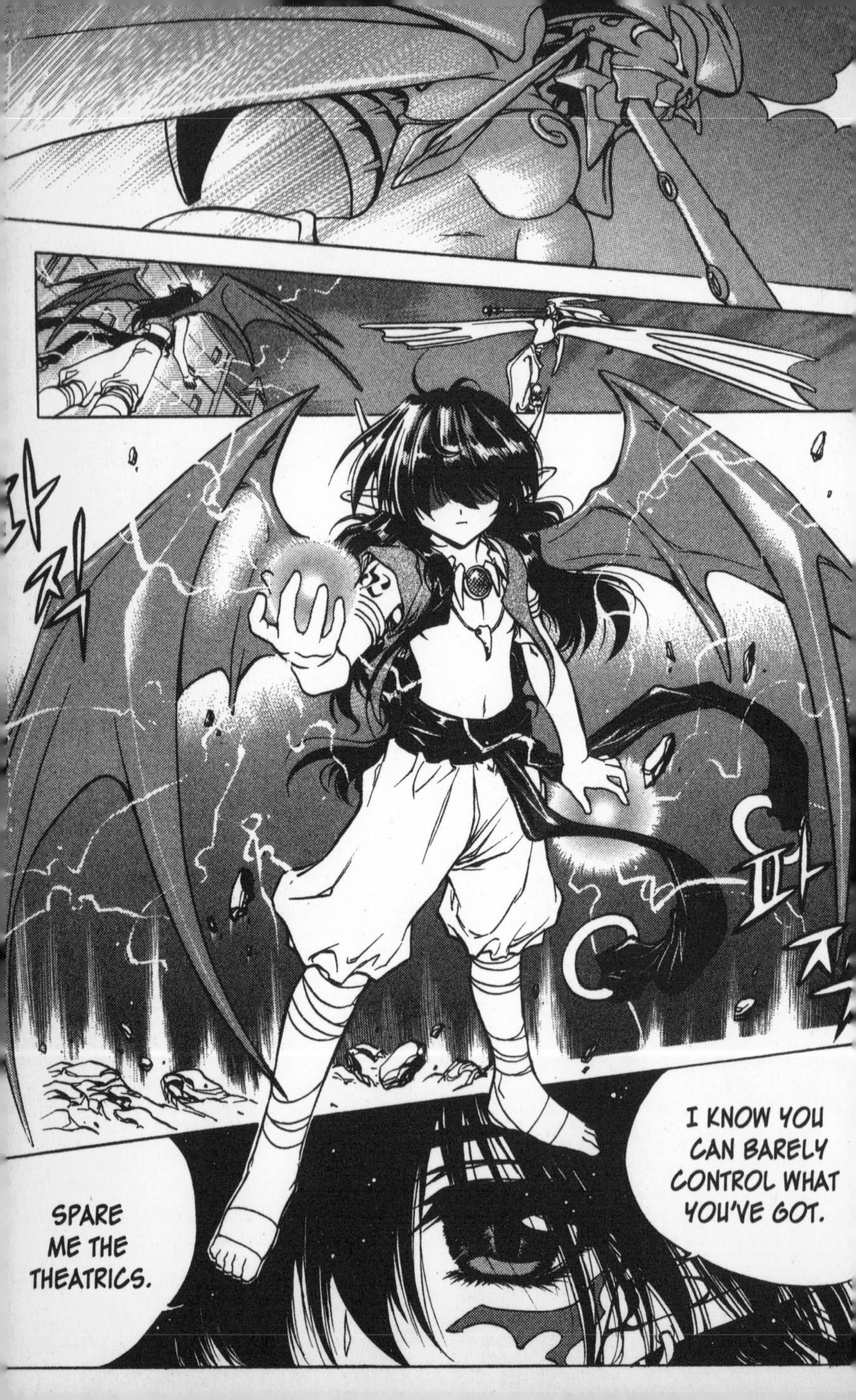

SPARE ME THE THEATRICS.
I KNOW YOU CAN BARELY CONTROL WHAT YOU'VE GOT.

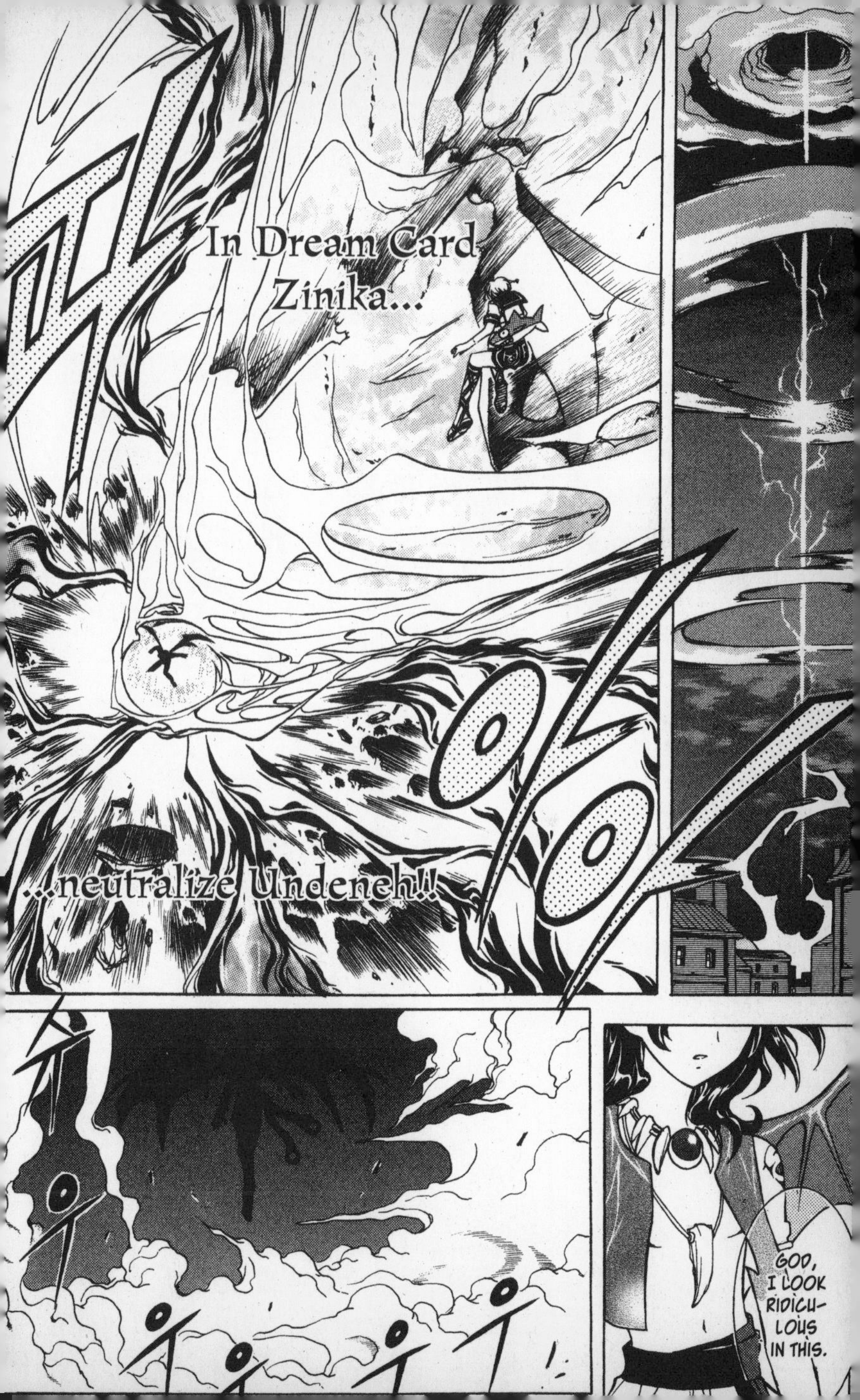
In Dream Card Zinika...
...neutralize Undeneh!!
GOD, I LOOK RIDICU-LOUS IN THIS.

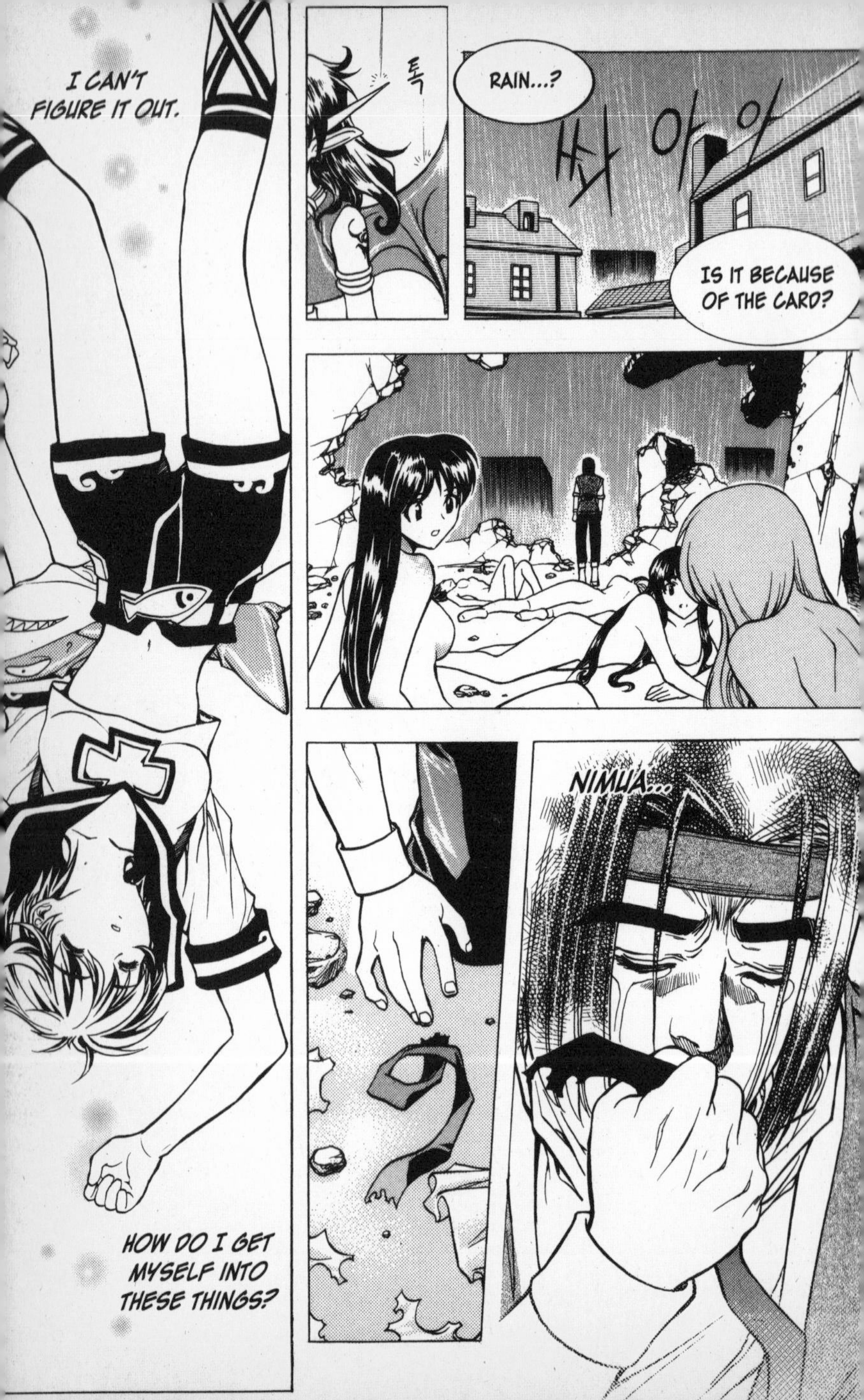
I CAN'T FIGURE IT OUT.
HOW DO I GET MYSELF INTO THESE THINGS?
톡
RAIN...?
쏴 아 아
IS IT BECAUSE OF THE CARD?
NIMUA...

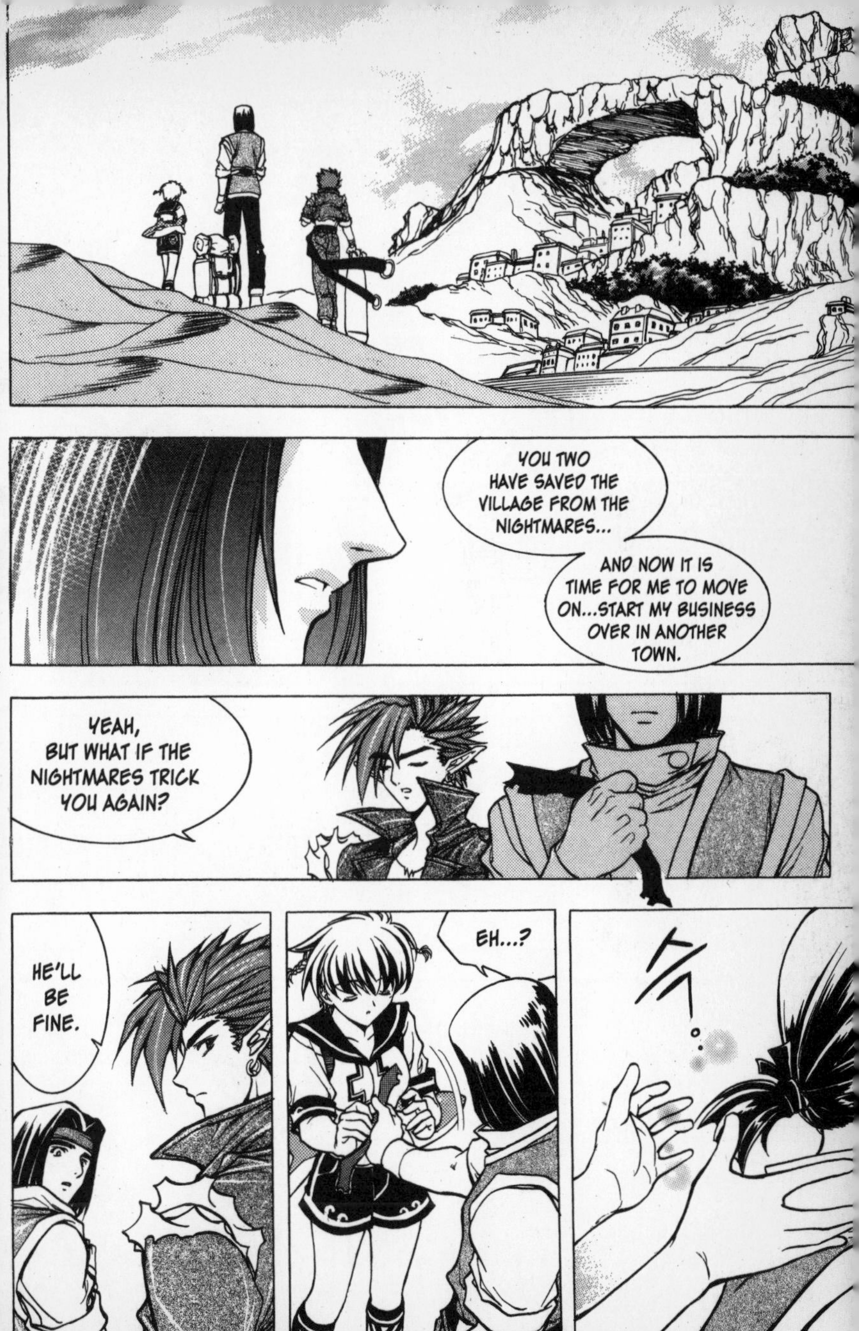
YOU TWO HAVE SAVED THE VILLAGE FROM THE NIGHTMARES...
AND NOW IT IS TIME FOR ME TO MOVE ON...START MY BUSINESS OVER IN ANOTHER TOWN.
YEAH, BUT WHAT IF THE NIGHTMARES TRICK YOU AGAIN?
HE'LL BE FINE.
EH...?

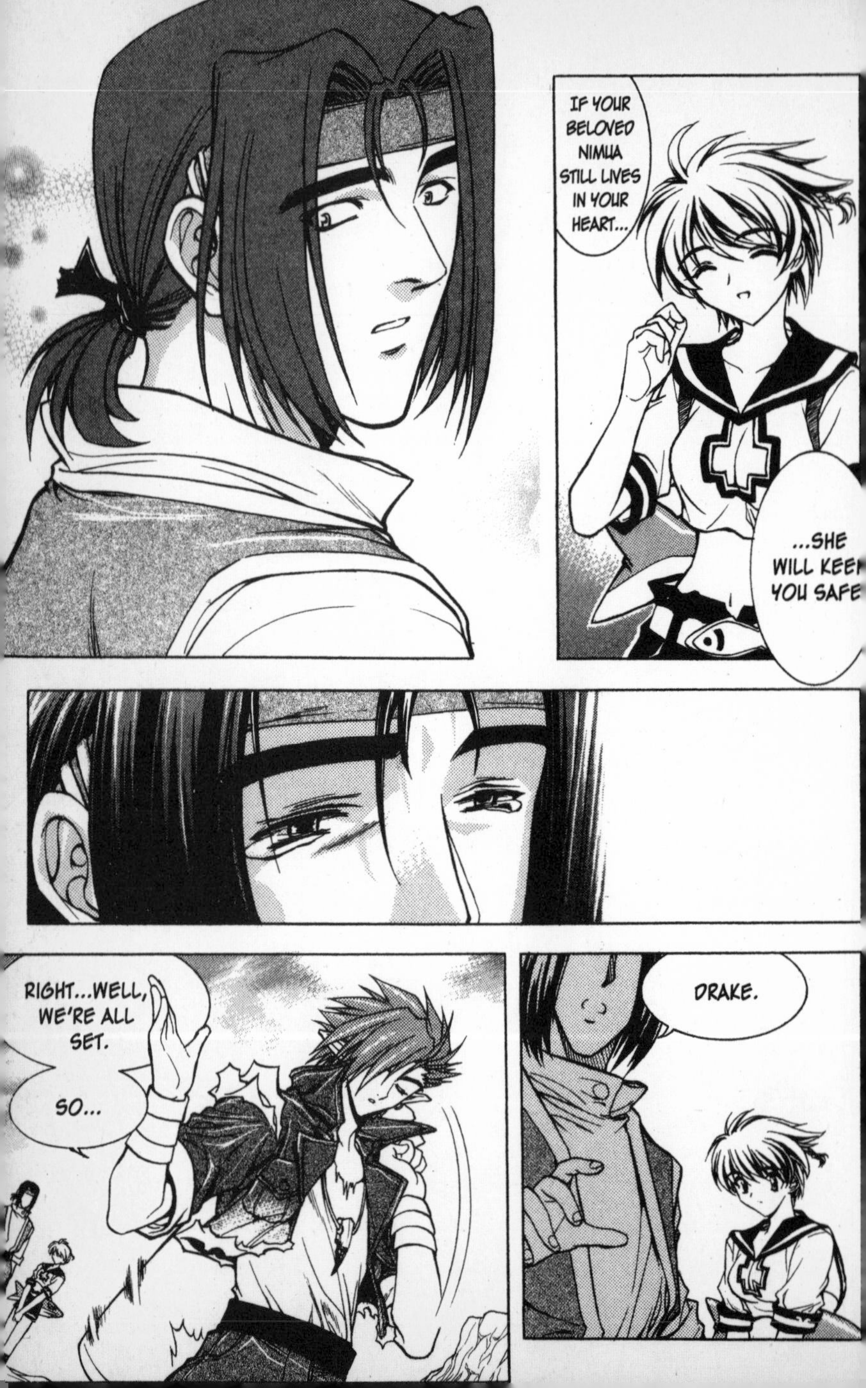
IF YOUR BELOVED NIMUA STILL LIVES IN YOUR HEART...
...SHE WILL KEEP YOU SAFE
RIGHT...WELL, WE'RE ALL SET.
SO...
DRAKE.

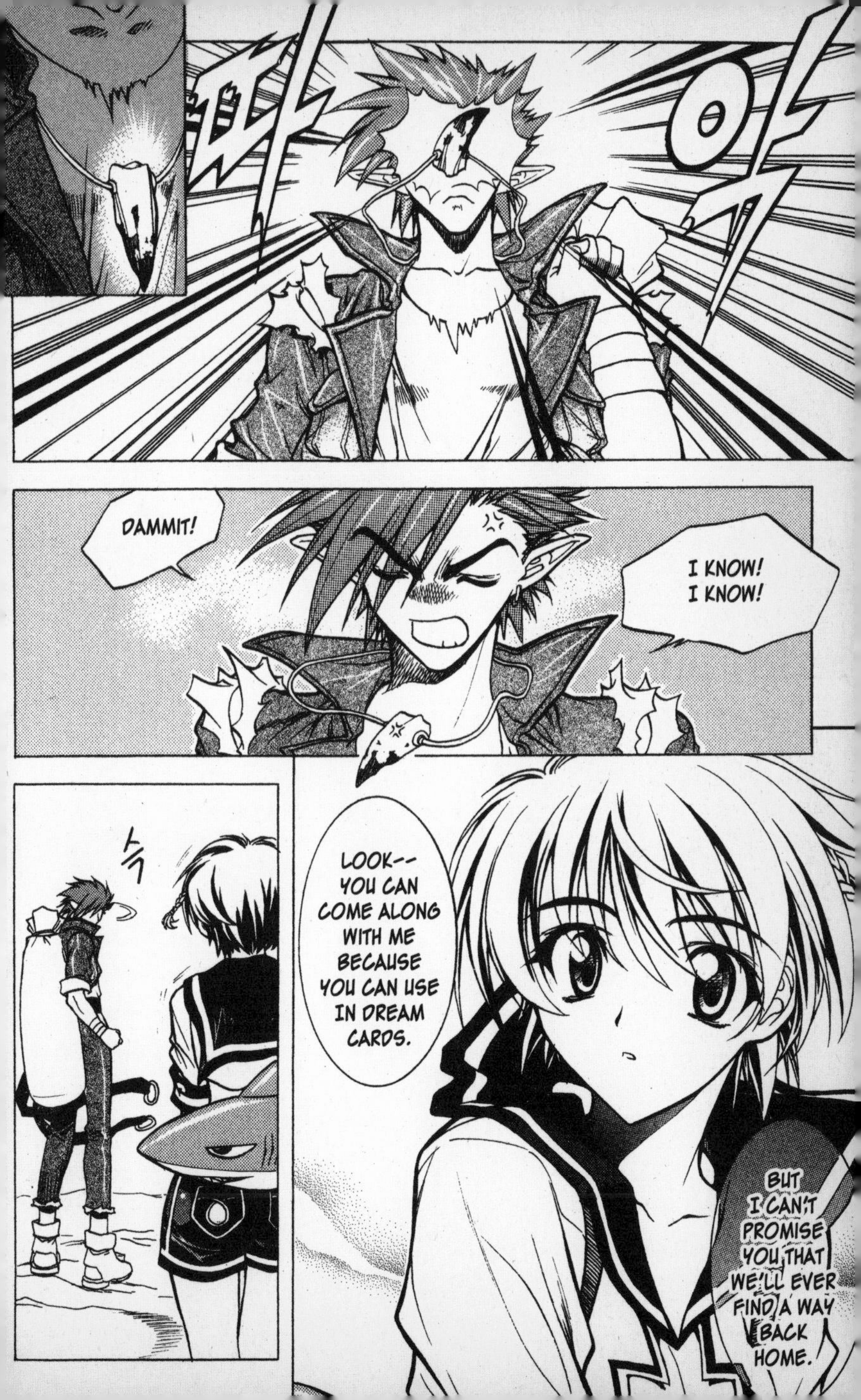
DAMMIT!
I KNOW! I KNOW!
LOOK-- YOU CAN COME ALONG WITH ME BECAUSE YOU CAN USE IN DREAM CARDS.
BUT I CAN'T PROMISE YOU THAT WE'LL EVER FIND A WAY BACK HOME.

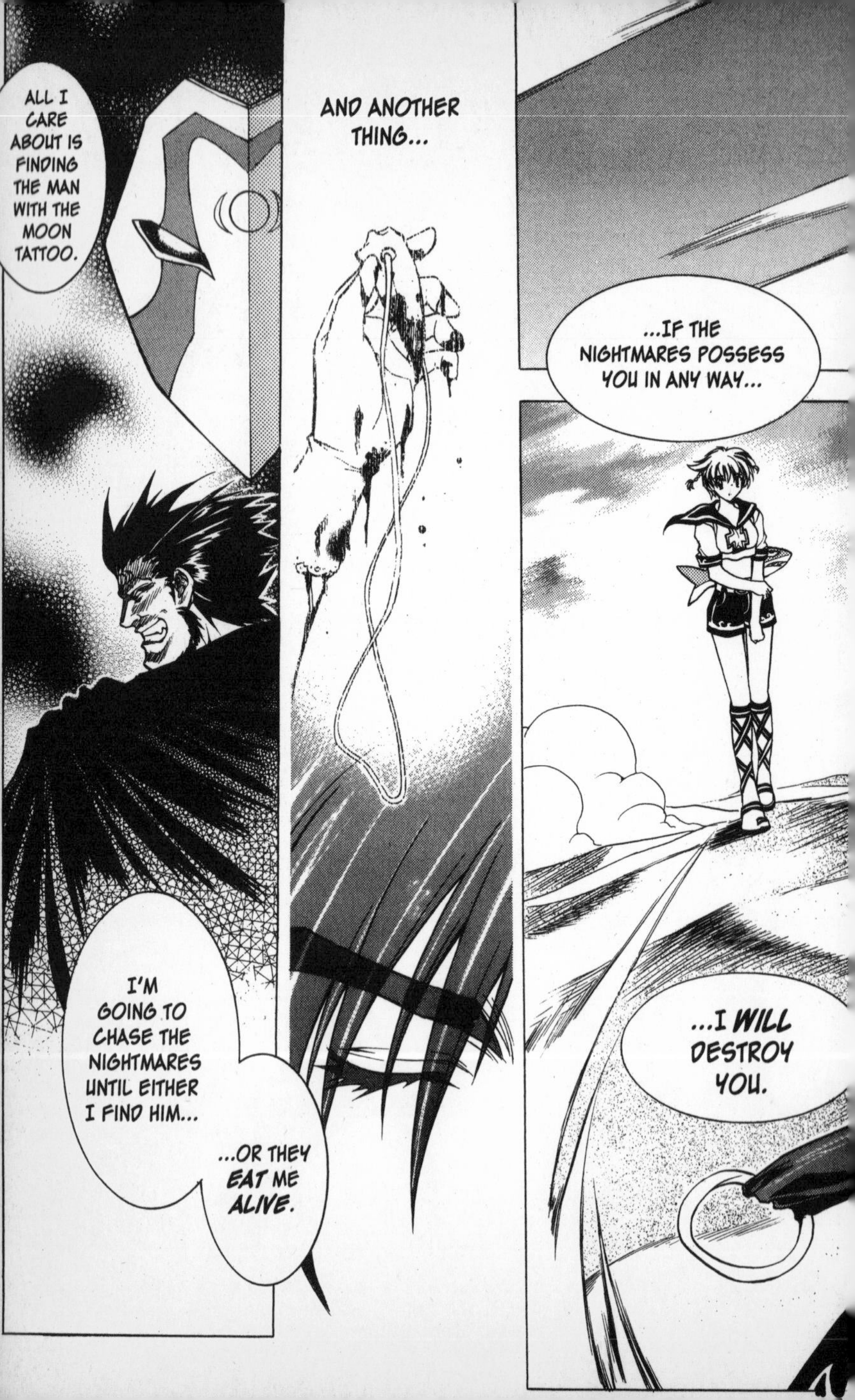
ALL I CARE ABOUT IS FINDING THE MAN WITH THE MOON TATTOO.
I'M GOING TO CHASE THE NIGHTMARES UNTIL EITHER I FIND HIM...
...OR THEY EAT ME ALIVE.
AND ANOTHER THING...
...IF THE NIGHTMARES POSSESS YOU IN ANY WAY...
...I WILL DESTROY YOU.

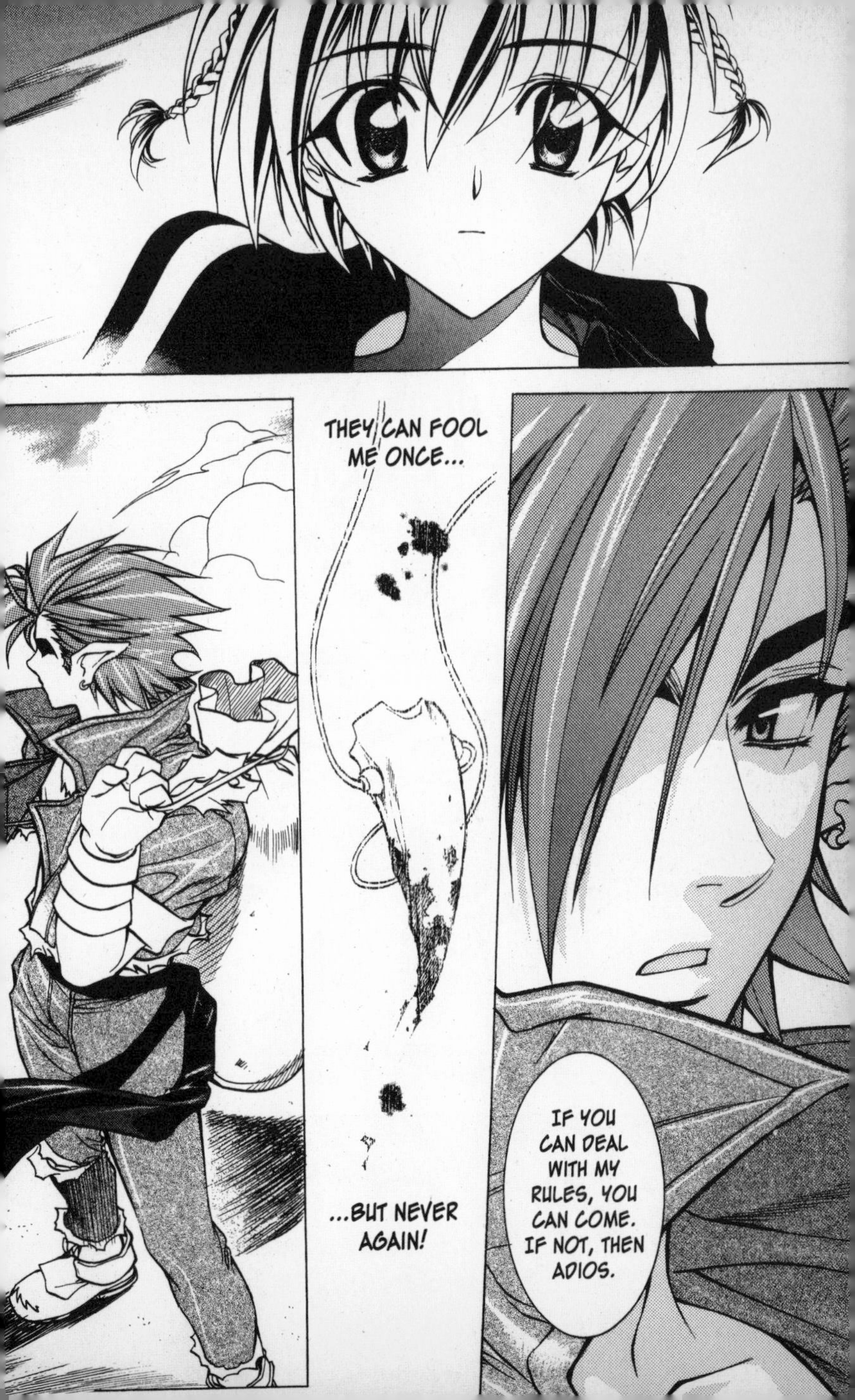
THEY CAN FOOL ME ONCE...
...BUT NEVER AGAIN!
IF YOU CAN DEAL WITH MY RULES, YOU CAN COME. IF NOT, THEN ADIOS.

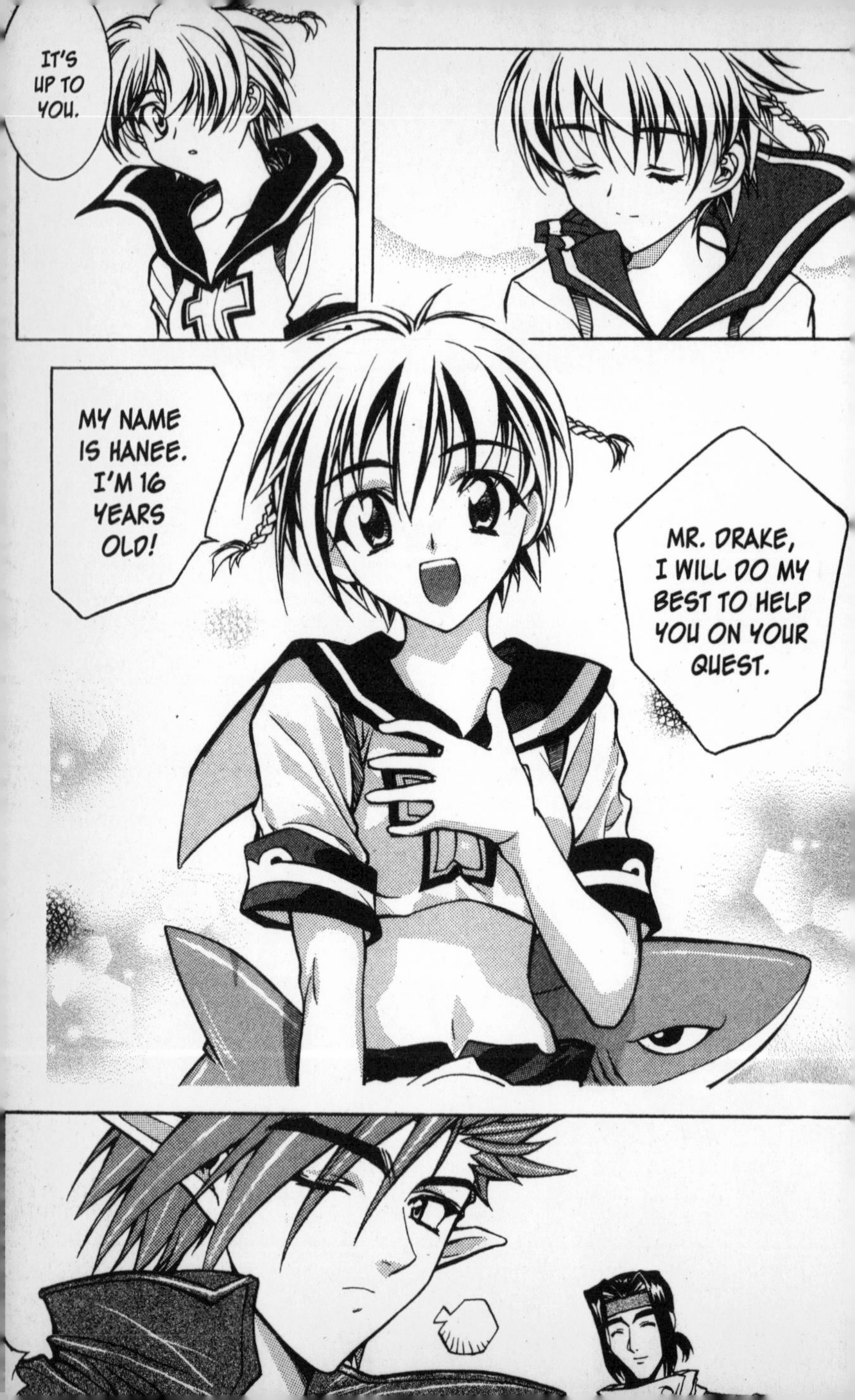
IT'S UP TO YOU.
MY NAME IS HANEE. I'M 16 YEARS OLD!
MR. DRAKE, I WILL DO MY BEST TO HELP YOU ON YOUR QUEST.

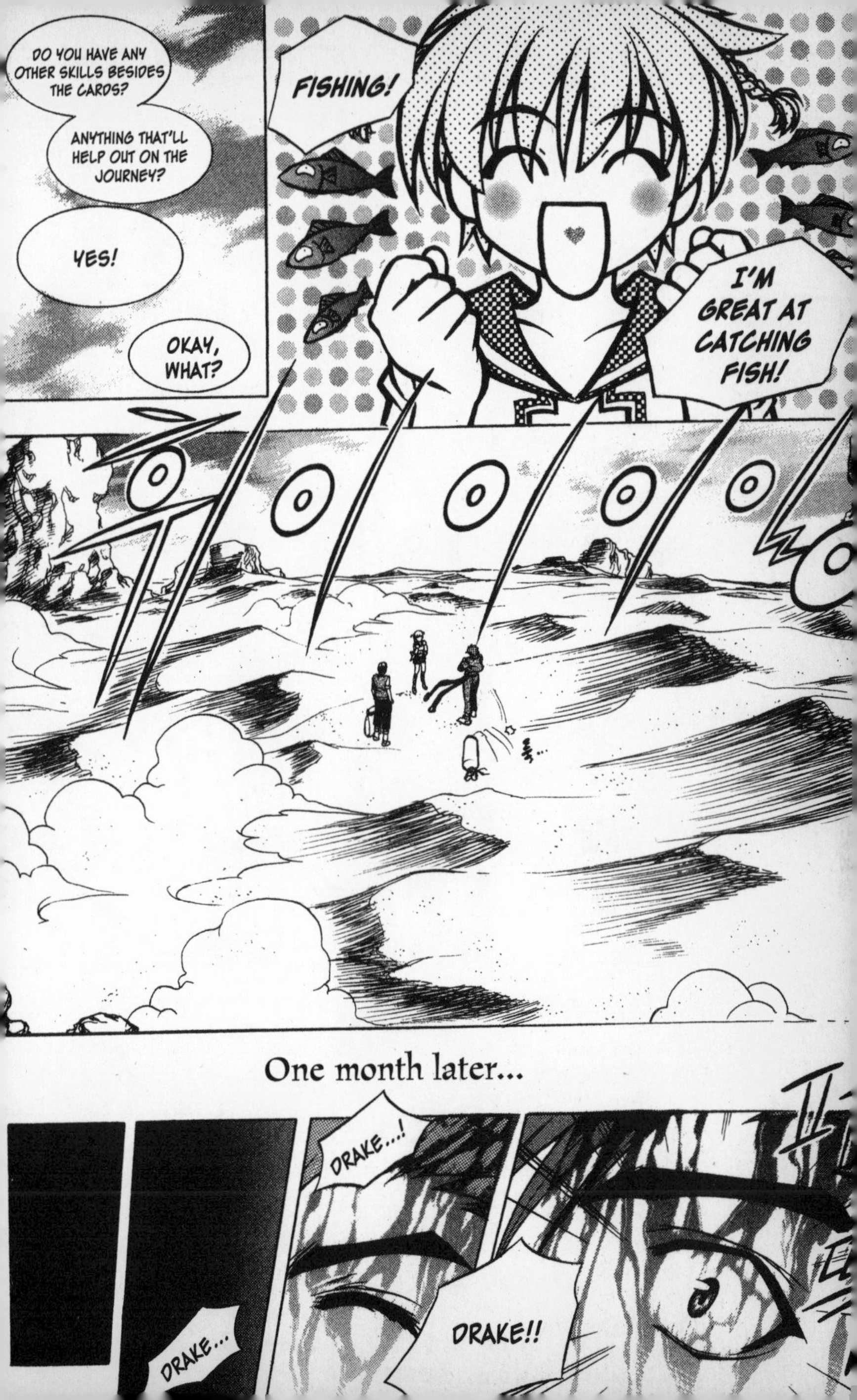
DO YOU HAVE ANY OTHER SKILLS BESIDES THE CARDS?
ANYTHING THAT'LL HELP OUT ON THE JOURNEY?
YES!
OKAY, WHAT?
FISHING!
I'M GREAT AT CATCHING FISH!
One month later...
DRAKE...
DRAKE...!
DRAKE!!

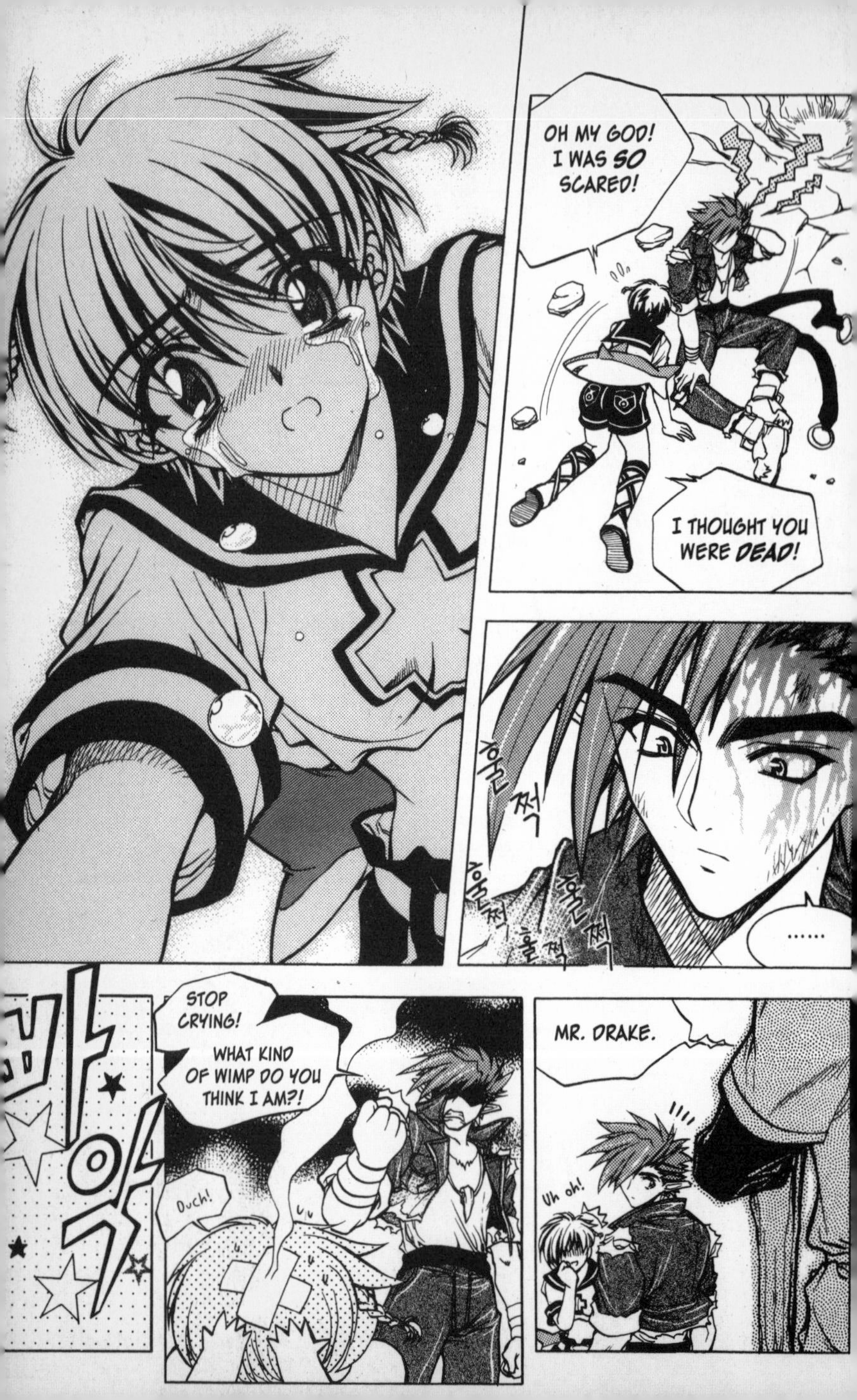
OH MY GOD! I WAS SO SCARED!
I THOUGHT YOU WERE DEAD!
훌쩍
훌쩍
훌쩍
훌쩍
......
STOP CRYING!
WHAT KIND OF WIMP DO YOU THINK I AM?!
Ouch!
MR. DRAKE.
Uh oh!

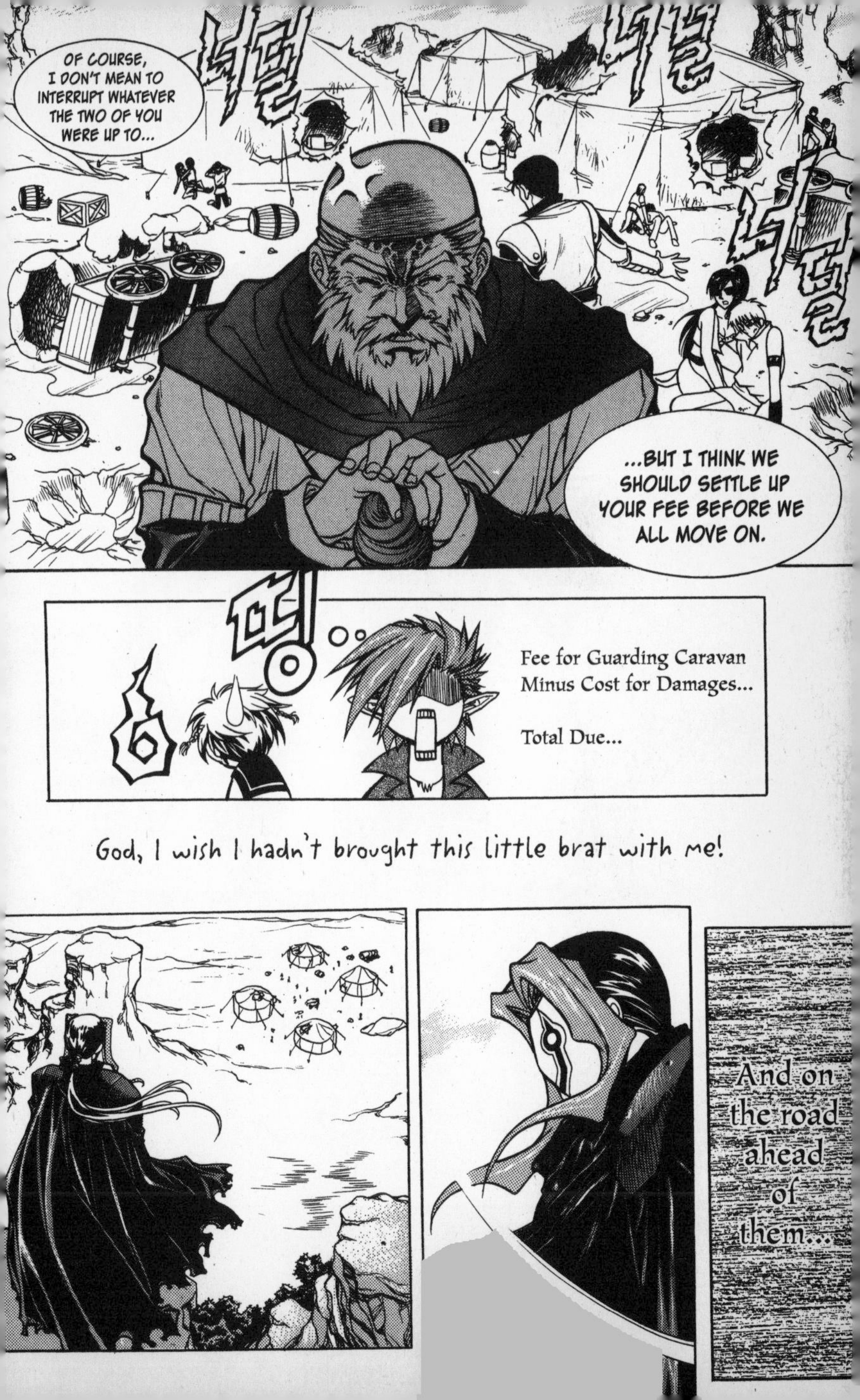
OF COURSE, I DON'T MEAN TO INTERRUPT WHATEVER THE TWO OF YOU WERE UP TO...
...BUT I THINK WE SHOULD SETTLE UP YOUR FEE BEFORE WE ALL MOVE ON.
Fee for Guarding Caravan
Minus Cost for Damages...
Total Due...
God, I wish I hadn't brought this little brat with me!
And on the road ahead of them...

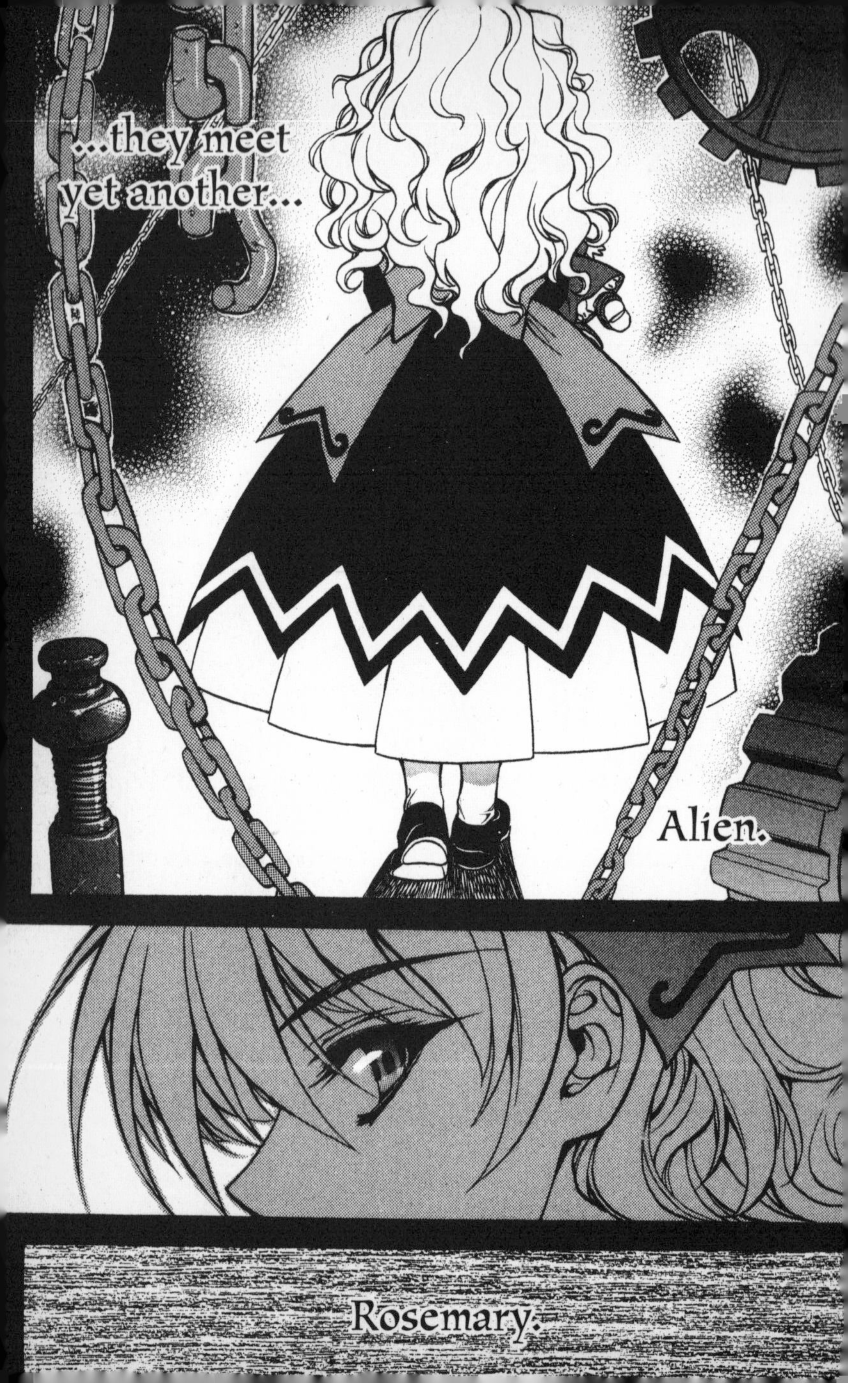
...they meet yet another...
Alien.
Rosemary.

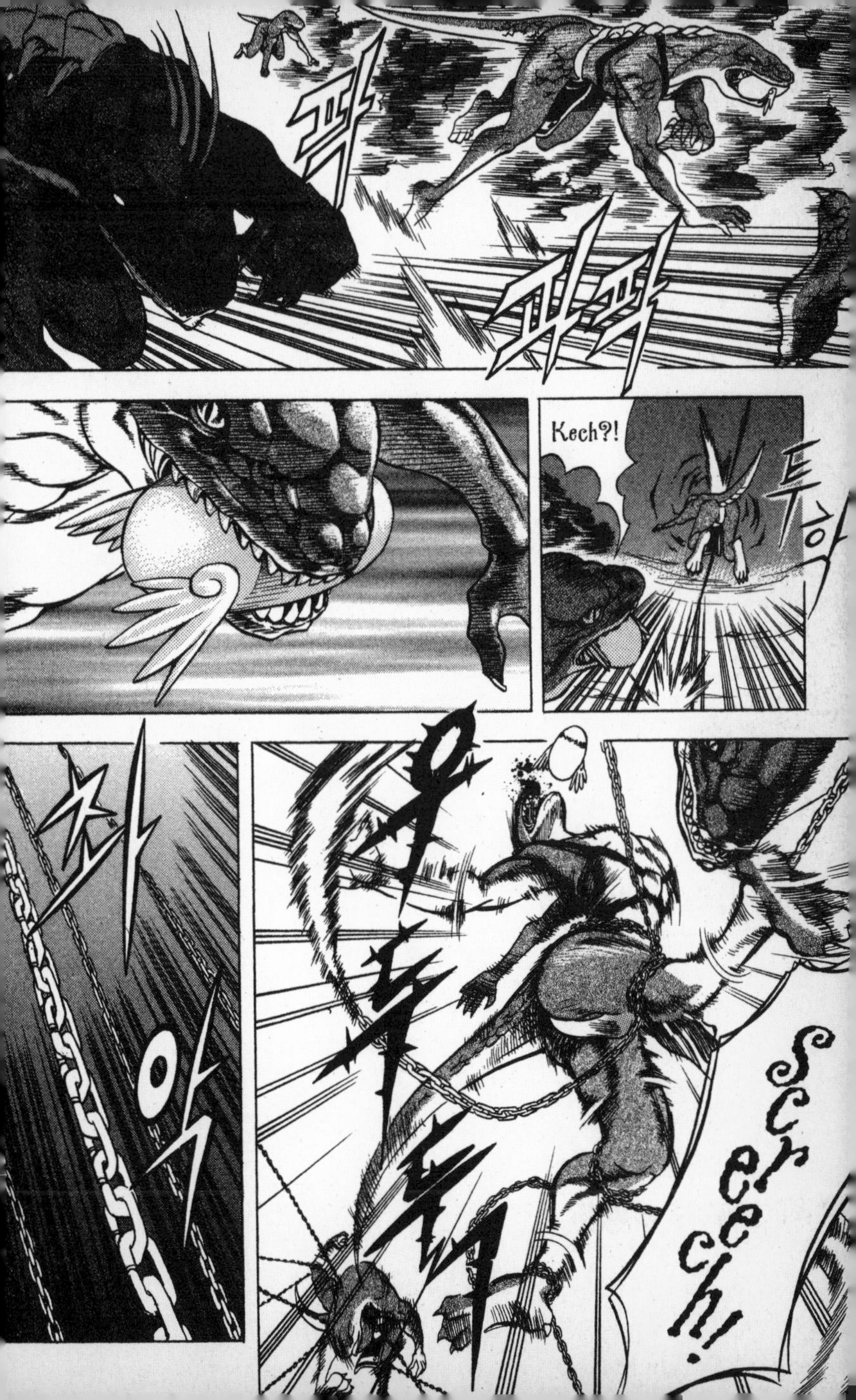
Kech?!
Screeech!!

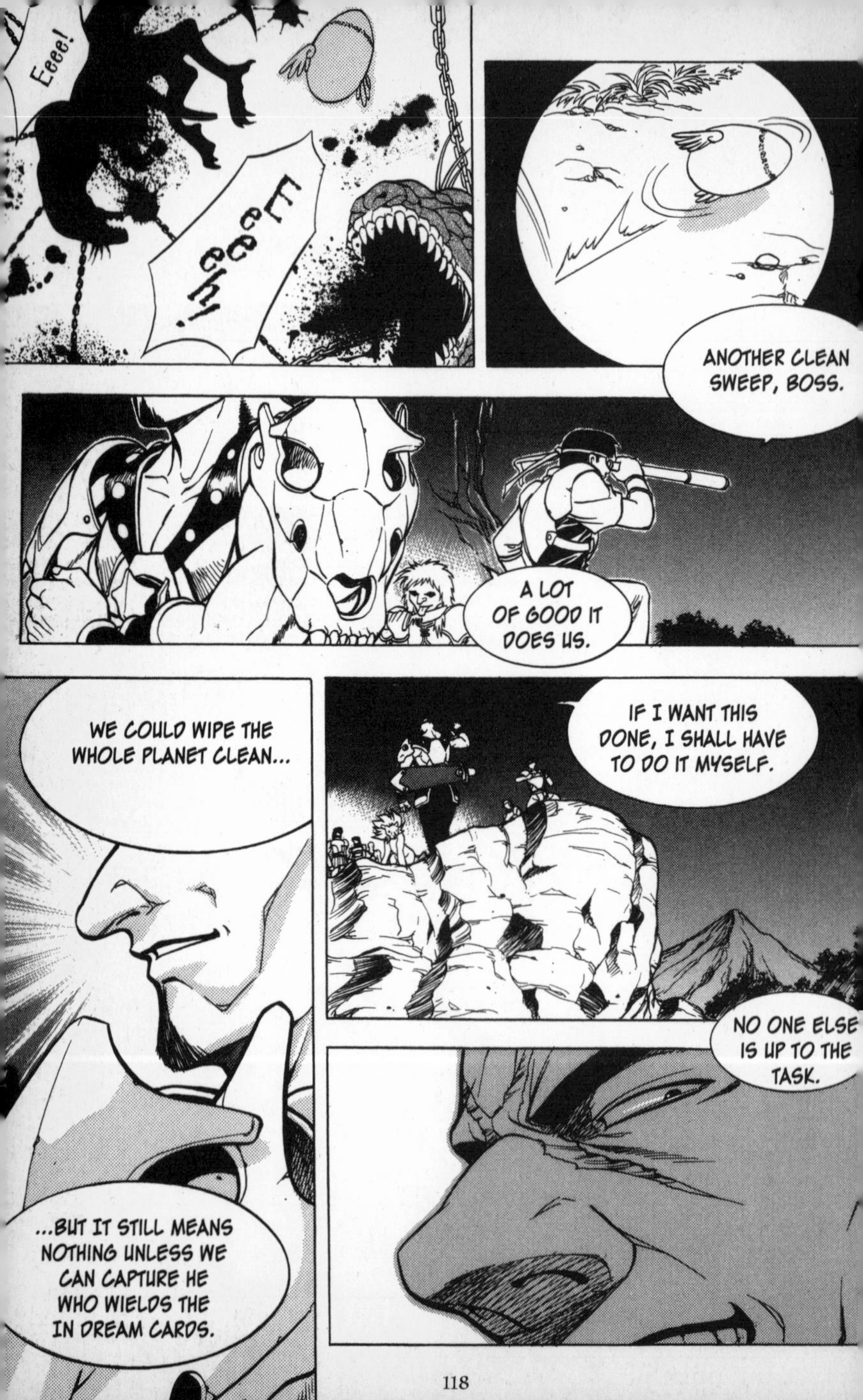
Eeee!
Eeeeh!
ANOTHER CLEAN SWEEP, BOSS.
A LOT OF GOOD IT DOES US.
WE COULD WIPE THE WHOLE PLANET CLEAN...
...BUT IT STILL MEANS NOTHING UNLESS WE CAN CAPTURE HE WHO WIELDS THE IN DREAM CARDS.
IF I WANT THIS DONE, I SHALL HAVE TO DO IT MYSELF.
NO ONE ELSE IS UP TO THE TASK.

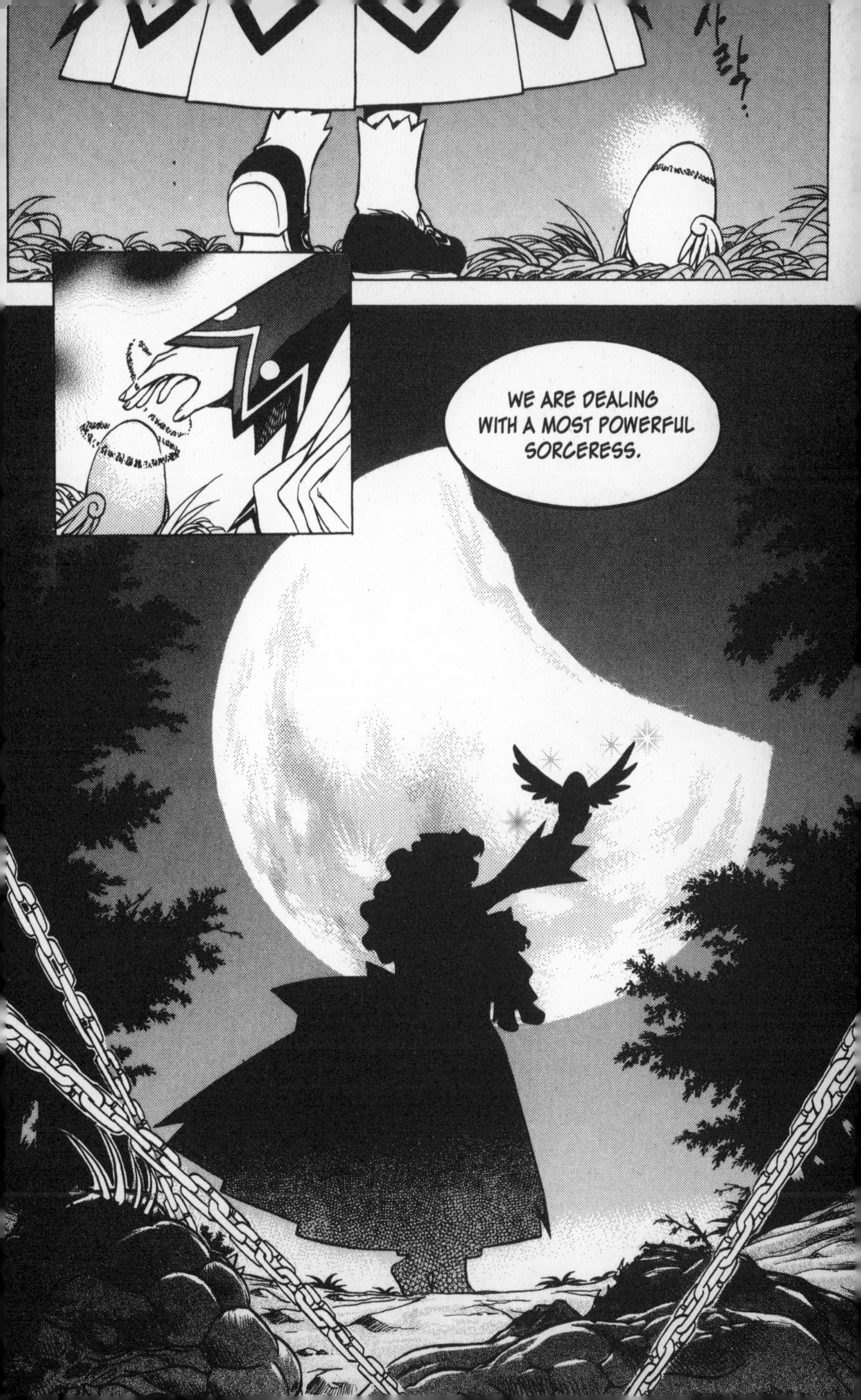
사락...
WE ARE DEALING WITH A MOST POWERFUL SORCERESS.

stage 6.

Rosemary

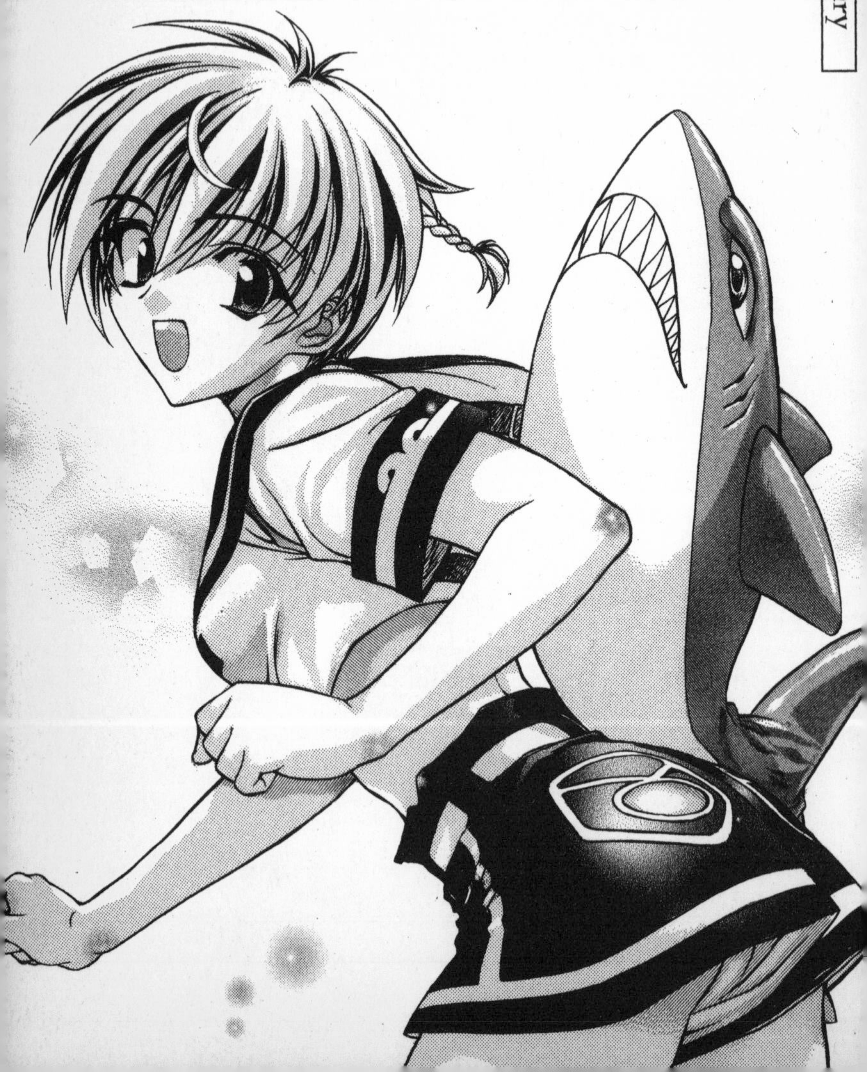

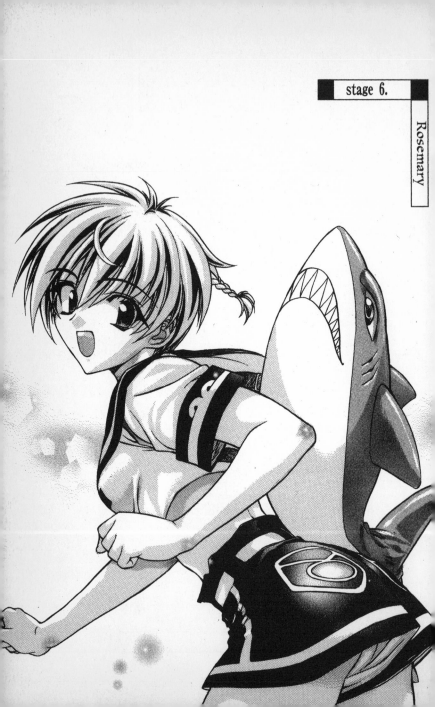

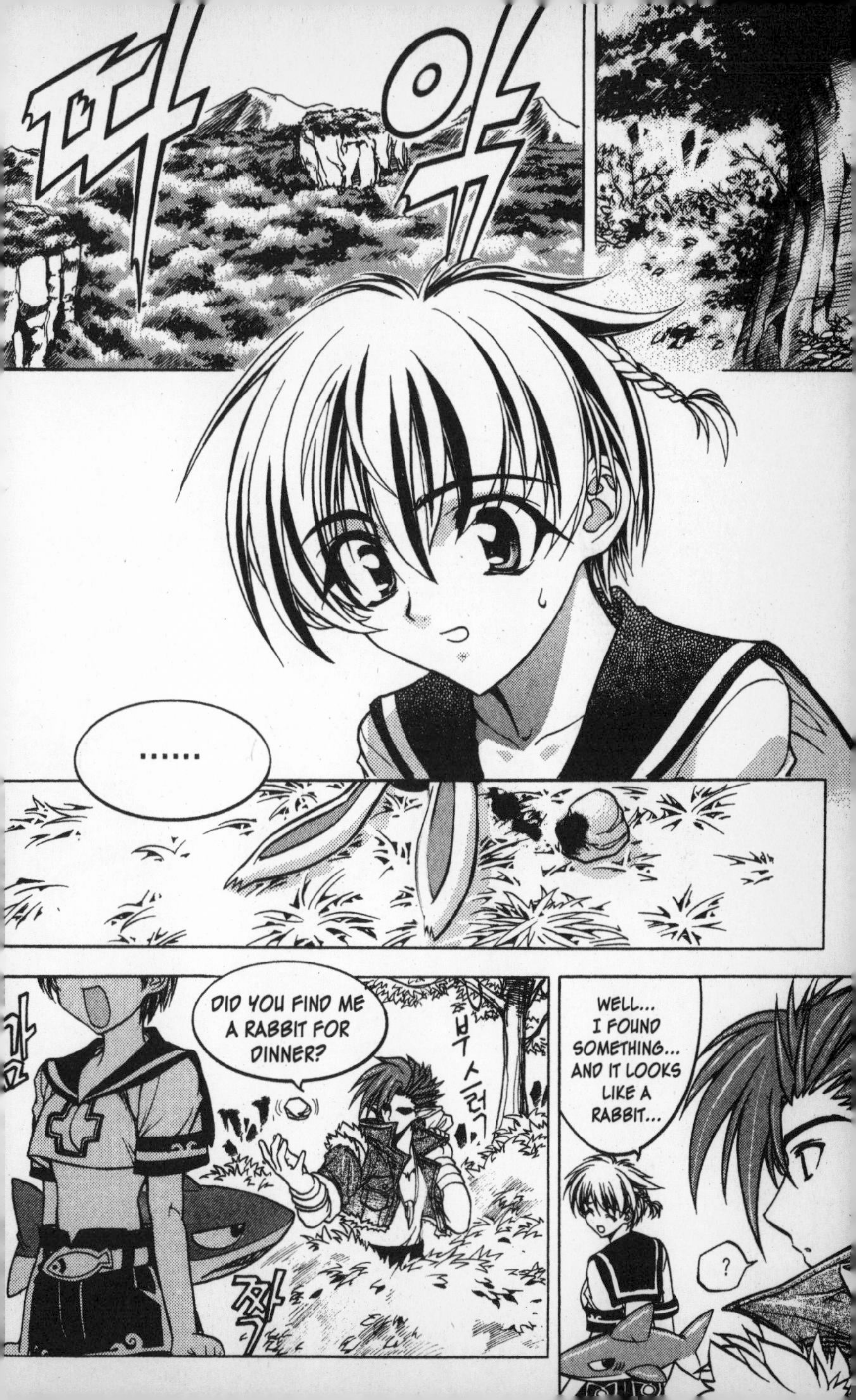
......
DID YOU FIND ME A RABBIT FOR DINNER?
WELL... I FOUND SOMETHING... AND IT LOOKS LIKE A RABBIT...
?

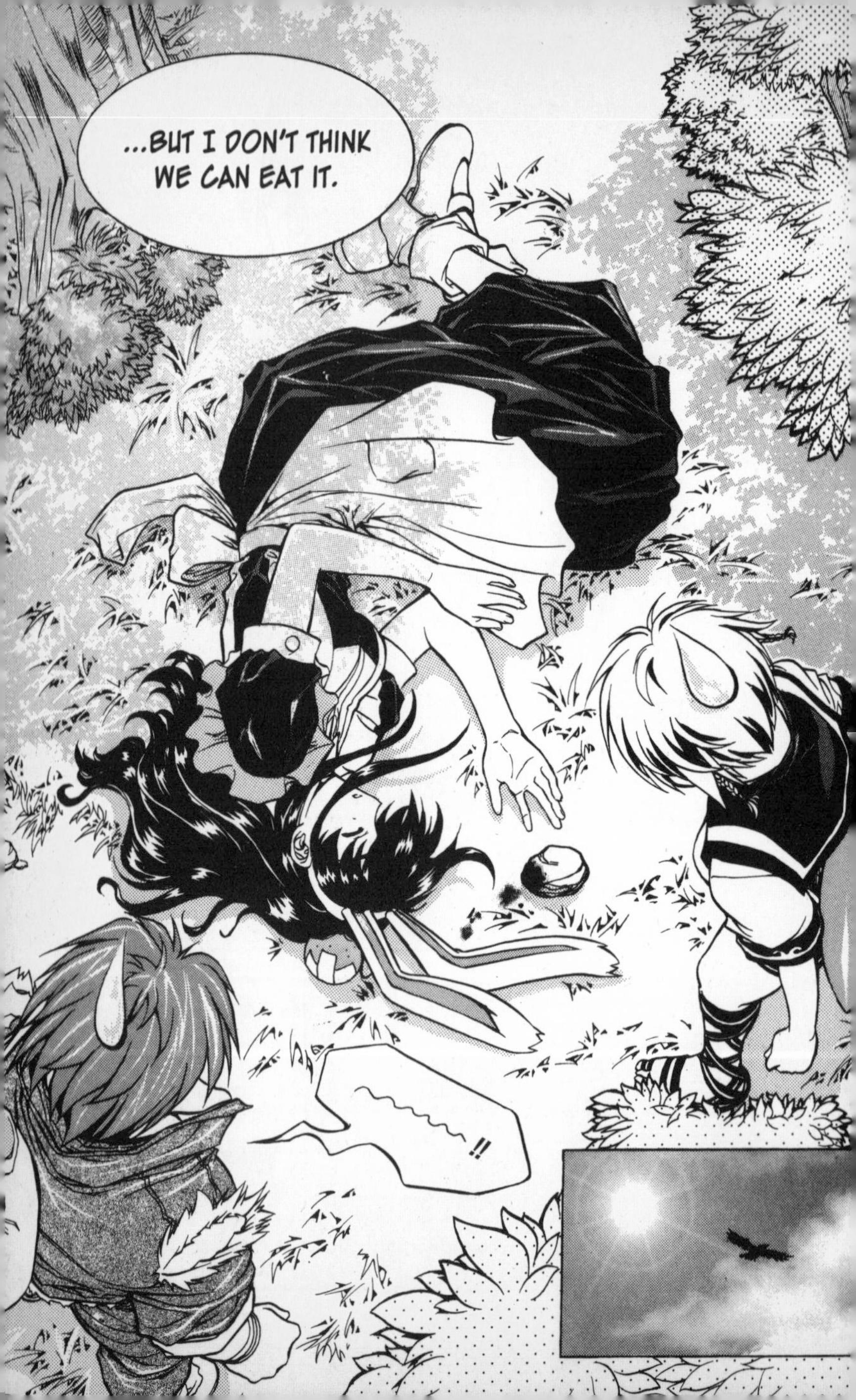
...BUT I DON'T THINK WE CAN EAT IT.
~~~~~~~!!
~~~~~~~

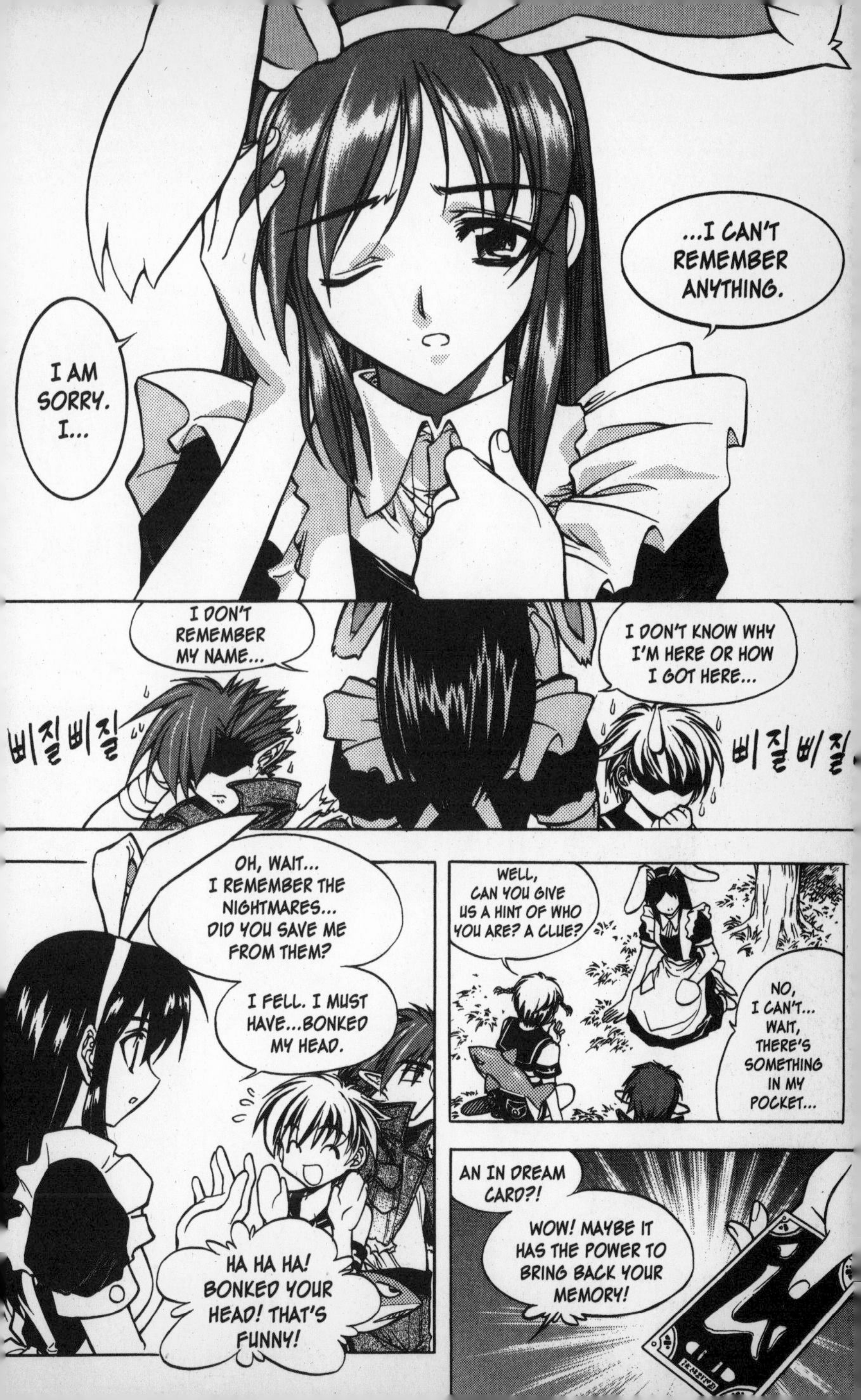
I AM SORRY. I...
...I CAN'T REMEMBER ANYTHING.
I DON'T REMEMBER MY NAME...
삐질삐질
I DON'T KNOW WHY I'M HERE OR HOW I GOT HERE...
삐질삐질
OH, WAIT... I REMEMBER THE NIGHTMARES... DID YOU SAVE ME FROM THEM?
I FELL. I MUST HAVE...BONKED MY HEAD.
HA HA HA! BONKED YOUR HEAD! THAT'S FUNNY!
WELL, CAN YOU GIVE US A HINT OF WHO YOU ARE? A CLUE?
NO, I CAN'T... WAIT, THERE'S SOMETHING IN MY POCKET...
AN IN DREAM CARD?!
WOW! MAYBE IT HAS THE POWER TO BRING BACK YOUR MEMORY!

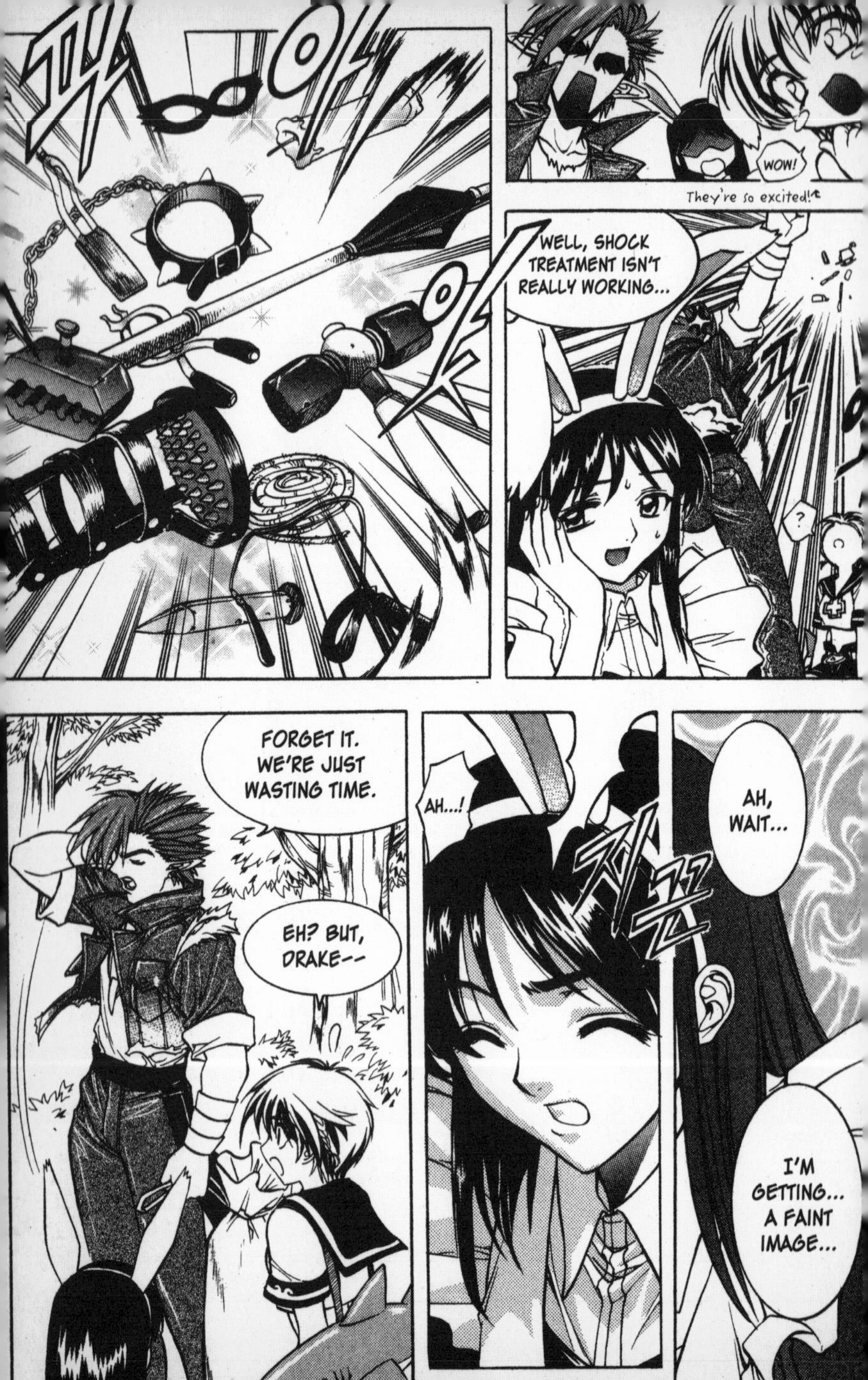
WOW!
They're so excited!
WELL, SHOCK TREATMENT ISN'T REALLY WORKING...
?
FORGET IT. WE'RE JUST WASTING TIME.
EH? BUT, DRAKE--
AH...!
AH, WAIT...
I'M GETTING... A FAINT IMAGE...

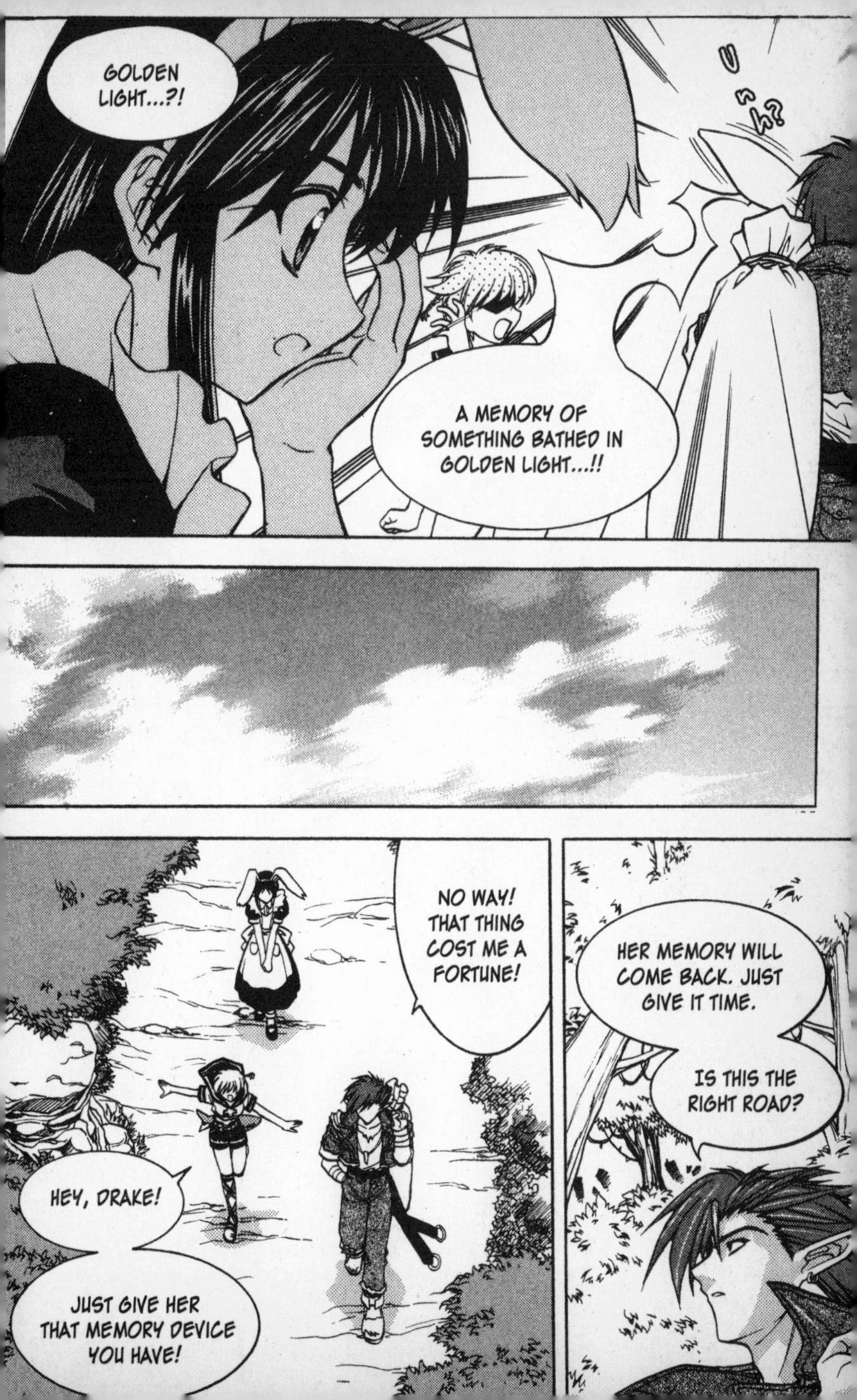
GOLDEN LIGHT...?!
Unh?
A MEMORY OF SOMETHING BATHED IN GOLDEN LIGHT...!!
NO WAY! THAT THING COST ME A FORTUNE!
HEY, DRAKE!
JUST GIVE HER THAT MEMORY DEVICE YOU HAVE!
HER MEMORY WILL COME BACK. JUST GIVE IT TIME.
IS THIS THE RIGHT ROAD?

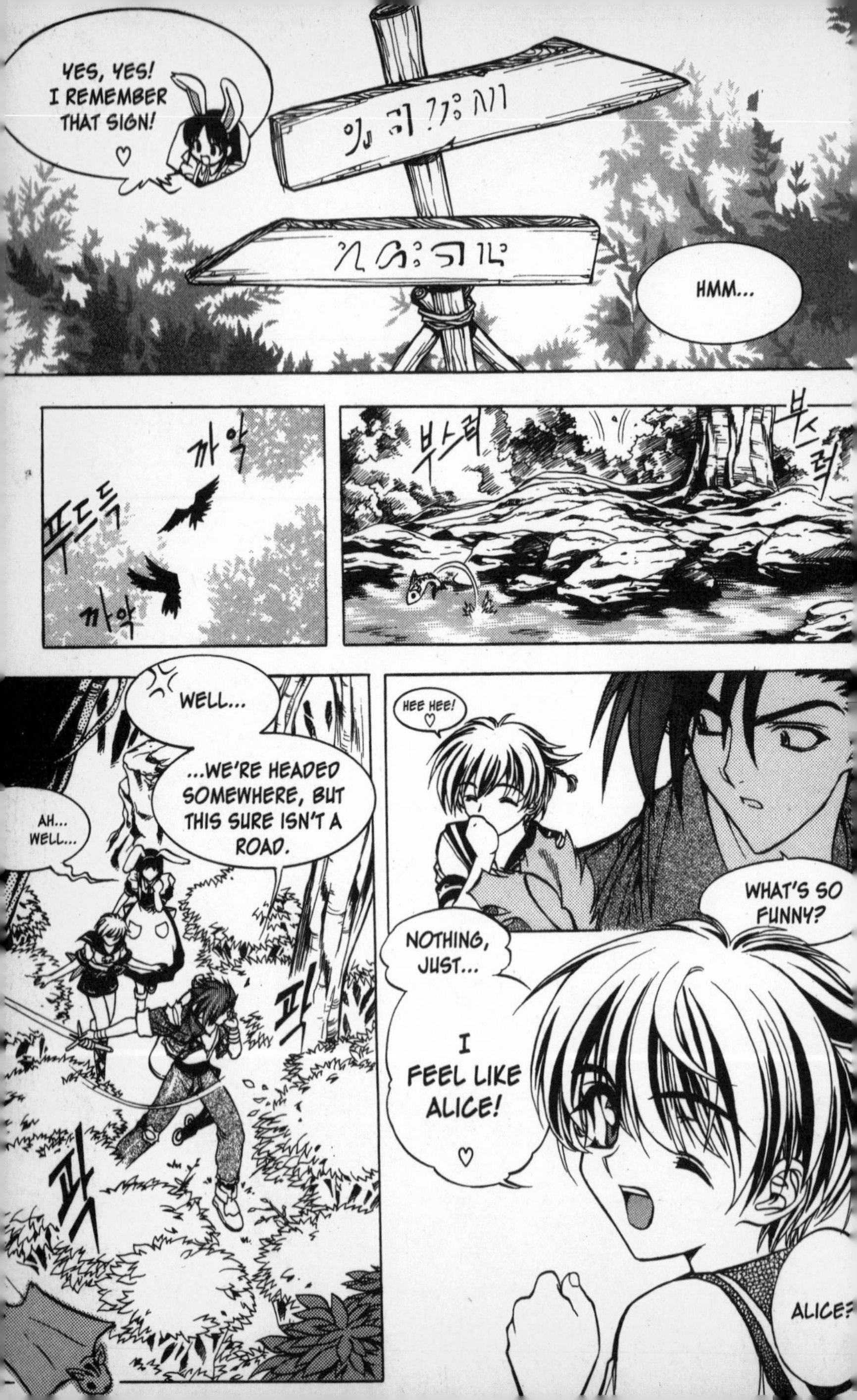

YES, YES! I REMEMBER THAT SIGN! ♡
HMM...
까악
푸드득
까악
부스럭
부스럭
WELL...
...WE'RE HEADED SOMEWHERE, BUT THIS SURE ISN'T A ROAD.
AH... WELL...
팍
팍
HEE HEE! ♡
WHAT'S SO FUNNY?
NOTHING, JUST...
I FEEL LIKE ALICE! ♡
ALICE?

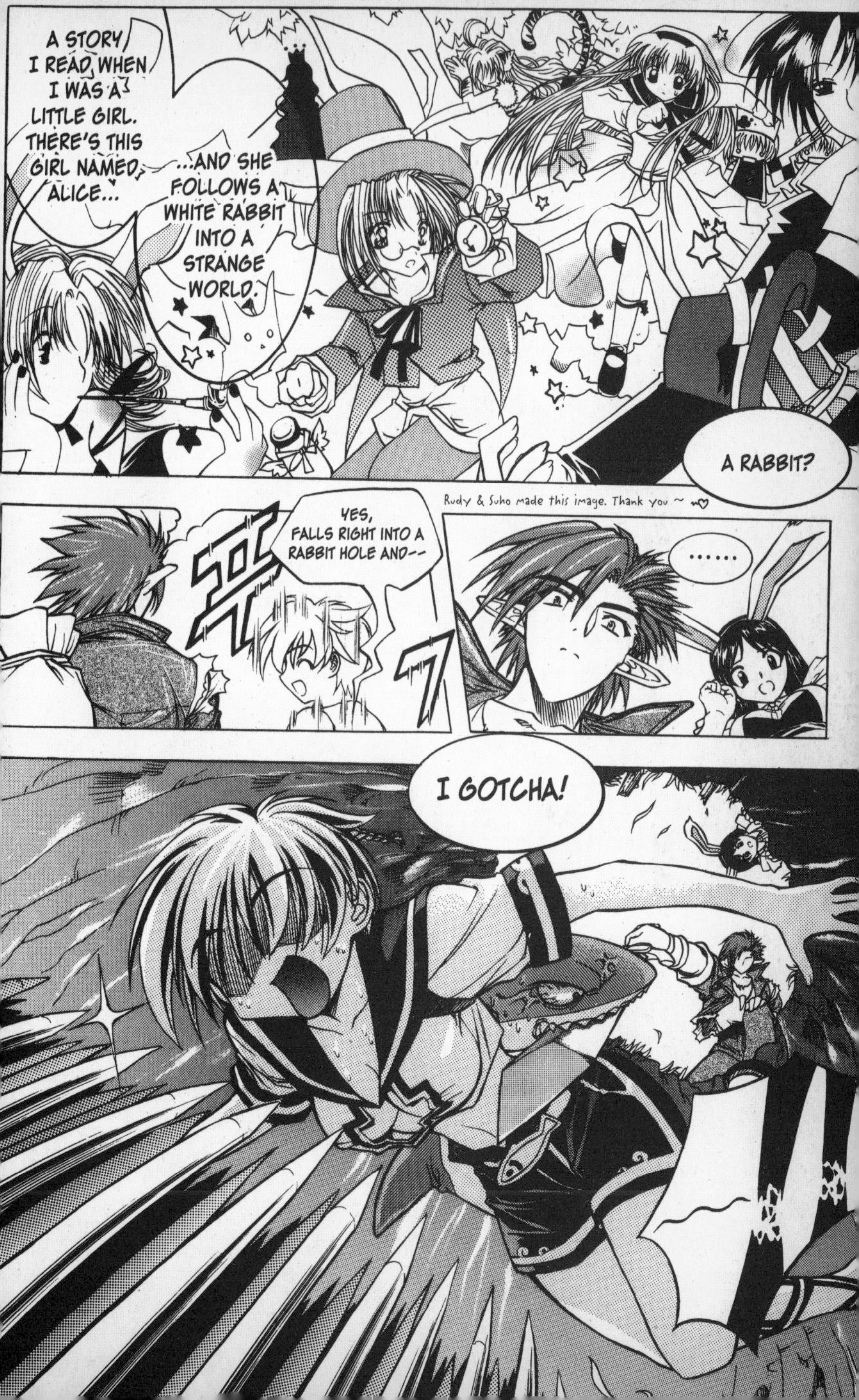
A STORY I READ WHEN I WAS A LITTLE GIRL. THERE'S THIS GIRL NAMED ALICE...
...AND SHE FOLLOWS A WHITE RABBIT INTO A STRANGE WORLD.
A RABBIT?
YES, FALLS RIGHT INTO A RABBIT HOLE AND--
Rudy & Suho made this image. Thank you ~
......
I GOTCHA!

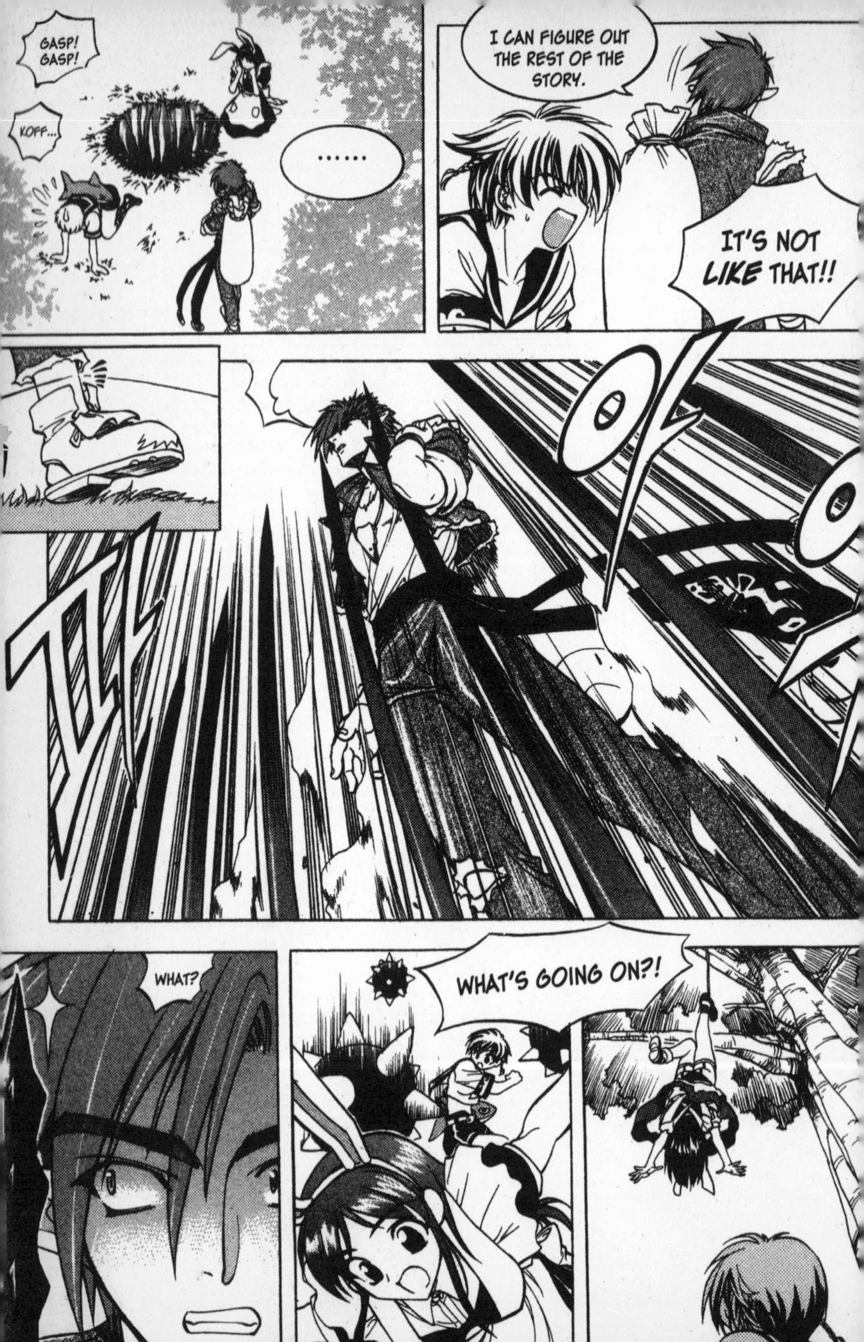
GASP! GASP!
KOFF...
......
I CAN FIGURE OUT THE REST OF THE STORY.
IT'S NOT LIKE THAT!!
WHAT?
WHAT'S GOING ON?!

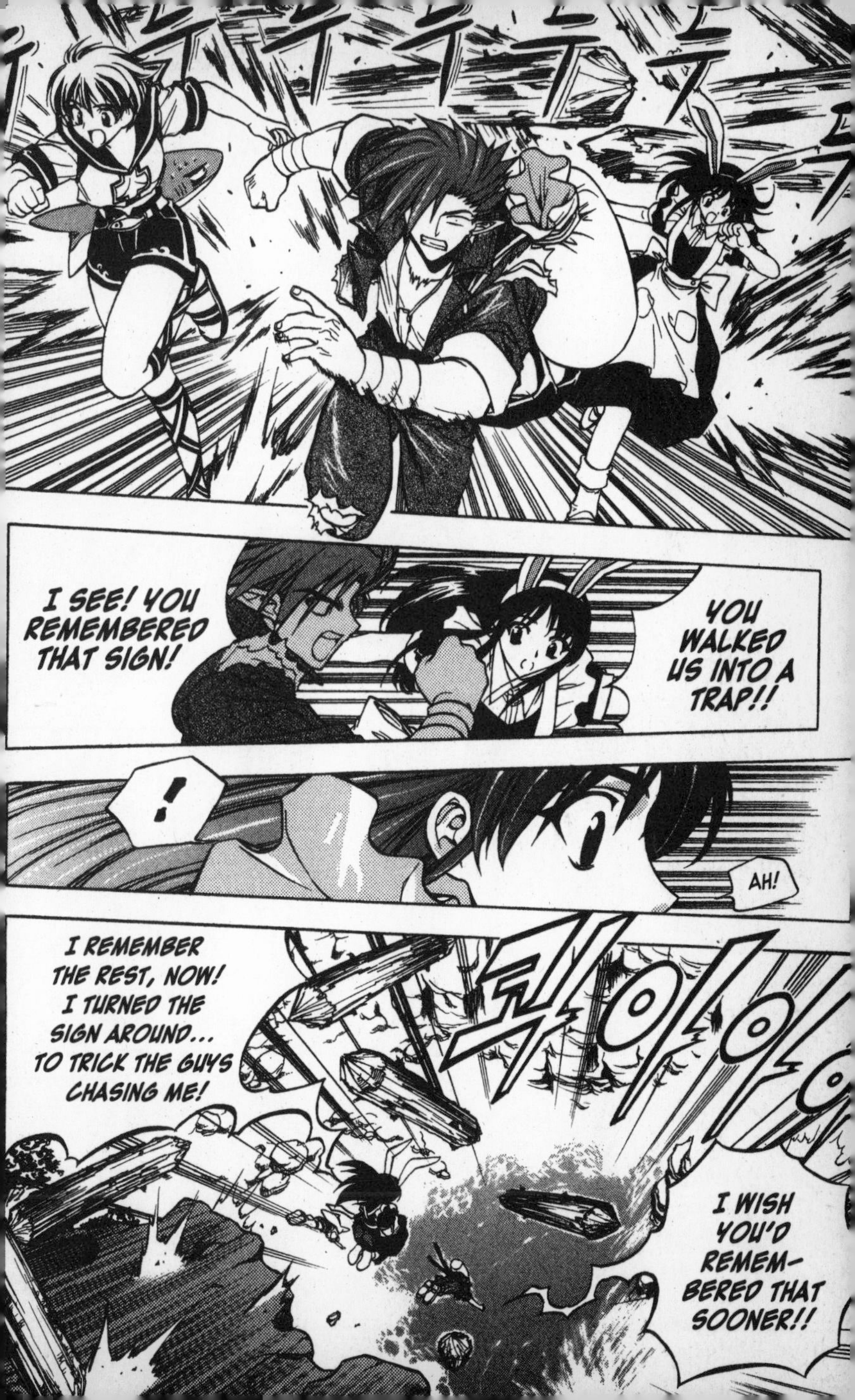
I SEE! YOU REMEMBERED THAT SIGN!
YOU WALKED US INTO A TRAP!!
!
AH!
I REMEMBER THE REST, NOW! I TURNED THE SIGN AROUND... TO TRICK THE GUYS CHASING ME!
I WISH YOU'D REMEMBERED THAT SOONER!!

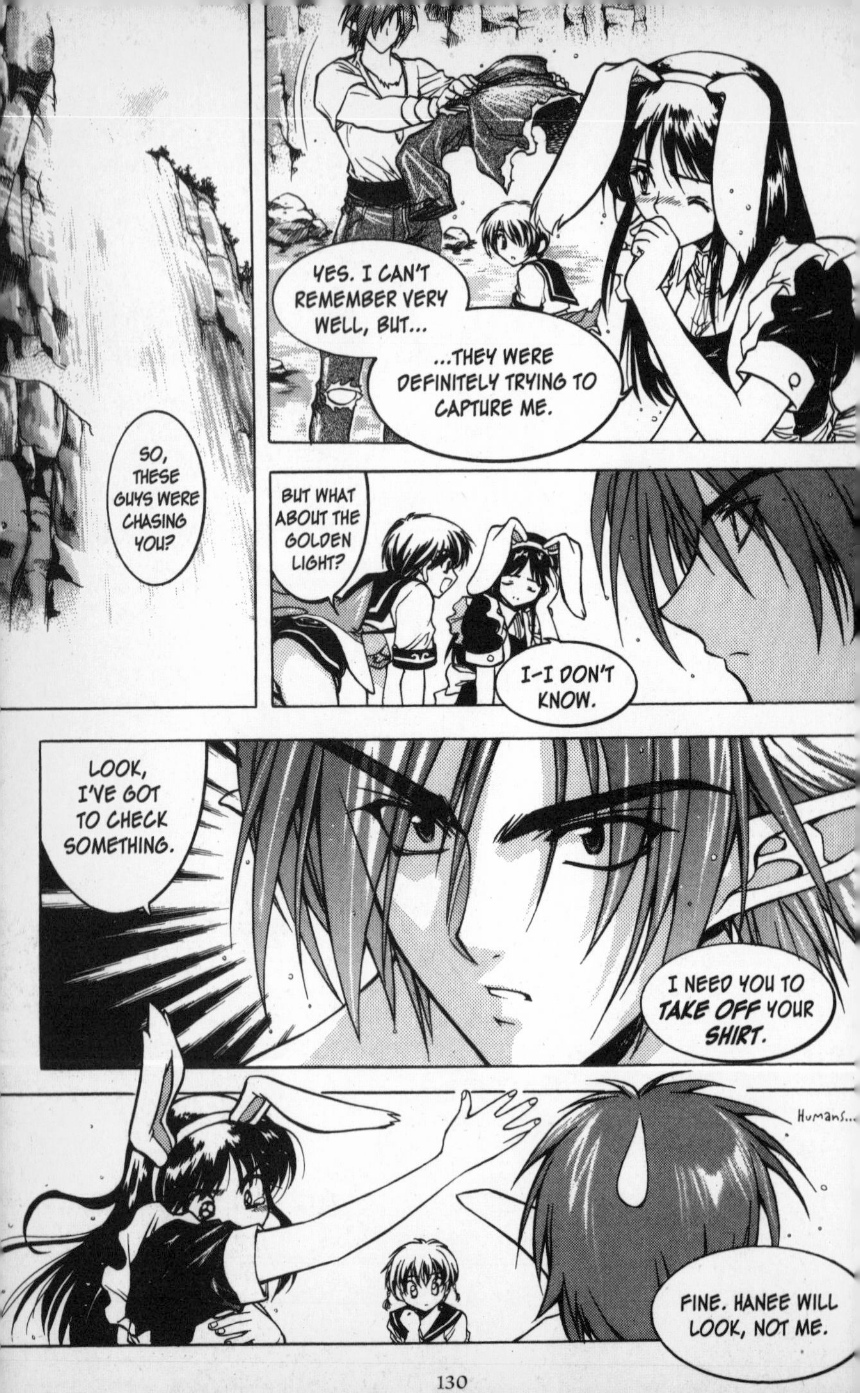
SO, THESE GUYS WERE CHASING YOU?
YES. I CAN'T REMEMBER VERY WELL, BUT...
...THEY WERE DEFINITELY TRYING TO CAPTURE ME.
BUT WHAT ABOUT THE GOLDEN LIGHT?
I-I DON'T KNOW.
LOOK, I'VE GOT TO CHECK SOMETHING.
I NEED YOU TO TAKE OFF YOUR SHIRT.
Humans...
FINE. HANEE WILL LOOK, NOT ME.

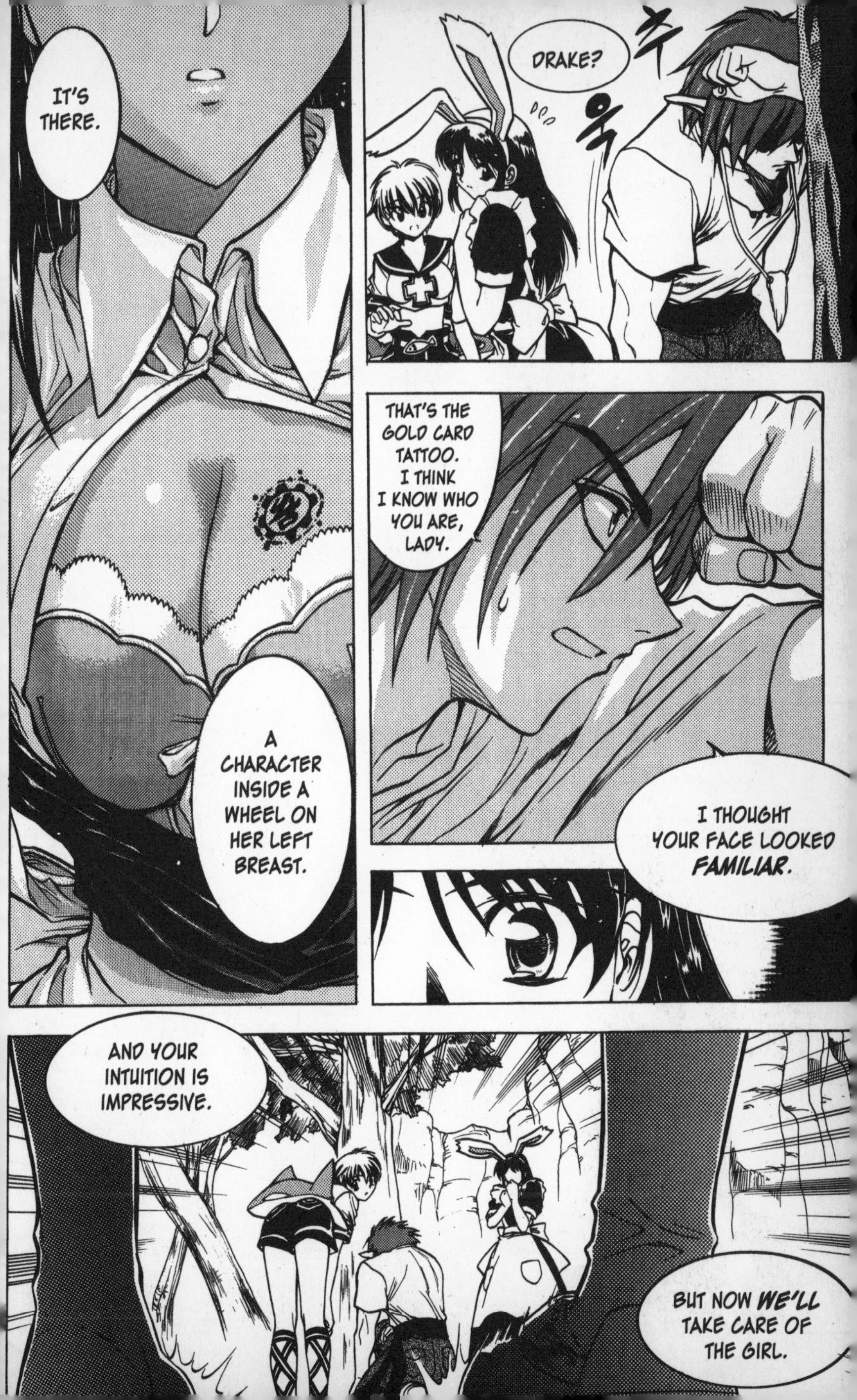
IT'S THERE.
A CHARACTER INSIDE A WHEEL ON HER LEFT BREAST.
DRAKE?
THAT'S THE GOLD CARD TATTOO. I THINK I KNOW WHO YOU ARE, LADY.
I THOUGHT YOUR FACE LOOKED FAMILIAR.
AND YOUR INTUITION IS IMPRESSIVE.
BUT NOW WE'LL TAKE CARE OF THE GIRL.

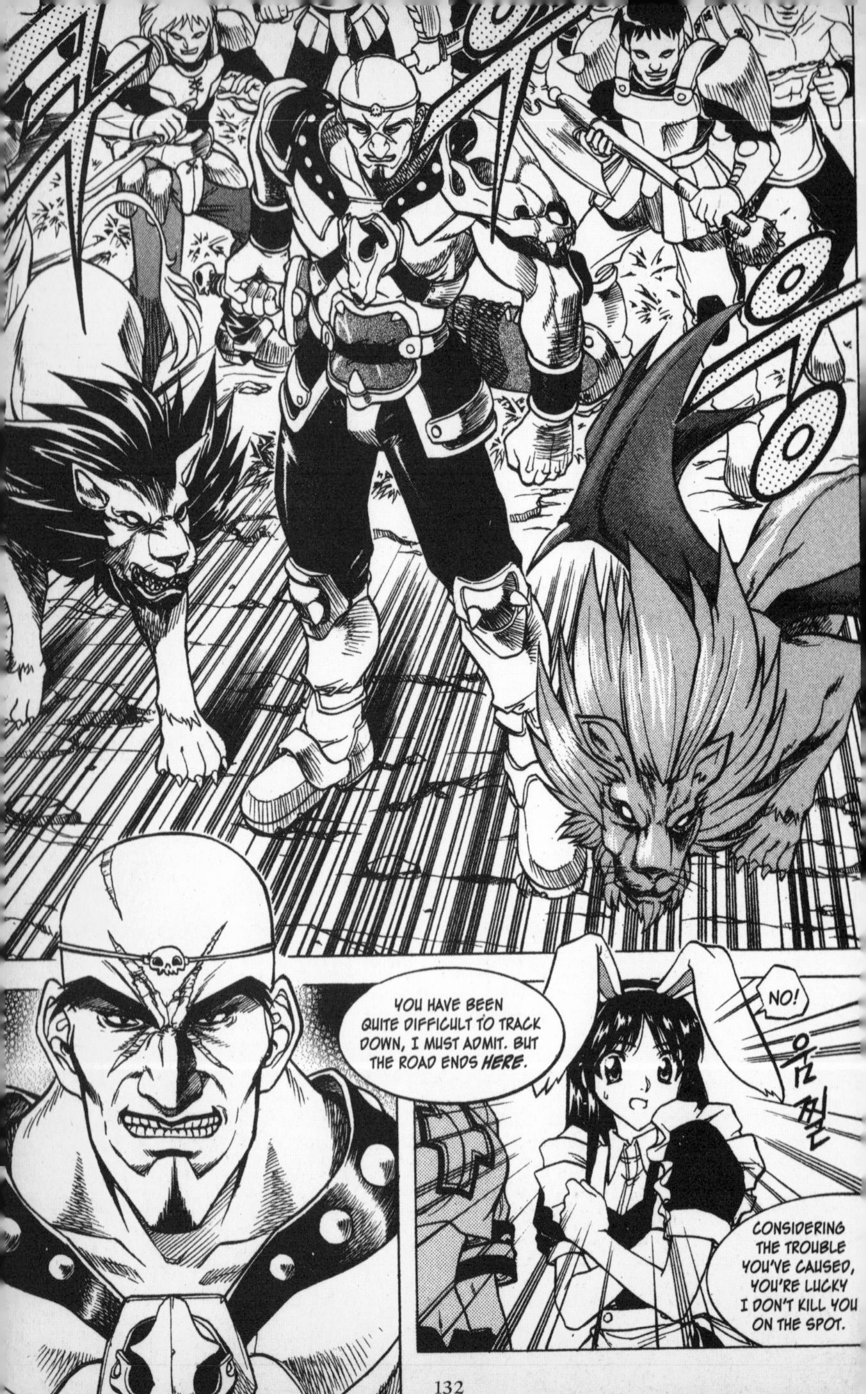
YOU HAVE BEEN QUITE DIFFICULT TO TRACK DOWN, I MUST ADMIT. BUT THE ROAD ENDS *HERE*.
NO!
CONSIDERING THE TROUBLE YOU'VE CAUSED, YOU'RE LUCKY I DON'T KILL YOU ON THE SPOT.

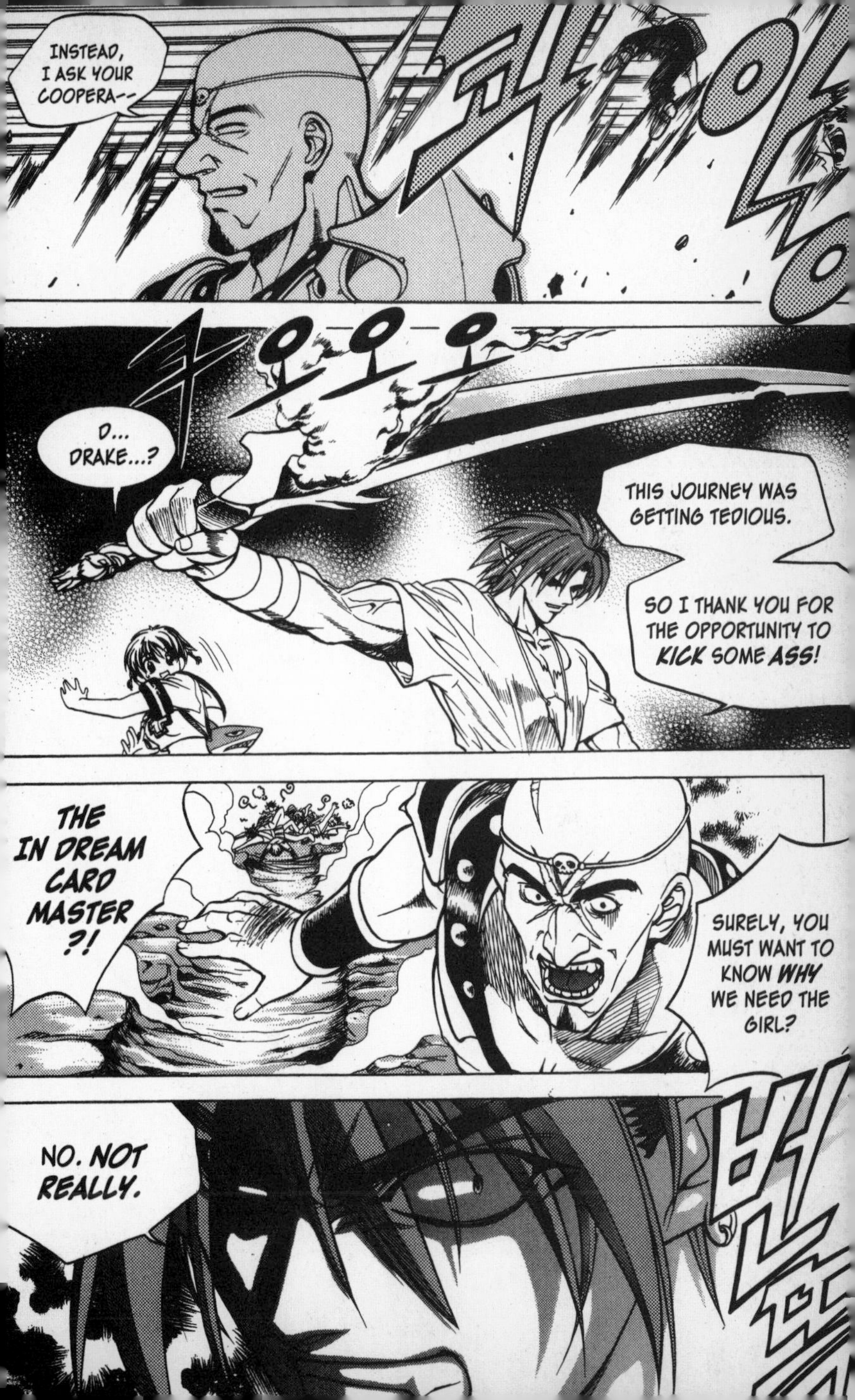
INSTEAD, I ASK YOUR COOPERA--
D... DRAKE...?
THIS JOURNEY WAS GETTING TEDIOUS.
SO I THANK YOU FOR THE OPPORTUNITY TO KICK SOME ASS!
THE IN DREAM CARD MASTER ?!
SURELY, YOU MUST WANT TO KNOW WHY WE NEED THE GIRL?
NO. NOT REALLY.

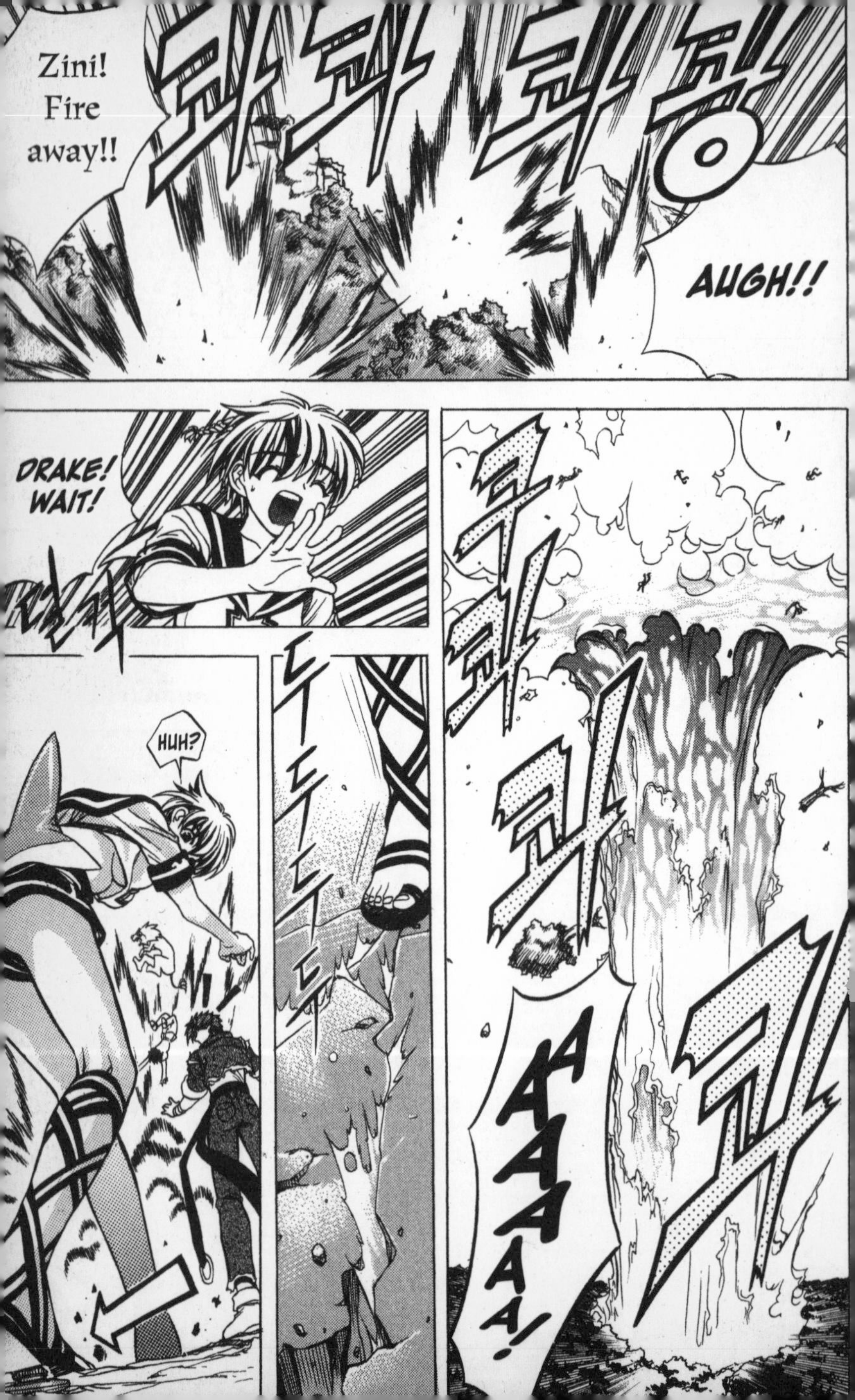
Zini! Fire away!!
AUGH!!
DRAKE! WAIT!
HUH?
AAAAAAA!

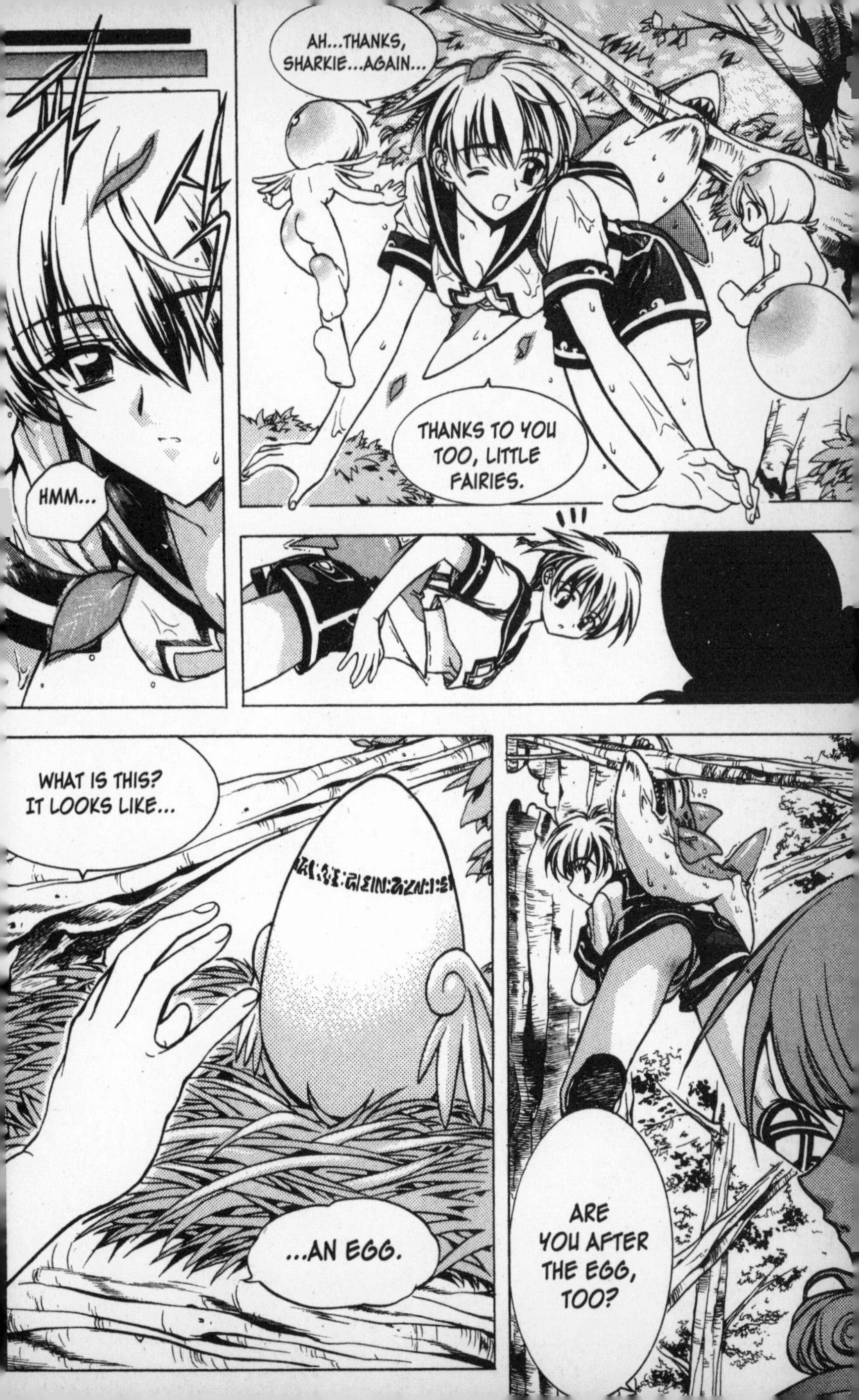
HMM...
AH...THANKS, SHARKIE...AGAIN...
THANKS TO YOU TOO, LITTLE FAIRIES.
WHAT IS THIS? IT LOOKS LIKE...
...AN EGG.
ARE YOU AFTER THE EGG, TOO?

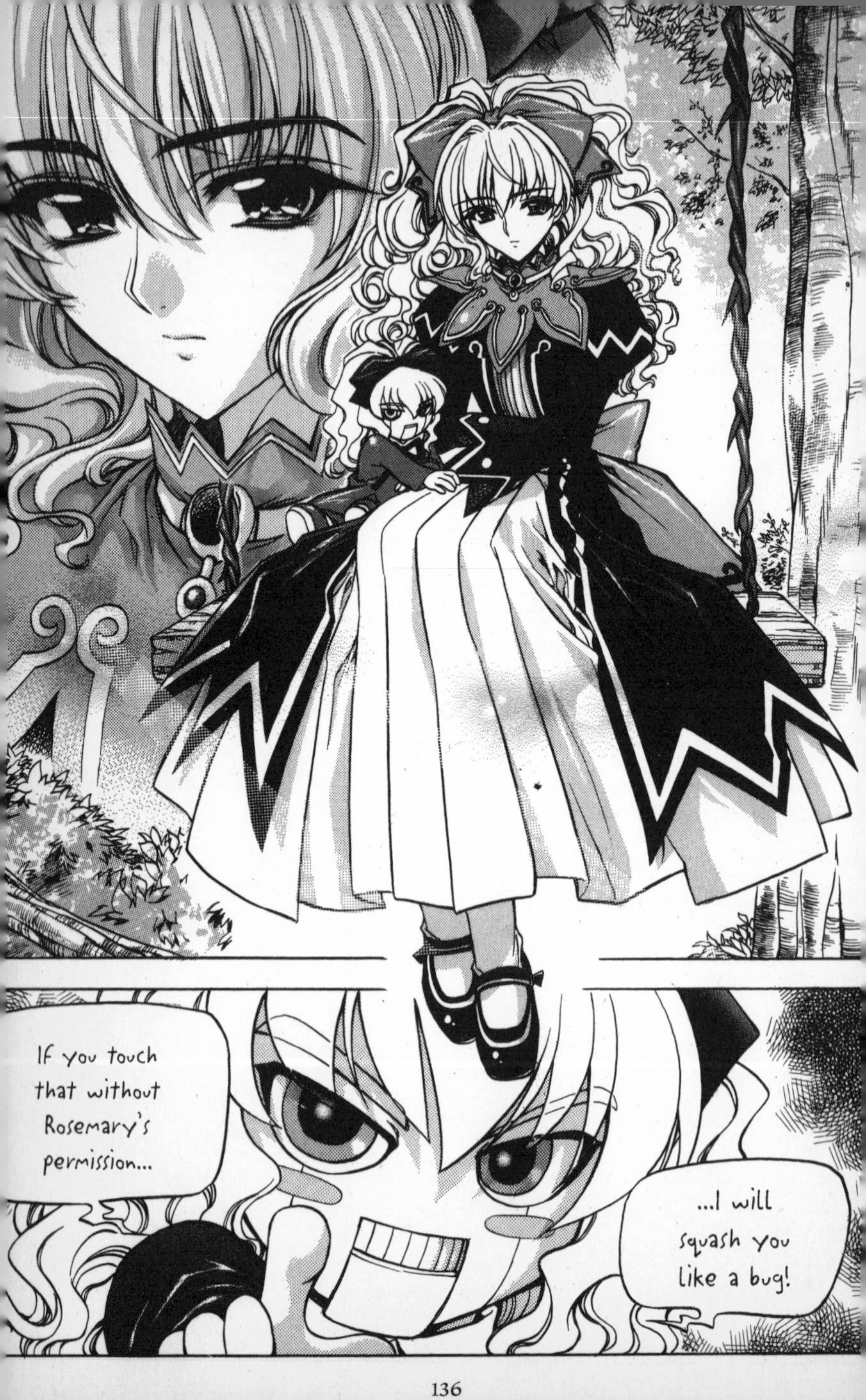
If you touch that without Rosemary's permission...
...I will squash you like a bug!

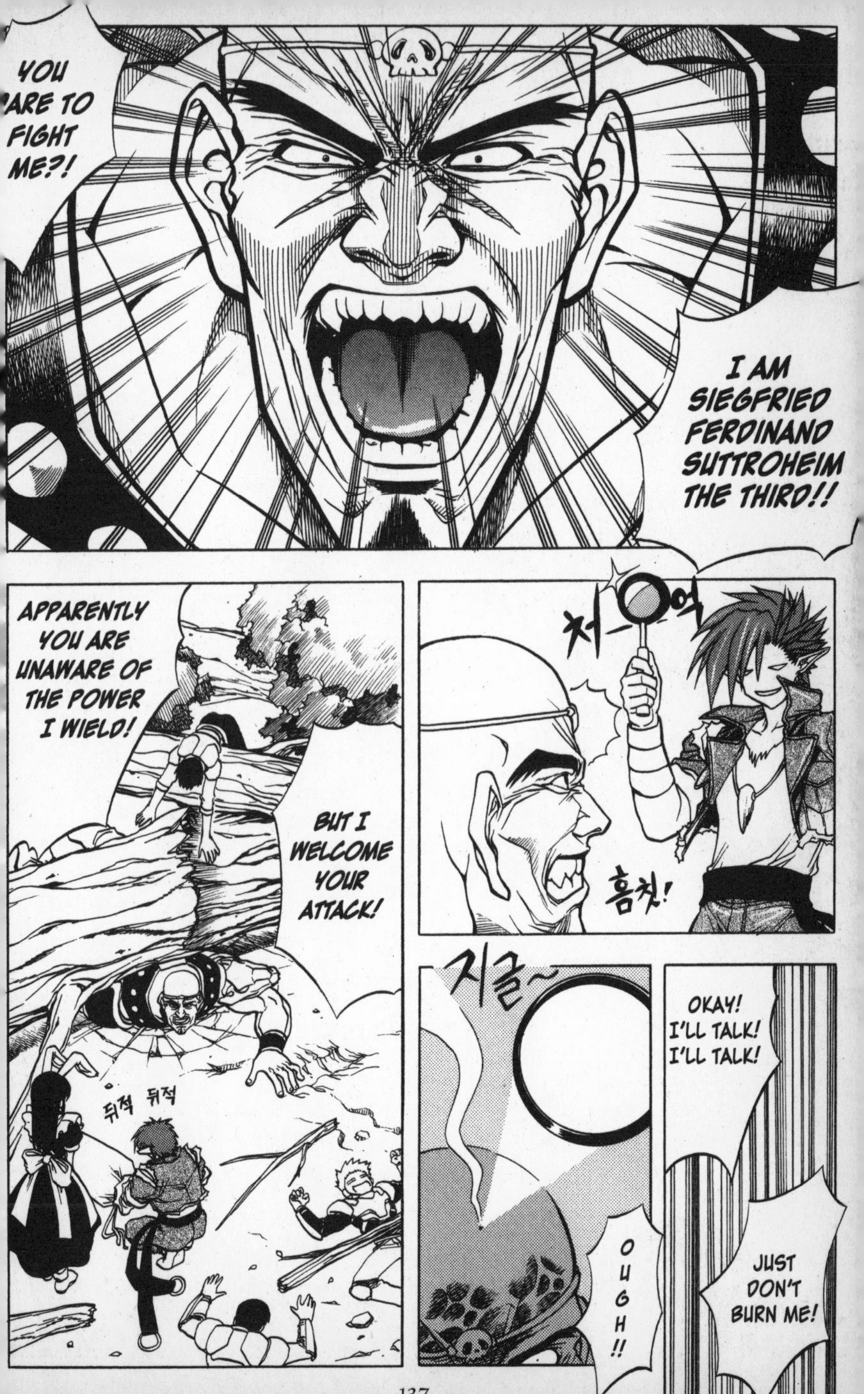
YOU ARE TO FIGHT ME?!
I AM SIEGFRIED FERDINAND SUTTROHEIM THE THIRD!!
APPARENTLY YOU ARE UNAWARE OF THE POWER I WIELD!
BUT I WELCOME YOUR ATTACK!
뒤적 뒤적
처-억
흠칫!
지글~
OUGH!!
OKAY! I'LL TALK! I'LL TALK!
JUST DON'T BURN ME!

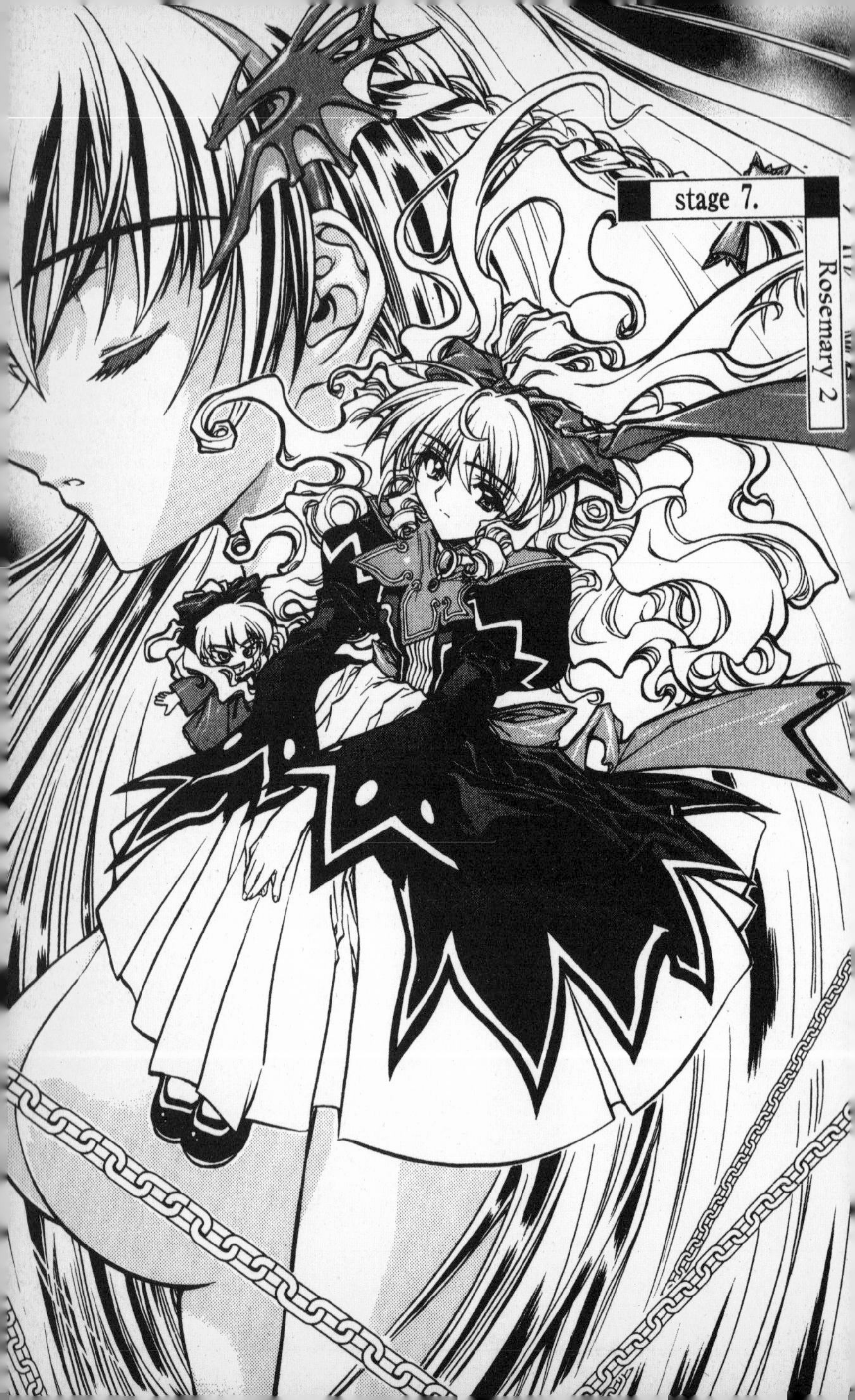
stage 7.
Rosemary 2

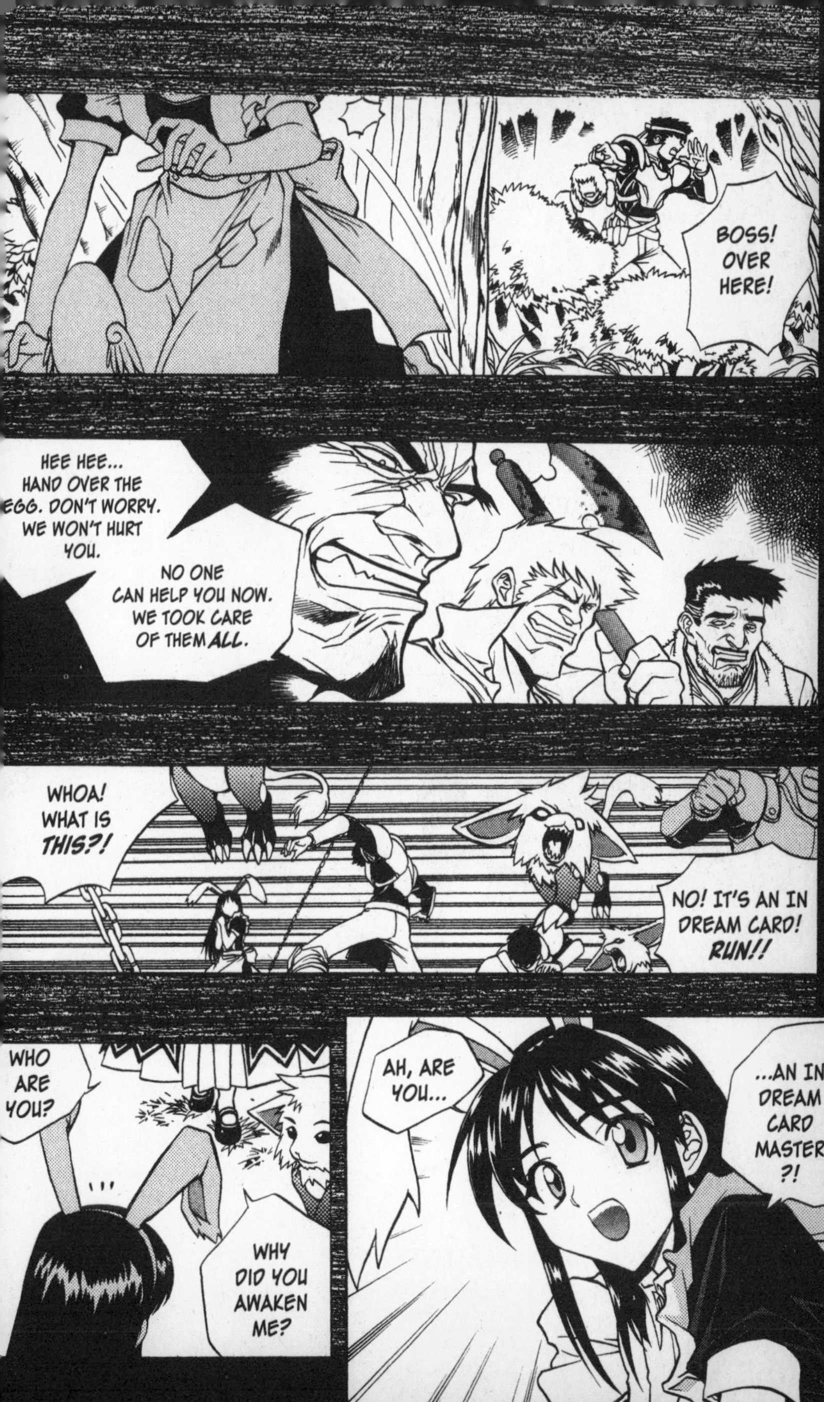
BOSS! OVER HERE!
HEE HEE... HAND OVER THE EGG. DON'T WORRY. WE WON'T HURT YOU.
NO ONE CAN HELP YOU NOW. WE TOOK CARE OF THEM ALL.
WHOA! WHAT IS THIS?!
NO! IT'S AN IN DREAM CARD! RUN!!
WHO ARE YOU?
...
WHY DID YOU AWAKEN ME?
AH, ARE YOU...
...AN IN DREAM CARD MASTER?!

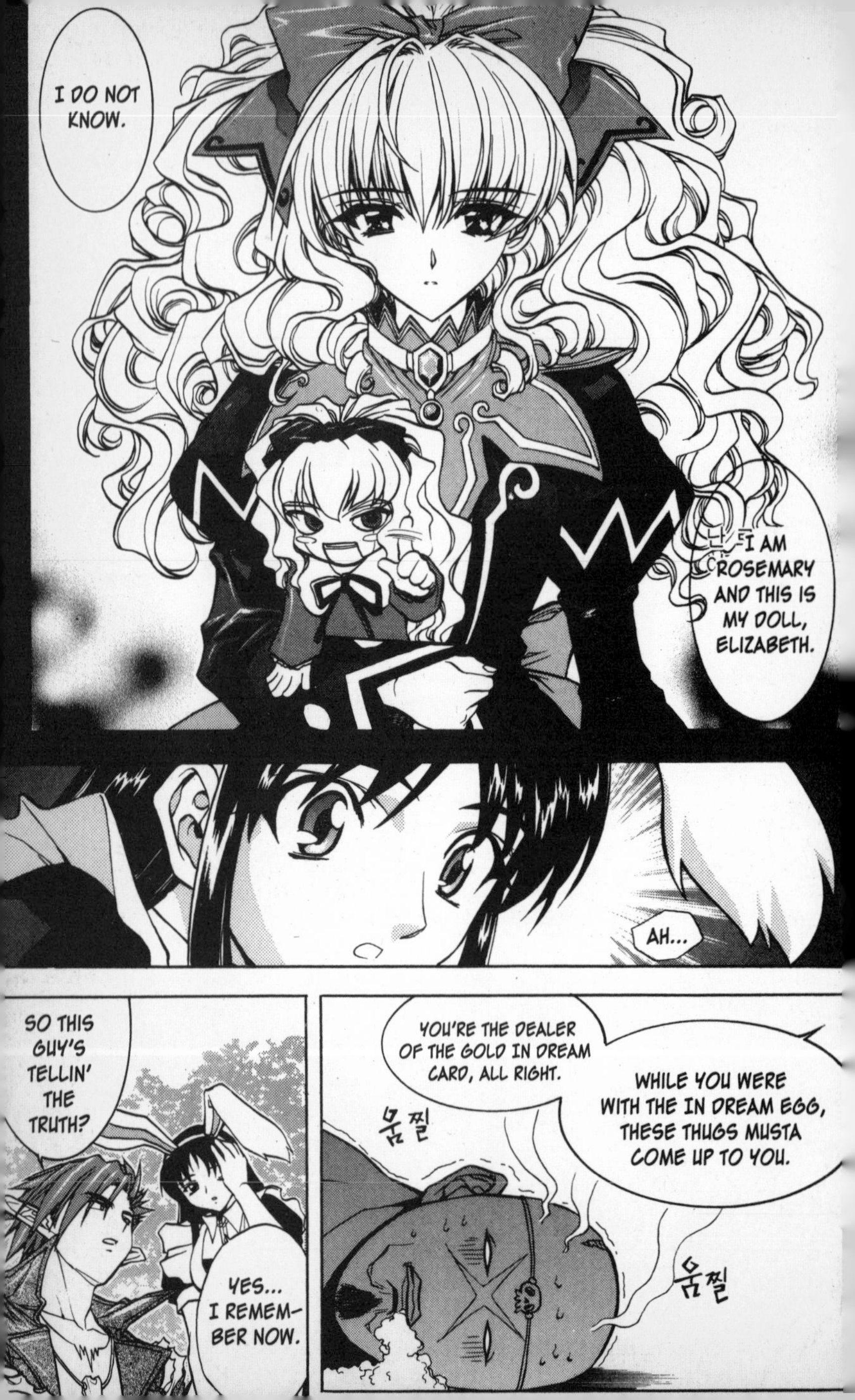
I DO NOT KNOW.
I AM ROSEMARY AND THIS IS MY DOLL, ELIZABETH.
AH...
SO THIS GUY'S TELLIN' THE TRUTH?
YES... I REMEMBER NOW.
YOU'RE THE DEALER OF THE GOLD IN DREAM CARD, ALL RIGHT.
움찔
WHILE YOU WERE WITH THE IN DREAM EGG, THESE THUGS MUSTA COME UP TO YOU.
움찔

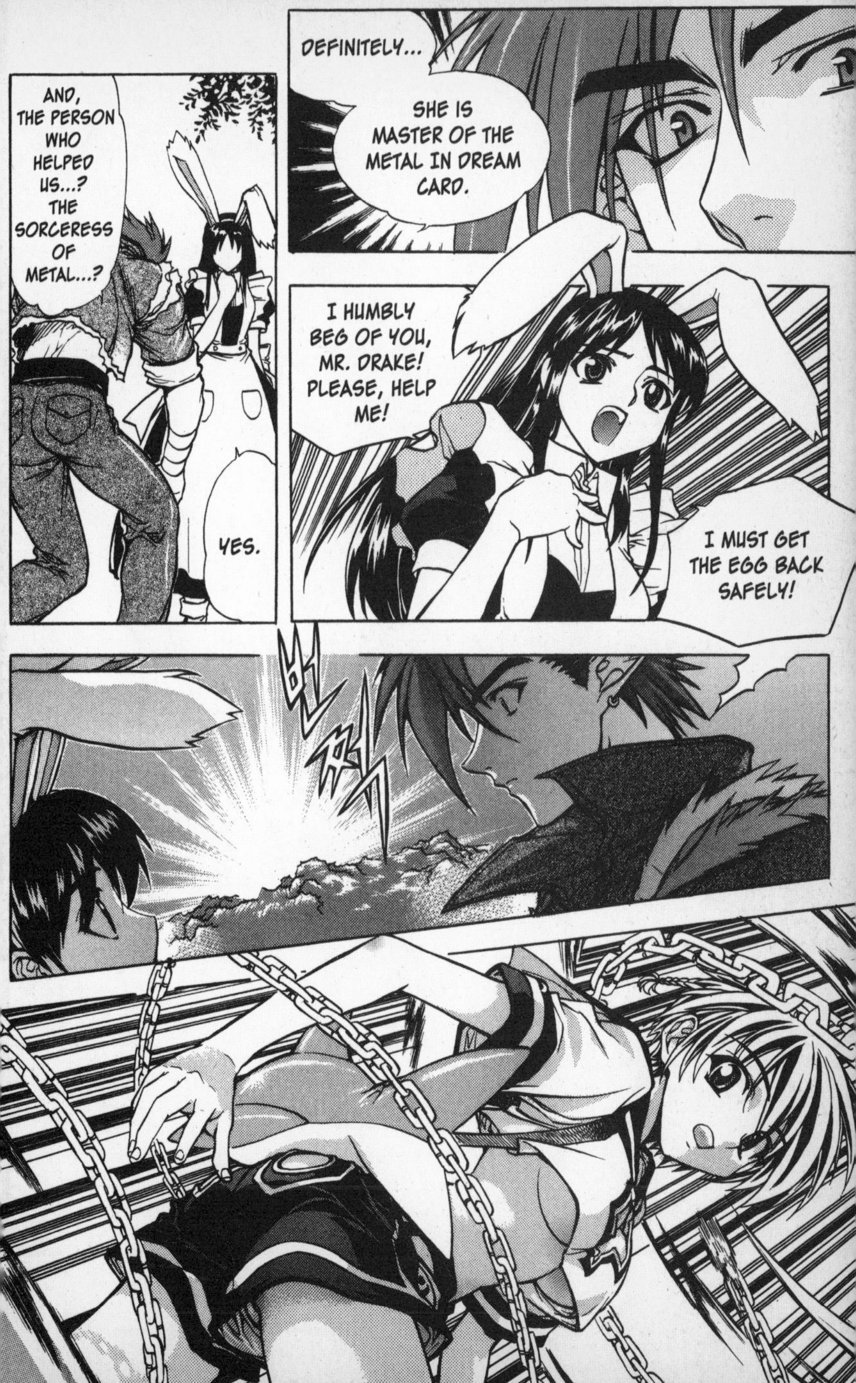
AND, THE PERSON WHO HELPED US...? THE SORCERESS OF METAL...?
YES.
DEFINITELY...
SHE IS MASTER OF THE METAL IN DREAM CARD.
I HUMBLY BEG OF YOU, MR. DRAKE! PLEASE, HELP ME!
I MUST GET THE EGG BACK SAFELY!

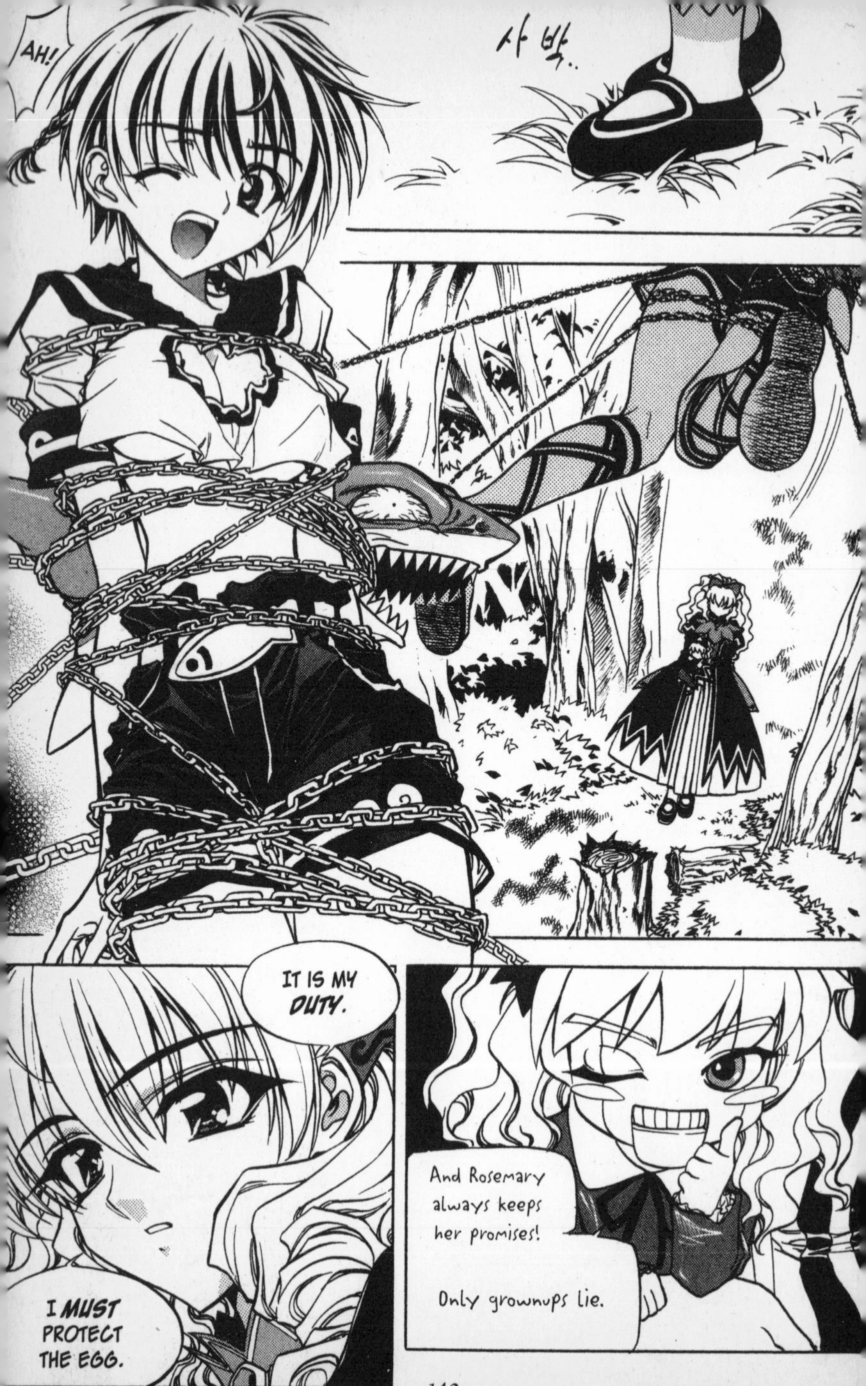
AH!
사박..
IT IS MY DUTY.
I MUST PROTECT THE EGG.
And Rosemary always keeps her promises!
Only grownups lie.

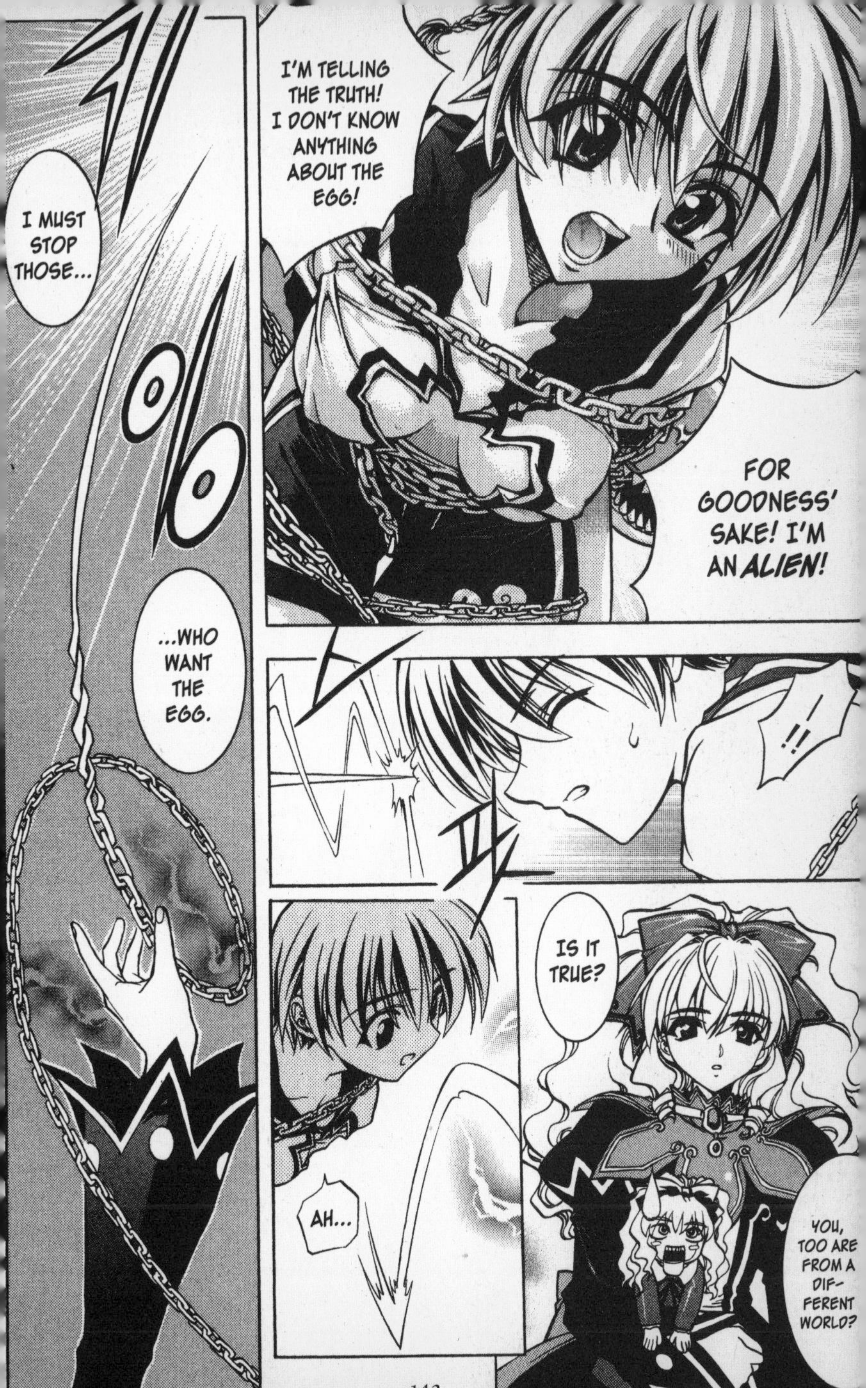
I MUST STOP THOSE...
...WHO WANT THE EGG.
I'M TELLING THE TRUTH! I DON'T KNOW ANYTHING ABOUT THE EGG!
FOR GOODNESS' SAKE! I'M AN *ALIEN*!
!!
IS IT TRUE?
AH...
YOU, TOO ARE FROM A DIF-FERENT WORLD?

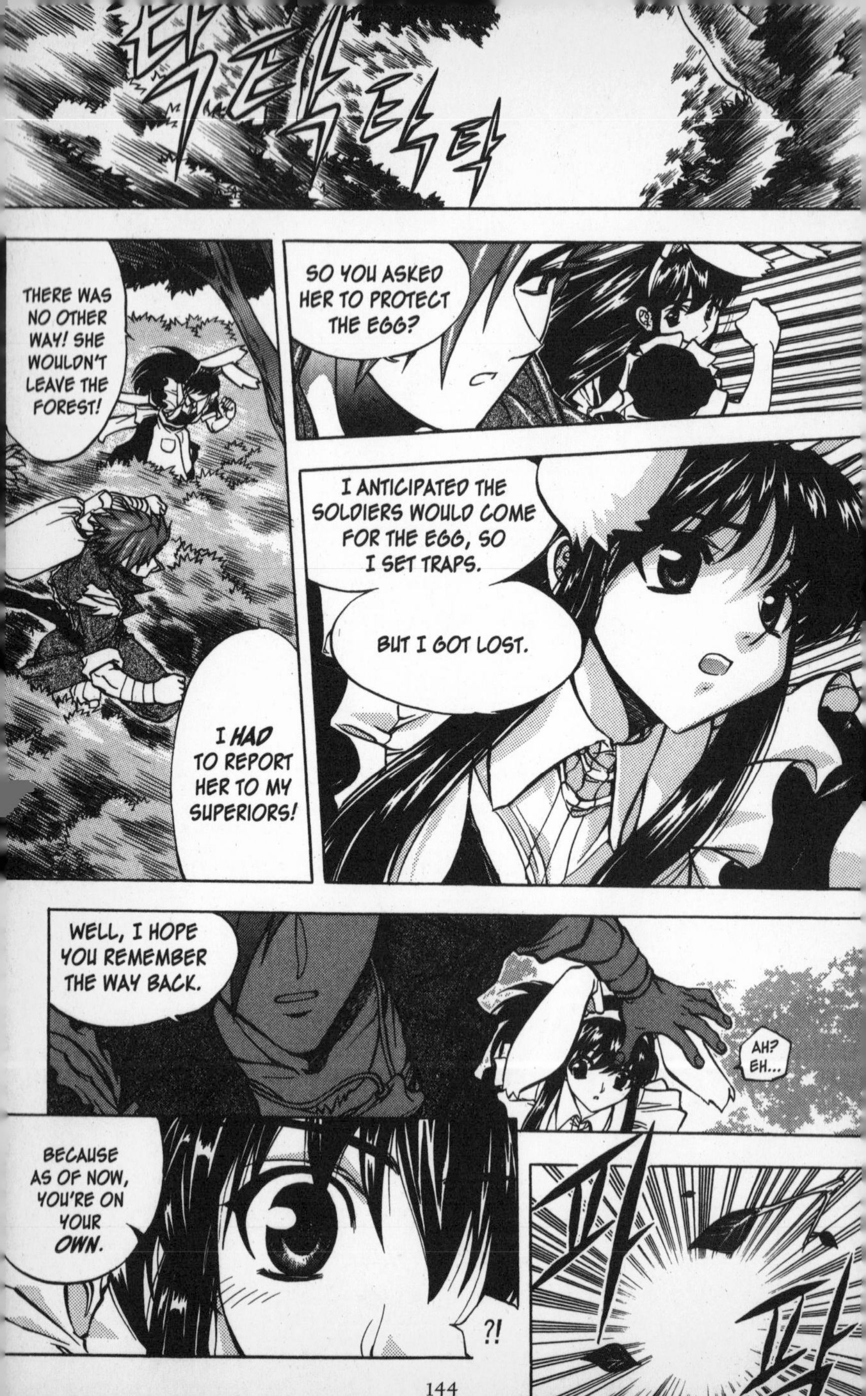
THERE WAS NO OTHER WAY! SHE WOULDN'T LEAVE THE FOREST!
I *HAD* TO REPORT HER TO MY SUPERIORS!
SO YOU ASKED HER TO PROTECT THE EGG?
I ANTICIPATED THE SOLDIERS WOULD COME FOR THE EGG, SO I SET TRAPS.
BUT I GOT LOST.
WELL, I HOPE YOU REMEMBER THE WAY BACK.
AH? EH...
BECAUSE AS OF NOW, YOU'RE ON YOUR *OWN*.
?!

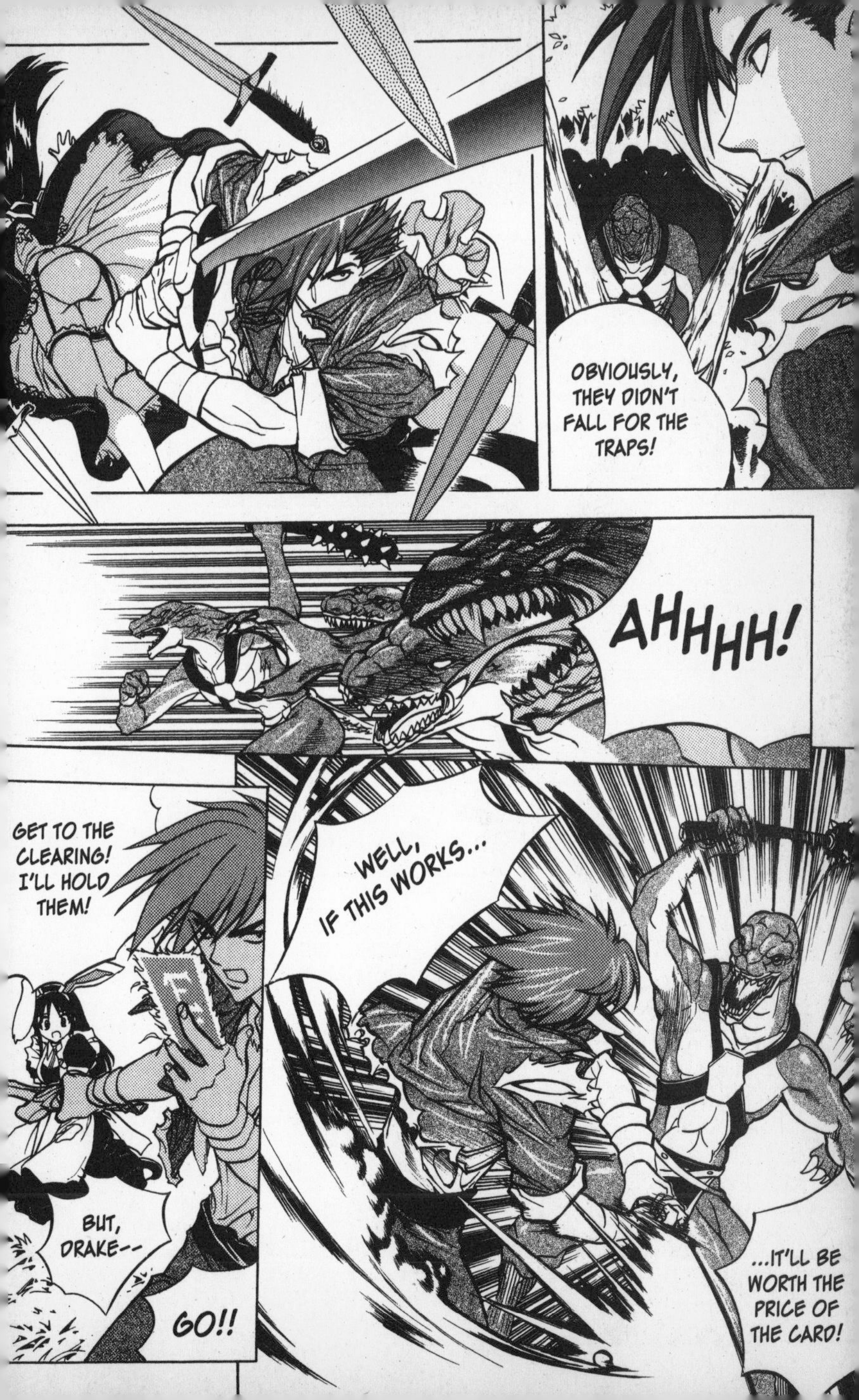
OBVIOUSLY, THEY DIDN'T FALL FOR THE TRAPS!
AHHHH!
GET TO THE CLEARING! I'LL HOLD THEM!
BUT, DRAKE--
GO!!
WELL, IF THIS WORKS...
...IT'LL BE WORTH THE PRICE OF THE CARD!

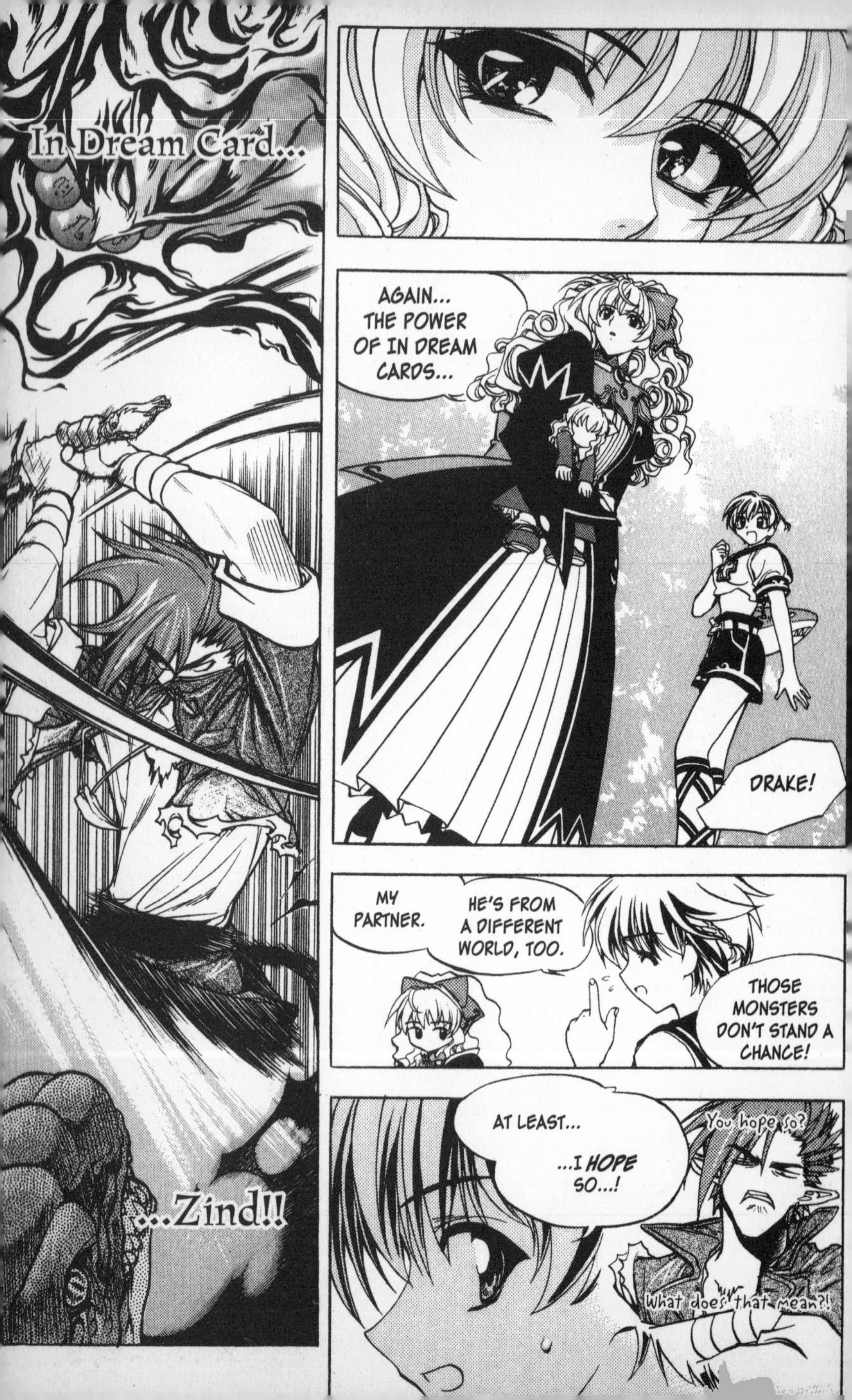
In Dream Card...
...Zind!!
AGAIN... THE POWER OF IN DREAM CARDS...
DRAKE!
MY PARTNER.
HE'S FROM A DIFFERENT WORLD, TOO.
THOSE MONSTERS DON'T STAND A CHANCE!
AT LEAST...
...I HOPE SO...!
You hope so?
What does that mean?!

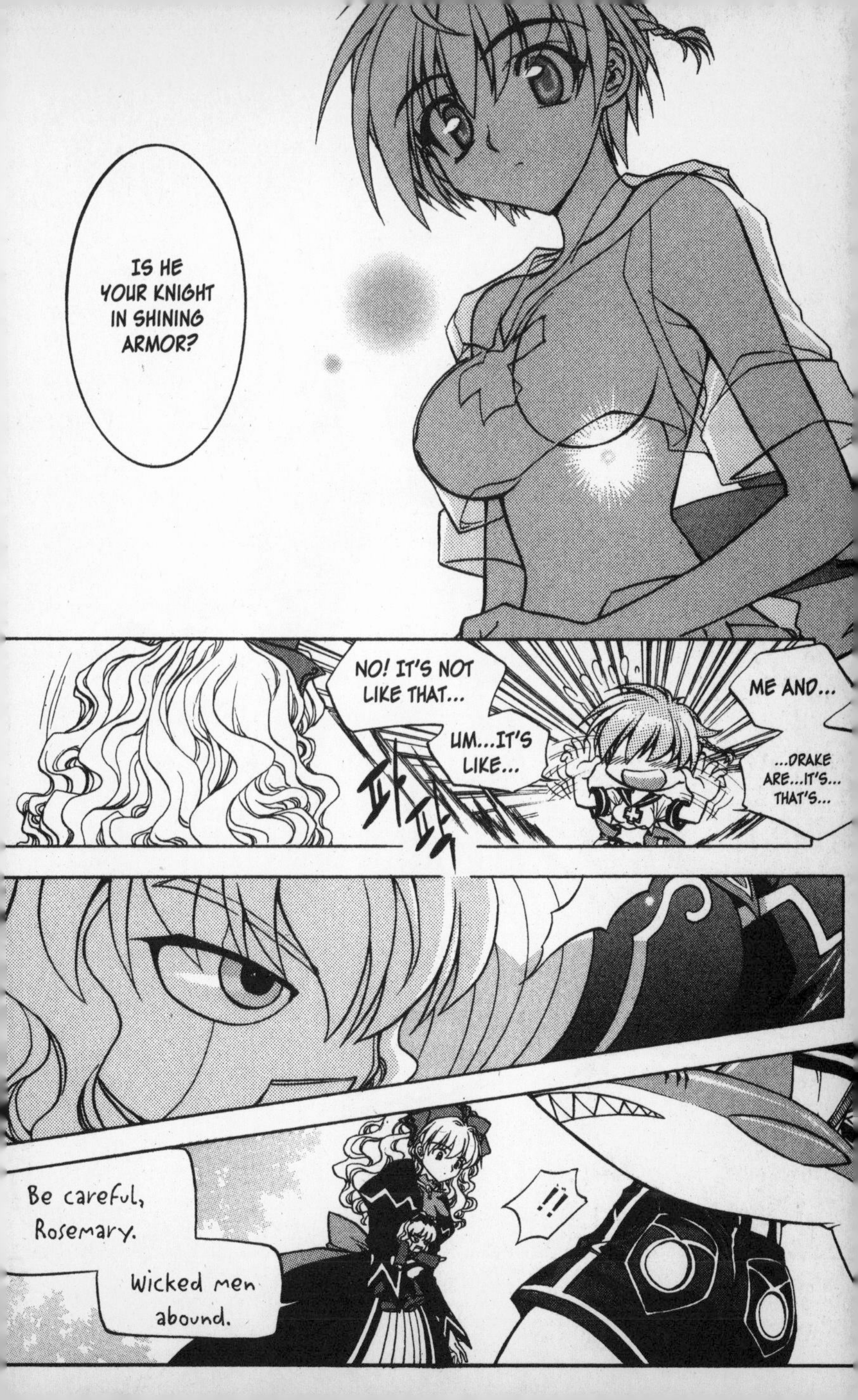
IS HE YOUR KNIGHT IN SHINING ARMOR?
NO! IT'S NOT LIKE THAT...
UM...IT'S LIKE...
ME AND...
...DRAKE ARE...IT'S... THAT'S...
Be careful, Rosemary.
Wicked men abound.
!!

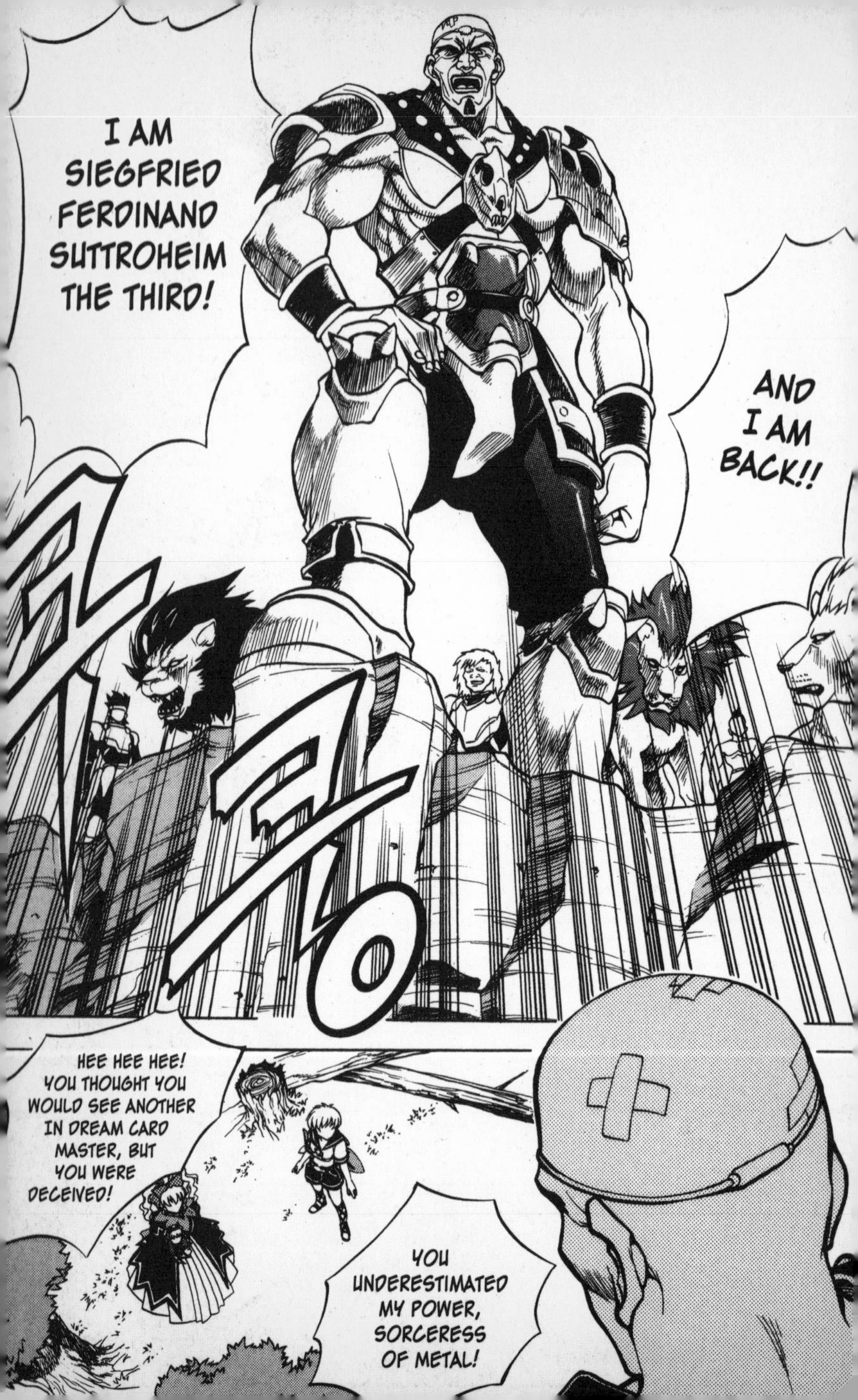
I AM SIEGFRIED FERDINAND SUTTROHEIM THE THIRD!
AND I AM BACK!!
HEE HEE HEE! YOU THOUGHT YOU WOULD SEE ANOTHER IN DREAM CARD MASTER, BUT YOU WERE DECEIVED!
YOU UNDERESTIMATED MY POWER, SORCERESS OF METAL!

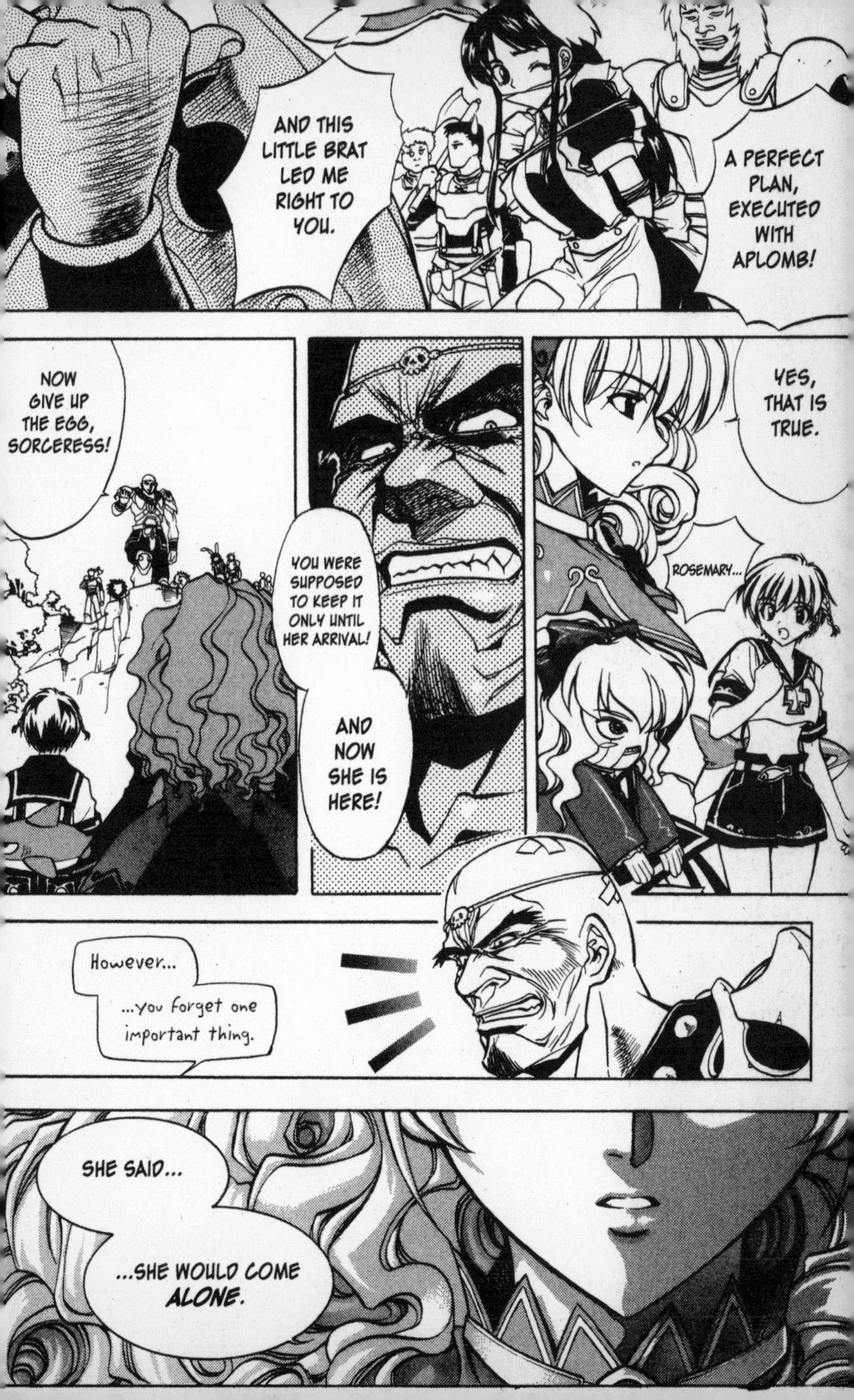
AND THIS LITTLE BRAT LED ME RIGHT TO YOU.
A PERFECT PLAN, EXECUTED WITH APLOMB!
NOW GIVE UP THE EGG, SORCERESS!
YOU WERE SUPPOSED TO KEEP IT ONLY UNTIL HER ARRIVAL!
AND NOW SHE IS HERE!
YES, THAT IS TRUE.
ROSEMARY...
However...
...you forget one important thing.
SHE SAID...
...SHE WOULD COME ALONE.

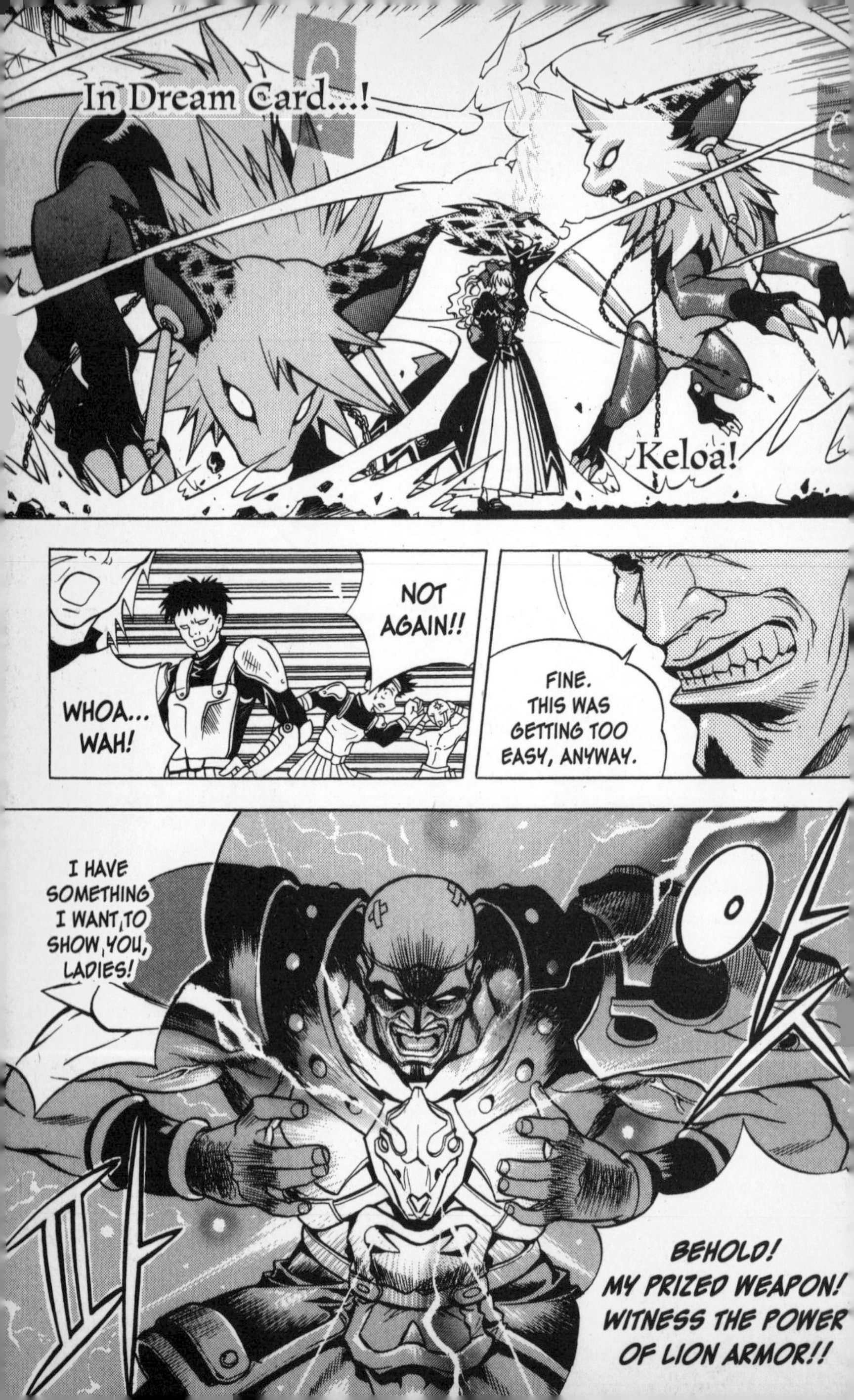
In Dream Card...!
Keloa!
NOT AGAIN!!
WHOA... WAH!
FINE. THIS WAS GETTING TOO EASY, ANYWAY.
I HAVE SOMETHING I WANT TO SHOW YOU, LADIES!
BEHOLD! MY PRIZED WEAPON! WITNESS THE POWER OF LION ARMOR!!

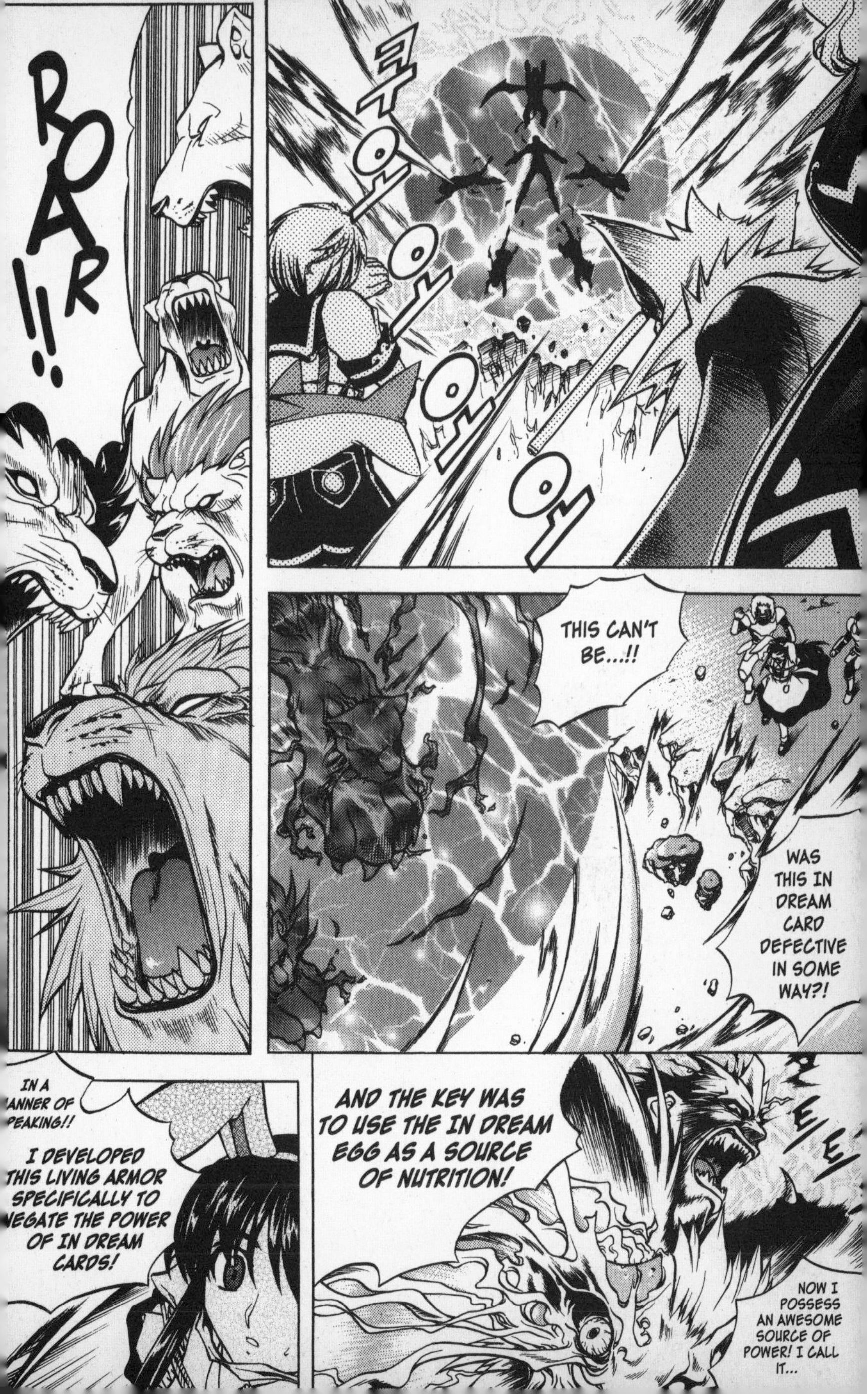
ROAR!!!
크오오오오
THIS CAN'T BE...!!
WAS THIS IN DREAM CARD DEFECTIVE IN SOME WAY?!
IN A ANNER OF PEAKING!!
I DEVELOPED THIS LIVING ARMOR SPECIFICALLY TO EGATE THE POWER OF IN DREAM CARDS!
AND THE KEY WAS TO USE THE IN DREAM EGG AS A SOURCE OF NUTRITION!
REE
NOW I POSSESS AN AWESOME SOURCE OF POWER! I CALL IT...

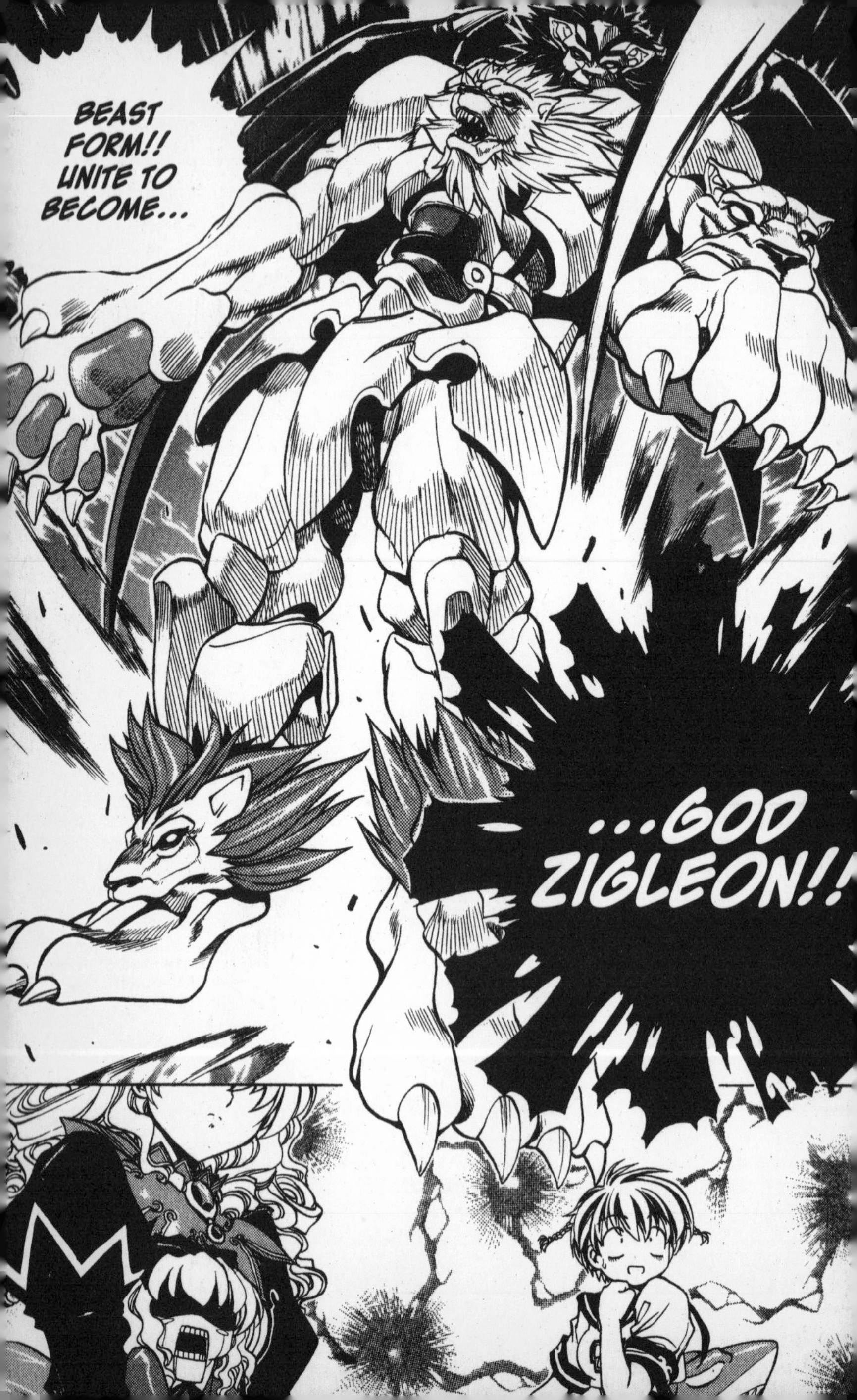
BEAST FORM!! UNITE TO BECOME...
...GOD ZIGLEON!!

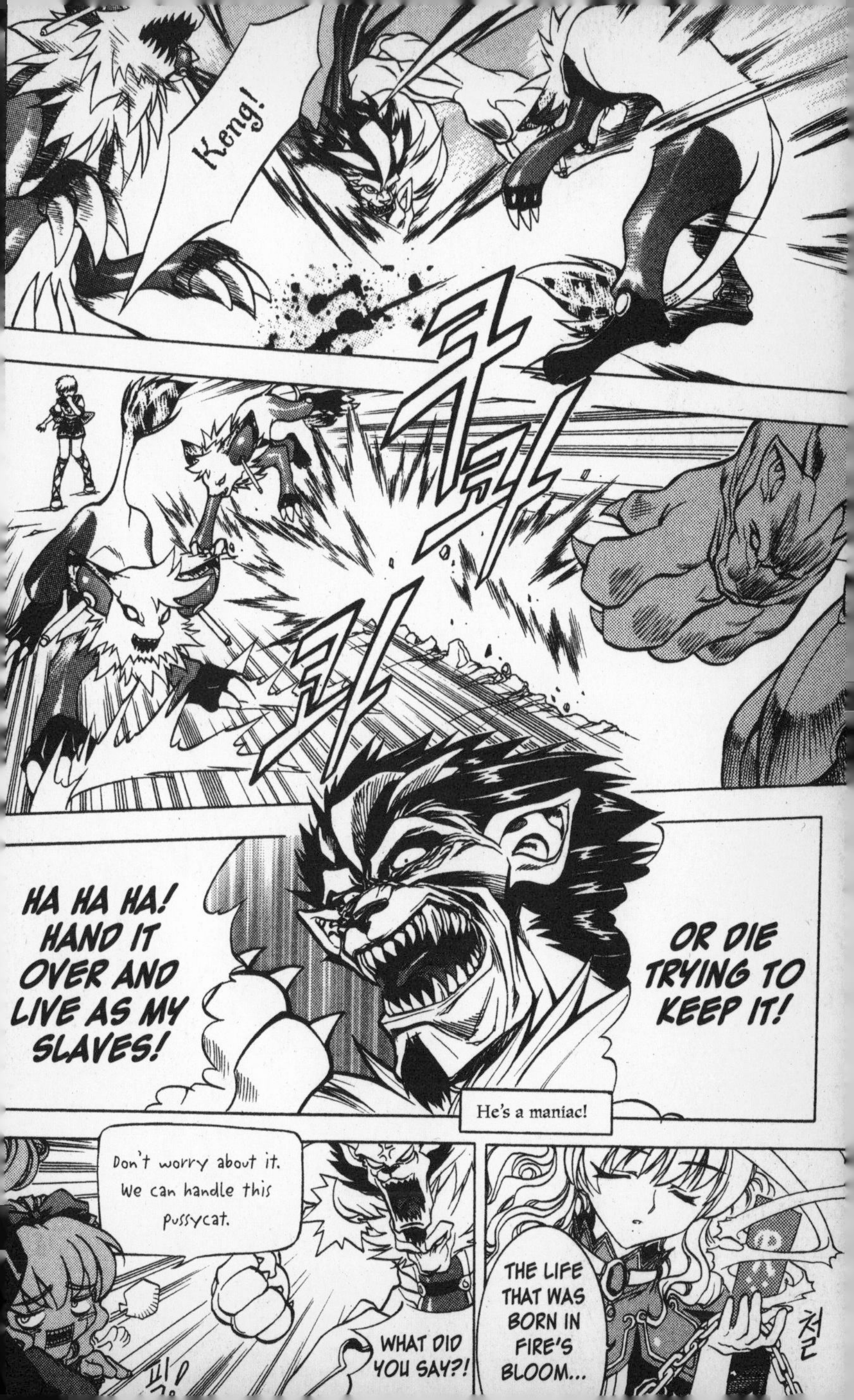
Keng!
HA HA HA! HAND IT OVER AND LIVE AS MY SLAVES!
OR DIE TRYING TO KEEP IT!
He's a maniac!
Don't worry about it. We can handle this pussycat.
WHAT DID YOU SAY?!
THE LIFE THAT WAS BORN IN FIRE'S BLOOM...

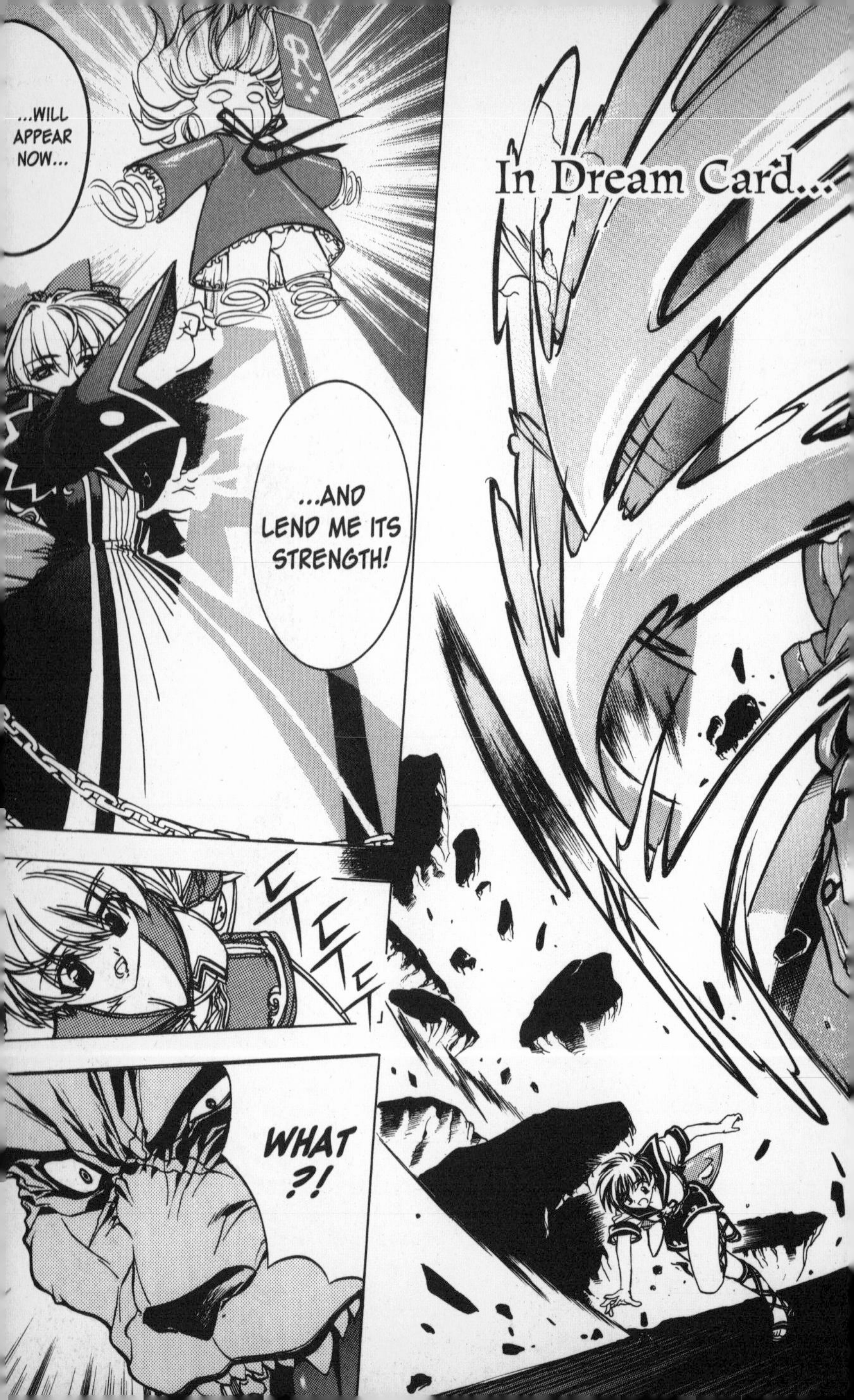
...WILL APPEAR NOW...
...AND LEND ME ITS STRENGTH!
WHAT ?!
In Dream Card...

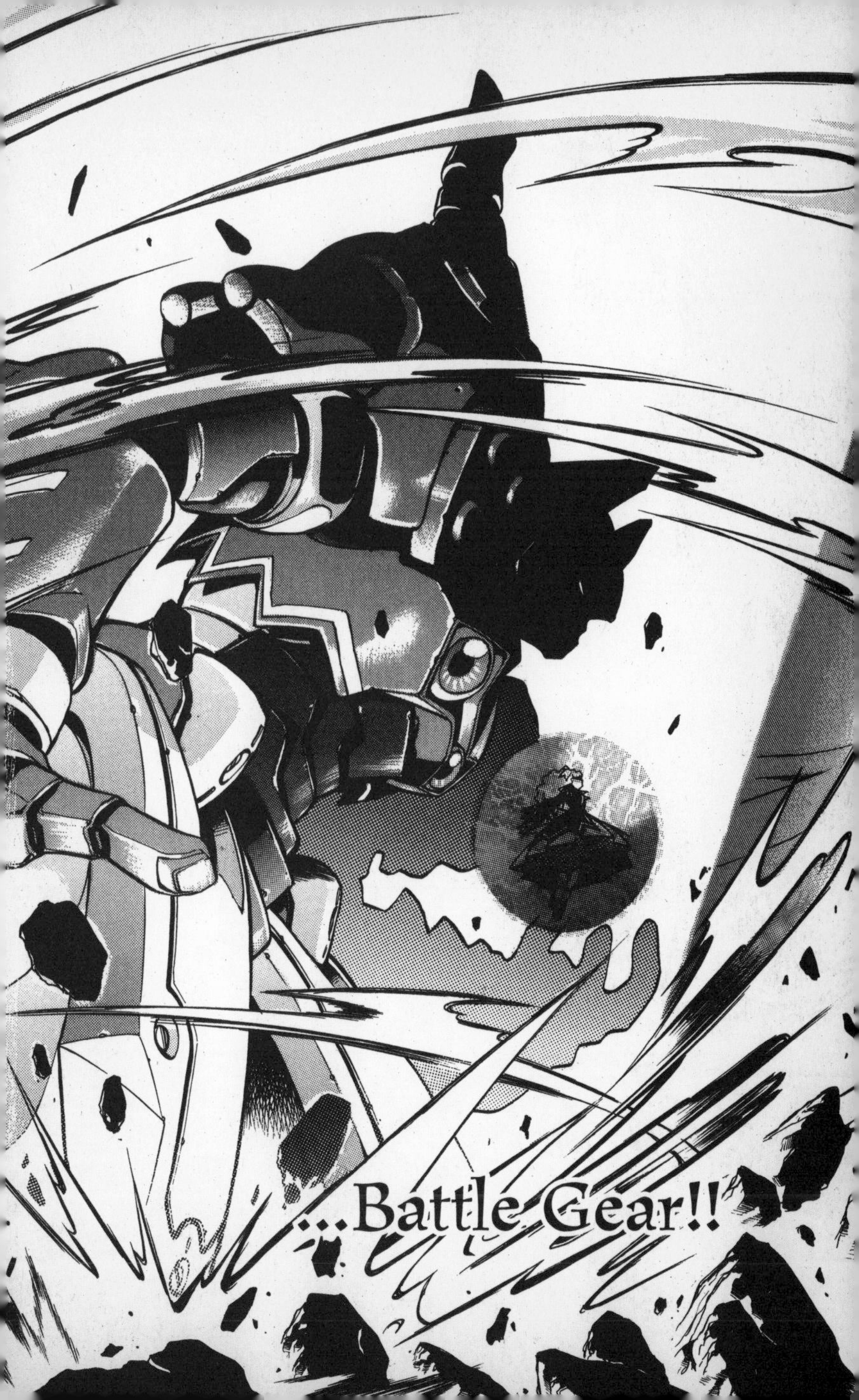
...Battle Gear!!

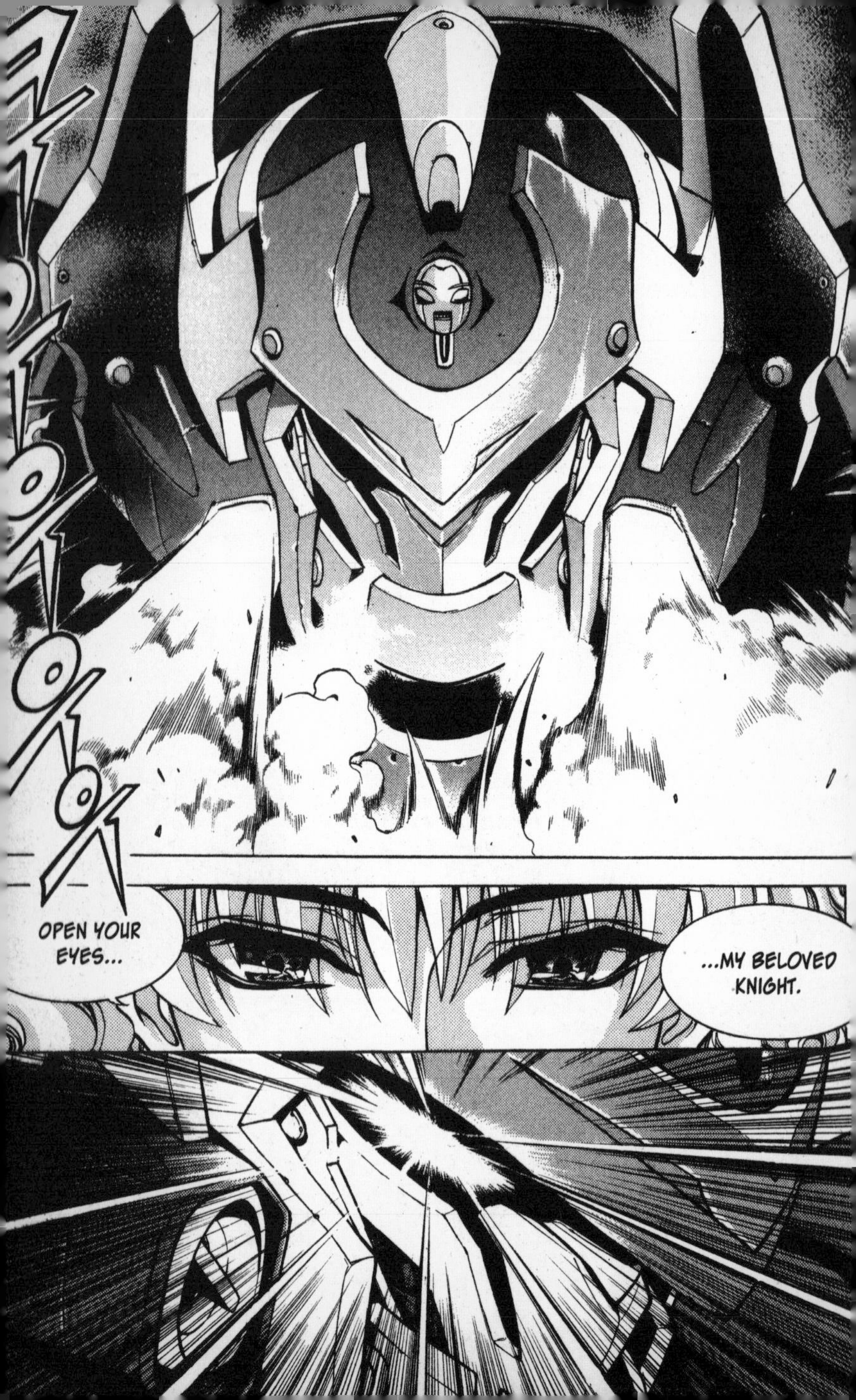
OPEN YOUR EYES...
...MY BELOVED KNIGHT.

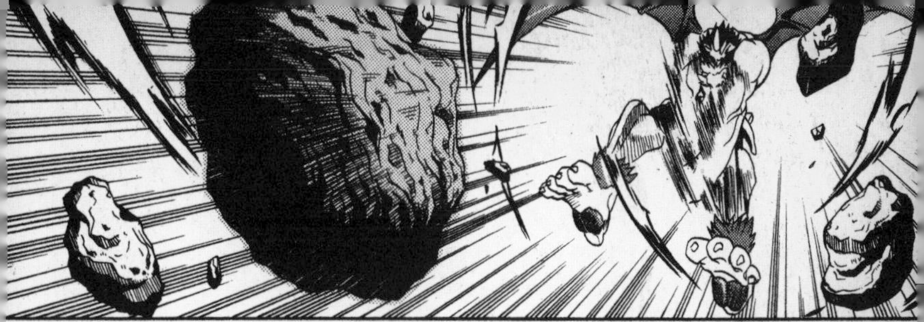

stage 8.

In Dream World

Rosemary 3

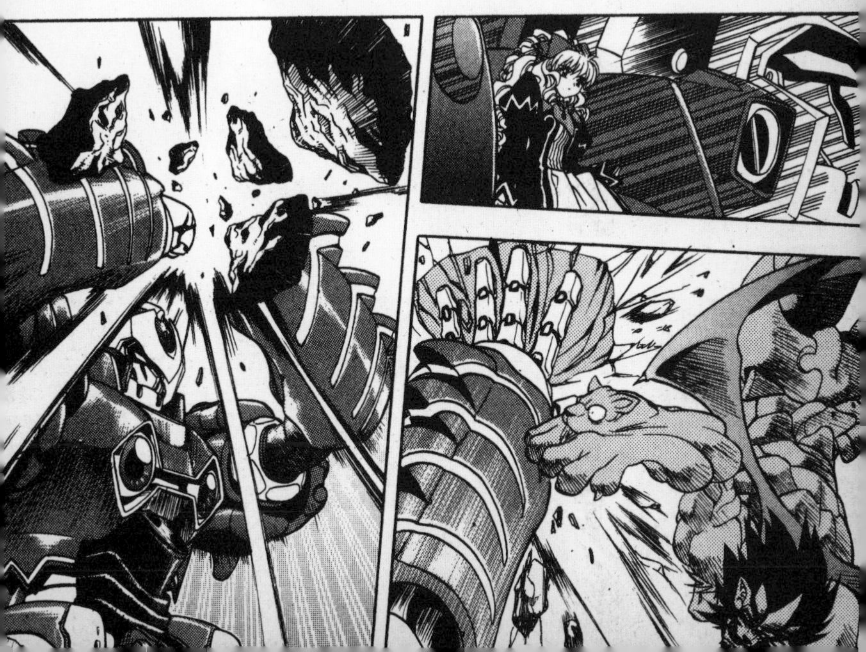

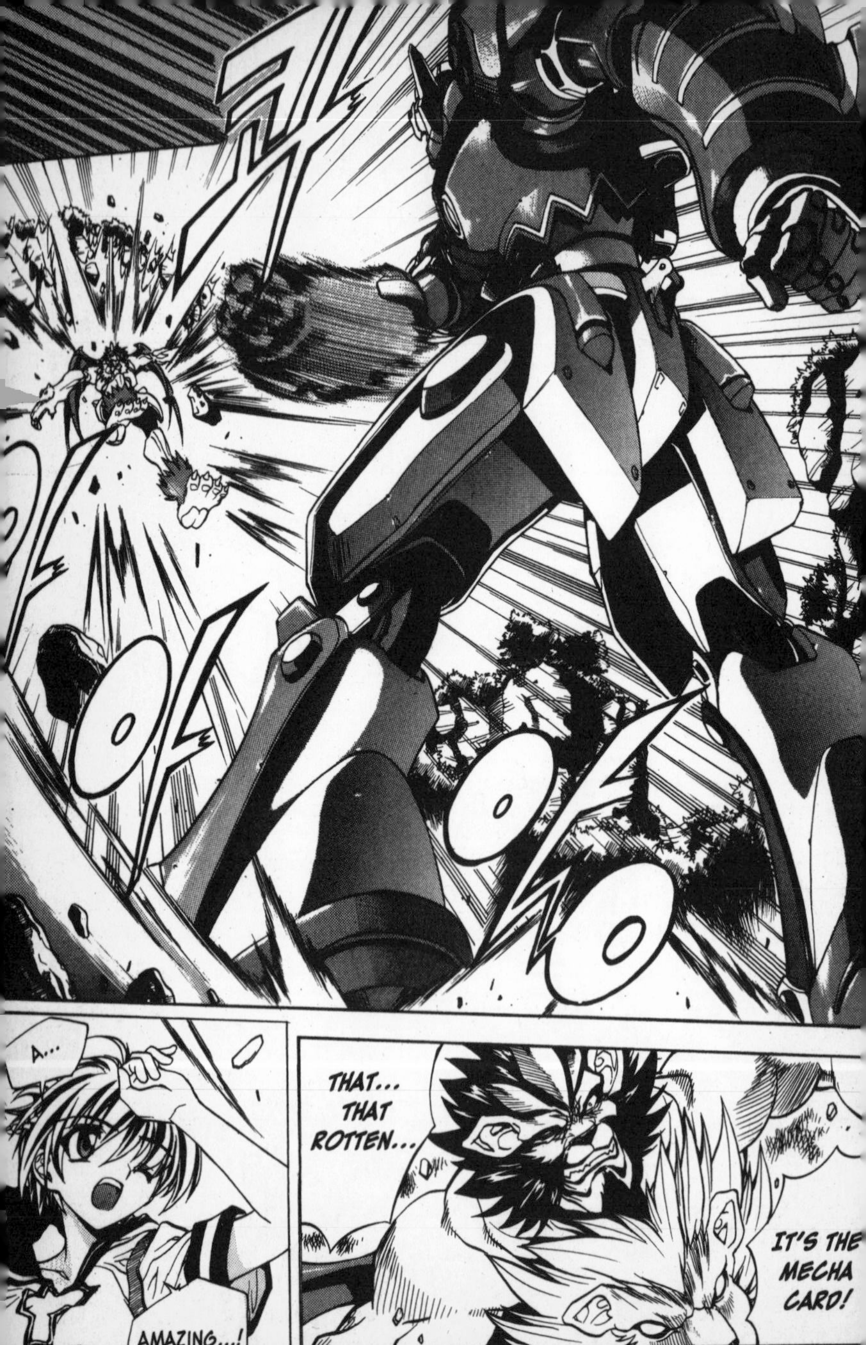
A...
AMAZING...!
THAT... THAT ROTTEN...
IT'S THE MECHA CARD!

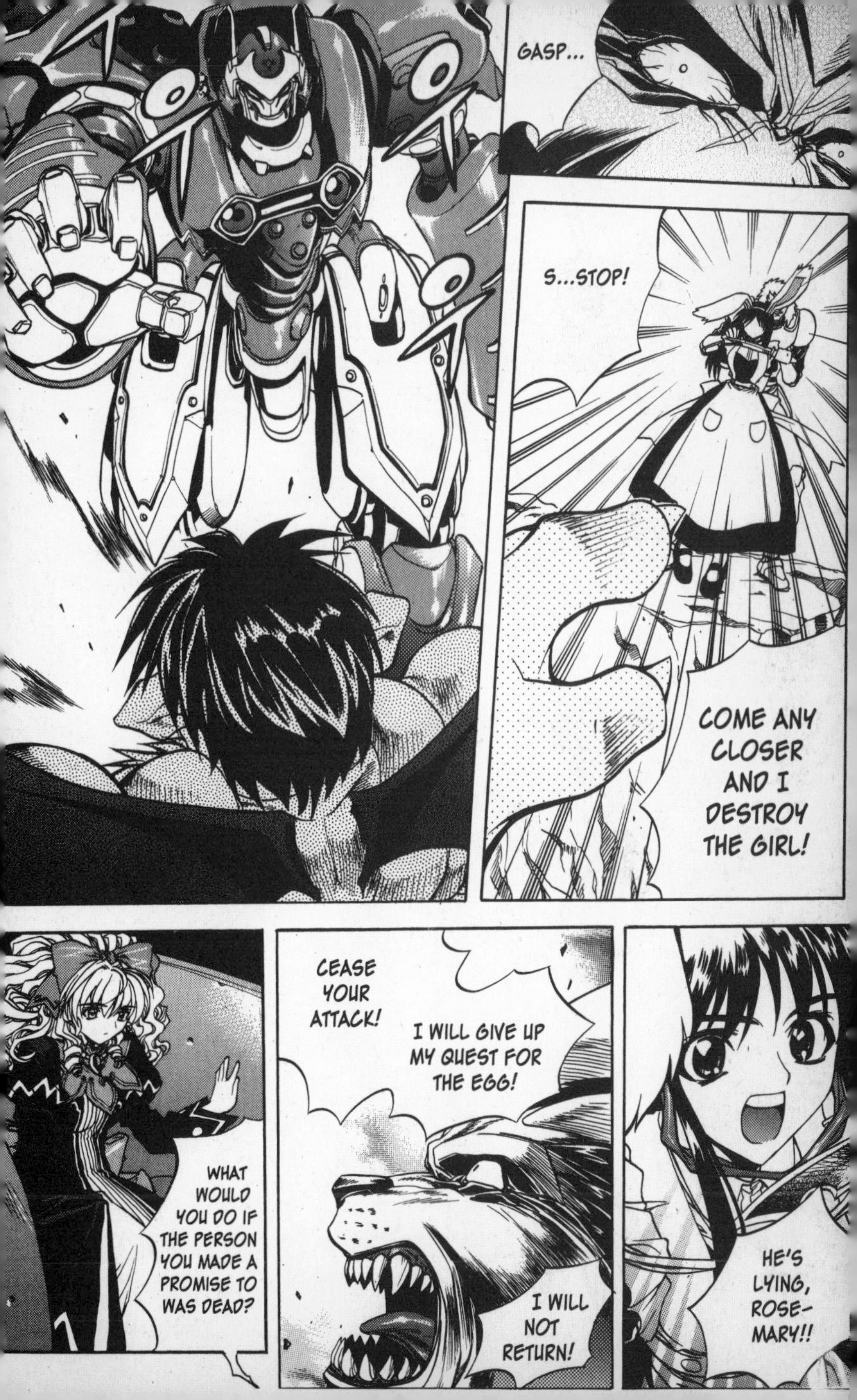
GASP...
S...STOP!
COME ANY CLOSER AND I DESTROY THE GIRL!
WHAT WOULD YOU DO IF THE PERSON YOU MADE A PROMISE TO WAS DEAD?
CEASE YOUR ATTACK!
I WILL GIVE UP MY QUEST FOR THE EGG!
I WILL NOT RETURN!
HE'S LYING, ROSE-MARY!!

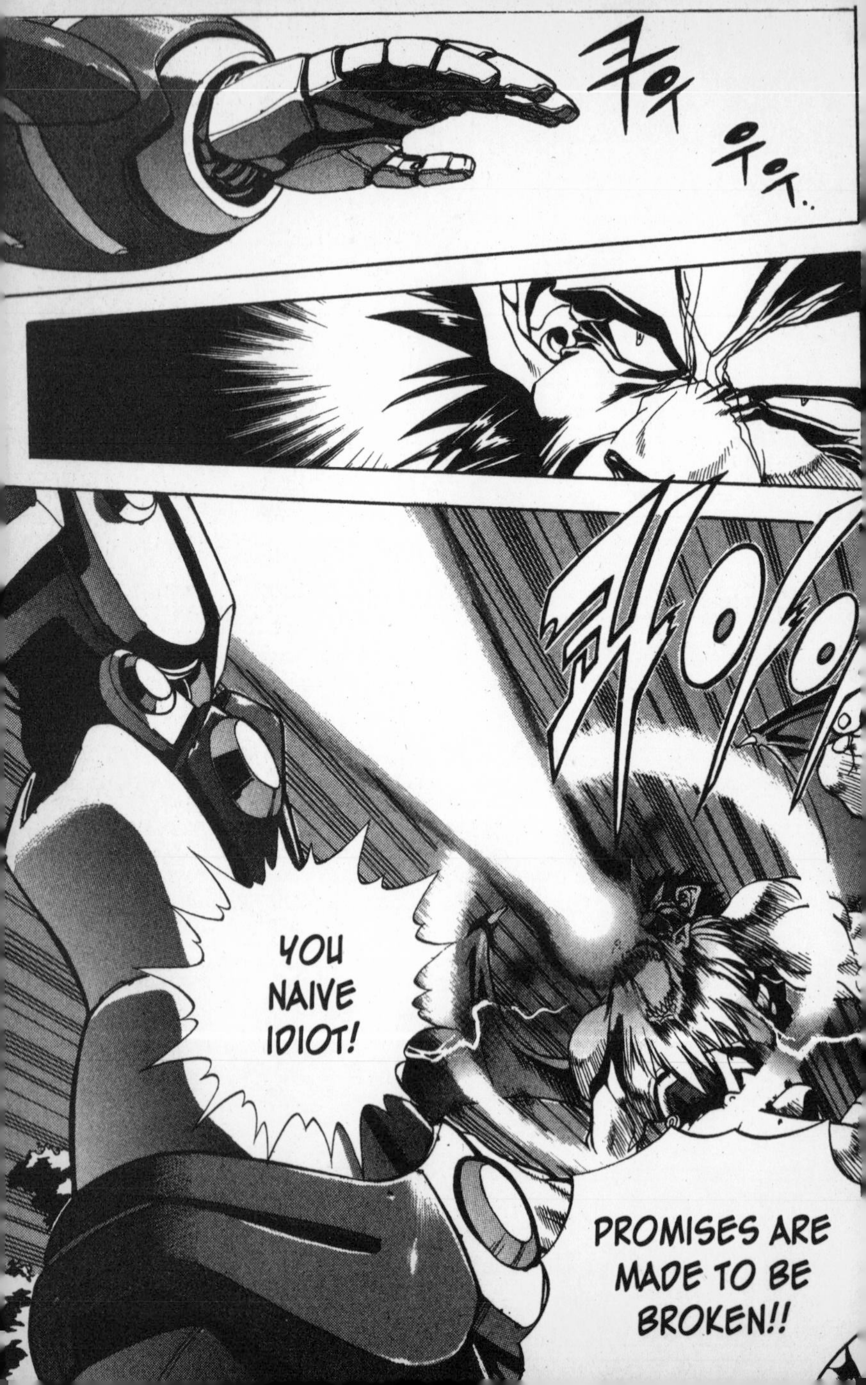
쿠우 우우..
콰아아
YOU NAIVE IDIOT!
PROMISES ARE MADE TO BE BROKEN!!

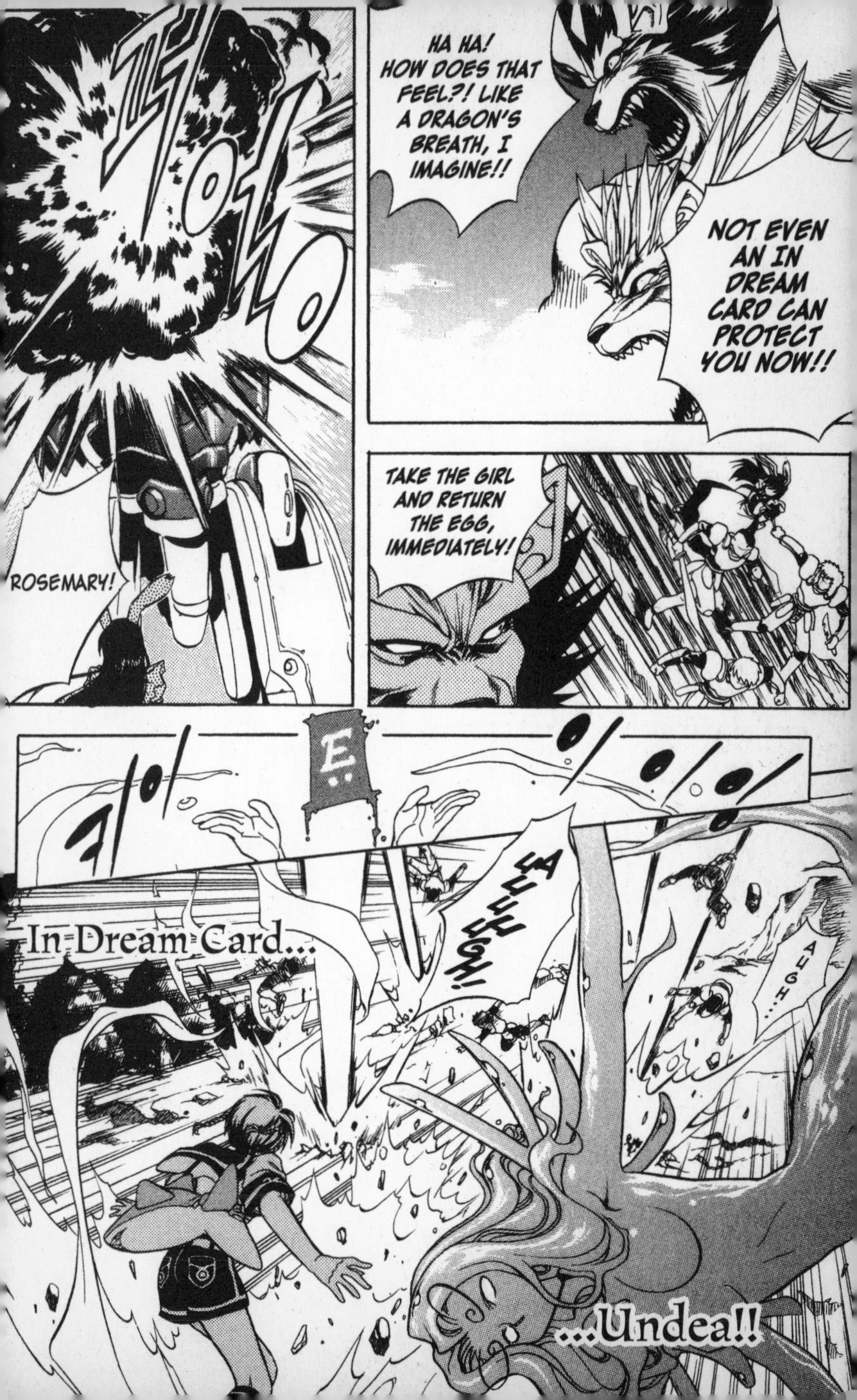
ROSEMARY!
HA HA! HOW DOES THAT FEEL?! LIKE A DRAGON'S BREATH, I IMAGINE!!
NOT EVEN AN IN DREAM CARD CAN PROTECT YOU NOW!!
TAKE THE GIRL AND RETURN THE EGG, IMMEDIATELY!
E
In Dream Card...
WAUUUGH!!
AUGH...
...Undea!!

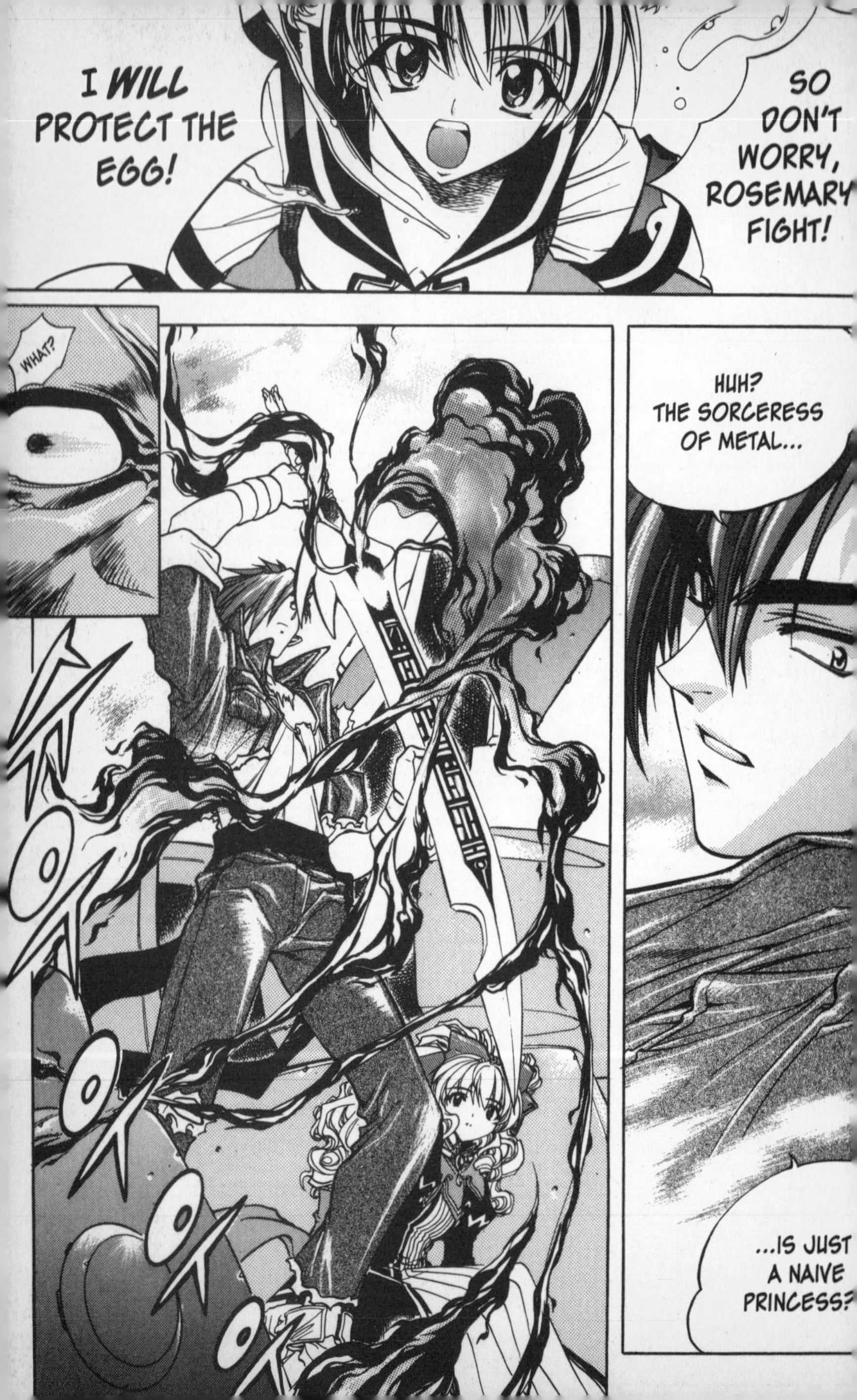
I WILL PROTECT THE EGG!
SO DON'T WORRY, ROSEMARY FIGHT!
WHAT?
HUH? THE SORCERESS OF METAL...
...IS JUST A NAIVE PRINCESS?

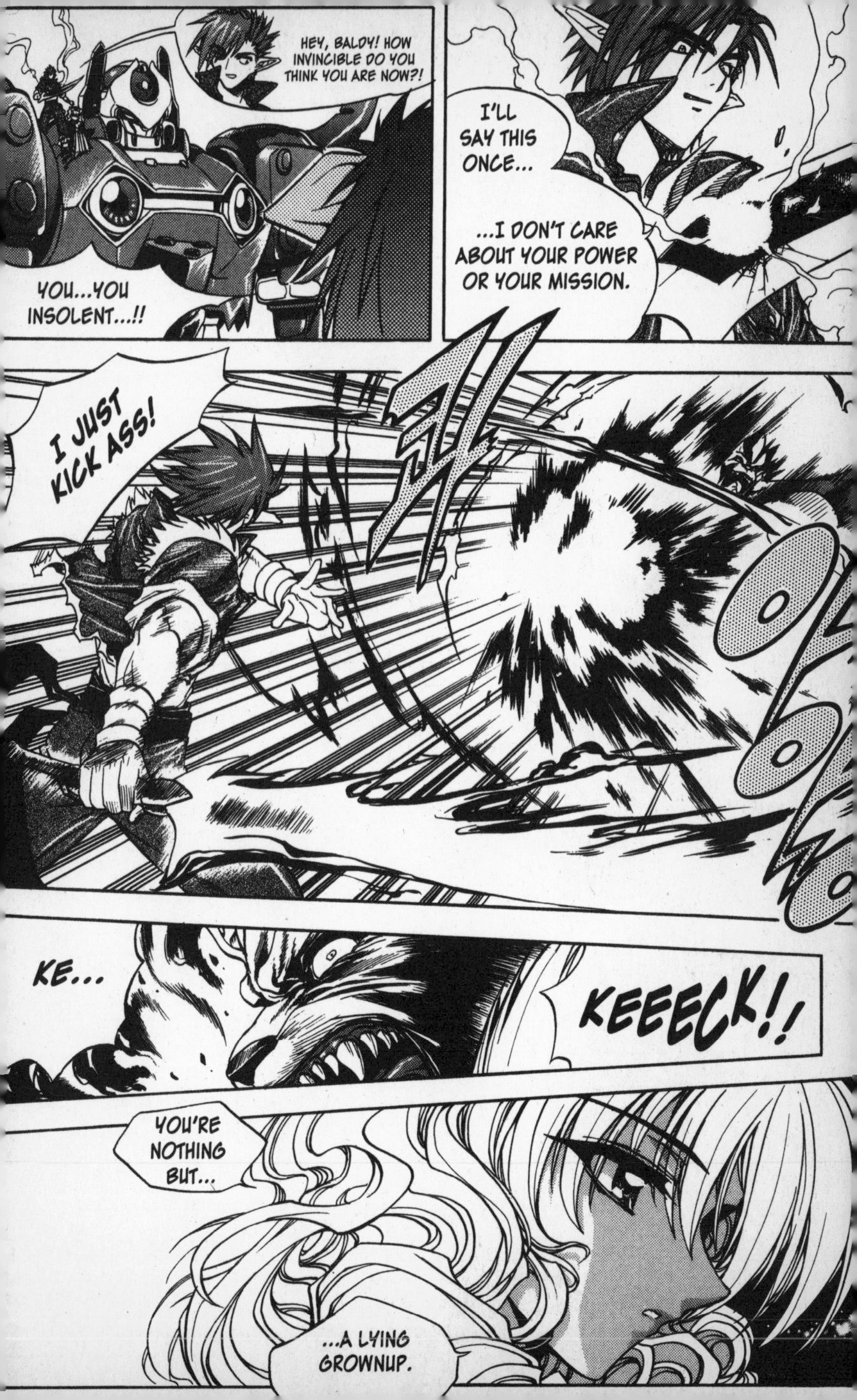
HEY, BALDY! HOW INVINCIBLE DO YOU THINK YOU ARE NOW?!
YOU...YOU INSOLENT...!!
I'LL SAY THIS ONCE...
...I DON'T CARE ABOUT YOUR POWER OR YOUR MISSION.
I JUST KICK ASS!
KE...
KEEECK!!
YOU'RE NOTHING BUT...
...A LYING GROWNUP.

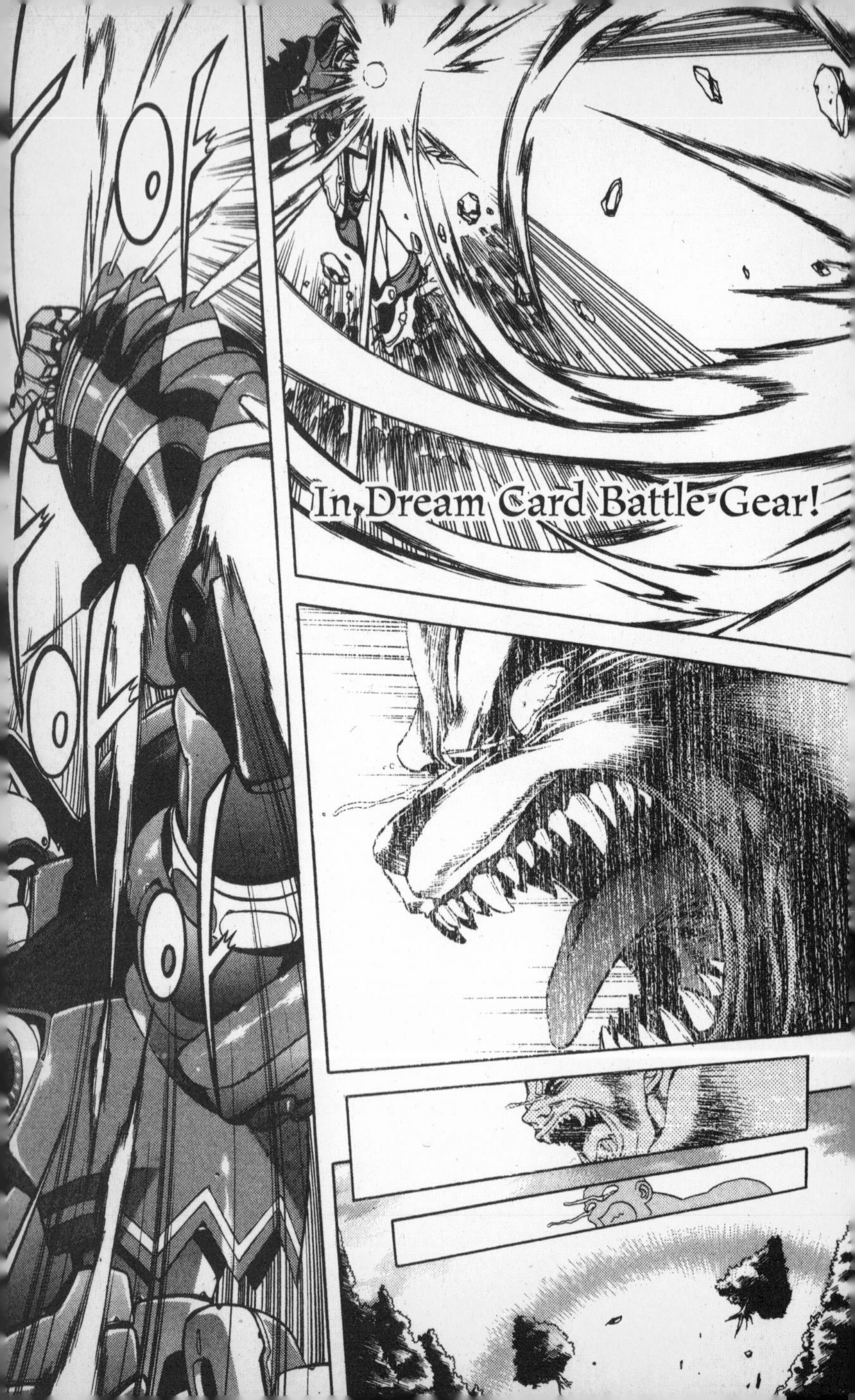
In Dream Card Battle Gear!

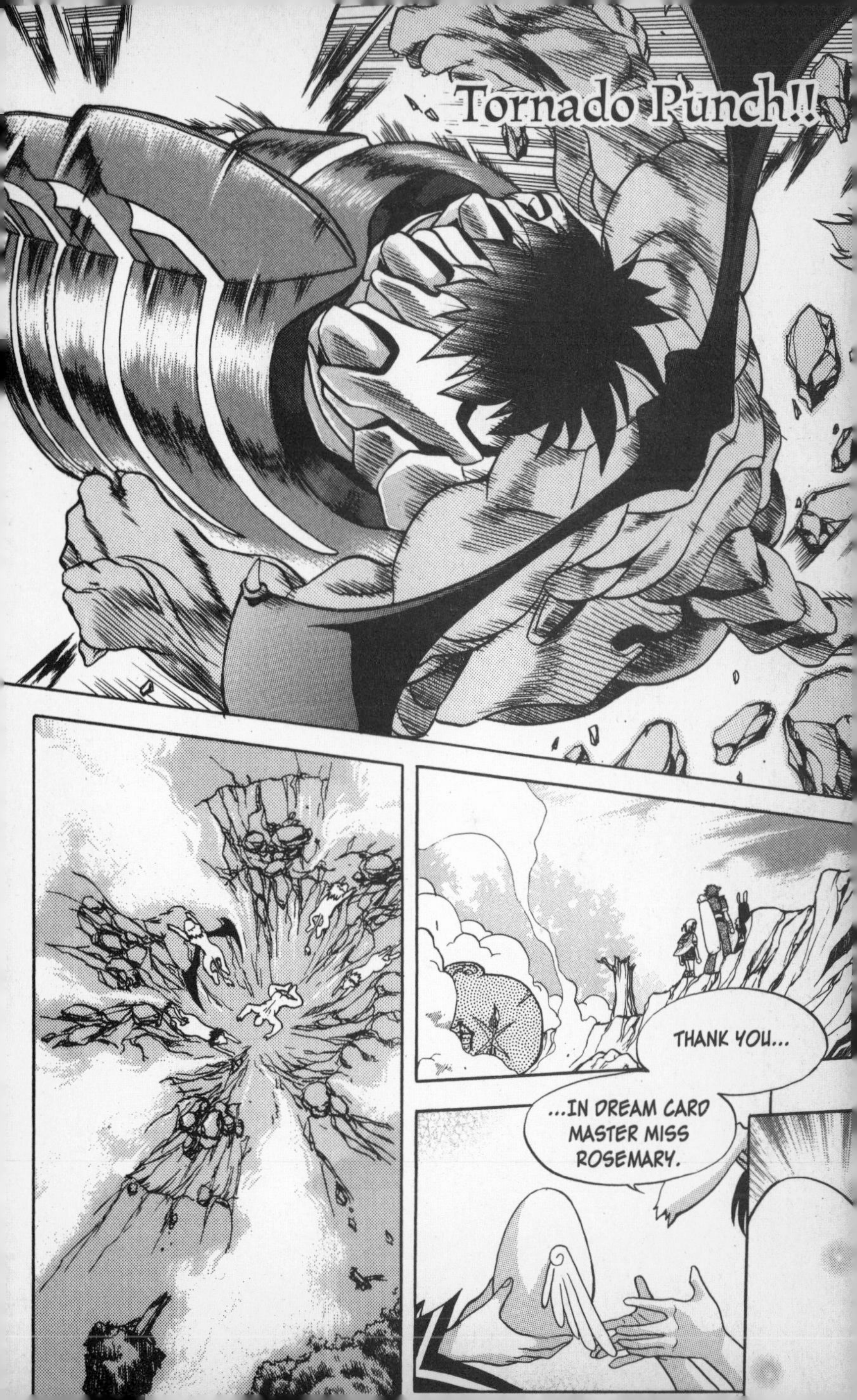
Tornado Punch!!
THANK YOU...
...IN DREAM CARD MASTER MISS ROSEMARY.

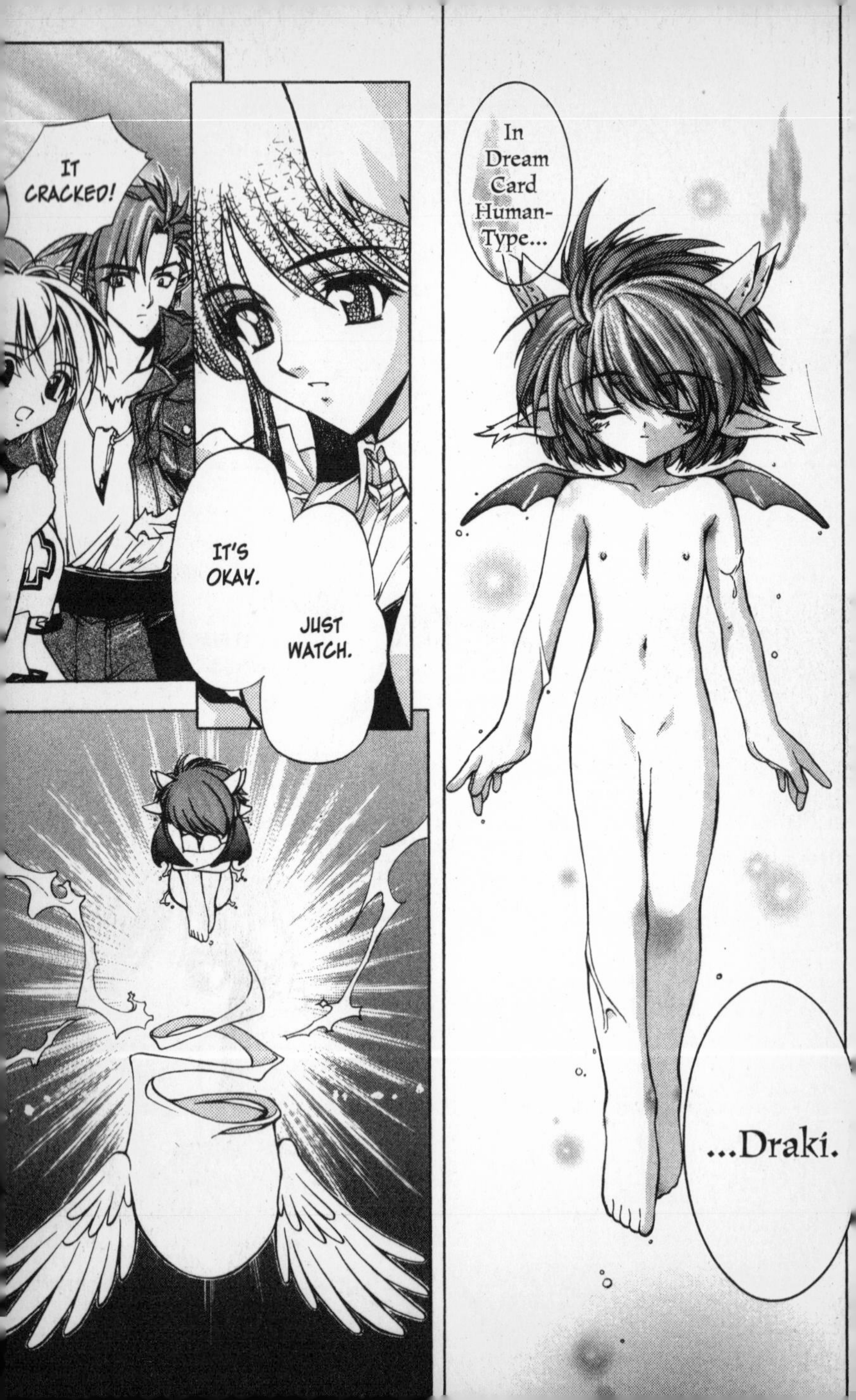
IT CRACKED!
IT'S OKAY. JUST WATCH.
In Dream Card Human-Type...
...Draki.

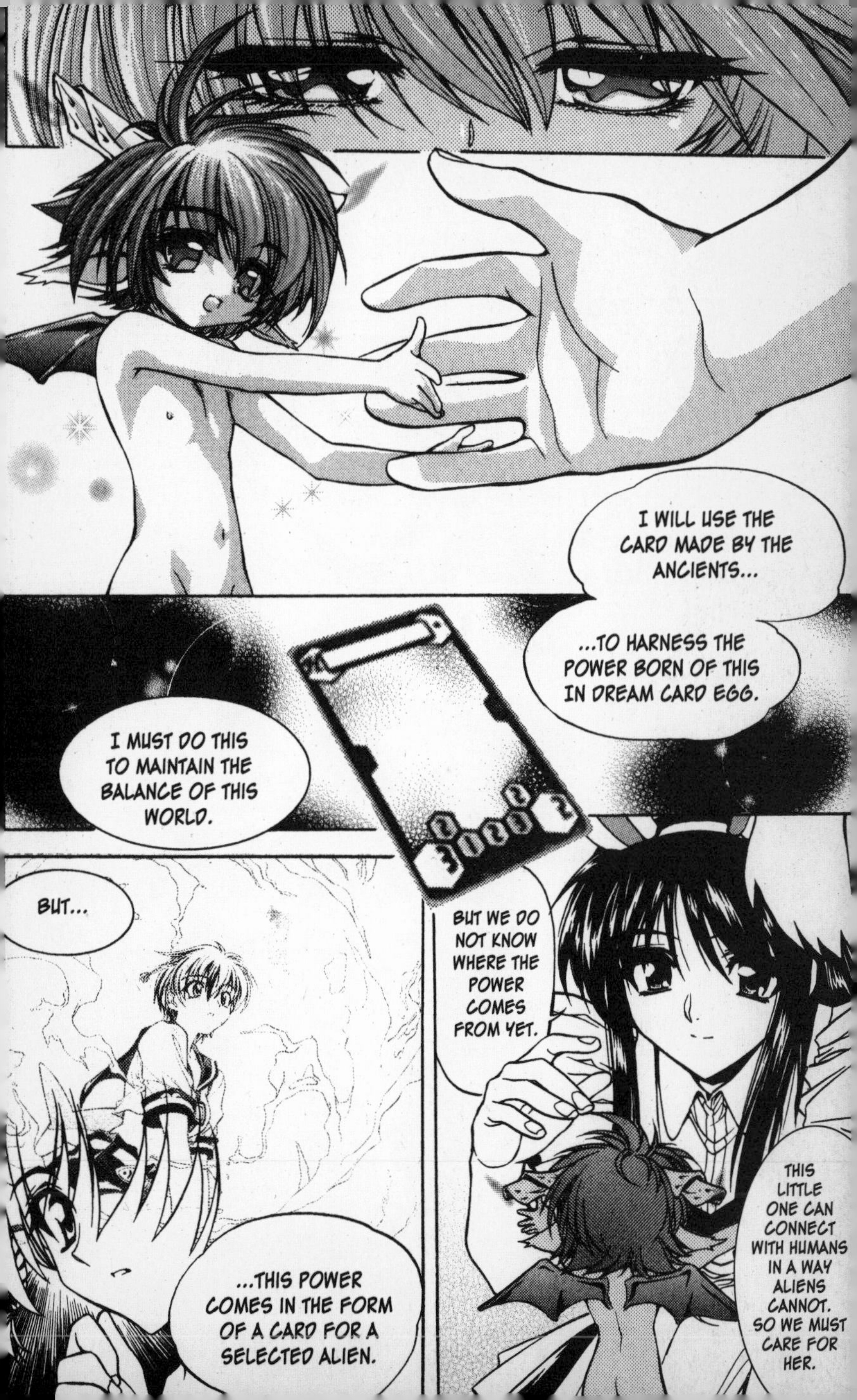
I WILL USE THE CARD MADE BY THE ANCIENTS...
...TO HARNESS THE POWER BORN OF THIS IN DREAM CARD EGG.
I MUST DO THIS TO MAINTAIN THE BALANCE OF THIS WORLD.
BUT...
...THIS POWER COMES IN THE FORM OF A CARD FOR A SELECTED ALIEN.
BUT WE DO NOT KNOW WHERE THE POWER COMES FROM YET.
THIS LITTLE ONE CAN CONNECT WITH HUMANS IN A WAY ALIENS CANNOT. SO WE MUST CARE FOR HER.

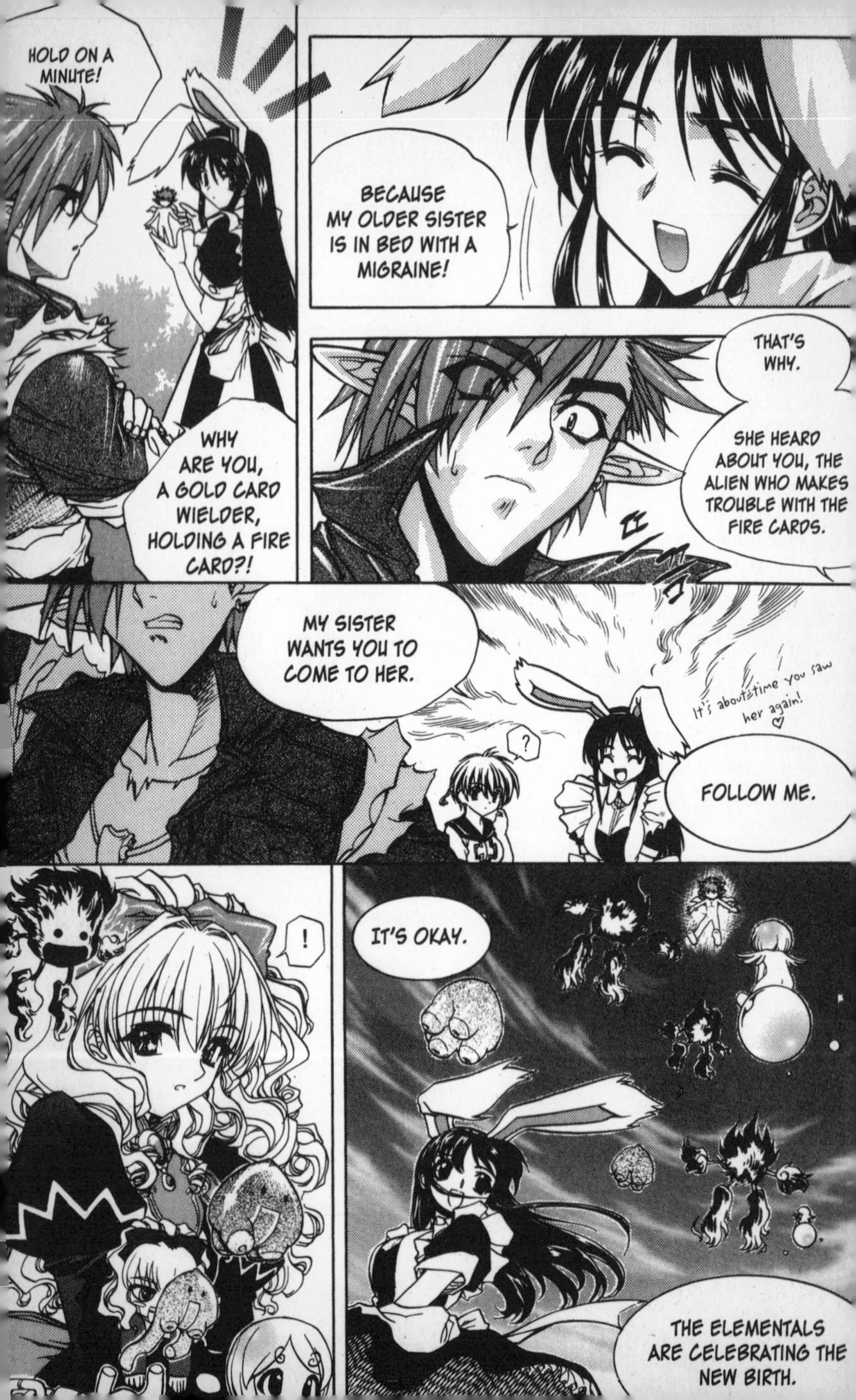
HOLD ON A MINUTE!
WHY ARE YOU, A GOLD CARD WIELDER, HOLDING A FIRE CARD?!
BECAUSE MY OLDER SISTER IS IN BED WITH A MIGRAINE!
THAT'S WHY.
SHE HEARD ABOUT YOU, THE ALIEN WHO MAKES TROUBLE WITH THE FIRE CARDS.
MY SISTER WANTS YOU TO COME TO HER.
?
It's about time you saw her again! ♥
FOLLOW ME.
!
IT'S OKAY.
THE ELEMENTALS ARE CELEBRATING THE NEW BIRTH.

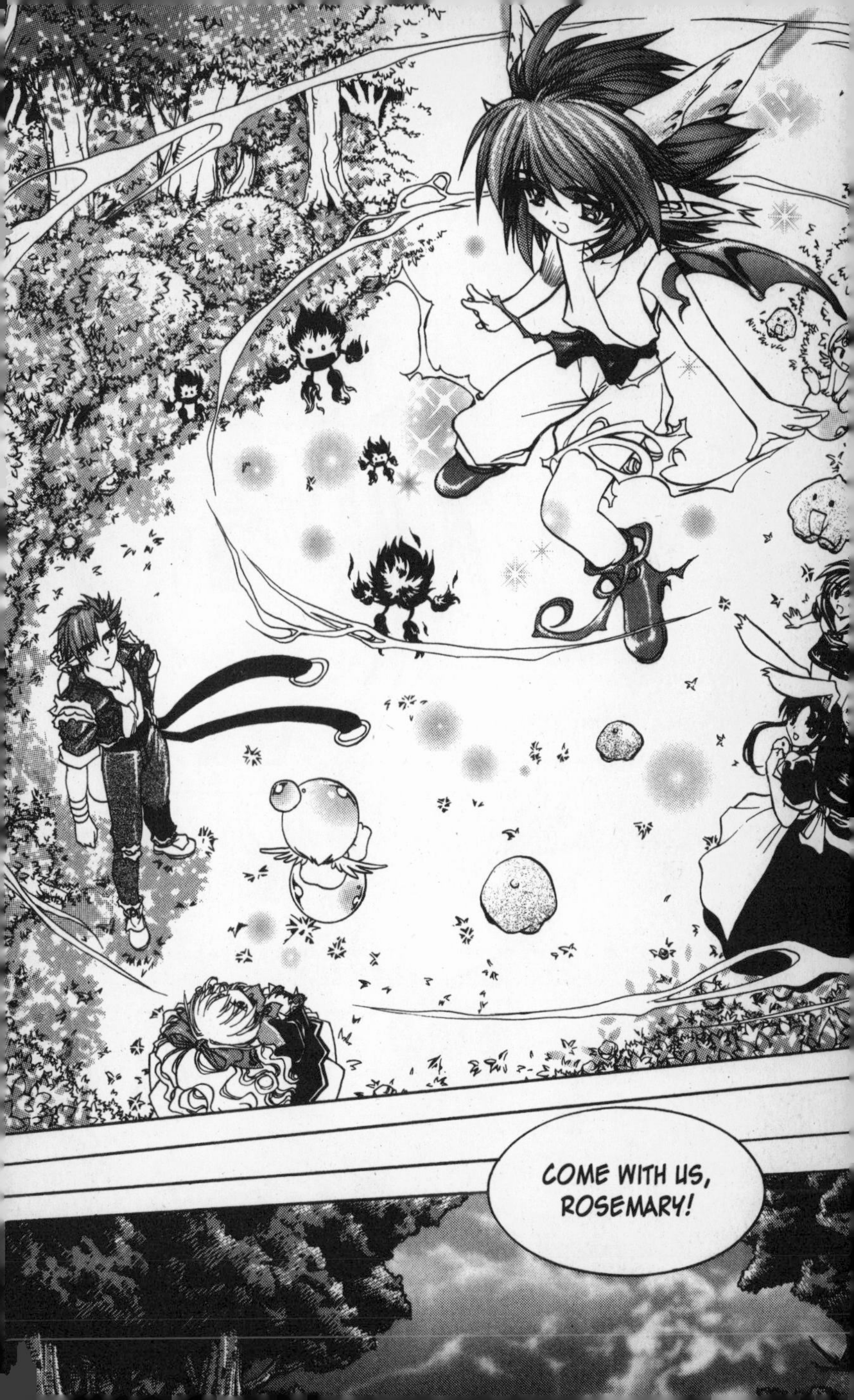
COME WITH US, ROSEMARY!

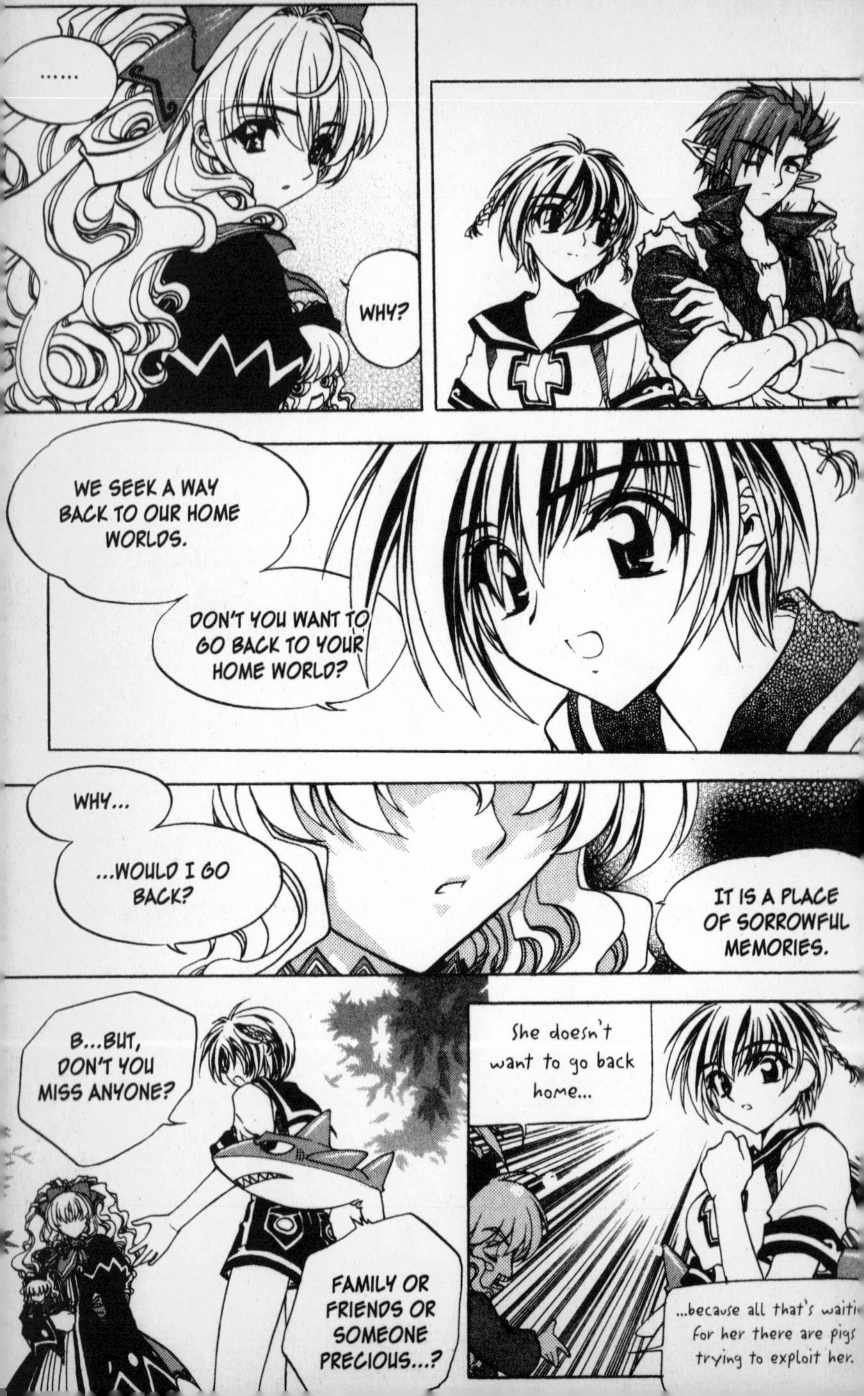
......
WHY?
WE SEEK A WAY BACK TO OUR HOME WORLDS.
DON'T YOU WANT TO GO BACK TO YOUR HOME WORLD?
WHY...
...WOULD I GO BACK?
IT IS A PLACE OF SORROWFUL MEMORIES.
B...BUT, DON'T YOU MISS ANYONE?
FAMILY OR FRIENDS OR SOMEONE PRECIOUS...?
She doesn't want to go back home...
...because all that's waiti for her there are pigs trying to exploit her.

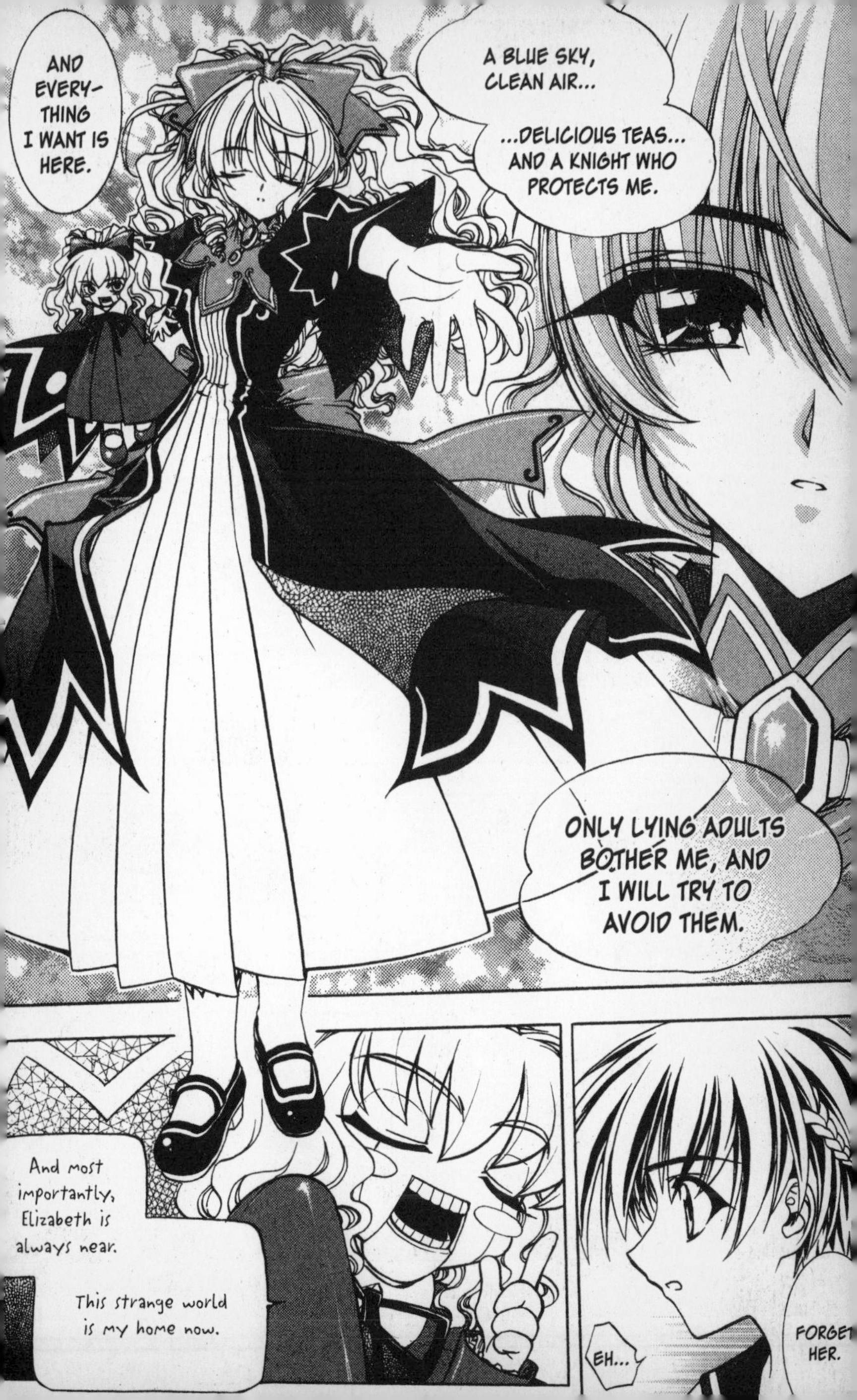
AND EVERY-THING I WANT IS HERE.
A BLUE SKY, CLEAN AIR...
...DELICIOUS TEAS... AND A KNIGHT WHO PROTECTS ME.
ONLY LYING ADULTS BOTHER ME, AND I WILL TRY TO AVOID THEM.
And most importantly, Elizabeth is always near.
This strange world is my home now.
EH...
FORGET HER.

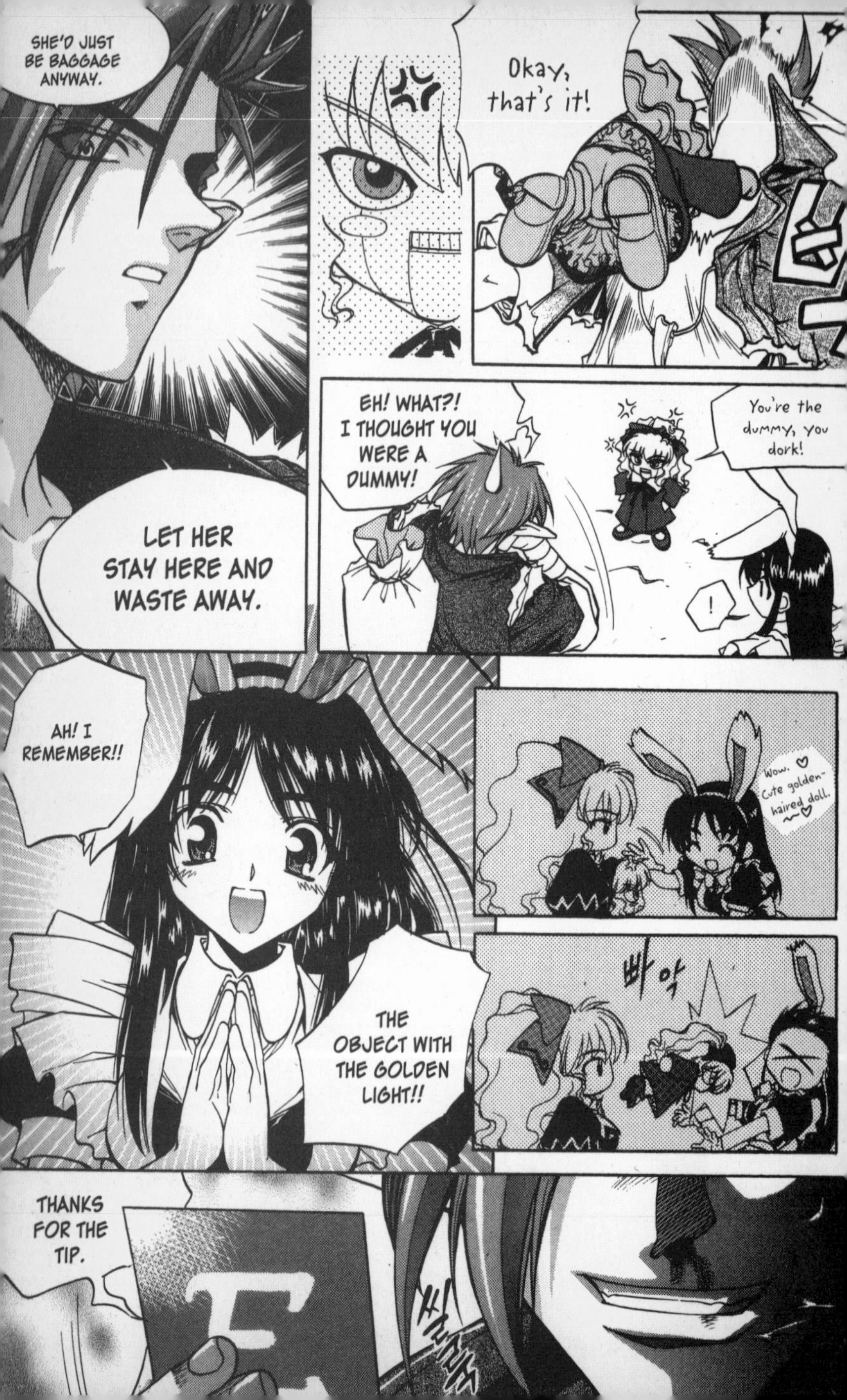
SHE'D JUST BE BAGGAGE ANYWAY.
LET HER STAY HERE AND WASTE AWAY.
Okay, that's it!
EH! WHAT?! I THOUGHT YOU WERE A DUMMY!
You're the dummy, you dork!
!
AH! I REMEMBER!!
THE OBJECT WITH THE GOLDEN LIGHT!!
Wow. ♡ Cute golden-haired doll. ~♡
빠악
THANKS FOR THE TIP.

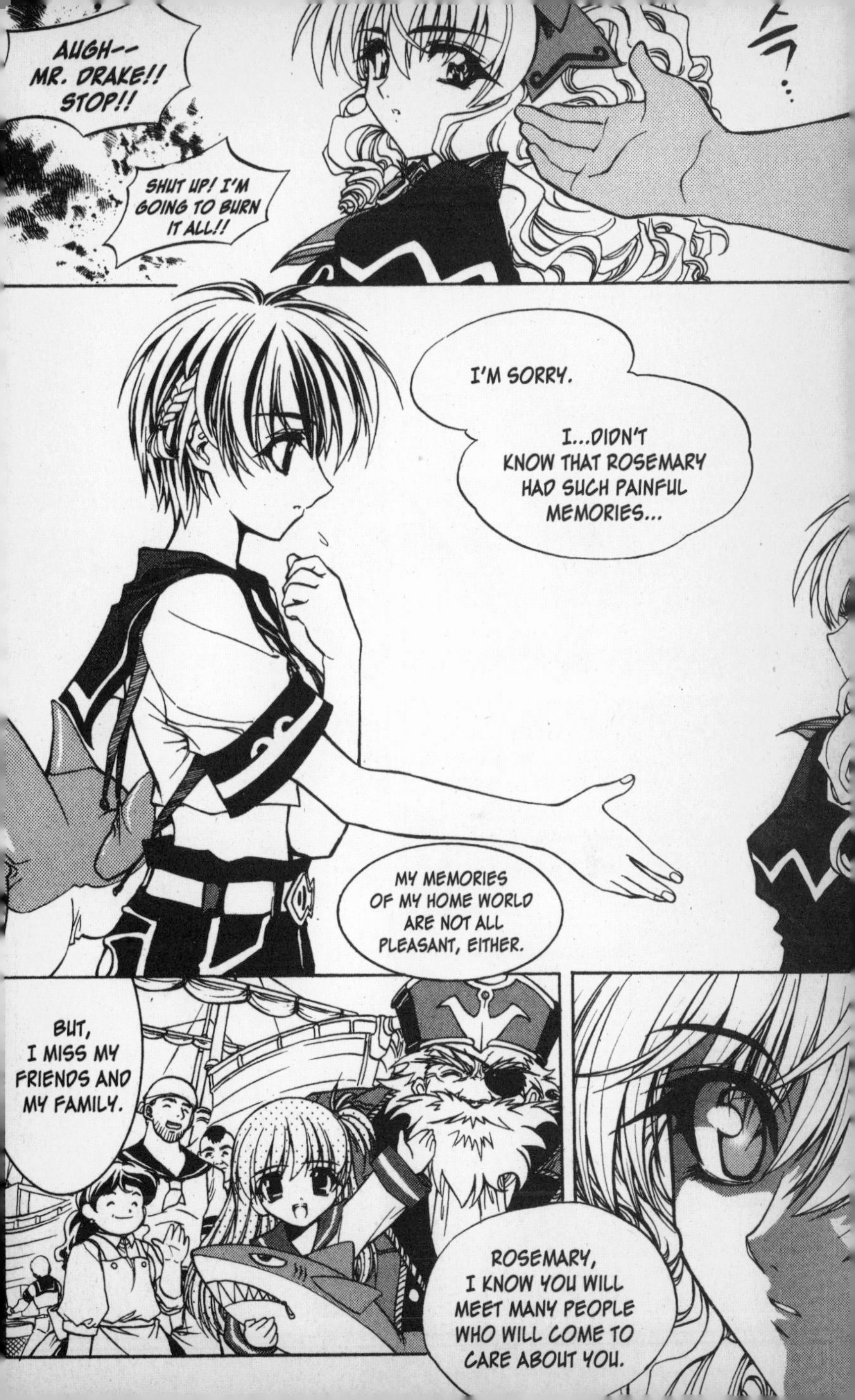
AUGH-- MR. DRAKE!! STOP!!
SHUT UP! I'M GOING TO BURN IT ALL!!
I'M SORRY.
I...DIDN'T KNOW THAT ROSEMARY HAD SUCH PAINFUL MEMORIES...
MY MEMORIES OF MY HOME WORLD ARE NOT ALL PLEASANT, EITHER.
BUT, I MISS MY FRIENDS AND MY FAMILY.
ROSEMARY, I KNOW YOU WILL MEET MANY PEOPLE WHO WILL COME TO CARE ABOUT YOU.

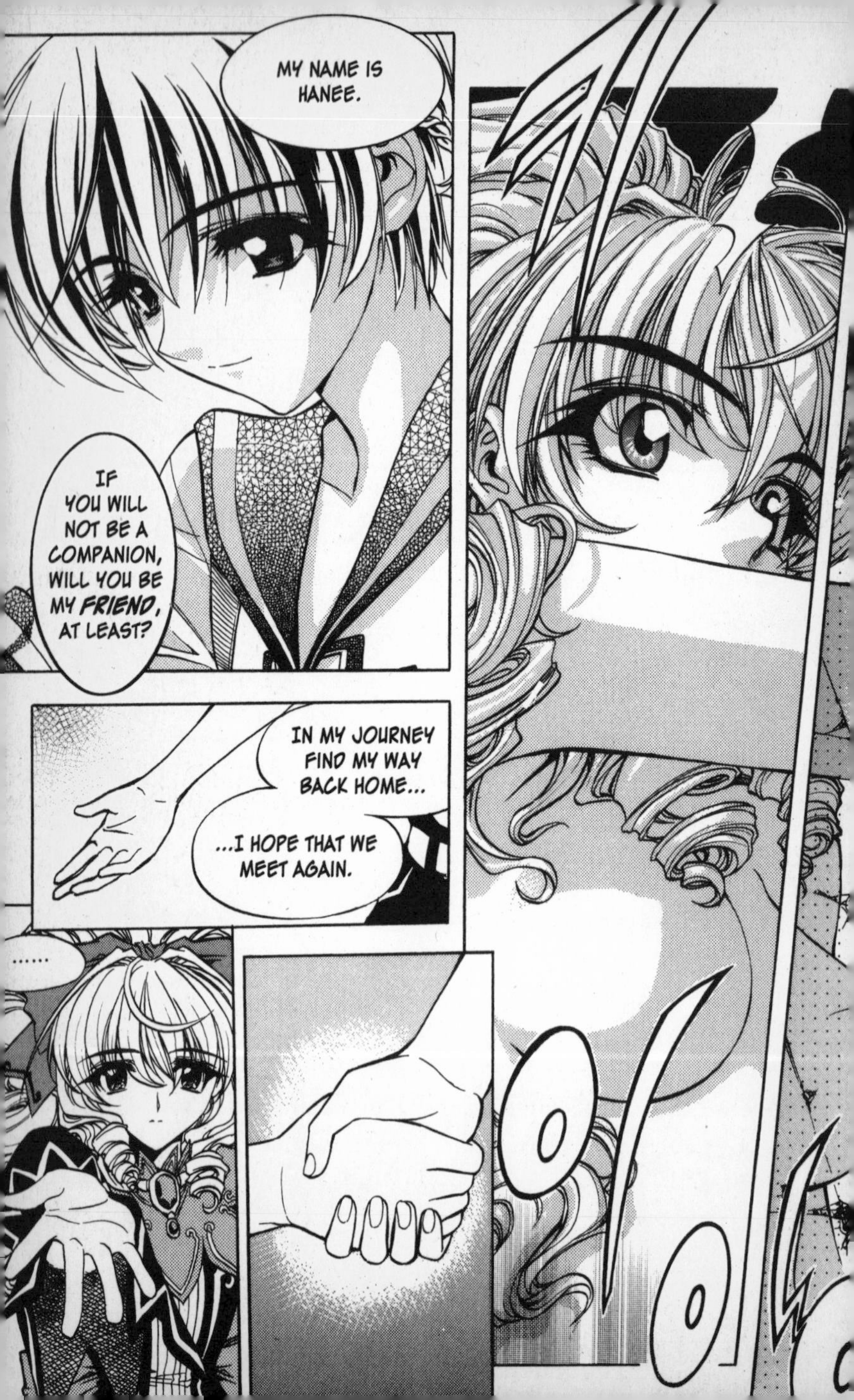
MY NAME IS HANEE.
IF YOU WILL NOT BE A COMPANION, WILL YOU BE MY *FRIEND*, AT LEAST?
IN MY JOURNEY FIND MY WAY BACK HOME...
...I HOPE THAT WE MEET AGAIN.
......

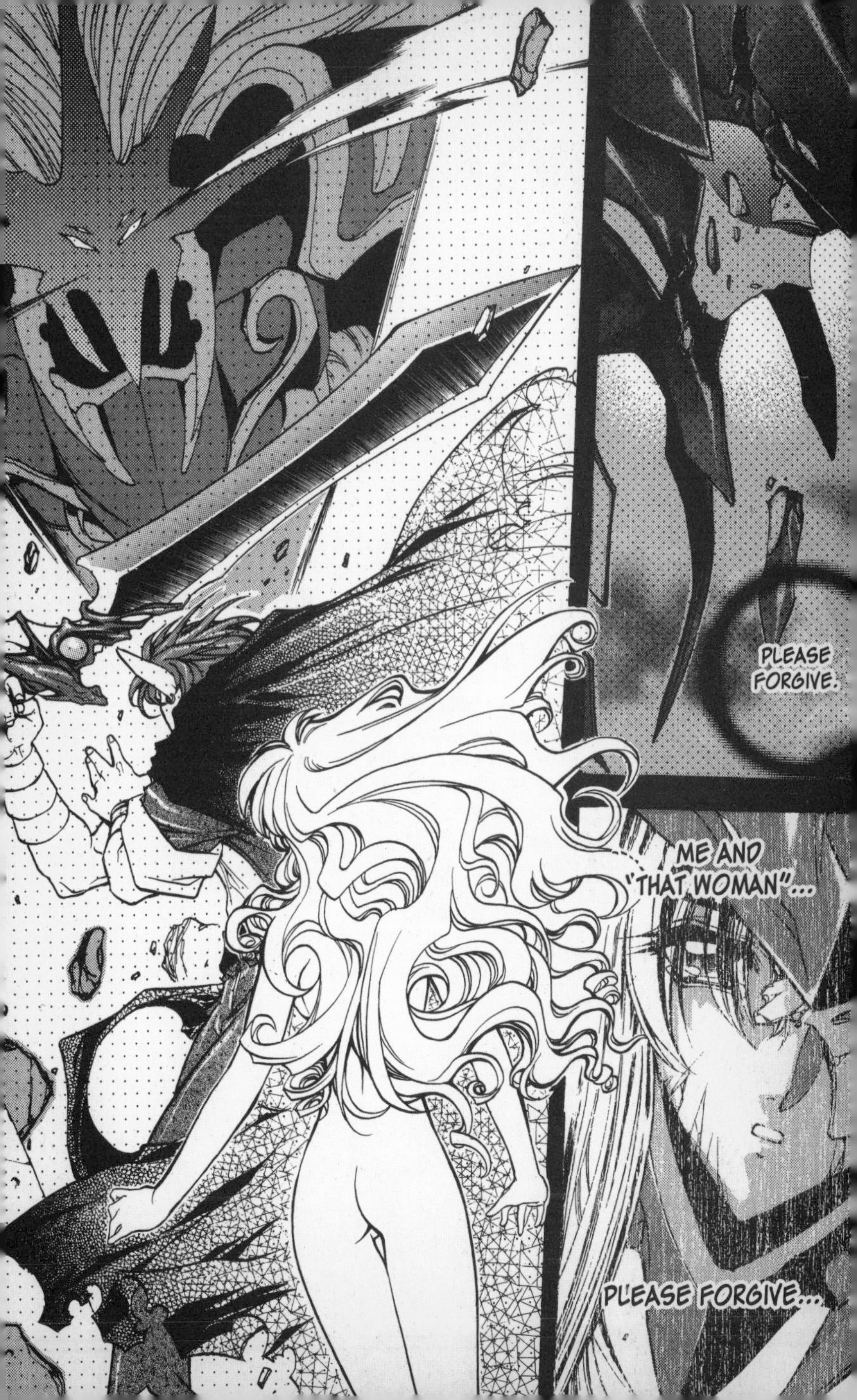
PLEASE FORGIVE.
ME AND "THAT WOMAN"...
PLEASE FORGIVE...

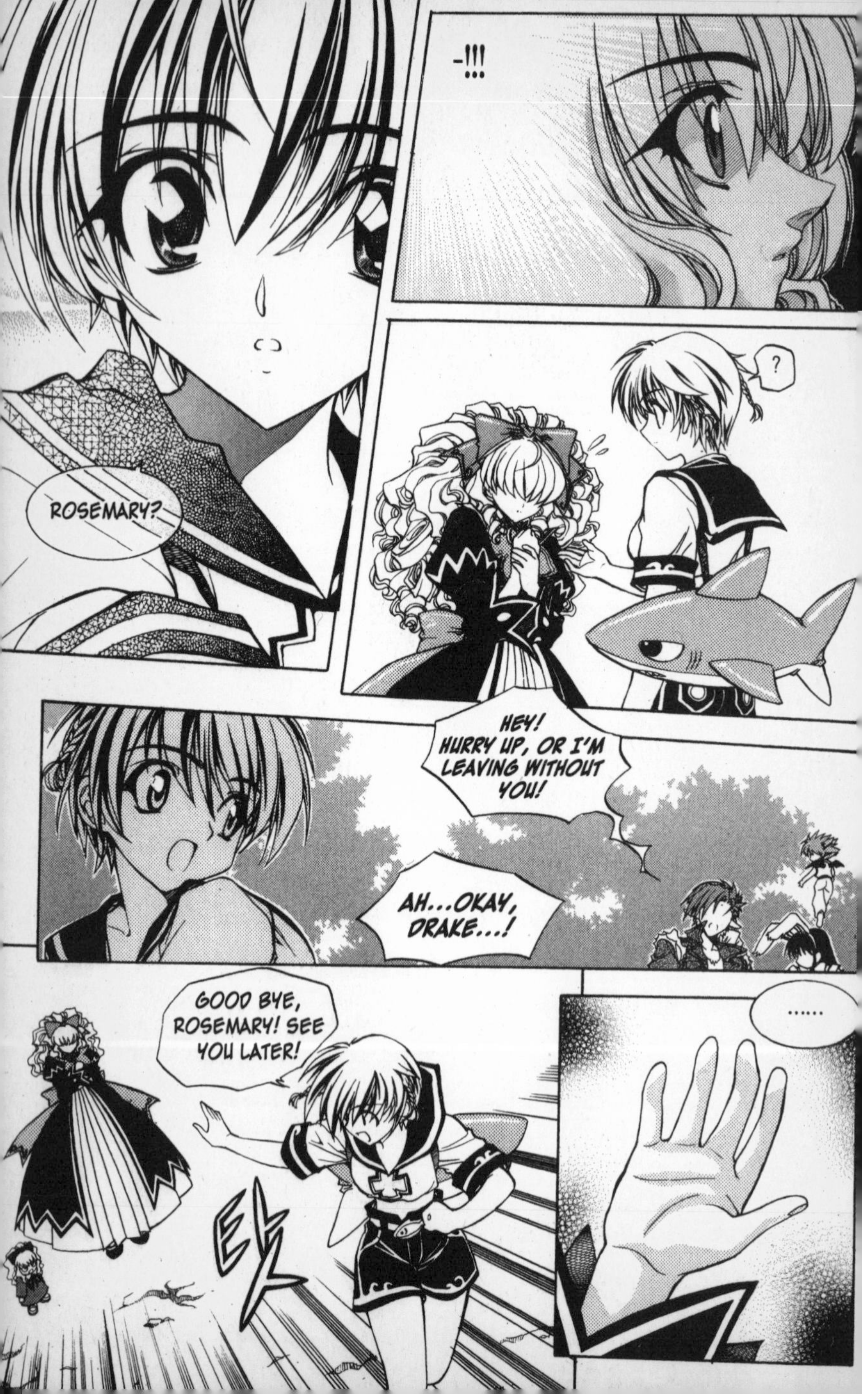
ROSEMARY?
-!!!
?
HEY! HURRY UP, OR I'M LEAVING WITHOUT YOU!
AH...OKAY, DRAKE...!
GOOD BYE, ROSEMARY! SEE YOU LATER!
EK
......

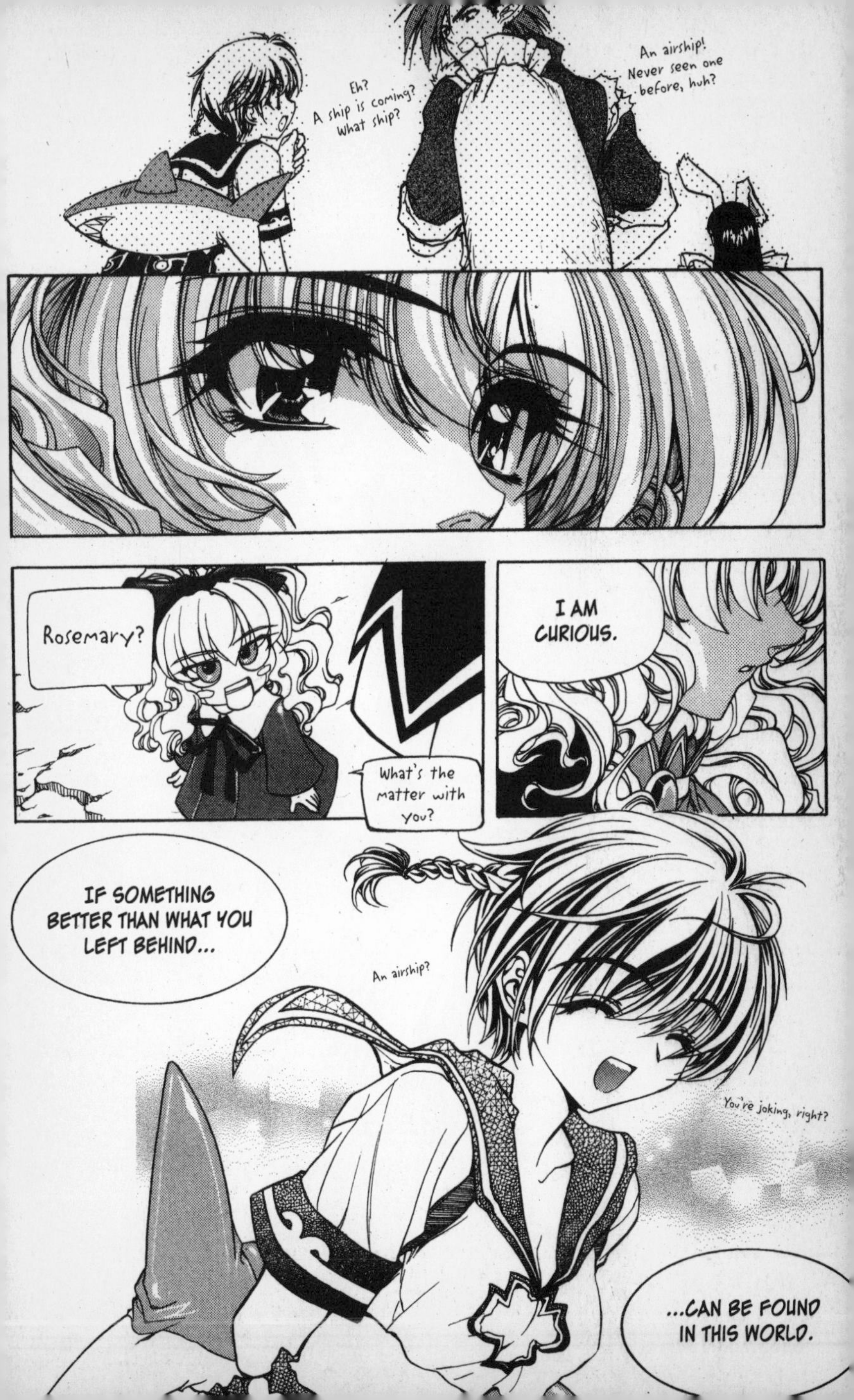
Eh?
A ship is coming?
What ship?
An airship!
Never seen one
before, huh?
Rosemary?
What's the matter with you?
I AM CURIOUS.
IF SOMETHING BETTER THAN WHAT YOU LEFT BEHIND...
An airship?
You're joking, right?
...CAN BE FOUND IN THIS WORLD.

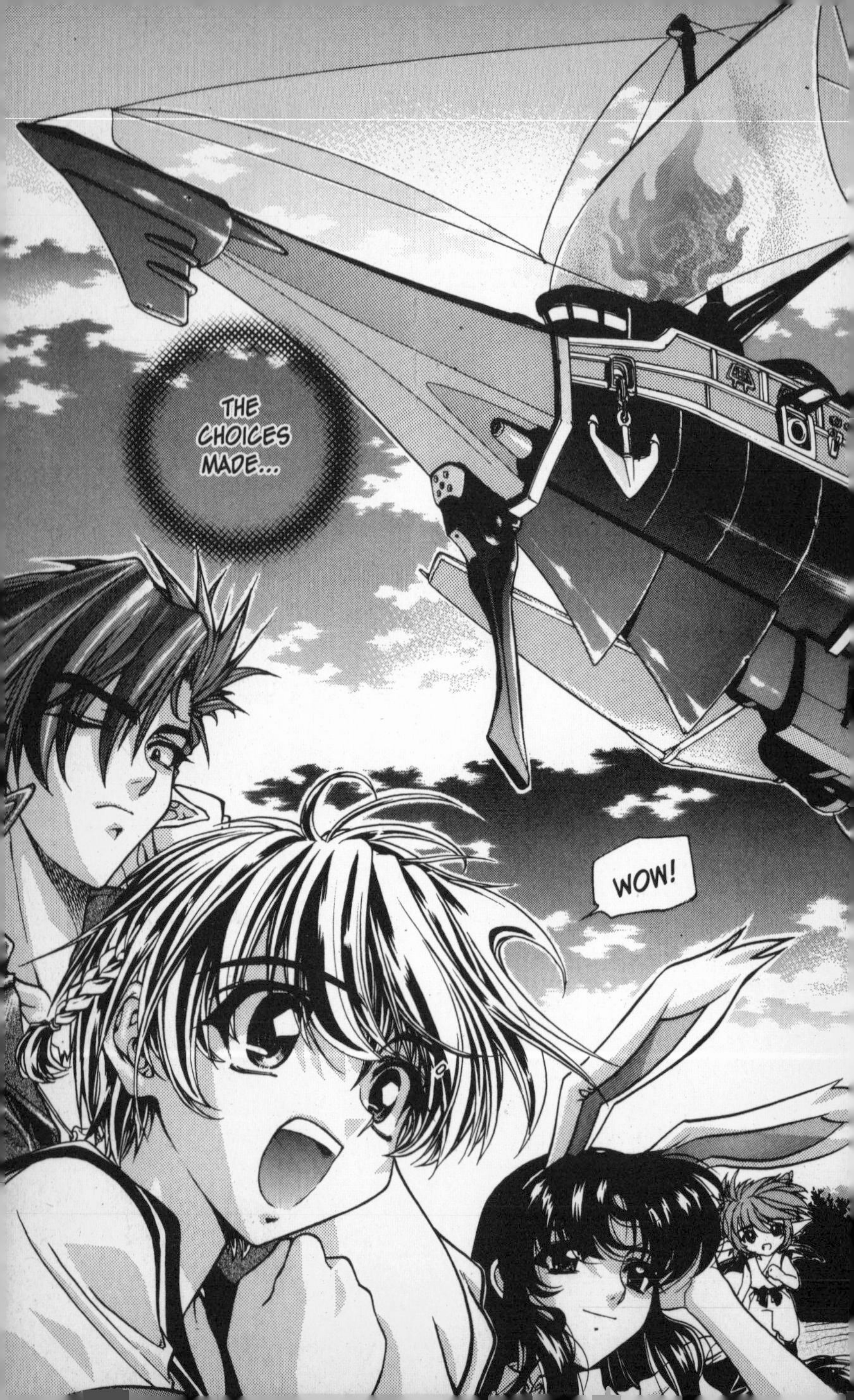
THE CHOICES MADE...
WOW!

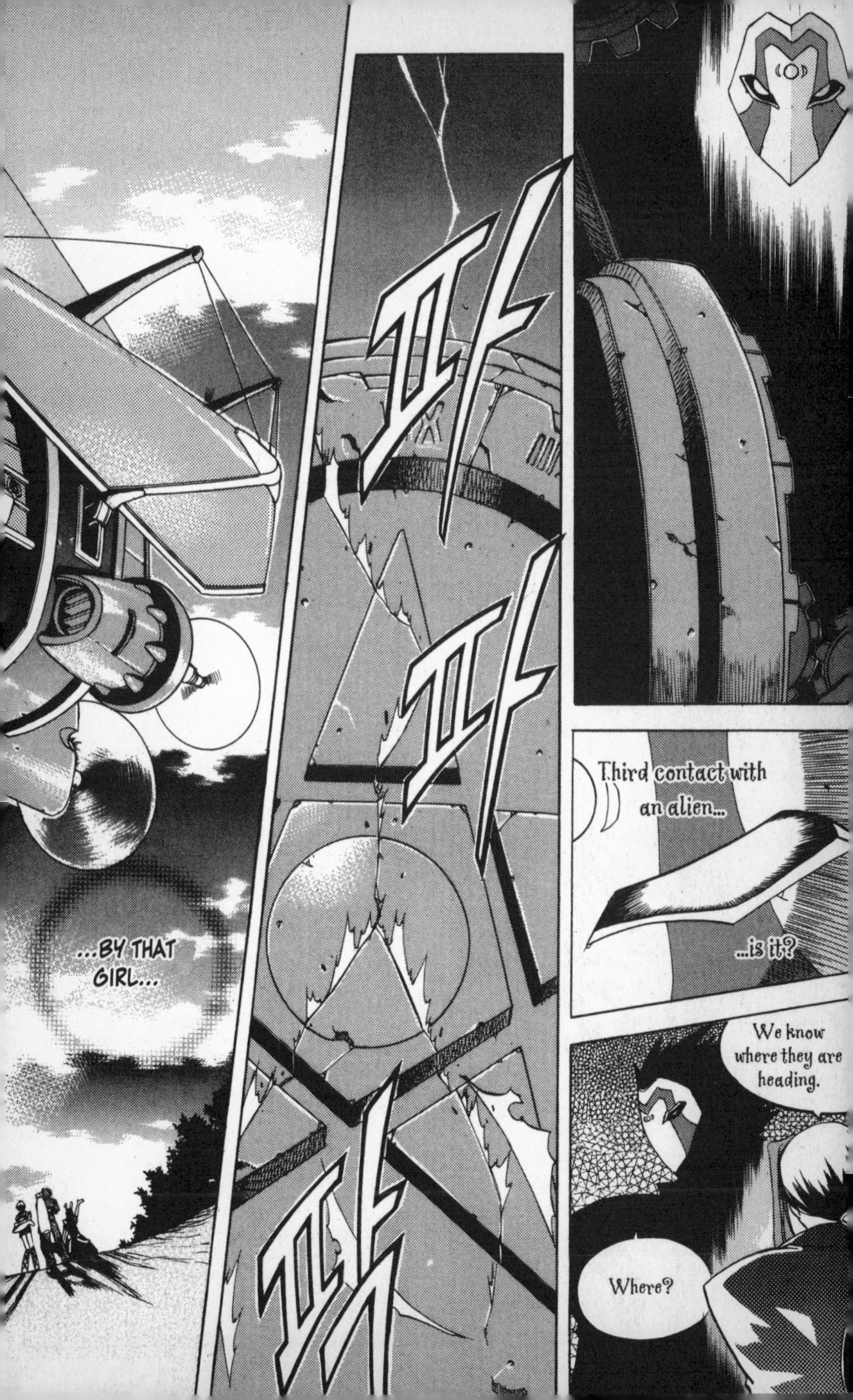
...BY THAT GIRL...
Third contact with an alien...
...is it?
We know where they are heading.
Where?

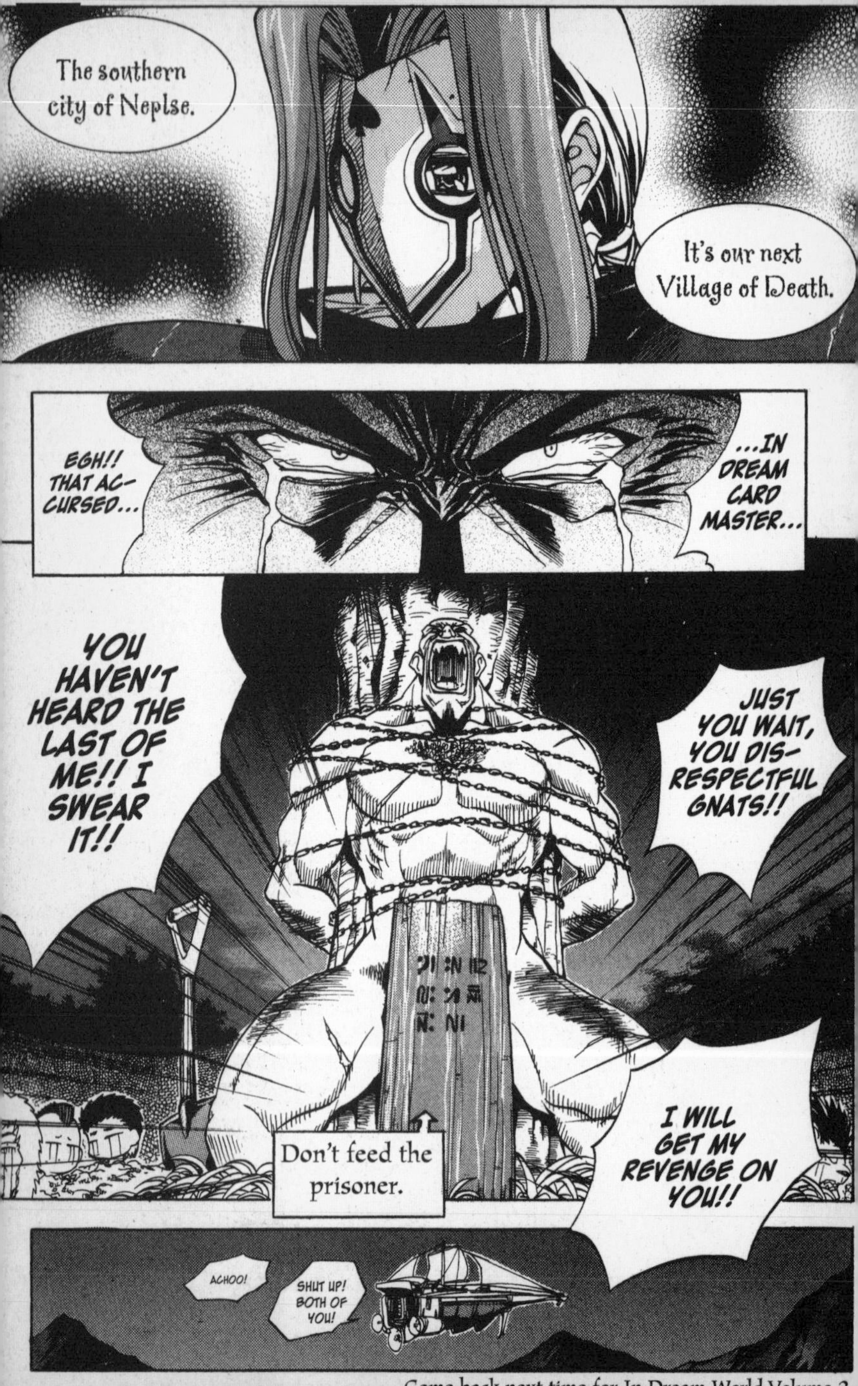
The southern city of Neplse.
It's our next Village of Death.
EGH!! THAT AC-CURSED...
...IN DREAM CARD MASTER...
YOU HAVEN'T HEARD THE LAST OF ME!! I SWEAR IT!!
JUST YOU WAIT, YOU DIS-RESPECTFUL GNATS!!
Don't feed the prisoner.
I WILL GET MY REVENGE ON YOU!!
ACHOO!
SHUT UP! BOTH OF YOU!

Come back next time for In Dream World Volume 2.

인드림카드 소개

In Dream World

In Dream Cards were created in ancient times to harness the power of five kinds of supernatural creatures. By placing the card on a weapon or a shield, you may transform into the creature depicted on the card, complete with all of that creature's tremendous power. But if an In Dream Card Player has witnessed the birth of a particular creature from its egg, he will not require a weapon to receive the creature's power.

Those who have received the power are the In Dream Card masters.

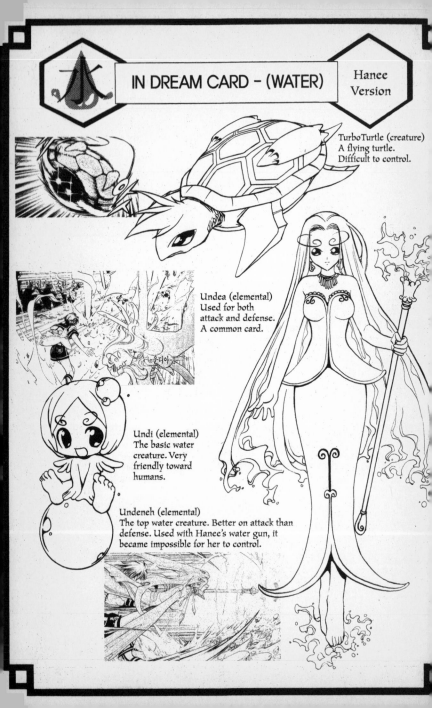

IN DREAM CARD - (WATER)

Hanee Version

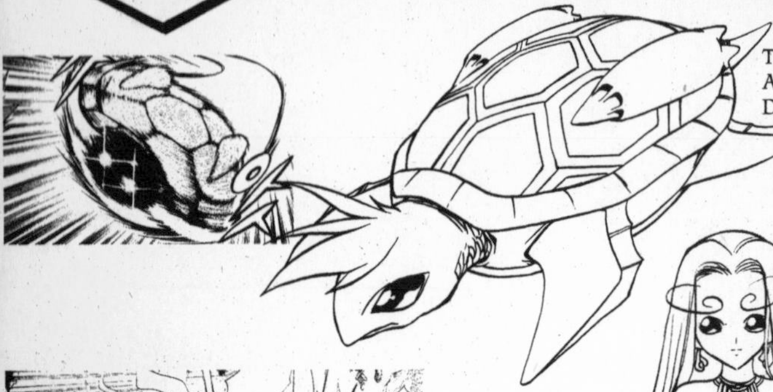

TurboTurtle (creature)
A flying turtle.
Difficult to control.

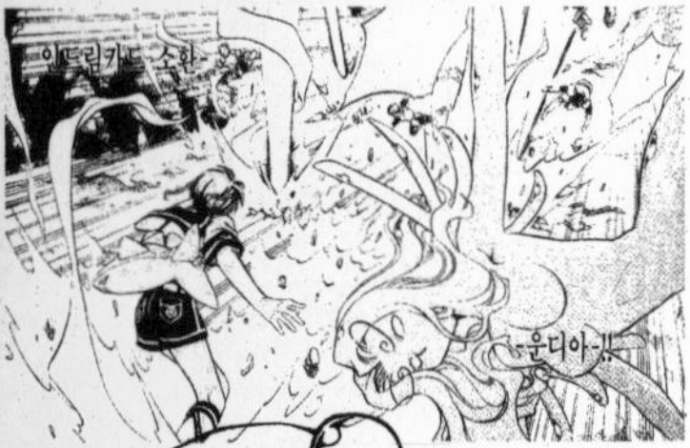

인드림카드 소환
-운디아-!!

Undea (elemental)
Used for both attack and defense. A common card.

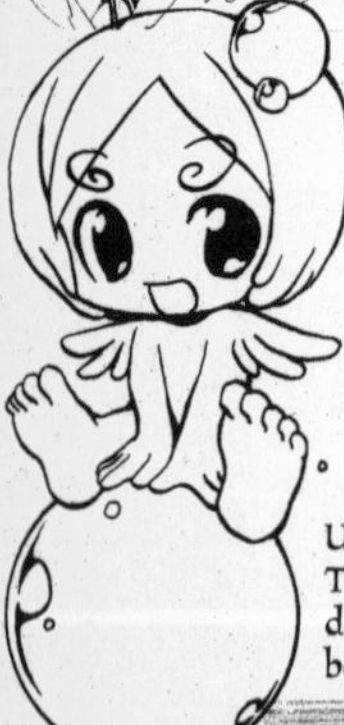

Undi (elemental)
The basic water creature. Very friendly toward humans.

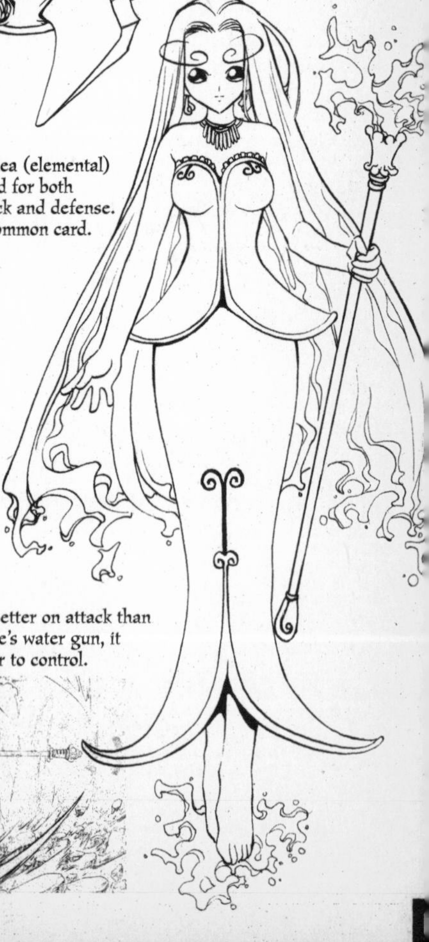

Undeneh (elemental)
The top water creature. Better on attack than defense. Used with Hanee's water gun, it became impossible for her to control.

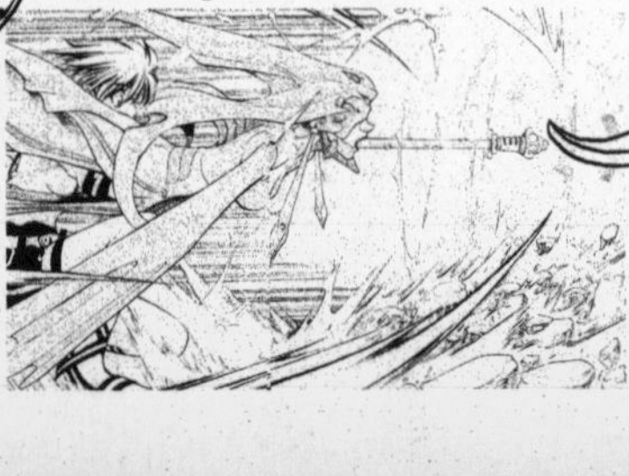

IN DREAM CARD - (FIRE)

Drake Version

Draki (human)
Looks like a child. Communicates easily with humans.

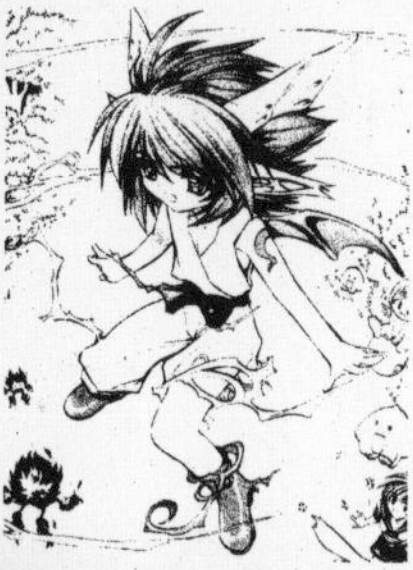

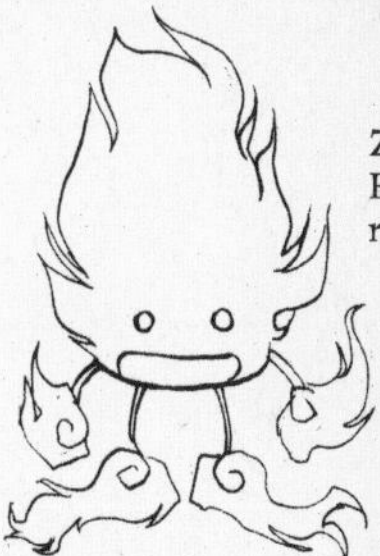

Zin (elemental)
Fire creature. Very rarely seen..

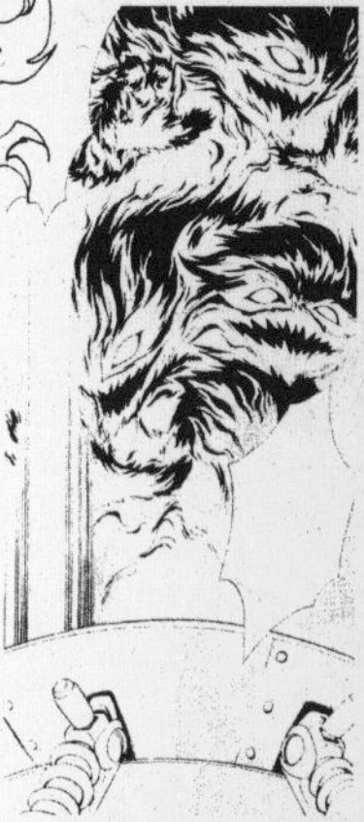

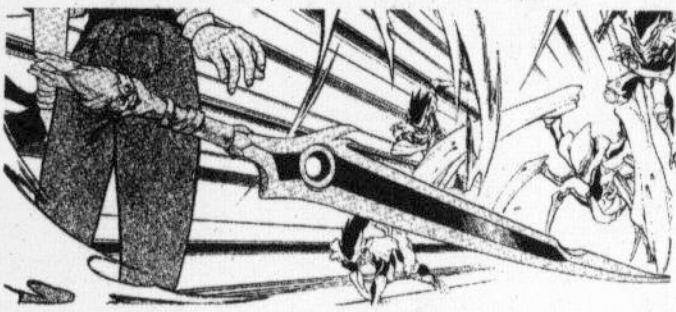

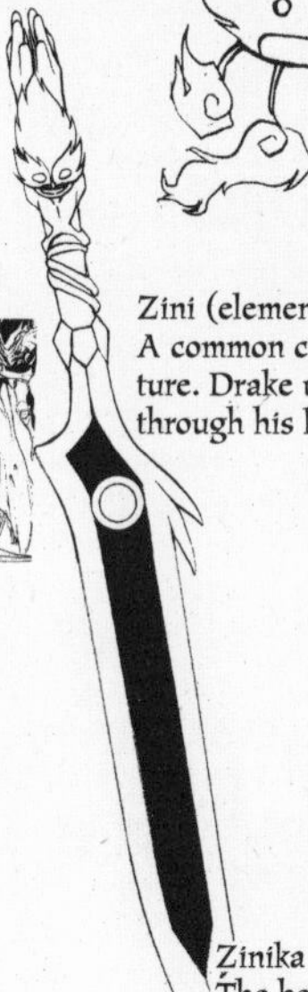

Zini (elemental)
A common creature. Drake uses it through his knife.

Zinika (elemental)
The best fighter of all. Its master takes on its appearance.

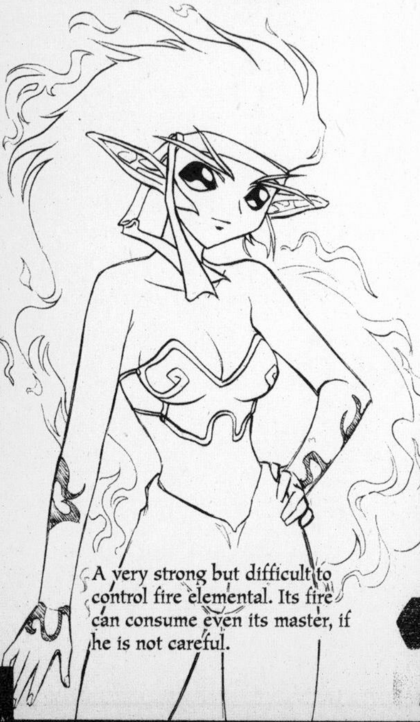

A very strong but difficult to control fire elemental. Its fire can consume even its master, if he is not careful.

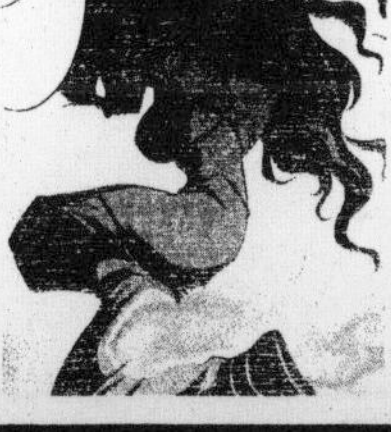

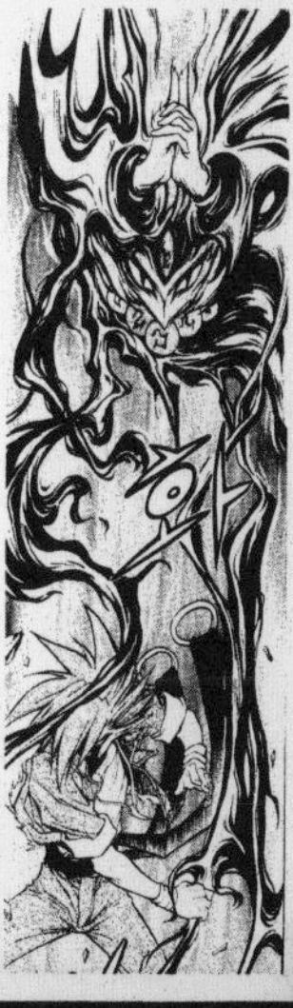

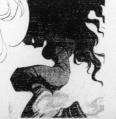

IN DREAM CARD - (METAR)

Rosemary's Version

Tini (elemental)
The basic metal creature.
Takes the shape of a
metallic chain.

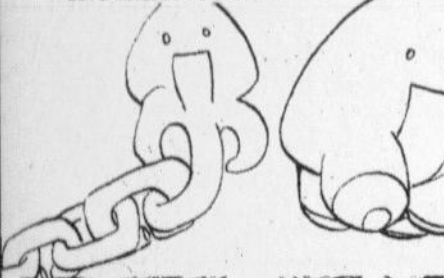

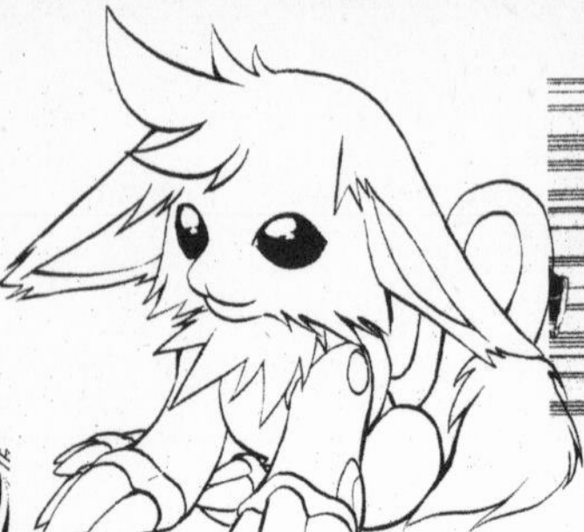

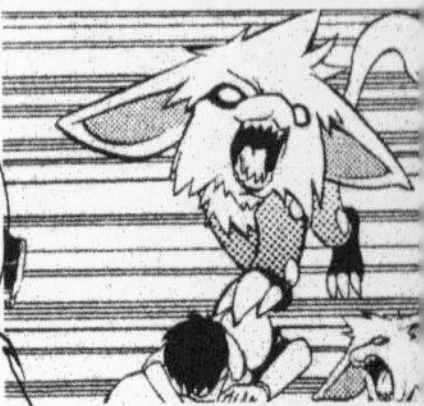

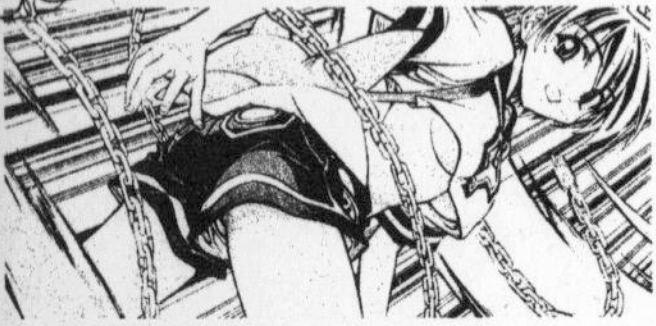

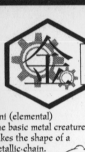

Kat (creature)
Looks like a cat, but don't
be fooled by how cute it is.
It can kill with ease.

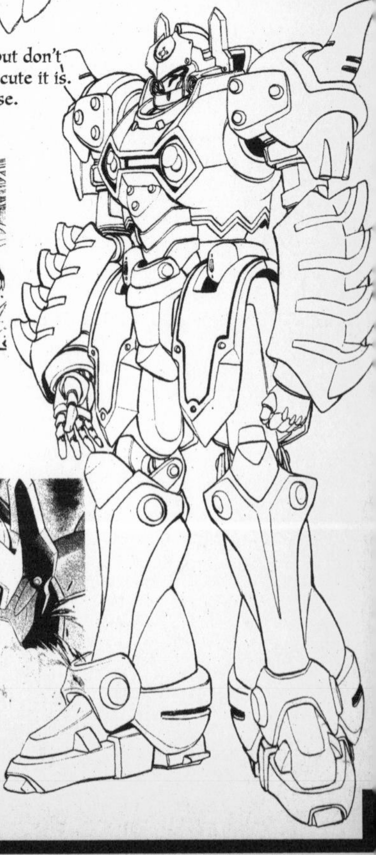

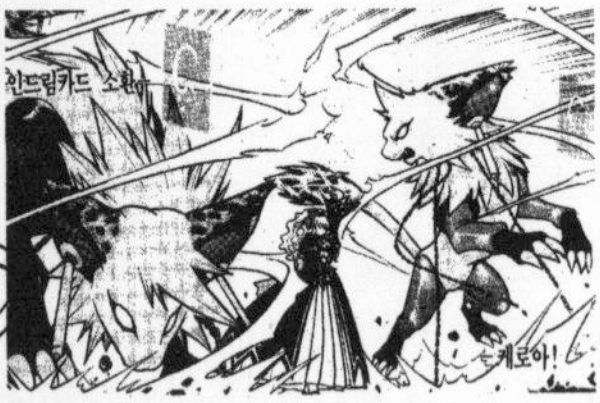

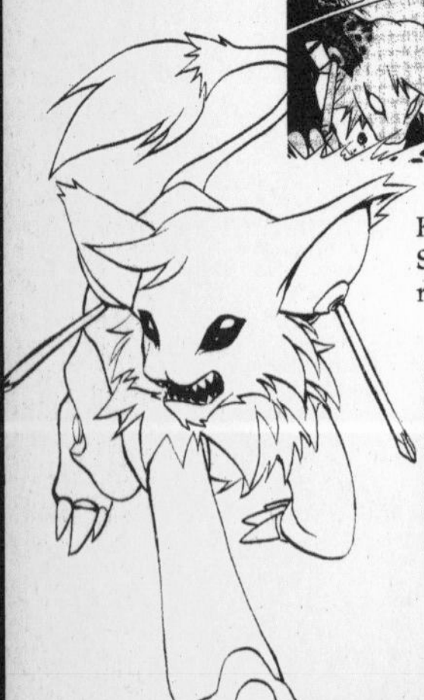

Keloa (creature)
Similar to Kat, but much
more powerful.

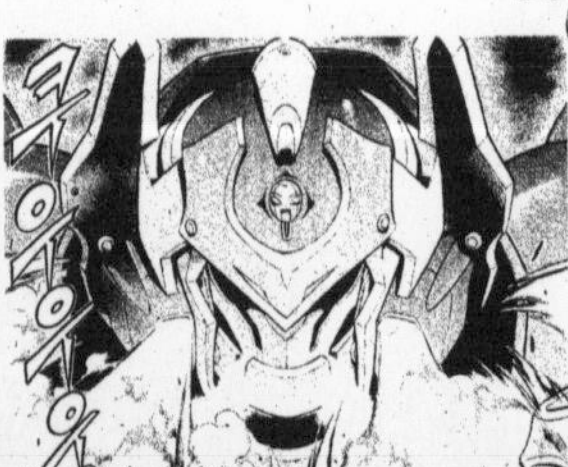

Battle Gear
Used with the doll Elizabeth, it
has human-shaped armor.
It is very faithful to Rosemary,
but it has a stubborn streak.

In the Next Volume...

The adventure continues!
Hanee, Drake and Bunny Girl
are traveling through In Dream
World by an airship powered by a
masterless elemental, El Forrest.
When the ship is attacked by
Nightmares, Hanee, Drake, Bunny
Girl and the stowaway Mei join
forces to defeat the enemy. Also,
find out Rosemary's past in the
human world and what brought her
to In Dream World!

TOKYOPOP SHOP

WWW.TOKYOPOP.COM/SHOP

HOT NEWS!
Check out
TOKYOPOP.COM/SHOP
The world's best
collection of manga in
English is now available
online in one place!

SOKORA REFUGEES

PLANET BLOOD

THE TAROT CAFÉ

WWW.TOKYOPOP.COM/SHOP

0 00000 00000 0

- LOOK FOR SPECIAL OFFERS
- PRE-ORDER UPCOMING RELEASES!
- COMPLETE YOUR COLLECTIONS

SPOTLIGHT TOKYOPOP MANGA SUPPLEMENT

IN DREAM WORLD: FOLLOW YOUR DREAMS... BUT BEWARE OF THE NIGHTMARES!

Nightmares are bad enough when you are asleep, but in Dream World, nightmares are real monsters! Drake, Hanee and Kyle battle these night terrors with special "In Dream Cards," magical cards that have unusual and devastating powers. Those who wield the cards gain the power of the elements, and our heroes must master the cards before they are put into a permanent state of sleep!

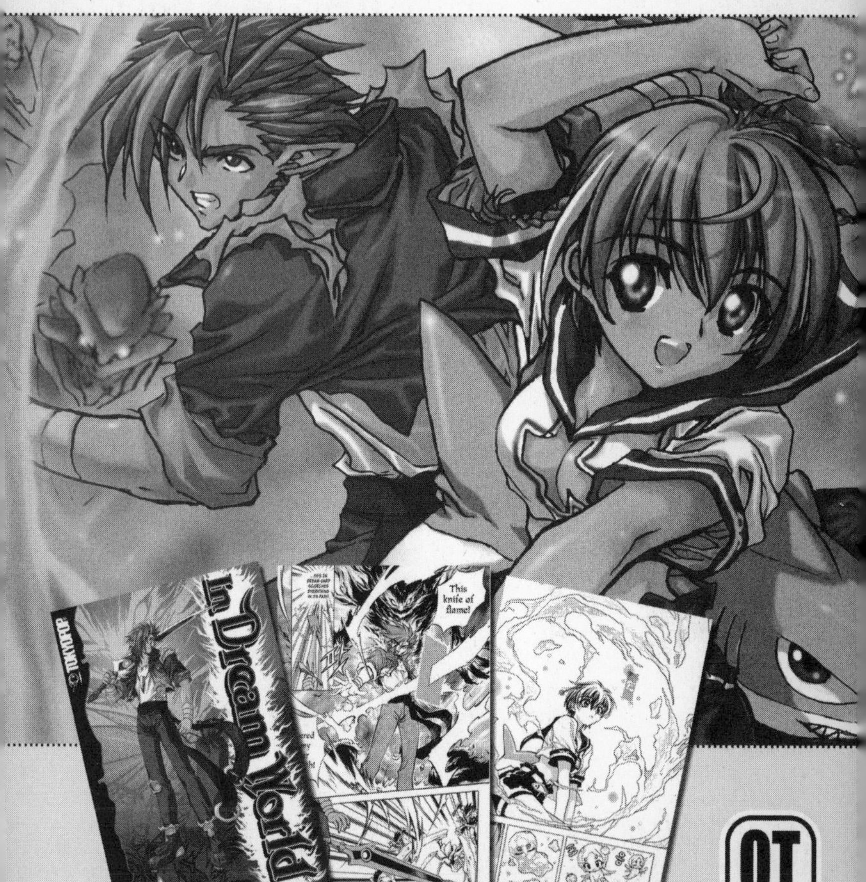
TOKYOPOP
In Dream World
1
JAE-HO YOON
This knife of flame!

OT
OLDER TEEN
AGE 16+

For more information visit: **www.TOKYOPOP.com**

VAN VON HUNTER

EVIL NEVER DIES...
BUT EVIL STUFF DOES!

FROM THE WINNERS OF TOKYOPOP'S FIRST RISING STARS OF MANGA™ COMPETITION

VAN VON HUNTER ™

In the dark ages long ago, in a war-torn land where tranquility and harmony once blossomed, tyranny ruled with a flaming fist! At last, a hero arose to defeat the evildoers and returned hope to the people and peace to the countryside. Now…the sinister forces are back with a vengeance, and in their hour of direst-est need, the commoners once again seek a champion to right wrongs and triumph over villainy! Unfortunately, they could only get the mighty warrior Van Von Hunter, Hunter of Evil…Stuff!

Together with his loyal, memory-challenged sidekick, Van Von Hunter is on a never-ending quest to smite the bad guys—and believe us, they're real bad!

Preview the manga at:

www.TOKYOPOP.com/vanvonhunter
www.VanVonHunter.com

T TEEN AGE 13+

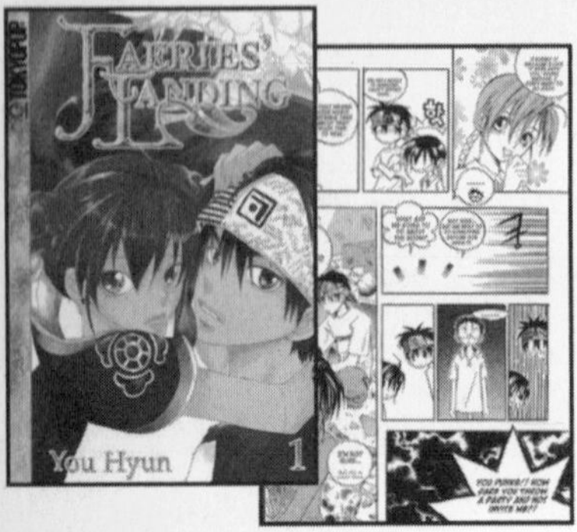
Faeries' Landing
TOKYOPOP
You Hyun
1

BY YOU HYUN

FAERIES' LANDING

Following the misadventures of teenager Ryang Jegal and Fanta, a faerie who has fallen from the heavens straight into South Korea, *Faeries' Landing* is both a spoof of modern-day teen romance and a lighthearted fantasy epic. Imagine if Shakespeare's *A Midsummer Night's Dream* had come from the pen of Joss Whedon after about a dozen shots of espresso, and you have an idea of what to expect from You Hyun's funny little farce. Bursting with sharp wit, hip attitude and vibrant art, *Faeries' Landing* is guaranteed to get you giggling.
~Tim Beedle, Editor

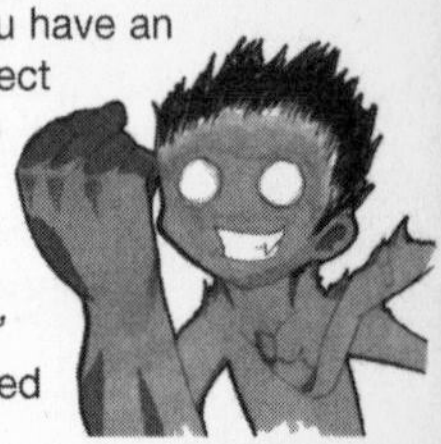

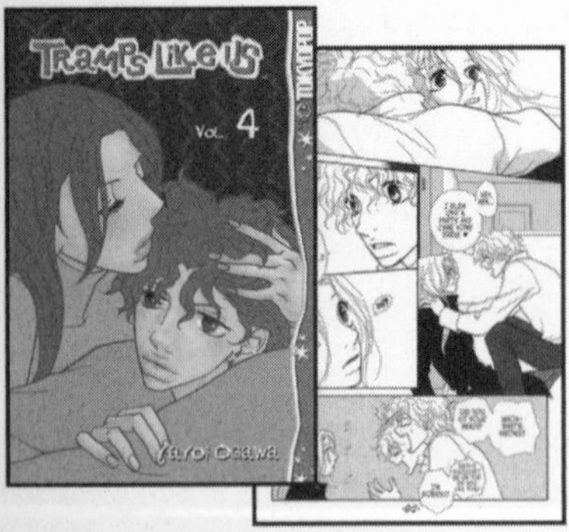
Tramps Like Us
TOKYOPOP
Vol. 4
Yayoi Ogawa

BY YAYOI OGAWA

TRAMPS LIKE US

Yayoi Ogawa's *Tramps Like Us*—known as *Kimi wa Pet* in Japan—is the touching and humorous story of Sumire, a woman whose striking looks and drive for success alienate her from her friends and co-workers...until she takes in Momo, a cute homeless boy, as her "pet." As sketchy as the situation sounds, it turns out to be the sanest thing in Sumire's hectic life. In his quiet way, Momo teaches Sumire how to care for another being while also caring for herself...in other words, how to love. And there ain't nothin' wrong with that.
~Carol Fox, Editor

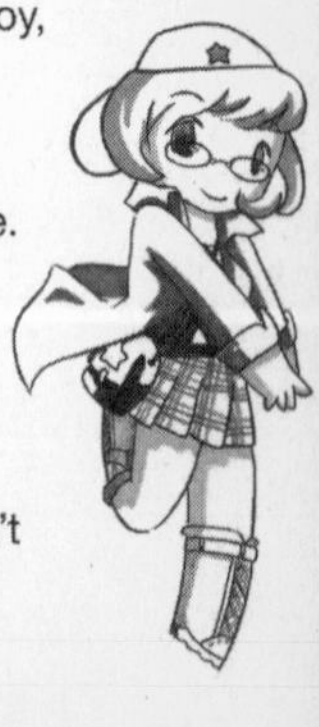

EDITORS' PICKS

TOKYOPOP MANGA SUPPLEMENT

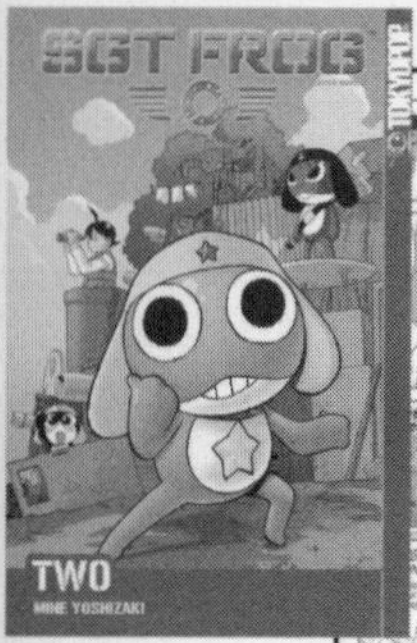
SGT FROG
TWO
MINE YOSHIZAKI

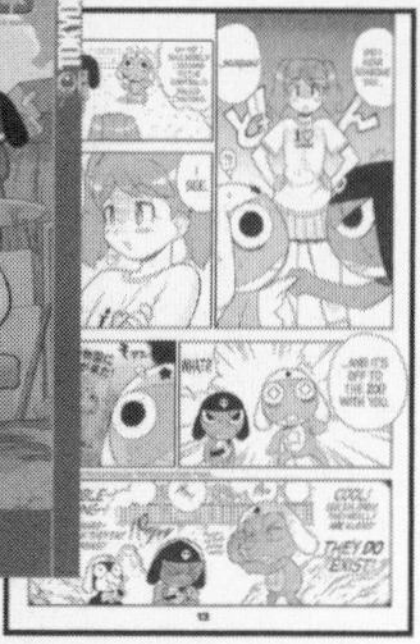

BY MINE YOSHIZAKI

SGT FROG

Sgt. Frog is so absurdly comical, it has me in stitches every time I edit it. Mine Yoshizaki's clever sci-fi spoof showcases the hijinks of Sergeant Keroro, a cuddly looking alien, diabolically determined to oppress our planet! While some E.T.s phone home, this otherworldly menace has your number! Abandoned on Earth, Keroro takes refuge in the Hinata home, whose residents quickly take advantage of his stellar cleaning skills. But between scrubbing, vacuuming and an unhealthy obsession with Gundam models, Keroro still finds time to plot the subjugation of humankind!

~ Paul Morrissey, Editor

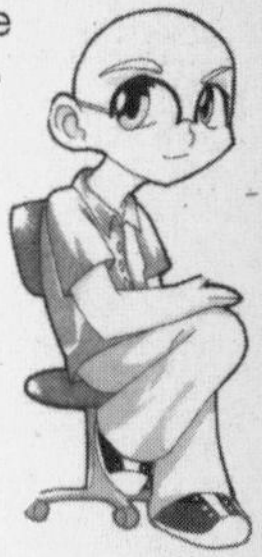

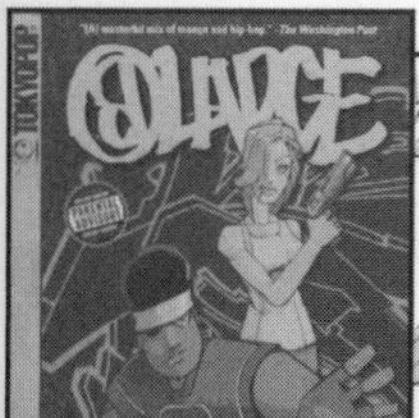
Ahmed Hoke
Two

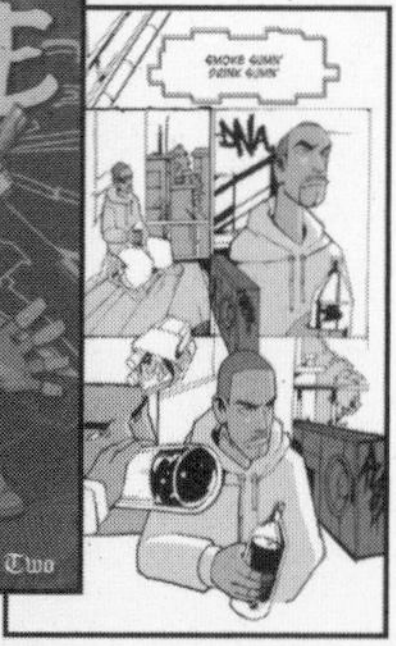

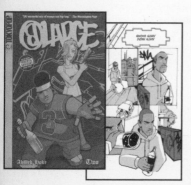

BY AHMED HOKE

@LARGE

Ahmed Hoke's revolutionary hip-hop manga is a groundbreaking graphic novel. While at first glace this series may seem like a dramatic departure from traditional manga styles, on a deeper level one will find a rich, lyrical world full of wildly imaginative characters, intense action and heartfelt human emotions. This is a truly unique manga series that needs to be read by everyone—whether they are fans of hip-hop or not.

~Rob Valois, Editor

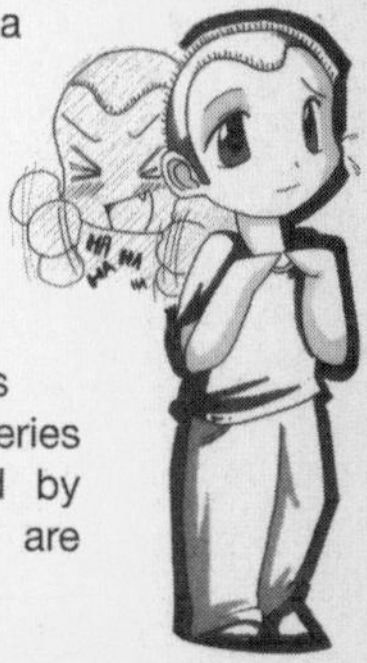

PASSION FRUIT
BY MARI OKAZAKI

Passion Fruit is a unique, unforgettable collection of stylish stories that touch upon our most private inhibitions and examine our deepest desires. This uncompromising blend of realism and raw emotion focuses on women exploring the vulnerability and frailty of the human condition. With uninhibited authenticity and pathos, passion proves to be stranger than fiction.

© Mari Okazaki

PLANET BLOOD
BY TAE-HYUNG KIM

Universal Century 0091. The Mars and Moon colonies fight for repatriation rights over the newly restored Earth. Amidst the bloody battle, one soldier, is rendered unconscious— only to awaken in an entirely different world enmeshed in an entirely different war...

© KIM TAE-HYUNG, DAIWON C.I. Inc.

T TEEN AGE 13+

LILING-PO
BY AKO YUTENJI

Master thief Liling-Po has finally been captured! However, the government offers a chance for Liling-Po to redeem himself. All he has to do is "retrieve" some special items—eight mystic treasures that are fabled to grant their owners any wish!

© Ako Yutenji

T TEEN AGE 13+